CATALYST

Also by John Hood

Our Best Foot Forward: An Investment Plan for North Carolina's Economic Recovery

Selling the Dream: Why Advertising Is Good Business

Investor Politics: The New Force That Will Transform American Business, Government, and Politics in the Twenty-first Century

The Heroic Enterprise: Business and the Common Good

To Know Such Liberty: An American Family History

Clear Creek and Rocky River: A Carolina Family History

CATALYST

JIM MARTIN AND THE RISE OF
NORTH CAROLINA REPUBLICANS

BY JOHN HOOD

John F. Blair, Publisher
Winston-Salem, North Carolina

John F. Blair, Publisher
1406 Plaza Drive
Winston-Salem, North Carolina 27103
blairpub.com

Library of Congress Cataloging in Publication Data

LCCN 2015027253

COVER
Image of Jim Martin courtesy of *The Fayetteville Observer* / Cindy Burnham
Background image of the North Carolina State Flag © Matt Trommer / Shutterstock

10 9 8 7 6 5 4 3 2 1

To my beloved Traci—my own, indispensable catalyst

CONTENTS

Prologue: A Second Southern Strategy   I

Chapter 1: Strong Bonds at the Start   9

Chapter 2: A Professor Turned Politician   23

Chapter 3: The Republican Breakthrough   53

Chapter 4: "At the Drop of a Rat"   73

Chapter 5: The Reagan Chain Reaction   94

Chapter 6: The Other Carolina Race of 1984   114

Chapter 7: Division Leads to Addition   131

Chapter 8: Governing by Twists and Turns   152

Chapter 9: Finding a Formula for Success   181

Chapter 10: "Better Schools, Better Roads, Better Jobs"   216

Chapter 11: A New Combination of Elements   243

Chapter 12: Home, Science, and Senior Statesman   284

Epilogue: A Catalyst for Change   307

Acknowledgments   316

Sources and Methods   319

Index   324

PROLOGUE

A SECOND SOUTHERN STRATEGY

Jim Martin spent 26 years representing North Carolina voters in local, state, and federal offices. But he isn't a native of the Tar Heel State. He was born in Georgia. He grew up in South Carolina. And to grasp the significance of Martin's political accomplishments, the best place to start may be in another neighboring state—Tennessee.

If you drive down Lamar Alexander Parkway about 30 miles south of Knoxville, you will find a resort called Blackberry Farm nestled against the Great Smoky Mountains. Boasting 4,200 acres of beautiful mountain scenery, a luxury hotel, and an award-winning restaurant, Blackberry is a working farm and a family retreat. For a small group of Republican politicians and strategists who met there one weekend in July 1985, however, retreat was the farthest thing from their minds. Just six months earlier, Ronald Reagan had rollicked to reelection over Walter Mondale by winning 49 states. Republicans had gained 16 seats in the United States House of Representatives and maintained their majority in the Senate. But below the federal level, the GOP remained firmly in the minority. Despite the impressive size of President Reagan's reelection wave, Republicans gained just one governorship in 1984, giving them 16 to the Democrats' 34. In most states, Democrats had long enjoyed control of both legislative chambers, often by wide margins. Republicans won majorities in only 11 state legislatures in 1984, a decline from the 15 they had won in the midst of the initial Reagan victory four years earlier.

The Republicans who convened at Blackberry Farm that sweltering summer were convinced that their party's electoral successes at the top of the ticket could be parlayed into greater gains in congressional, state, and local politics. Some attendees had already found success themselves. The host of the gathering, Lamar Alexander, was into his second term as governor of Tennessee. A native of Maryville, just a few miles from Blackberry Farm, Alexander had begun his political career by managing the 1970 campaign of Winfield Dunn, who became Tennessee's first Republican governor in half a century. Alexander attempted to follow in Dunn's footsteps in 1974 but was swamped by the post-Watergate Democratic tide. On his second try in 1978, he succeeded. Later, Alexander would run for president, serve as United States secretary of education and president of the University of Tennessee, and then enter the United States Senate.

Governor Alexander's short guest list for the weekend included Governors Dick Thornburgh of Pennsylvania and John Sununu of New Hampshire, who would later join him in the George H. W. Bush administration as attorney general and chief of staff, respectively. The guests also included two GOP consultants, Bob Teeter and Doug Bailey, and three key members of the Conservative Opportunity Society in the United States House: Carroll Campbell (soon to become governor of South Carolina), Connie Mack (soon to become a senator from Florida), and Newt Gingrich, who within a decade would become the first Republican speaker of the House in two generations.

A FOOT IN BOTH CAMPS

The ninth and final participant in the Blackberry Farm summit was Dr. James G. Martin. Although just 50 years old and elected governor of North Carolina only the previous November, Martin was actually the most experienced politician in the room. His first electoral win, to the Mecklenburg County Commission, occurred in 1966. The other politicians in attendance had won their first victories in the 1970s or early 1980s. By the time Martin won the governor's race in 1984, he had already spent 18 years in public office, including six two-year terms in Congress.

As a member of the first Republican commission majority in North Carolina's most populous county, and then a veteran of many battles on Capitol Hill, Martin was both a trailblazer and a bridge builder. While he was a congressman with a conventionally conservative voting record during the Nixon, Ford, Carter, and Reagan administrations, Martin had come to believe that the GOP needed a different message if it wanted to achieve success down the ballot as he had done in Mecklenburg in the late 1960s. Republicans needed a plan "to make us more effective in governing while also making us more effective in politicking," he said later. At Blackberry Farm, he used his experience to help bridge the gap between the governors, who tended toward political pragmatism, and his former congressional colleagues, who led a conservative insurgency on Capitol Hill during the early 1980s. Jim Martin—an ally of Newt Gingrich, Jack Kemp, Trent Lott, and others in that insurgency—had a foot in each camp. His presence proved essential in keeping the focus of the meeting on shared GOP principles and interests.

In addition to their shared partisan interests, Martin had much in common with two of the participants, John Sununu and Newt Gingrich. All three were former college professors. Sununu had a Ph.D. in mechanical engineering from the Massachusetts Institute of Technology and spent years as a professor and associate dean at Tufts University before beginning his political career in 1973 as a state legislator. Gingrich had a Ph.D. in education from Tulane and taught at West Georgia College for eight years before being elected to Congress (on his third try) in 1978. As for Martin, he had earned a Ph.D. in organic chemistry from Princeton University and then returned to his undergraduate alma mater, Davidson College, in 1960 to teach.

During their political careers, Martin, Sununu, and Gingrich never lost their professorial bent. To friends and foes alike, they at times came across as lecturing. But they were hardly the only intellectuals and passionate advocates in the room at Blackberry Farm. For example, Dick Thornburgh, who was then serving as chairman of the Republican Governors Association, had spent nearly a decade as a federal prosecutor and assistant United States attorney general before his election as Pennsylvania governor in 1978. Bob Teeter was a Michigan State–trained sociologist and polling pioneer. And Doug Bailey had earned his Ph.D. from the Fletcher School of Diplomacy at Tufts and then worked for Henry Kissinger at Harvard, a relationship that eventually led him into Republican politics. (Two years after the Blackberry Farm meeting, Bailey would found The Hotline, one of the first daily political briefing services in America.)

These were brainy, determined men. They included both establishment GOP figures such as Thornburgh and conservative revolutionaries such as Gingrich. What brought them together was a shared belief that the Republican

Party could become the majority party in state governments by developing an effective message, building a political and policy infrastructure at the state level, recruiting strong candidates, and broadening the donor base. Thornburgh called their emerging strategy the "Reagan Revolution Stage 2."

In the coming months, as Jim Martin and other Blackberry Farm participants focused on emerging GOP opportunities in the old Confederacy and border states, another name presented itself: the "Second Southern Strategy."

CONJUNCTION JUNCTION

The first "Southern Strategy" emerged in the 1960s from Republicans hoping to break the Democrats' electoral lock on the region. While Dwight Eisenhower and other GOP candidates had made some headway during the 1950s by targeting affluent or upwardly mobile voters in the South's growing metropolitan areas, the Republican strategists of the 1960s sought to broaden the playing field by leveraging the conservative views of rural and small-town whites on crime, civil rights, religion, and foreign policy into ticket-splitting votes for Republican candidates for president and other offices. One of the GOP operatives behind the 1960s Southern Strategy, Brad Hays, would later become Jim Martin's political consultant. Hays worked at the Republican National Committee in the late 1960s, when he helped turn the vague concept of appealing to traditionally Democratic voters into a specific political program of advertising, recruitment, and patronage. During the 1970s and 1980s, he ran Martin's campaigns for Congress and governor. Each was successful. Hays never stopped looking for ways to convert Democratic voters, and thus Democratic places, into Republican ones. Martin's ideas about political organizing and marketing bore the unmistakable imprint of Brad Hays.

While the initial Southern Strategy employed wedge issues to detach voters from their longtime home in the Democratic Party, that was insufficient to make Republicans competitive down the ballot. The Second Southern Strategy of the 1980s and early 1990s sought to attract new voters to GOP campaigns for governor, the legislature, and local offices by offering an appealing alternative to Democratic governance. This opportunity presented itself, as the Blackberry Farm participants recognized, after Ronald Reagan won the presidency in 1980 and began to change the party's brand. Merle and Earl Black, twins and influential political scientists at Emory and Rice universities, respectively, made this point in their 2002 book, *The Rise of Southern Republicans*. Reagan's "optimistic conservatism and successful performance in office made the Republican Party respectable and useful for millions of Southern whites," they wrote. "Many of them, for the first time in their lives, began to think of themselves as Republicans." This was only a partial realignment of traditionally Democratic voters, however. Bringing more along—convincing them to vote Republican for governor, the legislature, and other offices—meant addressing their demands for better schools, roads, and economic opportunities. It wasn't enough for GOP candidates to clutch the coattails of their presidential candidate. They needed a relevant, credible message of reformed and effective government. And they needed a realistic strategy for converting that message into electoral victories.

The strategy came into sharper focus within months of the Blackberry Farm meeting. Speaking at a Republican leadership conference in early 1986, Lamar Alexander challenged attendees to rethink their pitch to Southern voters. "Washington issues are tremendously important and so fascinating," he said. "But when we get together that's all we talk about, and the Democratic governors are running down the street proposing programs to improve the schools, clean up the garbage, fix the roads and make the children more healthy—and they get elected."

Later that year, Martin and Alexander convened a new group, the Southern Republican Exchange. Its purpose was to give Republican legislators, local officials, candidates, and strategists an opportunity to compare notes not simply on political tactics but also on new ideas for addressing issues such as education, crime, transportation, and health care. The formational meeting in August "was the politician's nightmare: everyone we invited came," quipped Alexander to veteran *Washington Post* reporter David Broder, who joined the 49 GOP activists at the Nashville gathering. Newt Gingrich was also there. He argued that conservative Republicans didn't need to compromise their principles to win state and local races. They could promise "lean but strong government," he said.

While Martin and Alexander focused their attention on cultivating new ideas and candidates to boost Republican fortunes in the South, other Blackberry Farm participants were hard at work elsewhere. For example, Gingrich decided in 1986 to assume control of a political action committee, GOPAC, that former Delaware governor Pete du Pont had founded in 1978 to train and support Republican candidates for state and local offices. Gingrich dramatically increased the budget and national impact of GOPAC beginning with the 1986 election cycle. As for Thornburgh and Sununu, the chairman and vice chairman of the Republican Governors Association, they spent much of 1985 and early 1986 recruiting a strong field of GOP candidates and raising a huge war chest to support them. Martin, Alexander, Gingrich, Thornburgh, and Sununu reassured the candidates, donors, and activists they were cultivating that although the political party of a reelected president tended to sustain major losses in his second midterm election—the so-called six-year itch—Republicans running for state office could effectively decouple themselves from the national trend with aggressive, well-funded campaigns on issues of local concern.

They were proven right. Although President Reagan's party lost seats in the House and its majority in the Senate in 1986, it enjoyed spectacular successes down the ballot. Republicans achieved a net gain of eight governorships, including victories by Bill Clements in Texas, Bob Martinez in Florida, Henry Bellmon in Oklahoma, Guy Hunt in Alabama, and Blackberry Farm participant Carroll Campbell in South Carolina. The down-ballot victories in 1986 were highly unusual for a president's party—which had lost an average of six governorships in midterm elections since World War II—and surprised nearly everyone in the national political establishment. The main exception was David Broder, who had reported on the Blackberry Farm summit in 1985 and interviewed Lamar Alexander, Jim Martin, and other key figures in the run-up to the 1986 elections. The summit's significance was more broadly understood after the elections, when *National Review* founder William F. Buckley labeled it "a historic way station in Republican politics in the South" on his TV show, *Firing Line.*

Over the next few years, Southern Republican Exchange meetings grew larger. Gingrich's GOPAC expanded, too. More of the party's financial and human capital began to flow into state and local politics. Other states started to emulate the party-building strategies pioneered in Tennessee and North Carolina. The breakout finally came in 1994, when Republicans won a majority of the nation's governorships and a plurality of the state legislatures. In North Carolina, the 1994 cycle gave the GOP its first majority in the state House of Representatives since Reconstruction.

Although it took several more election cycles, some tumultuous and frustrating, Tar Heel Republicans would eventually achieve their dream of unified control of state government in 2012 with the election of former Charlotte mayor Pat McCrory as governor and the reelection of Republican majorities in the legislature and the state supreme court.

AN UNLIKELY REVOLUTIONARY

In North Carolina, Jim Martin is not typically thought of as a political revolutionary. Outside North Carolina, his political career is not typically thought of at all. His contemporary, controversial senator Jesse Helms, is far better known. Furthermore, to those who meet Martin, a genial former professor who sometimes expresses his ideas in chemical formulas, the term *revolutionary* may seem ill-fitting. But appearances can be deceiving. From the beginning of Martin's political career in the mid-1960s through the 2012 elections, North Carolina politics went through a dramatic transformation. What was once a solidly Democratic state became a battleground. And what was once a solidly Democratic government by 2012 gave way to a Republican-led state government, as well as Republican commission majorities in most of the state's 100 counties.

Many events, trends, and personalities combined to produce North Carolina's political transformation. To suggest Jim Martin was solely responsible would be an overstatement. But more than simple coincidence was at work here. As a local politician, congressman, governor, and senior statesman, Martin helped prepare North Carolina's Republican Party for its historic rise to power. Unlike many other influential people in politics, he did not aspire to political activism in his youth. Martin's interests lay in science, music, sports, and friendships. The son of a Presbyterian minister, he developed a strong interest in matters of faith that has persisted throughout his life. He entered the political arena only after pursuing his chosen career in academia—and essentially by accident. Still, once he put his mind to it, Martin was determined to succeed at politics. Every time he campaigned for office, he won. Along the way, and not by accident, the fortunes of his political party rose as he did.

Martin was not simply a catalyst for political change, however. He also left his mark on government and policy. As a scientist serving in Congress during the 1970s and early 1980s, Martin was a leader in combating the excesses of federal regulation and the anti-nuclear movement. As governor, he reformed North Carolina's tax code and helped instigate one of the largest state public-works projects up to that time with the 1989 creation of the Highway Trust

Fund. As a county commission chairman in the 1960s and governor in the 1980s, Martin applied his scientific expertise to environmental policy, promoting new rules to protect air and water quality while keeping red tape and regulatory delay to a minimum. His eight years in Raleigh also served as a training ground for dozens of Republican leaders—some newly converted from the opposing party, some hailing from North Carolina's traditionally Republican western Piedmont and mountains—who would go on to serve as political strategists, lobbyists, candidates, and elected officials.

When Jim Martin, the newly elected North Carolina governor, traveled to East Tennessee in the summer of 1985, neither he nor anyone else at the Blackberry Farm summit was sure what would come of it. They had high hopes and bold ideas. But could they really engineer a Republican majority in Congress, in state governments, and in the formerly rock-solid Democratic South?

Now, we know that the answer to these questions was yes. By the end of this book, you will know more about the essential but under-appreciated role James G. Martin played in these and other events in North Carolina, the South, and beyond.

CHAPTER ONE

STRONG BONDS AT THE START

The tall, white steeple of the Independent Presbyterian Church towers over picturesque Chippewa Square in downtown Savannah, Georgia. If you've seen the movie *Forrest Gump*, you'll recall this commanding steeple in the opening scene as a feather floats by it.

Founded in 1755, Independent Presbyterian moved in 1800 to its current location in a building patterned after London's distinctive St. Martin-in-the-Fields. The structure today is an 1891 reconstruction of that original building, which had burned two years earlier. The Independent Presbyterian Church is a routine stop on tours of Savannah's historic buildings, both for its striking architecture and its contribution to the religious heritage of the region.

Another significant landmark of Southern Presbyterianism can be found north of Savannah near the South Carolina town of Winnsboro, which lies just off I-77 between Columbia and Charlotte. In 1788, Scots-Irish immigrants built a simple brick structure that would come to house the Ebenezer Associate Reformed Presbyterian Church. In 1803, ministers gathered there to create the Associate Reform Synod of the Carolinas. Later known as the Old Brick Church, it continues to be maintained as a historic property by local congregations as the unofficial "home church" of the ARP denomination.

Little Winnsboro, population 3,600, bears little resemblance to stately Savannah, the "Hostess City of the South." Nor does the humble Old Brick Church look anything like the towering Independent Presbyterian. Yet both places played host to key moments in the religious history of the American South. And both played important roles in the biography of James Grubbs Martin.

He was born in Savannah on December 11, 1935, while his father, the Reverend Arthur Martin, was an assistant minister at the Independent Presbyterian Church. Jim spent most of his childhood in Winnsboro while his father served as minister of Sion Presbyterian, located just a few miles from the Old Brick Church. The Martin family's religious roots ran deep. Their ancestors included notable Puritan missionaries, the first native South Carolinian to be ordained a Presbyterian minister, and even the founder of Scottish Presbyterianism himself, John Knox. Arthur Martin attended Davidson College, a Presbyterian-founded institution near Charlotte, and studied for the ministry at Louisville Presbyterian Theological Seminary, at the University of Edinburgh, and with the Protestant faculty of the University of Paris. He later served for 20 years as executive secretary of the Presbyterian Synod of South Carolina. In 1961, the Reverend Martin wrote that the Piedmont Presbytery was "becoming a part of the sprawling suburbia that joins Charlotte with Atlanta." He observed,

All over the area new industries arise where two hundred years ago pioneers watched for the feathers of Indian war bonnets. All over the landscape, where taut bowstrings once sent arrows singing, taut wires now transmit mighty power from waterfall to factory. The new day is here but it is only begun. The purposes and providence of God have marked this long trail from Indians to industry. His promises go before us into this new day, but most of all, His command compels us to meet the burgeoning opportunities of our time with faith and courage and our utmost commitment.

His second son, Jim, would enter public life to advance Arthur Martin's vision of Carolina progress through economic development. He would do so as a county commissioner, congressman, governor, and elder statesman. But Jim would also do so as a man of faith who never forgot the traditions and principles he learned as a minister's son.

FROM SAVANNAH TO WINNSBORO

Jim Martin's paternal grandfather, Joe Martin, was a longtime elder at the Independent Presbyterian Church and sold men's clothing in downtown

THE MARTIN FAMILY IN 1951. CLOCKWISE FROM TOP LEFT: JIM, JOE, BUBBA, NEAL, MARY, AND ARTHUR MARTIN FAMILY PHOTO

Savannah for 50 years. Arthur Morrison Martin, born in 1902, was the second son of Joe Martin and his wife, Adele, a South Carolina native. Growing up in Savannah, Arthur was an outstanding student, a talented singer, and a football star at Savannah High School, where he acquired the nickname "Piggy" after a newspaper reporter said he was "as strong as pig iron." Small for his age, he had learned to turn an apparent deficiency into an asset. Whenever the team was close to a first down or the goal line, he would get the snap. Then two larger teammates would lift him off the ground and throw him and the ball over the line.

Arthur Martin dreamed of scoring big in another field of endeavor: politics. According to personal correspondence discovered after his death in 1982, he aspired to attend West Point, to embark on a military career, and then to retire and run for Congress. But when it came right down to it, Arthur followed the path of so many other Southern Presbyterians and enrolled at Davidson College, where he continued his academic and musical pursuits while shifting his career aspirations from the military to the ministry. He threw himself headlong into college life, serving as an officer in eight different student groups while working as a research assistant and waiting tables. Although he graduated from Davidson in 1925, Arthur never really left the institution. Throughout his career as a Presbyterian minister and church official, he donated to and raised money for the college and made it a point to return at least once a year for an alumni gathering or sporting event. All four of his children attended Davidson, and he served on the school's Board of Visitors and cochaired its endowment campaign. In 1965, Davidson awarded him an honorary doctorate in divinity.

He became the Reverend Arthur Martin in 1928 when he was ordained at his home church, Independent Presbyterian in Savannah. Over the next decade, he served as an assistant minister there and then organized and served other churches around Savannah.

It was at Independent that he met Mary Grubbs, a church member and president of Savannah's Christian Endeavor Society. The two married in 1932. Two sons followed: Arthur M. Martin Jr., known as "Bubba," in 1934 and James Grubbs Martin in 1935. Jim was named after his maternal grandfather, James Elbert Grubbs of Savannah, who installed and serviced coal furnaces for a living.

Jim was nearly three years old when the Reverend Martin accepted the call to pastor Sion Presbyterian in Winnsboro, the seat of Fairfield County. As in many communities in South Carolina's Midlands and Upstate, Winnsboro's economy prospered during the heyday of cotton production in the antebellum period, experienced wrenching change during the Civil War, then reinvented itself in the late 19th and early 20th centuries as manufacturing moved south from New York and New England. By the time Arthur Martin and his young family arrived in 1938, the community was small but vibrant—and immensely proud of its rich heritage and clutch of historic buildings.

During their time in Winnsboro, the Martins welcomed two more sons to the family: Joseph B. Martin III and Neal A. Martin. All four boys would go to college and graduate school. Bubba earned a medical degree from Duke University and became a pathologist. Joe earned graduate degrees in literature from the University of Minnesota and Duke before going to work for Hugh McColl at what would become NationsBank and eventually Bank of America. The youngest brother, Neal, earned his graduate degree from Emory University and became a university and city librarian.

Both parents set high standards and held the Martin boys to them. But their approaches differed. Mary Martin made sure they did their homework and exercised their brains by memorizing lists such as the books of the Bible and the kings of Israel. Arthur Martin encouraged his sons to read for pleasure—the Hardy Boys series was a family favorite—and to play sports. As the sons of a small-town minister, the Martin boys were always under scrutiny. Naturally, their actions didn't always bear up to it. "Mom was the family disciplinarian," Jim later recalled, "although sometimes she would call on Pop to take on the boys, and he'd send us out to find our own switch." His brother Joe later described the parental division of labor this way: "I always thought Pop was there to set an example, and Mom was there to make sure we didn't miss the point." On one memorable occasion, she caught Jim and Joe playing ping-pong in the church fellowship hall on a Sunday afternoon. "That was absolutely forbidden," Joe said. "She spanked us with the ping-pong paddles. There was no rule against spanking on Sunday."

Music was a constant presence in the Martin home, a Victorian-style two-story frame house next door to Sion Presbyterian. At their mother's behest, the boys took piano lessons and sang in the choir. Jim and Bubba performed duets at local weddings. Arthur Sr. owned a windup phonograph and a collection of about a dozen recordings of works by Tchaikovsky, Brahms, and other composers. The records were a particular inspiration for Jim, who spent hours listening to each piece, pretending to conduct it, and drawing up outlines of where each instrument would be placed in the orchestra. "I'd draw the violins, the first over here, the seconds over here," Jim recalled. "Or I'd put the first here and the seconds there beside them, in different ways. I'd decide where the horns would be, the other brass, the woodwinds, percussion, the string basses—either around the back or in a group on one side." Much later, when Martin first ran for Congress, a reporter asked his mother what Jim had wanted to be when he grew up. "A symphony conductor," she replied. His childhood experiences fostered Jim's lifelong passion for music.

After grammar school, Jim joined his older brother, Bubba, at Mt. Zion Institute, the community's public high school. He joined the band, choosing to play tuba because it was the only instrument provided free of charge by the school. He was also a standout offensive and defensive end for the Mt. Zion Wildcats, making the all-state second team his senior year. Like his dad before him, Jim had to find ways to excel on the football field despite his relatively small stature. Joe Martin later told the story of a game in which Jim found himself facing an opponent not just larger but faster than himself. When the player got the ball and started to run, "Jim yelled at the guy so forcefully that the guy turned around, and he stumbled," thus allowing Jim to make the play, Joe said. "I was a 165-pound tight end," Jim recalled. "I've often wondered whether, if wide receivers had been invented back then, I might have amounted to something."

In addition to football, Jim played basketball and baseball, ran track, worked on the school newspaper and annual, and excelled at South Carolina's statewide academic competitions in Columbia, called "Mental Contests." He also sang in the school's glee club and male quartet. His musical abilities came in handy when he decided to pursue the state presidency of the Beta Club, a national academic and service organization founded in South Carolina in 1934. To campaign for the job, Jim marched into the state convention playing his sousaphone. It worked. He was elected president of the South Carolina Beta Club in 1952.

THE CHEMISTRY SET

At Mt. Zion, the course of Jim's life was profoundly affected by W. R. Price, the school principal. "Monk" Price was also the head coach of the football team and taught science. During Jim's junior year, he and Bubba took Price's physics class. Their rivalry was, as usual, intense. The following year, Jim took chemistry. Although Price had no formal education in chemistry, he had served in the United States Army Chemical Corps and had a solid understanding of chemical principles and applications. Jim was immediately fascinated by the field—by the intricate bonds, the elaborate models, the idea that laboratory experiments could lead to a visualization of particles too small to be seen directly. Although there wasn't much doubt about where Jim would go to college, it wasn't until his last year at Mt. Zion that he began to think of science as his future. His brother and role model, Bubba, a Davidson freshman by the time, aspired to be a physician. But to Jim, the greater attraction was theoretical chemistry, not practical application. "It's the way I was wired to think," Jim said later. "I was more interested in trying to visualize the shape of chemicals and how that related to their effectiveness." He explained it this way:

In biochemistry, for example, which studies how some drugs would work because they fit like a key in a lock, if you had the mirror image it wouldn't fit. So only one design would work to cure something or cause a disease, whether it was vitamins or proteins that had active sites that could only be approached by a certain shape. If you could figure that out, the shape that would fit in that keyhole, you could design the drug. I could think more readily in spatial terms like that, rather than [in terms of] an apparatus, about how to improve the machinery.

In 1953, Jim graduated as salutatorian from Mt. Zion (Bubba had been valedictorian the previous year) and headed off to his father's alma mater, Davidson College, to major in chemistry. Although his athletic pursuits ended after his first year—Jim tried out for freshman football but soon realized making the varsity team was unlikely—he once again threw himself into a wide spectrum of campus activities. He was a member of the male chorus, president

JIM (*LEFT*) CLOWNING
AROUND WITH FRATERNITY
BROTHER ZELL McGEE IN
FRONT OF A HISTORICAL
MARKER
MARTIN FAMILY PHOTO

of the concert band, an active member of the Omicron Delta Kappa leadership fraternity and the Phi Mu Alpha Sinfonia music fraternity, treasurer of the inter-fraternity council, and rush chairman for the Beta Theta Pi social fraternity (he later served as national president of Beta Theta Pi in the 1970s). During his senior year, Jim even auditioned for the Charlotte Symphony and won a seat playing tuba.

JIM MEETS DOTTIE

Both during high school and college, church played a major role in the social life of Jim and his brothers. Teenagers from the three largest churches in Winnsboro—Presbyterian, ARP, and Methodist—got together after Sunday services as a combined youth group to eat, socialize, sing, and study the Bible. Jim and his brothers also frequently attended Presbyterian youth conferences around the state.

It was at one such conference, a summer program at South Carolina's Lake

Greenwood when Jim was in 10th grade, that he met Dorothy Ann "Dottie" McAulay, a little over a year his junior. He liked her from the start. Jim already knew Dottie's father, the assistant manager of a Belk department store in Columbia. The company's founder, William Henry Belk of Charlotte, was a generous patron of Presbyterian causes, including churches, hospitals, and orphanages. When Belk sent Ben McAulay to help run his store in Columbia, there was a related assignment: to help found a new church, Eastminster Presbyterian, and to assist Presbyterian ministers in the area. The Reverend Arthur Martin was one of those ministers. He regularly took Jim and the other boys to Ben McAulay's Belk store in Columbia to buy shoes and clothes from a wider selection than they could find in Winnsboro.

Over the next few years, Jim Martin and Dottie McAulay saw each other at various church gatherings. But it wasn't until Jim was a student at Davidson that his relationship with Dottie took a different turn. One spring weekend, he came home to Winnsboro to escort a friend to the prom. The following day, Saturday, Jim's mother, Mary, hosted a meeting of Presbyterian youth leaders at the Martin home. One of the attendees was Dottie McAulay of Columbia. After the meeting, the young people went swimming. Jim decided that Dottie "was a right interesting young lady" and decided to get to know her better. That summer, he worked as a lifeguard at a Presbyterian conference center near Asheville, North Carolina, called Montreat (short for "mountain retreat"). He invited Dottie up for the week, showing her the frigid lake where he worked and taking her dining, sightseeing, hiking, and square dancing—though always "with a good chaperon." The two continued to date throughout Jim's undergraduate studies at Davidson.

As he thought about his career after college, Jim concluded that practical experience in chemistry might help clarify his options. During his sophomore year, he applied for a summer job at Esso Research and Engineering Company (EREC), an affiliate of Standard Oil based in Linden, New Jersey. For weeks, he heard nothing. Then he got a call from EREC's Lyman Parrigin, a Davidson graduate. Parrigin said sheepishly that the application had been mislaid under a desk blotter—and offered Jim the job right then and there.

The decision proved fortuitous. Jim worked each summer at EREC's Linden lab from his sophomore to his senior year. During his second stint, in 1956, he even received his first patents, for three applications of butyl rubber he developed with colleagues. Also that summer, Jim met Bob Miner, a Ciba

JIM ESCORTING DOTTIE
MCAULAY TO A FORMAL
DANCE
DAVIDSON COLLEGE

pharmaceutical company executive, while both were attending a local church. Miner had earned his graduate degree in chemistry at Princeton. Learning that Jim was majoring in the subject at Davidson and considering graduate studies, Miner discouraged him from choosing such schools as Harvard and MIT. If he wanted an excellent education in a friendly environment, he told Jim, he should make a different choice. "I twisted his arm to go to Princeton," Miner said. His argument proved persuasive, as did the fact that Princeton's upper-level chemistry program had a strong focus on theory.

In preparation for graduate studies at Princeton in the fall of 1957, Jim took two fateful steps. The first, and more important, was proposing marriage to Dottie—not that the proposal came as any great surprise. Once Jim's Princeton plans grew definite, she said, "I just wasn't going to let him go that far away." They married on June 1, 1957. The other step was to apply to the St. Louis–based Danforth Foundation for a slot in its national fellowship program. Danforth Fellows were required to meet three criteria: espouse a commitment to a religious faith, pledge to teach at a university after graduation, and attend weeklong programs each summer at Michigan's Camp Miniwanca. Jim found all three stipulations easy to meet. He had already decided he would rather teach chemistry than work as an industrial chemist. And he had always loved the water, so the prospect of spending part of his summer at a camp on Lake Michigan was a welcome one. In fact, it was at Camp Miniwanca that Jim met another Danforth Fellow, Tony Abbott, who would become his neighbor, Davidson faculty colleague, and lifelong friend. Another Danforth Fellow Jim befriended, William Bowen, became an influential labor economist and president of Princeton University.

At Princeton, Jim threw himself into his studies with the goal of finishing his doctorate in three years. His specialty was organic stereochemistry, the study of how atoms and molecules are arranged in three-dimensional space to form organic compounds. He was particularly interested in the Diels-Alder reaction, named for the two German chemists who won the 1950 Nobel Prize for their discovery. Among other applications, the Diels-Alder reaction was useful to chemists creating synthetic steroids, cholesterols, and other compounds commonly employed in medicine and manufacturing. Jim's doctoral dissertation, completed in 1960 and typed up by Dottie, was entitled, "Stereochemistry of the Diels-Alder Reaction." He published a version of the paper the following year in the academic journal *Chemical Reviews*, with Princeton chemistry professor Richard Hill, his thesis advisor, listed as coauthor.

BACK TO DAVIDSON

While Jim completed his Ph.D., Dottie took a secretarial course and got a job in the university's Industrial Relations Department. Their first child, James G. Martin Jr., was born during their stay in Princeton. Later, his parents and siblings would tease Jimmy for being a "Jersey boy."

As the final year of his doctoral program began, Jim began to consider teaching offers from Arkansas State, St. Lawrence University, and other schools. Still, the tug of home was strong. During his last year at Davidson, his organic chemistry professor, Dr. John Gallent, had pointedly mentioned his advanced age and urged Jim not to leave Davidson out of his future plans. Three years later, as Jim approached the end of his doctoral studies, he heard from the dean of the Davidson faculty, Dr. Frontis Johnston, who had been Jim's history professor. Johnston told his former student that Jim could become

"Mr. Chemistry in 10 years" at Davidson. But there was no need for a hard sell. The Martins were delighted at the opportunity to move back to the Carolinas. Jim joined the Davidson faculty in time for the 1960–61 school year. He would remain there for 12 years, until being elected to Congress in November 1972.

Jim expected to love teaching chemistry. His expectation proved correct. The challenge of translating complex principles into ideas that students could readily grasp appealed to him. "He was always prepared," said Dr. James Fredericksen, a colleague in Davidson's Chemistry Department. "He did his homework when he was getting a lecture up." A tough but fair grader, Jim quickly became a popular professor and threw himself into campus life much as he had during his undergraduate days, serving as faculty advisor for several student organizations. He sang tenor in the Davidson College Presbyterian Choir and rejoined the Charlotte Symphony in what he described as "first chair" in tuba (there was only one player). Jim also returned to the football field as a referee for high-school games and became an active member of the Davidson College Presbyterian Church, eventually serving as a deacon. The Martin family's first home was a small, rented log cabin on Thompson Street. They lived there while building a house of their own, made possible by the college's policy of offering low-interest loans to faculty members.

During Jim's undergraduate days, Davidson had been led by longtime president Dr. John Rood Cunningham. While Jim was at Princeton, Davidson got a new president, Dr. David Grier Martin, a lawyer who had served as college treasurer under Cunningham. President Martin took an instant liking to Jim (no relation). In 1964, Grier Martin called the young chemistry professor into his office and told him that a friend, a Charlotte obstetrician, had a lot he no longer wanted to use on Lake Norman, an artificial lake created a few years earlier when Duke Power Company erected a dam on the Catawba River to generate electricity. The lot happened to be next to President Martin's own lakefront property, which had a dock both families shared. He asked if Jim and Dottie might be interested in leasing the lot. At the time, Jim saw it as a mysterious but exciting opportunity. "He could have offered it to any of the established faculty members," Jim remarked. He and Dottie jumped at the chance, not just because they enjoyed the water but also because the college president would be their neighbor. At first, they could afford no more than a hammock, a small boat, and water skis. Later, the state utilities commission pressed Duke to sell some of its property along Lake Norman to leaseholders.

Duke made a special offer to those willing to put houses on their lots, as that would create new electricity customers. Jim and Dottie jumped at that chance, too, even though the deal put a major strain on the family finances. That lake house, enlarged several times over the ensuing decades, remains the Martins' home. Brothers Joe and Neal Martin also built lake houses nearby, as did Tony Abbott and his wife, Susan.

The family continued to grow as well. A daughter, Emily Wood Martin, arrived a couple of years after Jim and Dottie returned to Davidson. A decade later, they had another son, Ben. Finances were tight. Jim earned a modest faculty salary and got $35 for every concert he played with the Charlotte Symphony. For a time, Dottie supplemented the family income by working as a teacher's aide. Another source of extra revenue was renting rooms in their house to girls visiting Davidson to see their boyfriends for dates (the college didn't go fully coed until 1973). Each room went for five dollars a night. When there was a school dance, football game, or other large event, the Martins would room four girls and make $20. Every little bit helped.

Jim Martin had arrived in 1960 at a college ripe for transformation. Davidson had a proud tradition and a loyal, active base of alumni. But its leaders saw opportunities to move the institution forward by reforming its curriculum, admissions, and policies. In 1962, the college dropped its racial barriers to admissions. Thanks to financial support from the Duke Endowment and other donors, it also began a program of upgrading its library, physical plant, and academic programs. With help from Jim Martin and other faculty members, Davidson designed and introduced its multidisciplinary Blue Sky Curriculum, which broadened course offerings and encouraged independent study.

South Carolina native John Napier was an undergraduate at Davidson in the late 1960s and drew Jim Martin as his faculty advisor. According to Napier, both faculty and students saw Jim as a "rising star" on campus who was destined for "bigger things"—as an award-winning chemist, perhaps, or a future president of Davidson. As Jim had by this time won election to the county commission, some were already speculating that he might end up in Congress. An older colleague, history professor Chalmers Davidson, told Napier that Jim's natural leadership abilities had come to the fore early in his academic career. Other, more experienced faculty members often looked to Jim as someone who could "bring divergent factions together to see the other point of view," Davidson told Napier, who would later serve with Jim Martin in Washington as a congressman from South Carolina.

As Davidson underwent significant changes during the 1960s, most alumni and donors came to see them as positive. But not everything happening at the college struck them the same way. In particular, as student protests and left-wing activism became increasingly prominent on campuses across the country, some longtime supporters began to wonder about the political climate at Davidson. For example, they read frequent columns in the *Charlotte Observer*, the *Davidsonian*, and other publications by Ernest Patterson, a Davidson economist whose Marxist beliefs and apologetics for Soviet foreign policy won him the epithets "Red Ernie" and "Pink Patterson." They also learned that in 1962, the college's first drama instructor, Bill Goodykoontz, had produced some plays laced with controversial political content, and that he had resigned the following year after clashing with college administrators.

Among those grumbling about a possible ideological divide between the college's faculty and its donor base was one of its most generous benefactors, Charles Cannon, president of Kannapolis-based Cannon Mills. He repeatedly mentioned his concerns to President Grier Martin, who assured Cannon that Patterson, Goodykoontz, and other professors didn't let their personal politics influence their teaching or grading practices. Still, it seemed to President Martin that it would be helpful if donors such as Cannon knew that Davidson was a place of diverse views and political allegiances.

As luck would have it, shortly after one of his tense conversations with Charlie Cannon in early 1966, Grier Martin received a request for a meeting from a young chemistry professor who said he was thinking about running for political office—as a Republican.

Given the circumstances, the president of Davidson College wasn't just comfortable with Jim Martin's idea. He was ecstatic.

CHAPTER TWO

A PROFESSOR TURNED POLITICIAN

Jim Martin never lost a campaign. But he did lose an election. The distinction is important. When he approached his Davidson College superiors in early 1966 about running for county commission, it was not his first foray into electoral politics.

In 1963, Martin had decided to enter a nonpartisan race for Davidson's town council, aspiring to be of service to a community he loved. Shortly after filing for office, he was heading toward his office on campus and ran into Dr. John T. Kimbrough, a respected mathematics professor and incumbent council member. Kimbrough said he'd heard the 27-year-old Martin would be a candidate in the upcoming election. "Well, now," Kimbrough confided, "you understand that in Davidson we don't campaign actively. We just rely on the people who know us."

Martin accepted the advice with equanimity. He'd done the math. During the previous municipal election in 1961, the lowest-polling victor had gotten a little over 100 votes. Martin pulled out a Davidson phone directory and picked out at least 100 good friends he'd made since his return from Princeton. Assuming most of them turned out to vote, plus a few others who knew him by reputation, he figured he had an excellent chance of winning the election without breeching the local political etiquette by running an active campaign.

Martin figured wrong. Left out of his equation was that Davidson had four bond referendums on the ballot to fund water, sewer, and electricity projects. As a result, voter turnout for the municipal election on May 7, 1963, was higher than it had been two years before. Martin got 114 votes. But this time, it took at least 166 to win one of the at-large seats. "The bond referendums

IN THE CHEMISTRY LAB
WITH PROFESSOR MARTIN
DAVIDSON COLLEGE PHOTO

succeeded," he said. "I didn't." He would never make that mistake again. In all his subsequent races—six primary and general elections for county commission, 12 primary and general elections for Congress, and four primary and general elections for governor—Jim Martin ran energetic, creative, and aggressive campaigns, even when the advantages of incumbency seemed to render the effort unnecessary. He never took an election for granted again. And he went 22–0.

A NATIONAL REVIEW OF LOCAL POLITICS

As a high-school and college student, Jim Martin hadn't paid much attention to politics. His parents were conservative-leaning Democrats, as were the majority of their fellow Georgians and Carolinians. But Arthur and Mary's views did diverge from the conventional wisdom of the day on a key issue: race relations. They were "very progressive" on racial issues, Martin said later. As a church leader and, most notably, as executive secretary of the Presbyterian

Synod of South Carolina, the Reverend Arthur Martin decried extremism and counseled moderation during periods of racial strife.

Behind the scenes, he went farther. During the mid-1950s, the Reverend Martin was one of the founding members of a group of Columbia-area clergy known informally as the "Displaced Pastors." It included church leaders, editors of denominational newspapers, and faculty members from local seminaries and the University of South Carolina. The group offered assistance to fellow ministers who, by speaking out against racism, had lost their jobs. It also worked "quietly and consistently behind the lines" to encourage constructive dialogue and racial reconciliation within the denominations and their institutions, according to civil-rights historian Elaine Lechtreck. Later, the Reverend Martin created South Carolina's first biracial association of ministers, served as founding chairman of the state's first ecumenical council of churches, and helped organize an interfaith group of Protestant, Catholic, and Jewish leaders. When Harvey Gantt enrolled as the first black student at Clemson University in 1963, Arthur Martin worked with other church leaders to calm tensions, ensuring that South Carolina's integration experience would not be like Mississippi's. In an interesting twist of fate, Gantt would go on to serve as mayor of Charlotte from 1983 to 1987, overlapping Jim Martin's tenure as Charlotte's congressman and North Carolina's governor.

While Jim was hardly a political junkie as a young man, growing up in Arthur and Mary Martin's household did produce a love of reading and a strong sense of civic responsibility. These characteristics would eventually put him on the path to a political career. During his studies at Princeton, he became close friends with Bill Purcell, a fellow graduate student in the Chemistry Department. Martin was drawn to Purcell, a devout Catholic, because he was one of his few colleagues in the department who matched Martin's strong religious faith.

One day, Purcell handed him a copy of *National Review*, the conservative magazine William F. Buckley had founded just a few years earlier. Martin was fascinated. He took particular interest in subjects to which he had not previously given much thought, such as foreign policy. Coming from the solidly Democratic South, Martin also found *National Review*'s frequent discussions of the principle of federalism compelling. While he agreed with the conservative argument that Washington was drawing too much power to itself on transportation, education, and other issues best left to states and localities,

AT THE BLACKBOARD WITH PROFESSOR MARTIN. DAVIDSON COLLEGE PHOTO

Martin saw a problem with applying the idea. At least in the nation's capital, there was robust partisan debate and competition. That wasn't true back home. For federalism to work properly, Martin came to believe, state and local officials needed to be held accountable through frequent, competitive general elections. In the South, that would require a Republican Party capable of challenging Democrats outside of a few mountain counties and urban enclaves. To be competitive, the party would need more than just good candidates, strategists, and resources. It would need a governing philosophy for delivering public services such as education and transportation in an effective, efficient way, a philosophy Martin would later call "constructive conservatism." If states and localities "were going to establish themselves with a bulwark against the federal government telling them what they had to do," he concluded, "then they had to meet those responsibilities themselves."

Martin continued to read *National Review* and other periodicals as he completed his studies at Princeton and began his work as a professor. In 1962, he changed his voter registration from Democratic to Republican. But his involvement in political matters went no farther. "I thought that there was a need to inject some degree of competition" into North Carolina politics, Martin later reflected, "though I had no idea that I'd ever be a part of helping to make that come about." Then a group of students approached him about the idea of forming a Conservative Club on the Davidson campus. They needed a faculty advisor. Martin agreed. When the students decided to convert it into a College Republicans chapter, Martin continued his role. The group hosted events and volunteered to walk precincts during election campaigns, compiling and using an extensive set of voter records on index cards. It was Martin's first taste of partisan politics at the retail level. He found that he liked it.

A NEW BREED OF REPUBLICANS

Local GOP leaders took note of Davidson's active College Republicans chapter. They were convinced they needed a new breed of younger, more energetic candidates to market the Republican Party—and that 1966 might just be the year to present them to increasingly restless voters. Boasting nearly 300,000 residents at the time, Mecklenburg County was the state's most populous. It was also one of the few counties in the state represented in Washington by a Republican, Charles Raper Jonas. Widely known as "Mr. Republican" for his efforts to build the GOP brand, Charlie Jonas was first elected to Congress in 1952 in what was then North Carolina's 10th District. He was the first Republican in the state to hold a United States House seat since 1930, when two freshmen GOP congressmen—George Pritchard and Charlie's father, Charles Andrew Jonas—lost their reelection bids amid voter discontent with the Herbert Hoover administration.

The younger Jonas stayed in Congress for 20 years. He even survived an attempt to gerrymander him out of office after the 1960 census, which had revealed that North Carolina's then-anemic population growth would cost the state a congressional seat. Democratic legislators responded by moving Democratic-leaning precincts from the neighboring district of Representative Hugh Quincy Alexander into Jonas's district in hopes of ridding the delegation of its lone GOP member. Their hopes were dashed in 1962, as Jonas coasted to reelection while Alexander, his base weakened by the gerrymander, lost to a GOP challenger, Lenoir furniture executive Jim Broyhill. Never again would Republicans be shut out of North Carolina's congressional delegation, or even relegated to a single seat.

While Charlie Jonas played a pivotal role in the growth of North Carolina's Republican Party, he was from Lincolnton. Mecklenburg County routinely delivered sizable vote totals for Congressman Jonas, but the partisan relationship didn't extend down the ballot. Democrats occupied all six of the county's seats in the North Carolina House and both of its seats in the state Senate. All of Mecklenburg's county commissioners were Democrats, as was the sheriff. Only two Republicans had ever been elected to the county commission, both in 1962, and they'd lost their reelection bids two years later. More than three-quarters of the county's voters were registered Democrats. Statewide, North Carolina had a Democratic governor and two Democrats in the United States Senate. In the 1964 presidential race, the state had voted for Lyndon Johnson (unlike neighboring South Carolina and Georgia, both of which went for Barry Goldwater). The 1964 election cycle had also slashed the GOP's already-scant presence in the state legislature by eight seats, leaving just 14 Republicans in the 120-seat House and a single Republican in the 50-seat Senate.

Joining the GOP in Mecklenburg County in the mid-1960s, then, looked more like an act of protest than a serious effort at influencing local politics. But looks can be deceiving. By early 1966, Republican leaders in North Carolina had come to believe they were on the verge of a political breakout. For one thing, the national environment would be favorable. After winning one of America's largest popular-vote majorities in his 1964 election campaign, President Johnson saw his approval ratings plummet over the next two years. Popular discontent with both his foreign and domestic policies played a role, as did Southern resentment of federal action on segregation and voting rights.

Looking to capitalize on the trend in North Carolina, Republican leaders sought to recruit a solid slate of candidates. While the state's incumbent Democrat in the United States Senate, Everett Jordan, would feel little threat in 1966 from Republican nominee John Shallcross, other Democratic incumbents weren't so fortunate. In eastern North Carolina, the longtime chairman of the House Agriculture Committee, Harold Cooley, faced a rematch with Jim Gardner, the 33-year-old Republican businessman who nearly beat him in 1964. (Gardner had been elected state party chairman in 1965 and moved the party headquarters from Charlotte to Raleigh.) Another Democratic congressman in the east, freshman Walter Jones, faced a serious challenge from East Carolina University political scientist John East, who had run surprisingly strong against Jones in a special election a few months earlier. Meanwhile, in the Piedmont and western counties where the GOP had always enjoyed a stronger foothold, Republicans put up strong candidates for dozens of legislative and county commission seats. "Get away from LBJ!" was their slogan. It proved to be a popular one.

A BUSINESS CONTACT
TURNS POLITICAL

Mecklenburg GOP leaders initially focused on recruiting candidates for the General Assembly. The county's rapid growth resulted in an additional seat in each chamber for the 1966 cycle. Its delegation, all elected at-large, now would consist of seven representatives and three senators. County chairman Marcus Hickman, a Charlotte attorney who cofounded what became the Kennedy Covington law firm, first approached Ken Harris, a Charlotte banking executive and member of the politically influential Rhyne clan of neighboring Iredell County. But Harris, who would later serve in the state legislature and become Charlotte's first Republican mayor, wasn't yet ready to list his name on the ballot. However, he agreed to help Hickman recruit other candidates. One of the names on Harris's list was a business client, Professor Jim Martin.

When pitched the idea of running for the state legislature, Martin was intrigued but doubtful it would be consistent with his duties to family and faculty. Hickman and Harris then switched gears and talked about the county commission. Elected at-large like the legislative delegation, Mecklenburg's commission had five members, all Democrats. Hickman and Harris said they wanted to run five strong Republicans as a county-wide ticket, hoping to take advantage of an anti-Johnson, pro-Republican tide in 1966. Seeing an opportunity to pursue public service locally without encumbering his professional and personal responsibilities, Martin said he would run the idea by his Davidson College superiors, Grier Martin and Frontis Johnston.

The subsequent meeting went better than he could have expected. Textile magnate Charlie Cannon wasn't the only Davidson donor who had expressed unease about what was perceived as the increasingly leftward tilt of the faculty. Davidson leaders saw Jim Martin's proposal as a great opportunity to mollify the critics. As Tony Abbott, Martin's faculty colleague and close friend, would later put it to a television reporter, "Davidson is sort of like an island of liberalism in a sea of conservatism." The way President Martin and Dean Johnston saw it, even if Martin didn't win the election, his candidacy would serve to showcase the college's ideological diversity. And if he did end up on the county commission, so much the better for Davidson. The two gave Martin their full support.

Martin reported back to Hickman and Harris and confirmed his intention to run. But in his eagerness, he forgot to consult the most important person of all: his wife, Dottie. When she found out he had agreed to run for county commission without talking to her first, she "wasn't amused," Martin later recalled. Dottie put it this way: "I don't think I was ugly, but I did want to know what he was going to do." She ultimately supported her husband's decision. Still, he learned a valuable lesson. From then on, he always sought Dottie's trusted counsel before making big decisions.

For the 1966 cycle, the Mecklenburg GOP fielded its strongest slate of candidates in decades, including a highly competitive nominee for county sheriff, former SBI agent Donald Stahl. In addition to Martin, four other Republicans were running for county commission. Each was making his first run for public office. Robert Potter was a 43-year-old attorney who would later join the federal bench. Charles Tull, 47, owned an oil distribution company. John A. Campbell, who went by "Gus," was a 47-year-old accountant and business executive. At 67, life-insurance executive M. W. "Pete" Peterson was the most experienced hand on the team. At just 30, Jim Martin was the youngest candidate of either party. The five Democrats were all incumbent county commissioners: Chairman Sam Atkinson, Vice Chairman and former Matthews mayor W. A. "Lex" Hood, retired state employee Frank Blythe, businessman Henry Thrower, and building contractor Mason Wallace.

THE DOCTOR IS IN

Martin and the other Republicans knew their opponents would benefit from massive financial and organizational advantages. So they husbanded their resources carefully. Most of their newspaper ads and billboards featured all five candidates together. Each promoted the other four during campaign appearances. As Election Day approached, however, some solo display ads appeared. One featured a picture of the youthful candidate with the headline, "Dr. Jim Martin for County Commissioner," accompanied by this text: "It's time we

THE BUMPER STICKERS REVEAL THE TRUTH: JIM SUPPORTED BARRY GOLDWATER AND DOTTIE SUPPORTED LYNDON JOHNSON IN 1964. MARTIN FAMILY PHOTO

elected someone concerned enough to look into the Court House, the School House, and the Jail House. Jim Martin is such a man!" The description "Dr. Jim Martin" also graced the candidate's posters and streamers in distinctive red type on black backgrounds. More than a few voters may have drawn the conclusion that he was a medical doctor, not a chemistry professor. But how many actually saw the messages in the first place? Martin's entire campaign fund consisted of $435. Of that amount, $400 came from a successful Charlotte businessman, Reitzel Snider, who had been Martin's fraternity brother at Davidson. His other two contributions came from his mother ($25) and his own pocket ($10). The Martin campaign relied on a team of volunteers to hand out leaflets and put up signs. Perhaps the most prodigious volunteer was Jim Gill, Dottie's uncle, who tossed piles of "Dr. Jim Martin" signs in the back of his pickup truck and went from street corner to street corner putting them up.

Media coverage of the race was sporadic at best. Indeed, to the extent the local media covered the Mecklenburg campaigns, as opposed to regional or national ones, they put most of their emphasis on the sheriff's race between Stahl, the Republican challenger, and incumbent Democrat Clyde Hunter, who had held the office for 22 years. County commission candidates spoke at occasional public forums hosted by the League of Women Voters and other community groups. But the events were lightly attended and sparsely covered.

Martin and his teammates emphasized three major issues: school funding, open government, and city-county cooperation. The education issue was the most contentious. As population growth began to take off in the early 1960s, demand surged for new teachers, support staff, and facilities for the newly merged Charlotte-Mecklenburg Schools (CMS). Democratic-majority commissions sought to keep pace while also funding other county programs— and while avoiding large hikes in the county's property-tax rate. Although real-estate values were rising along with the population, residential property wasn't revalued every year. In 1966, CMS asked for a budget increase that would have required a massive increase in the property tax. It was so large, in fact, that Martin and other Republicans suggested it had never been seriously intended—that the initial proposals were inflated to allow Democratic incumbents to "get credit" for protecting taxpayers by approving small funding amounts later in the process.

Whatever the motivation, the Democratic commission did reject the initial spending request despite strong pressure from the local teachers' association, newspaper editorial boards, and some civic leaders who favored more money for education regardless of the effect on the property-tax rate. The pressure was so intense, in fact, that county commissioners agreed to put the matter to a public referendum in May 1966. By a large margin, voters rejected a six-cent increase in the property tax to fund higher teacher salaries. Democratic commissioners subsequently enacted a far leaner budget, all the while arguing that the state legislature ought to give Mecklenburg authorization to levy sales or cigarette taxes to fund school improvements. Martin and the other Republicans actually took the same position on alternatives to the property tax, but they also argued that the Democratic commissioners had failed to set firm priorities with county revenues—that the incumbents could have been more generous to the school system while keeping property taxes down by spending less on lower-priority programs.

The Democrats spoke with one voice on school funding. Indeed, they rarely disagreed about anything, at least in public. When Democratic commissioner Mason Wallace voted no at one mid-1966 meeting, it actually made front-page news—because it interrupted a string of 355 unanimous votes by the board, dating back to the previous fall. The Republicans argued that the incumbent commissioners were making decisions in secret caucuses, then presenting the results in public meetings with little discussion and unanimous votes. Playing off his background in music, Martin took to calling the commission a "one-man board," referring to Chairman Sam Atkinson's dominant influence. The Democrats would "say their decisions weren't unanimous in their private meeting," Martin said. "We answered, 'Well, so what? Let's hear what the arguments are.' "

Another range of issues involved relations among Mecklenburg County, the city of Charlotte, and the smaller municipalities. For years, local officials had tried but failed to work out arrangements for extending Charlotte's water and sewer lines into the county. Charlotte officials, in turn, had tried but failed to get the county to help fund projects of mutual interest, such as charity care at Charlotte Memorial Hospital (which later became the anchor institution of Carolinas Medical Center). Some local leaders had a broader goal: merging county and municipal services, such as animal control and law enforcement, with the eventual aim of consolidating the various localities into a single Mecklenburg government. The Republican candidates favored consolidation where it would save money and faulted the Democrats for not fostering greater intergovernmental cooperation. Jim Martin, however, was careful to stress that the county commission shouldn't chart a new course on anything, such as new taxing authority or governmental mergers, without building a public consensus first. "It is important not to get too far away from what the people want," Martin insisted. "I would educate the people to the needs, not force it down their throats, until they are persuaded that this is what we must do." This concept became integral to Martin's philosophy of how best to resolve difficult public-policy disputes.

ASSEMBLING A WINNING COALITION

By the homestretch of the 1966 campaign, Mecklenburg Democrats were privately fretful, while Mecklenburg Republicans were publicly gleeful. For the first time anyone could remember, the GOP outpaced Democrats in new voter registrations, although Republicans were still overwhelmingly the minority party. At the legislative level, Democratic incumbents who had once fielded coordinated campaigns were now running their own individual races, suggesting a lack of unity. As for the county commission, the incumbent Democrats had until the last weeks of the race acted as though Election Day would be just another Tuesday in November. In particular, they continued interviewing candidates to replace County Manager Harry Weatherly, whom they'd let go after complaining that his performance did not justify his $22,500 salary (about $163,000 in 2015 dollars). Weatherly was scheduled to leave the job a week after Election Day. Commission chairman Sam Atkinson announced that the board was planning to have a new manager in place by early December. The notion that the Democrats might not be in a position to make that decision went unmentioned, at least in public.

At a November 2 event in Charlotte, the state's Democratic governor and United States senators joined other leaders in rallying Democratic voters to the polls. Senator Sam Ervin joked that Republicans were like a cross-eyed man for whom it didn't matter whether he "looked where he was going 'cause he didn't go where he was looking." The Democratic leaders may have been engaging in a bit of bluster, but even outside observers still saw a GOP breakout in Mecklenburg as improbable. Joe Doster, the reporter covering the race for the *Charlotte Observer*, matter-of-factly described the five incumbent Democratic commissioners as "favored for re-election as a group" just days before the vote.

Both sides were indeed running five-man slates. But voters retained the right to pick and choose among the candidates. So did Doster's colleagues on the editorial board of the *Observer*. In a November 7 endorsement editorial, they recommended the reelection of three Democratic incumbents: Chairman Sam Atkinson, Vice Chairman Lex Hood, and longtime commissioner Frank Blythe. For the other two slots, however, they suggested voters pick from three candidates: Democratic incumbent Mason Wallace, Republican Gus Campbell, and Republican Jim Martin, whom the paper singled out as "worthy of special consideration." While Martin "lacks experience in public affairs," the editorial stated, "his serious-minded approach and the work he has done on his own in analyzing budget trends in local education are impressive and show considerable understanding. His open-minded attitude and his obvious intelligence would be an asset to the board." The evening paper, the *Charlotte News*, described Martin as "an engaging candidate who has made a good impression despite his youth" but did not endorse him, urging instead that voters reelect Democrats Atkinson, Hood, and Wallace and add two Republicans, Peterson and Potter, to the board.

While Martin expected a strong turnout among Republican-leaning voters and hoped that favorable media coverage might win him crossover votes from conservative and moderate Democrats, he didn't stop there. Inspired by his father's example, Martin reached out to leaders of another traditionally Democratic constituency: black voters. He particularly focused on black ministers who shared his deep religious faith. Other local Republicans were thinking along similar lines. On the weekend before Election Day, the party targeted black neighborhoods with leaflets encouraging residents to "elect Republicans and get some action instead of just promises." The piece went on to link the entire Democratic slate to I. Beverly Lake Sr., whose name appeared on the ballot as a Democratic candidate for election to the North Carolina Supreme Court. Lake had run for governor in both 1960 and 1964 as a defender of segregation. The victor in the latter race, Governor Dan K. Moore, had appointed Lake to the supreme-court seat he now aspired to win outright. The Republican leaflet reproduced a portion of the ballot with Lake's name circled. It also argued that Mecklenburg's black residents were poorly treated by local Democratic officeholders. "Why is it that Negro deputy sheriffs are not allowed to serve papers in the county?" it asked. "How many Negroes have good jobs at the county courthouse? How many Negroes have been named to county boards and commissions?"

THE REPUBLICAN EARTHQUAKE

Whether Martin's efforts and other GOP appeals were responsible for attracting black voters or at least dampening enthusiasm for the Democratic ticket would be hard to prove. But on Election Day, Democrats did win fewer votes in Mecklenburg County's majority-black precincts than they usually polled. At the same time, turnout was higher than expected in Republican-leaning areas—the *Observer* called them "silk-stocking districts"—thanks to effective voter mobilization and strong anti-Johnson sentiment. The effect was evident as the balloting began on the morning of November 8, 1966. "You could tell it was our day when the voters started coming in to the polls," one Mecklenburg Republican said. "They looked mad and they didn't stay in there very long. We knew that was a straight Republican vote."

The results in Mecklenburg were the political equivalent of an earthquake. On the county commission, only the incumbent chairman, Sam Atkinson,

survived. County voters replaced the other four Democrats with Gus Campbell, Robert Potter, Pete Peterson, and Jim Martin. The Democratic sheriff
lost, too, while Republicans claimed two of the county's seven House seats.
The legislative gains in Mecklenburg were part of a larger trend. Statewide,
the GOP gained 12 seats in the House and six in the Senate, giving the party
a total of 33 members in the General Assembly—the highest number to date
in the 20th century. North Carolina Republicans also upped their number of
congressional members to three with the victory of Jim Gardner over Harold
Cooley, although John East ended up falling short in his bid against Walter
Jones.

Jim Martin didn't just win a seat on the Mecklenburg commission. He
was the highest-polling Republican, winning 26,494 votes. By tradition, he
should have been elected chairman at the new board's first meeting. As a first-
time elected official just shy of 31 years of age, however, Martin didn't consider
himself ready. And as a Davidson resident, his knowledge of Charlotte's issues
and personalities was limited. He suggested that Gus Campbell serve as chairman for the first few months while Martin got up to speed. Campbell and the
other Republicans agreed. They had run on an agenda of opening up county
government and prioritizing education. The first issue on their plate, however,
was a leftover. Rather than moving quickly to replace County Manager Harry
Weatherly, as the previous Democratic commission had planned, the new Republican board asked him to stay in the job. What may have been intended
as a temporary arrangement became permanent, Weatherly serving as county
manager for most of Martin's six-year tenure on the commission.

Shortly after taking office, the members of the new Republican majority
began acting on their campaign promises. They moved more board discussions
from private caucuses onto the agenda for public meetings. In charge of county
government for the first time, the Republicans also decided it would be wise
to divvy up oversight responsibilities by agency, so each commissioner would
more rapidly gain expertise. Robert Potter became the commission's point
man on water and sewer issues. The new chairman, accountant Gus Campbell, took on primary responsibility for the budget. Pete Peterson focused on
health and human services. The former chairman, Sam Atkinson, got the assignment of working with the county's legislative delegation, most of whom
were Democrats like himself.

As for Jim Martin, he assumed the lead role on education. His immediate challenge was to address the longstanding dispute about school funding. In doing so, Martin exhibited what became a characteristic element of his leadership style: bringing people of different views together to facilitate dialogue and develop consensus. Working with his neighbor, school-board member Julia Maulden, Martin set up a dinner at Davidson College for members of both boards, plus key staff members including Harry Weatherly, the recently retained county manager, and Charlotte-Mecklenburg Schools superintendent Craig Phillips, who would later serve 20 years as North Carolina's superintendent of public instruction. After sharing a private meal at the student union, the participants opened their policy discussion to the media. School-board members made their pitch for greater funding. The newly elected Republican commissioners expressed their willingness to listen. Over the subsequent months, members of the two boards met frequently. Rather than hearing from school-system representatives at the end of budget meetings, as previous commissions had, the Republicans scheduled them first.

The Mecklenburg commissioners also acted quickly on another priority: extending water and sewer lines into rural areas to encourage development. On a party-line vote, they made a deal with the city to approve service to the University of North Carolina at Charlotte in time for the 1967 session of the state legislature, when campus officials planned to seek expansion funds. UNCC had joined the Consolidated University of North Carolina only two years earlier as its fourth campus (after UNC–Chapel Hill, North Carolina State, and UNC-Greensboro). While some criticized the UNCC deal for being too generous to the city's Water Department, the county commissioners were actually buying time to prepare a far more ambitious idea: creating a county-run water utility to replace or merge with Charlotte's existing system. After a series of proposals and counterproposals, what initially emerged was a formal city-county water agreement. The county paid to extend lines to growing areas outside Charlotte while actually purchasing the water from the city. By the last year of Martin's tenure on the commission, 1972, the city and county had finally merged their systems into a single entity, the Charlotte-Mecklenburg Utility Department, which came to provide water and sewer service to most county households and businesses.

Working with his county commission colleagues on these and other policy issues gave Martin the opportunity to build relationships and learn new things. Not all of them had to do with politics. One afternoon, Martin and Peterson went to inspect a piece of real estate Mecklenburg County was purchasing. Discovering during their conversation that Peterson was a Freemason, Martin asked, "What would I need to do to become a Mason?" Peterson smiled and replied, "You just did." The inquiry would prove a momentous one for Martin, who soon joined Phalanx 33 Lodge. He would later become a 33rd-degree Mason (both Scottish and York rites), as well as a Shriner. Martin was eventually elected Grand Cross Knight of the Scottish Rite, a recognition held by only a few dozen American Masons.

A FRESH FACE BECOMES CHAIRMAN

In June 1967, Gus Campbell announced that he was giving up the gavel as commission chairman after six months in the job. The board unanimously chose Jim Martin to replace him. "At 31," reported the *Charlotte Observer*, "Martin is the youngest commissioner anyone at the courthouse can remember. He hardly even looks that old."

Among the new chairman's first duties was presiding over a series of hearings about a proposed county-wide zoning ordinance. It faced strong opposition from landowners. But proponents pointed out that municipalities were already imposing zoning restrictions on much of the county, including land in the extraterritorial jurisdiction of municipal officials for whom the affected residents could not vote. Martin and other commissioners approved the ordinance, thus adopting the first county-wide zoning in North Carolina.

Martin's leadership skills were simultaneously put to the test as the Republican board fashioned its first county budget. A combination of escalating service demands, higher debt service from voter-approved school bonds, and other factors led county staff to propose an initial 13 percent increase in the property-tax rate. Martin and the other new commissioners had resigned themselves to a tax hike, given Mecklenburg's prior fiscal commitments. But they kept it to 9 percent by cutting agency expenses and rejecting some requested increases, particularly from the county's Welfare Department and the Charlotte Area Fund, a nonprofit that administered antipoverty programs. The latter had been founded four years earlier as an outgrowth of the North Carolina Fund, a project created by three private grant makers—the Ford Foundation, the Z. Smith Reynolds Foundation, and the Mary Reynolds Babcock Foundation—at the instigation of former governor Terry Sanford.

Although Martin and other commissioners expressed their support for the stated goals of the Charlotte Area Fund, they questioned the governance and effectiveness of its programs. Their efforts to demand more accountability for taxpayer funds met with strident opposition not only from the fund's staff and board members but also from Charlotte mayor Stan Brookshire, the newspapers, and state officials. Brookshire argued that appropriating tax dollars to the organization was a matter of public safety. "We have been spared the traumatic experience of hundreds of other cities that have been caught up in civil strife," Charlotte's mayor said. "Our continuing to be spared will depend on our continuing efforts to meet human needs in our community." This argument didn't sit well with Martin. During the escalating tensions about the Charlotte Area Fund's request for additional money, he had attended a public meeting at which one fund supporter had threatened to slash his tires if the request wasn't honored. "You can't buy peace with money," Martin told Brookshire.

The county commission decided not to fund the organization's entire request. It further insisted that as a condition for receiving future amounts, the Charlotte Area Fund would need to provide documentation that its programs were successfully moving recipients into self-sufficiency. As chairman, Martin also had the opportunity to appoint additional members to the fund's board of directors, slots he filled with local business leaders and county health director Wallace Kuralt, the father of legendary CBS broadcaster Charles Kuralt. It later came out that one of the fund's most controversial hires, Noble Coleman, had a criminal record and was using the organization's resources to recruit activists to lobby for more government spending on welfare. Coleman and the executive director who hired him eventually resigned.

The enactment of a Mecklenburg County budget for the 1967–68 fiscal year was only the start of an extensive public debate about education funding. While the Republican-led county commission was crafting its spending plan, Mecklenburg's mostly Democratic legislative delegation was in Raleigh seeking permission to impose a local sales tax. The bill that finally passed the General Assembly authorized any county with a population exceeding 250,000 to hold a November 1967 referendum to levy a 1 percent local sales tax on top of the statewide rate of 3 percent. While the language of the measure didn't specify Mecklenburg, it was the only county in the state that met the standard. State lawmakers chose this language in an attempt to head off a potential constitutional challenge to a local-option sales tax.

It didn't work. Mecklenburg voters did indeed approve the one-cent hike in the sales tax in the November referendum, but three months later a group of local retailers and citizens sued to block its implementation, citing a provision of North Carolina's constitution that forbade the state legislature from authorizing any "class or subject" to be taxed unless "every classification shall be uniformly applicable in every county, municipality and other local taxing unit of the state." The plaintiffs argued that because Mecklenburg was the only county authorized to levy the sales tax, it was unconstitutional. Attorneys for the city, county, and state argued that the constitutional provision applied only to the uniform classification of land and buildings for local property taxes, and thus didn't prevent sales-tax rates from varying across the state.

During the 1967 referendum campaign, Jim Martin joined most other elected officials in urging voters to support the sales-tax hike, assuring them that if they voted in the sales tax, the county commission would then be able to reduce the property-tax rate. Shortly after the voters said yes to the sales tax, however, the school system and other agencies began lobbying to use the proceeds to raise employee salaries. Throughout 1968, both the constitutional challenge to the tax and the tussle over how to spend it clouded Mecklenburg's budget picture. In midsummer, citing the legal uncertainty surrounding the sales tax, the county commission voted to keep the property-tax rate level for the 1968–69 fiscal year but also to reject most agency requests for new spending.

For many politicians in Mecklenburg and other communities, the discussion of local taxing authority was only a subset of a larger conversation about how best to modernize local government. Political, business, and community leaders formed a task force to devise concrete steps for merging county and municipal governments. Among the participants was Jim Martin's mentor, Grier Martin, who remained active on the issue even after retiring as Davidson College's president in 1968. The effort took formal shape the following year, during the 1969 session of the North Carolina General Assembly, when lawmakers created the Charlotte-Mecklenburg Charter Commission to craft a merger plan for voter approval. While Jim Martin favored city-county consolidation in broad outline, he believed it was at least as important to encourage the region's localities to cooperate even if they were to remain legally separate. After reading about regional governmental councils already in operation in other states, Martin approached mayors and commission chairmen in surrounding counties about forming a similar body. The result was the Central

Piedmont Regional Council of Governments, founded in 1968 and comprising localities in Mecklenburg, Gaston, Iredell, Lincoln, Rowan, Cabarrus, Union, and Stanly counties. Martin served as the initial leader of its governing board. By 1972, some 16 other regional councils of government existed across North Carolina.

COMMUNITY LEADERS AVERT A CRISIS

On April 4, 1968, prison escapee James Earl Ray shot and killed Dr. Martin Luther King Jr. at the Lorraine Hotel in Memphis, Tennessee. As news spread of King's assassination, so did local protests. Some of them turned into riots, producing burglaries, arsons, assaults, and other violent incidents across the South and beyond. In Raleigh, hundreds of protestors threw rocks and bricks, broke windows, looted stores, and battled police along Fayetteville Street. Vandalism was also committed during street protests in Winston-Salem, Wilmington, Goldsboro, and Weldon. In Greensboro, National Guardsmen and snipers exchanged gunfire around the campus of North Carolina A&T State University. Across the United States, King's closest associates and most other civil-rights leaders preached nonviolence while most public officials strongly condemned the assassination and called for calm. Although places such as Chicago, Baltimore, and Washington, D.C., experienced large-scale rioting, leaders of other communities including New York and Los Angeles avoided that fate through strong local leadership and eloquent calls for reconciliation.

Charlotte was among them. On the first two nights after King's assassination, hundreds of young African-Americans took to the streets to express dismay. But little violence occurred. The community's two most prominent elected officials—Democratic mayor Stan Brookshire and Republican county commission chairman Jim Martin—declared April 6 to be a day of mourning and organized a memorial service at the city's Ovens Auditorium. Speakers at the service included the two political leaders, plus state NAACP chairman Kelly Alexander, Charlotte Chamber of Commerce president Donald Denton, and George Leake, a local civil-rights leader and minister of Little Rock AME Zion Church. During his remarks, Martin restated one of his fundamental political beliefs: that local governments should take the lead on difficult issues, rather than deferring to or being usurped by Washington. To that end, Martin told the crowd local governments should adopt their own ordinances against racial discrimination in housing. His position brought praise from some quarters and condemnation from others, including supporters of his 1966 campaign. "I heard immediately of people who had said they wouldn't support me for county commissioner again," Martin said.

Two days later, on April 8, leaders of Charlotte's black community hosted their own memorial service for King at St. Paul's Baptist Church. One of the speakers was, again, Kelly Alexander. He stressed the importance of honoring King's principles of nonviolence. "We can understand but cannot condone violence," Alexander said.

Among the 2,000 attendees, white and black, who flocked to the Sunday-evening service was Jim Martin. "I didn't believe you'd come," the Reverend Leake told Martin. The lengthy controversy about the Charlotte Area Fund may have been one reason some were surprised to see the Republican commissioner at the service. Another was the prominent role played at the various King memorial events by another local politician, Democratic businessman Charles M. Lowe, who had formerly chaired both the Mecklenburg commission and the Charlotte Area Fund's board. During 1967, Charlie Lowe had become one of Martin's fiercest critics. He spent months lining up candidates, volunteers, and donors to "take county government back" for the Democratic Party in the 1968 elections. Lowe filed for a commission seat himself in early 1968. The day after the memorial service at St. Paul's, Lowe joined Leake and three other Democratic candidates at the head of a march through the streets of Charlotte. Despite Lowe's prominent role in the public memorials to King, Martin thought it important to participate himself to encourage civic dialogue and discourage violence.

On the Republican side, two of the party's four members on the board— Robert Potter and Gus Campbell—decided against running for a second term. Chairman Jim Martin and Vice Chairman Pete Peterson filed for reelection. Three other Republicans joined them on the ballot: architect Alan Ingram, attorney and consultant Bill Robinson, and attorney Paul Whitfield. The only Democratic incumbent, former chairman Sam Atkinson, also bowed out of the race, so the Democratic ticket for county commission in 1968 consisted of Charlie Lowe, attorney Wallace Osborne, former sports broadcaster Phil Agresta, former zoning-board chairman David Kelly, and attorney Charles T. Myers, who chaired the county's Democratic Party in 1964 and 1965.

A CHAIRMAN AGAINST A CHAIRMAN

Lowe was clearly the leader of the Democratic slate. Although Martin recalled him as a "genial, colorful raconteur," Lowe ran an aggressive campaign against Mecklenburg's first Republican-led commission. He and Martin sparred repeatedly about the commission's performance. Lowe criticized the Republicans for assigning too many duties to commissioners rather than county staffers and refusing to use the proceeds of the new county sales tax to fund pay raises and benefits for teachers. But he aimed some of his most strongly worded attacks at the board's handling of welfare policy. He questioned why Republican commissioners had clashed repeatedly with the Charlotte Area Fund and had not reappointed the county welfare board's only black member, Dr. James Wertz. "They're fighting a national battle on the local level," Lowe said, referring to the broader Republican critique of President Johnson's Great Society agenda. He added that the Charlotte Area Fund was treated "like a red-headed stepchild" by "forcing them to come hat in hand begging for money."

Martin and other Republicans defended their record just as forcefully. They pointed out that in the run-up to the sales-tax referendum, county voters had been promised an offsetting property-tax decrease. Although willing to spend some of the new revenue on county programs such as capital needs and a health plan for public employees, they rejected the idea of committing the bulk of it to pay raises or anything else, particularly because its constitutionality was still under review. Just before Election Day, the North Carolina Supreme Court declared Mecklenburg's local-option sales tax to be legal, ruling that provisions of the state constitution cited by the plaintiffs served only to limit local property taxes. Even then, while Democratic commission candidates demanded immediate expenditure of the sales-tax revenue on pay raises and county programs, Martin and his colleagues responded that the current budget shouldn't be dramatically altered and that in 1969 the commission should follow through on its promised property-tax reduction.

Defending their record on education, the Republicans further argued that, unlike their Democratic predecessors, they had increased the share of local property-tax revenue devoted to education. In 1968, some $1.25 of the county's per-$1,000 tax rate was earmarked for schools, compared to $1.16 when the GOP majority took charge. Overall, county funding for education had risen by an annual average of 11 percent. Martin and the other Republicans freely admitted that other, lower-priority spending hadn't grown as much under their tenure. Rather than seeing the dispute with the Charlotte Area Fund as politically damaging, they cited it as evidence that they were being more careful than their predecessors in spending tax dollars wisely and discouraging longtime dependency on government handouts. "I feel quite a lot has been accomplished in this area," Martin said, "by assuring a reorganization and stabilization of the Area Fund."

Mecklenburg County's entire slate of Democratic candidates ran a well-funded, coordinated campaign in 1968, in sharp contrast to its lackluster effort two years earlier. The campaign's theme was "Mecklenburg Democrats: A Tradition of Good Government." It included signs, banners, newspaper ads, brochures, and mailers sent to more than 100,000 households. To support the five Democratic commission candidates, one of the party's newspaper ads suggested "five ways to improve your county government" would be to vote for Lowe, Osborne, Agresta, Kelly, and Myers.

The GOP candidates published their own brochures and ads touting the current board's policy accomplishments, including the city-county water agreement and the replacement of patchwork rules with county-wide zoning. Martin's campaign literature also noted his role in forming the Central Piedmont Regional Council of Governments and observed that he had received editorial endorsements from both the *Charlotte Observer* and the *Charlotte News*, although both favored turning control of the board back to the Democrats. "Despite his relative newness to politics and public service," the *News* wrote of Martin, "he led the board well through some difficult undertakings."

Despite the Democrats' advantage in fundraising and organization, Republicans in Mecklenburg County hoped to benefit from two external forces in the 1968 election cycle: presidential candidate Richard Nixon's "Southern Strategy" play for the electoral votes of North Carolina and Republican congressman Jim Gardner's strong campaign for North Carolina governor against Democratic lieutenant governor Bob Scott, the son of former governor Kerr Scott. Just weeks before Election Day, both of these factors were clearly working in the party's favor. Nationally, Nixon had a double-digit lead in the polls. A Gallup survey taken September 20–22 gave him a 15-point lead, 43–28, over Democratic nominee Hubert Humphrey. North Carolina polls also showed Nixon in a strong position to win the state. In the governor's race, even

Democrats were publicly admitting that Gardner posed the greatest threat to their party's control of the office since the end of the 19th century. As in 1966, Republicans had recruited an impressive slate of candidates up and down the ballot. All signs pointed to another strong showing for the GOP in the state's most-populous county.

But it was not to be. Although Republicans won some North Carolina elections in 1968, there was no wave. Nixon did get the state's electoral votes, albeit with only 40 percent of the popular vote. Independent candidate George Wallace, the segregationist former governor of Alabama, pulled votes in North Carolina from both major-party nominees and came in second with 31 percent of the state's vote, to Humphrey's 29 percent. As for Jim Gardner, he had proclaimed his loyalty to Nixon but declined to criticize Wallace, hoping to win the votes of eastern Democrats who liked Wallace. Some analysts believed the strategy proved too clever by half, alienating traditionally Republican voters in the Piedmont and west. In any event, Gardner underperformed expectations and Scott ended up keeping the governor's office in the Democratic column, garnering 53 percent of the vote. Republicans fared better in the state's congressional races, in which they elected two more members to the United States House: former professional baseball star Wilmer "Vinegar Bend" Mizell in the Fifth District and Salisbury mayor pro tem Earl Ruth, Catawba College's former basketball coach, in the Eighth. Republicans also gained eight seats in the General Assembly.

In Mecklenburg County, Republicans underperformed expectations. While Nixon won a majority of the county's votes for president, Scott edged Gardner in the gubernatorial balloting. One of the county's two GOP representatives in the North Carolina House lost his reelection bid. As for the county commission, incumbent Republicans Jim Martin and Pete Peterson led the county-wide polling with 53,299 and 49,107 votes, respectively, but the other three GOP candidates fell short. Democrats Charles Lowe, Charles Myers, and Wallace Osborne won the remaining three seats on the commission. After two years of service in the majority, most of that time as chairman, Martin would now be relegated to the minority faction.

Or would he? The course of political events in Mecklenburg County over the next two years proved a bit more interesting than that.

LEARNING A NEW WAY TO LEAD

Relations between the Democratic and Republican blocs were initially tense. Under the new chairman, Charles Lowe, the majority abandoned several initiatives begun under the previous administration. Martin objected, noting that the water projects, in particular, had been approved by voters in a referendum.

A few months later, in March 1969, the county commission voted to spend much of the revenue collected from the new local sales tax on pay raises for teachers and county employees. However, one of the three Democrats on the board, Vice Chairman Charles Myers, announced that he agreed with the Republicans that when the commission approved a new budget for the 1969–70 fiscal year, Mecklenburg voters should get the property-tax reduction they were promised during the 1967 sales-tax referendum.

Myers's announcement didn't come out of the blue. Martin had spent months developing a working relationship with him and persuading him that the tax cut was warranted. The other two Democrats, Lowe and Osborne, were noncommittal. While saying they didn't feel obligated to roll back the tax rate, they agreed to consider it. In the end, the 1969–70 budget contained both spending increases and a property-tax cut. It also contained another idea Martin had originally championed: establishing a separate savings reserve to ensure that unforeseen expenses, particularly in education, wouldn't lead to a subsequent tax hike. (Much later, as North Carolina's governor, he would advocate a similar policy for the state.)

About a week later, Myers voted with the Republicans on another controversial issue: purchasing land to build a county landfill on Harrisburg Road in the Wilgrove community, east of Charlotte. While Lowe and Osborne sided with neighbors of the proposed landfill, who feared traffic problems and lower property values, Martin and Peterson convinced Myers that adding landfill capacity was the most responsible and cost-effective response to population growth. If the commission yielded to neighborhood opposition against the Wilgrove site, they asked, would it really be able to find a more welcoming place? Myers worked with Martin and Peterson to devise an action plan for addressing the legitimate concerns of Wilgrove residents. It included limiting the times that trucks could deliver waste to the facility, purchasing other property around it to create a buffer, and planning a future park and golf course on the site.

Over the ensuing months, Myers repeatedly voted with his two Republican colleagues on other issues. "It's become increasingly apparent that the Mecklenburg Board of County Commissioners is 'Democratic-dominated' in name only," the *Charlotte Observer* stated in late 1969, arguing that what had emerged instead was "a new bipartisan coalition consisting of one Democrat and two Republicans." Just as his initial two years in elective office had given Martin his first experience serving as a political leader and policymaker, his next two years taught him how to be an effective member of a minority faction. That second set of lessons would prove critical to his future successes as a Republican member of a Democratic Congress and as a Republican governor who helped broker a historic bipartisan arrangement to share power in the North Carolina House.

Martin exerted leadership on another environmental issue, water pollution, although in this case all of his fellow commissioners were in agreement. Studies showed deteriorating conditions in many creeks and streams. Martin suggested that the commission ask the county Health Department to draw up a pollution-control program. He also asked the Central Piedmont Regional Council of Governments to help devise a broader solution for waterways that crossed county boundaries. Homebuilders and developers were among the strongest proponents of the new program and of expanding the city-county water agreement into a full-fledged county-wide system. Martin argued that, to the extent Mecklenburg County could take the lead on providing clean, affordable water service in the towns and unincorporated communities surrounding Charlotte, it would encourage growth outside the urban core, which he considered desirable. "If dispersal of population can be achieved," Martin explained, "it will have a tremendous influence on the quality of life in the area."

ANOTHER ELECTION, ANOTHER ELECTION ISSUE

During the rest of 1969 and much of 1970, the Mecklenburg commissioners devoted their attention primarily to coping with growth. Work began on planning a new county hospital. The commissioners approved new spending on water and sewer lines, schools, and Central Piedmont Community College. But there were signs that Mecklenburg residents were becoming less accepting of new debts and higher taxes. In a May 1970 referendum, county voters said no to five of nine proposed bond issues. A month later, voters rejected a large tax-hike proposal to fund recreation projects. The commissioners took note of the trend, rejecting the county staff's proposed budget for 1970–71, which called for dramatic increases in spending and a 23-cent hike in the property tax to pay for them. Still, they did approve higher expenditures and a 15-cent (or 9 percent) tax hike. It was a compromise between Republicans Martin and Peterson, who pushed for more spending restraint to lessen the effect on taxpayers, and Democrats Lowe and Osborne, who wanted to spend more. Myers acted, as usual, as a swing vote.

By mid-1970, Martin found himself with a leadership role that was both entirely unexpected and hugely important to his political career. After finishing his service on the Central Piedmont Regional Council of Governments, he traveled to Wilmington for the annual meeting of the North Carolina Association of County Commissioners. He had been invited to discuss regional cooperation. Following his presentation, Martin checked out of the hotel and prepared to leave. However, two Lincoln County commissioners he'd met through the regional council, Jim Warren and John Gamble, approached him. They asked him to remain in Wilmington and file as a candidate for president of the association. Warren and Gamble strongly supported the next-in-line candidate, Commissioner Bob Martin of Pitt County, but others had pushed him aside in favor of an unprecedented second term for the incumbent head of the association, Livingstone Stallings of Craven County. The vast majority of the state's county commissioners were Democrats.

During the subsequent infighting, supporters of Bob Martin told other members that "if you're not going to take a Democratic Martin, we'll run a Republican Martin." Following the first ballot, Jim Martin found himself tied with Stallings. After a tactical recess failed to locate or convert more votes for Stallings, he withdrew in favor of Martin. Quite to his surprise, Martin found himself elected the first-ever Republican head of the county commissioners' association. His year of service yielded a valuable new circle of contacts, taught him much about issues beyond his home county, and brought him to the attention of state Republican activists such as Frank Rouse, who was elected chairman of the North Carolina GOP in 1971.

Back home, the water-system precedent and rising costs for local services prompted advocates of a consolidated Charlotte-Mecklenburg government to believe they were on the cusp of accomplishing their objective. One of them, former Democratic commission chairman Sam Atkinson, even decided to run for the county commission again, on the grounds that political experience would be needed "with this consolidation business." Other Democratic nominees for the 1970 board included incumbents Charles Myers and Wallace Osborne, as well as W. T. "Bill" Harris, head of the Harris Teeter supermarket chain and former chairman of the Charlotte Chamber of Commerce. The sitting chairman, Democrat Charlie Lowe, had initially decided not to run, in part because of Martin's success in convincing Myers to vote with the Republicans on some issues. "I would probably run again if we could get some fellows on [the commission] who think like I do," Lowe stated matter-of-factly. "But the ones we've got now don't." Once like-minded Democrat Bill Harris confirmed his candidacy, however, Lowe changed his mind and filed for reelection. On the Republican side, incumbents Jim Martin and Pete Peterson filed for reelection. Joining them on the GOP ticket were former commission chairman Gus Campbell, lawyer Paul Whitfield, and Daniel Hennigan, a minister and real-estate agent who was the first African-American to be nominated by either major party for county office.

Several of the candidates said they expected the 1970 race to be Mecklenburg's last county-wide election for county commission, since the future consolidated government would have a very different governing board. But consolidation never happened. (The charter commission's plan was defeated in a subsequent referendum.) And as the 1970 political season unfolded in Mecklenburg, an entirely different issue came to dominate the news: school desegregation. Like many other states with long histories of racial segregation, North Carolina had initially responded to the Supreme Court's 1954 decision in *Brown v. Board of Education of Topeka* with a glacially slow approach, to put it charitably. A decade after the *Brown* decision, the vast majority of black students in the Charlotte-Mecklenburg Schools and other North Carolina districts continued to attend highly segregated (and patently inadequate) schools.

In 1964, a legal intern at the NAACP Legal Defense Fund in New York City, Julius Chambers, returned to his native North Carolina to open a law practice in Charlotte. One of the first major cases he took in 1965 was that of six-year-old James Swann and nine other black students, whose families demanded immediate action to desegregate CMS. Under pressure from the federal government as well as the plaintiffs in *Swann v. Charlotte-Mecklenburg Board of Education*, the school system adopted a desegregation plan. It began by merging schools in a few willing communities, including Davidson. (Jim and Dottie Martin's son Jim Jr. enrolled in the newly desegregated Davidson Elementary School.) Although ambitious by national standards, the plan still left the vast majority of the system's 24,000 black students attending segregated schools.

Chambers took the *Swann* case back to court in 1968. It landed in the lap of James B. McMillan, who had just become the federal district-court judge for the western part of the state. McMillan first ordered the school board to revise its desegregation plan. Although he largely accepted the district's approach for elementary schools, the judge eventually imposed a cross-county busing plan devised by an outside consultant to integrate junior and senior high schools. The school system appealed the decision but lost in the Fourth Circuit Court of Appeals. In September 1970, it proceeded with court-ordered busing of some 43,000 students, more than double the number bused during the previous school year. In the meantime, the case went to the United States Supreme Court. During September and October, media outlets produced nearly daily stories about the implementation of the busing plan and the status of the *Swann* case.

Jim Martin approached the issue with caution. On one hand, he opposed segregation and favored efforts not only to end race-based assignment but also to provide greater educational opportunities to black students. On the other hand, Martin had long opposed forced busing as the proper route to racial diversity. After initially supporting a resolution in March 1970 to put the Mecklenburg commissioners on record against busing, Martin changed his mind. He argued that they should withhold comment and let the legal process unfold.

DISSENSION COSTS THE DEMOCRATS

While the Supreme Court's consideration of the *Swann* case dominated the headlines and public disaffection with the county's rising property taxes put the majority party on the defensive, the Democratic candidates for county commission were struggling with another disadvantage: dissension. Early on, the chairman of the county party, banking executive Luther Hodges Jr., tried to repair the very public rupture between Lowe and Myers. As the campaign unfolded, however, it became evident that the Democratic slate was really composed of two groups of candidates. Lowe and Harris, essentially running as a team, formed one of them. Atkinson, Myers, and Osborne formed the other. In their campaign statements, Lowe and Harris signaled a willingness to raise the property tax to fund educational improvement, while Myers stressed the need to "keep taxes down." Atkinson and Osborne talked mostly about government consolidation, which Myers opposed. The Democrats clearly did not have a unified message.

On the other hand, the Democrats didn't face in 1970 what they had in 1966 and 1968: an energized Republican Party poised to make gains across the state and nation. It was the first midterm election under President Richard Nixon. Across the nation, Democrats did well in the 1970 cycle, posting a net gain of 11 governorships and 12 seats in the United States House, although they lost four seats in the Senate. In North Carolina, Democrats took back 10 of the 26 legislative seats they'd lost to the GOP during the previous two cycles. None of the state's congressional seats changed hands.

So Jim Martin and the rest of Mecklenburg's Republican slate had no GOP wave to surf in 1970. That they did well anyway confirmed that the local party's rise to competitiveness during the 1960s was quite real. Martin's campaign ads featured four accomplishments: (1) four straight years of substantial budget increases for education, (2) initiatives to combat air and water pollution, (3) the creation of the Central Piedmont Regional Council of Governments and Martin's service as head of the state association of county commissioners, and (4) consistent opposition to "special favors of political patronage," a reference to the Democrats' frequent awarding of county contracts to Democratic-leaning firms. Other campaign materials on behalf of the Republican ticket as a whole stressed the need for change after two controversial years of Democratic control.

Voters heeded this message and put a Republican majority back in charge of the county commission while also reelecting the Republican sheriff and electing Mecklenburg's first Republican solicitor, or district attorney. As in 1966, the 1970 results demonstrated the dangers local Democrats faced when they were divided. Charlie Lowe and Bill Harris, running to the left of the other three candidates, secured the base Democratic vote. But many conservative Democrats ended up abandoning the candidates most like them—Sam Atkinson and Charles Myers—in favor of the Republicans.

Once again, Martin was the top-polling candidate, garnering 30,153 votes, followed by fellow Republican incumbent Pete Peterson (26,752), former Republican member Gus Campbell (26,521), and Democrats Harris (24,266) and Lowe (23,505). By making these selections, Mecklenburg voters spurned the editorial advice of the *Charlotte Observer* (whose only Republican endorsements were of Martin and the African-American candidate, Dan Hennigan) in favor of the very five candidates endorsed by the *Charlotte News*. Another factor in the outcome may well have been the historic campaign of Hennigan, who ended up in seventh place, winning 22,801 votes. Not only did thousands of white Republicans and Democrats vote for him, but he also got strong support among overwhelmingly Democratic black voters, many of whom seemed to have cast single-shot votes for Hennigan. That was a common tactic for electoral minorities in multi-member districts, and would have had the effect of reducing the vote totals for white Democratic nominees.

Just as media coverage of local elections before Election Day had been largely supplanted by near-daily stories on the status of the school system's busing plan, the news that Mecklenburg County had again elected a Republican-majority commission didn't linger on the front page for long. During the last two months of 1970 and the first three months of 1971, Charlotte's news outlets devoted significant attention to the arguments made before the United States Supreme Court in the *Swann* case. On April 20, 1971, the court unanimously upheld Judge McMillan's order. Large-scale busing for racial balance would remain CMS policy for a quarter-century.

For Jim Martin, the course of his final term on the county commission would be very different from his first two for a singular reason: his preparations to run for Congress.

CHAPTER THREE

THE REPUBLICAN BREAKTHROUGH

As early as 1967, Charlotte political observers speculated that Dr. Jim Martin might one day replace Charles Jonas in Congress. In October 1969, as doubts surfaced that Jonas would run for reelection the following year, reporters began peppering Martin with questions about the congressional seat. When Martin told them he was running for the Mecklenburg commission again, they interpreted that as a sign Jonas was staying in Congress. The conventional wisdom, in other words, was that the two decisions were automatically linked: if and when Jonas decided to retire, Martin would be nominated as his successor.

The conventional wisdom proved prescient. Congressman Jonas had indeed approached Martin earlier in 1969 to say he was considering retirement and to urge Martin to run for the seat Jonas had held since 1952. Ultimately, however, Jonas filed for reelection in 1970, telling Martin that retiring after a full two decades in Congress would be better than retiring after 18 years. A few months later, in mid-1971, the 66-year-old Jonas confirmed to Martin that the seat would be open the following year. "I talked with Dottie first this time around," Martin said ruefully. He also spoke with other confidants such as his brother Joe, an executive at NCNB (now Bank of America), and influential Republican lawyer Bob Bradshaw, who helped found one of the pillars of Charlotte's legal community, the firm that became known as Robinson, Bradshaw and Hinson. Virtually everyone urged Martin to run.

Still, he had a lot to think about. By 1971, Martin had won three competitive county-wide elections and spent the better part of five years in public service. But serving in Congress would be more than just another steppingstone in a political career. It would be a fundamental change in his life. He'd no longer be a chemistry professor at his beloved Davidson College. His young and growing family—Dottie was pregnant with their third child, Arthur Benson Martin—would have to relocate to the nation's capital. He'd also be leaving a political arena in which he had significant influence, Mecklenburg County, to enter what was then an overwhelmingly Democratic Congress. So the decision was hardly an easy one. It helped that his family was supportive. "We saw it as an exciting opportunity for him—and actually for us, too," Dottie said. But the chief reason Martin decided to run for Congress was that he thought he could make a difference there. As a county commissioner, he had criticized federal encroachment on state and local matters. As a member of the House, he might be in a position to do something about it.

WHOSE TURN?

Of course, to decide to run was not to become a congressman. Martin would have to win the Republican nomination and overcome what would likely be a strong Democratic candidate for the open seat in the fall of 1972. Furthermore, he'd have to do all that after sustaining some political damage in Mecklenburg County during the tumultuous political year of 1971, the most challenging of his career to date. And it began with an internal party squabble about who should chair the new Republican-majority commission.

Tradition argued for Martin, the top-polling candidate in 1970, to become chairman once again. But his interest in a congressional run was widely assumed. And Pete Peterson, the only Republican commissioner who had yet to chair the board, told reporters the day after the election that it was his turn. "I might take [the chairmanship] for a year and then give it to Jim," Peterson said. On the other hand, he explained, if Martin's future hinged on his being chairman again, Peterson wouldn't stand in his way. "It's not worth hurting Jim's political image," he said.

After several weeks of public speculation and private conversation, Peterson and Gus Campbell decided to support Martin as chairman for 1971. Martin promised the board would act on several major issues: solid-waste disposal, the location of a new public hospital, and—above all—funding for the Charlotte-Mecklenburg Schools.

While awaiting a final decision on the *Swann* case, the school system was obliged to obey Judge James B. McMillan's order to begin cross-district busing. CMS had received about $119,000 from the county to implement a busing plan that, it turned out, was going to cost close to $800,000 (about $4.8 million in 2015 currency). And that didn't include the cost of purchasing additional buses for the next school year. On April 20, 1971, the Supreme Court unanimously affirmed McMillan's order. In response, the county significantly increased appropriations to CMS. These higher funding levels for cross-district busing would continue for a quarter-century, until parents filed a successful lawsuit against the district's race-conscious assignment plan. (It was Martin's former Republican colleague on the county commission, Robert Potter, who as a federal district judge declared the system to be a "unitary" district in 1999, leading to the end of court-ordered busing in Charlotte-Mecklenburg.)

A SEASON OF POLITICAL BRUISES

The *Swann* decision in April 1971 was the second heavy shoe to drop in local politics. The first had occurred the previous month, when the long-debated Charlotte-Mecklenburg consolidation plan finally went to the voters in a county-wide referendum. The idea enjoyed significant support among civic leaders, the chamber of commerce, and the editorial boards of both daily newspapers. C. C. "Cliff" Cameron, the well-respected head of First Union National Bank, stepped forward to lead the pro-referendum campaign. But just weeks before the March 22 referendum, it drew strong opposition from a new group, the Committee to Ensure Good Government, headed by local businessman Allen Bailey. Prominent consolidation opponents included Democratic school-board chairman William Poe, state representative Larry Cobb (the only Republican in the county's legislative delegation), Democratic state senators Eddie Knox and Herman Moore, Jim Martin's fellow Republican commissioners Pete Peterson and Gus Campbell, county GOP chairman Henry Wilmer, prominent Republican lawyer Bob Bradshaw, the mayors of the county's five other municipalities besides Charlotte, and Philip Van Every, the head of snack-food giant Lance Inc. and a former Charlotte mayor. Pointing out that local public schools, water and sewer, and health programs were already merged or headed in that direction, opponents questioned whether or not full-fledged consolidation of the two governments would really have net benefits.

NEWLY ELECTED
UNITED STATES REPRE-
SENTATIVE JIM MARTIN
POSES WITH JIMMY,
EMILY, AND DOTTIE.
MARTIN FAMILY PHOTO

With regard to the referendum, Jim Martin found himself in the same place he was on forced busing: he had mixed feelings. On one hand, he had long supported the general concept of consolidation, provided it truly brought cost savings and was approved by referendum, rather than forced down the throats of county residents. During the 1970 campaign, however, Martin had voiced two objections to the merger plan. First, he thought the new governing board relied too much on district representation, without enough at-large members to ensure accountability to Mecklenburg residents as a whole. Second, he argued that citizens in unincorporated areas would end up shouldering a disproportionate share of taxes to pay off bonds for projects primarily benefiting Charlotte residents. Without a resolution of these two concerns, Martin said shortly after his second election to the chairmanship, he'd "have to think long and hard" about endorsing the consolidation referendum.

Other prominent leaders such as former Charlotte mayor Stan Brookshire and even Cliff Cameron had previously expressed similar reservations. They ultimately endorsed the merger plan, however, as an improvement over the status quo. Would Martin? The political risks were obvious. Two weeks before the vote, a *Charlotte News* poll found that opponents outnumbered supporters by a 3–2 margin.

Martin decided to follow his best judgment, not the political winds. Two days after the poll came out, he called reporters into his office to endorse the merger and respond to its critics. He argued that small-town interests would be protected and that if local taxes rose in the coming years, it would be due to court-ordered busing and cuts in federal funding for localities, not consolidation.

These arguments proved unpersuasive. Of the nearly 57,000 Mecklenburg voters who turned out for the March 22 referendum, 70 percent said no. Not only did those residing outside Charlotte vote overwhelmingly against it, but the merger plan even failed to draw majority support among city residents. The margin was so decisive that the idea didn't get a serious airing again until the 1980s. (It didn't happen then either.)

Party chairman Henry Wilmer and other local GOP leaders were so energized by the smashing success of their anti-merger effort that they sought to turn it into momentum for gains on the Charlotte council in 1971 and in county and state races in 1972. Gus Campbell put it bluntly: "This is a conservative county and that was a liberal document. That's what beat it."

As one of the few prominent Republicans who had endorsed the merger plan, Martin now seemed out of step with his party and the direction of county politics. Nor was the referendum defeat his only political headache. Another was the growing unpopularity of a plan he supported to build a new 450-bed hospital at a county-owned site on Charlotte's Randolph Road. Local officials and consultants had recommended the site for its proximity to three other major facilities—publicly owned Charlotte Memorial Hospital, the private Presbyterian Hospital, and the Catholic Mercy Hospital. Having the institutions close together would facilitate coordination of services and attract the best medical workforce, they said, while using land already owned by the county would reduce the cost. But residents to the north and west complained that their needs weren't being met. Some alleged the proximity of the Randolph Road location to some of Charlotte's most affluent neighborhoods exhibited elitism. Moreover, the county commissioners had originally proposed a May 7, 1971, referendum to authorize a $23 million bond and a property-tax increase to finance the new hospital. To residents already concerned about rising debts and taxes, this would have been a hard sell in any event. But selling it less than two months after the decisive defeat of the city-county merger would have been impossible. Martin and his colleagues bowed to the inevitable and canceled the referendum.

THE FIELD NARROWS

On October 1, 1971, Martin told reporters that he would not be running for reelection to the county commission. Three days later, Charlie Jonas used a simple two-paragraph written statement to announce that he would be retiring. Although speculation immediately centered on the 35-year-old Martin as a potential replacement, he confirmed only that he was weighing his options to "determine what my own political stock is. I have got to be careful not to deceive myself." Other Republicans were also weighing their prospects. Among them were Charles Jonas Jr., the congressman's son, and the other two Republicans on the Mecklenburg commission, Gus Campbell and Pete Peterson. On the Democratic side, school-board chairman William Poe was giving the office serious consideration. Two Charlotte politicians, Mayor John Belk and city councilman Milton Short, also made the short list of potential Democratic candidates, along with local broadcaster Cy Bahakel, who'd been the party's nominee against Representative Jonas in 1970, and Jim Beatty, a three-term state representative and executive of a cleaning-supply company.

All had political experience, but only Beatty was a bona fide celebrity. As an undergraduate at UNC–Chapel Hill, he had been a standout runner who won the ACC championship in the mile run in 1955 and 1956. His best time during his collegiate career was 4:06. After moving to Los Angeles in 1960, Beatty continued to train relentlessly. His goal? To become the first person to run a mile on an indoor track in less than four minutes. On February 10, 1962, he did it with a run of 3:58 while competing in the Los Angeles Invitational. Beatty set records in other events as well. He was the ABC *Wide World of Sports* Athlete of the Year in 1962 and won a silver medal at the Pan American Games in 1963.

Beatty and the other potential candidates spent the next several weeks gauging their support. For Martin, this "pre-primary" process proved to be awkward because of a fellow commissioner's interest in the race. In late November, Gus Campbell approached him to suggest that Martin not seek reelection as chairman of the county board for 1972. Campbell argued that serving as chairman would inhibit Martin's ability to run an effective congressional campaign. Martin demurred, thinking to himself that Campbell was more likely concerned that the chairmanship would boost Martin's candidacy for the Republican nomination, not hamper it. Campbell then got more explicit. "You're not going to make it," he told Martin, because the other four commissioners had already agreed to elect Pete Peterson as chairman for the coming year. Campbell advised Martin to announce he'd voluntarily decided to step down. But Martin decided to play it differently. At the December board meeting, Campbell nominated Peterson. The commissioners voted 4–0 on the nomination, with Martin abstaining. In the press, the dominant narrative was that the other Republican commissioners had conspired with the Democrats to overthrow Martin. GOP chairman Henry Wilmer criticized Campbell and Peterson for engaging in intra-party "cannibalism." Other Republicans were also put off by the maneuver. Campbell's nascent candidacy for the United States House fizzled. Martin had managed to turn a tactical defeat into a strategic victory.

On December 20, 1971, Martin formally announced his congressional campaign in the meeting room of the Mecklenburg County Board of Commissioners. He promised to use the seat in Congress to combat federal encroachment on state and local prerogatives. Surrounded by his wife, children, parents, and 200 Republican activists from the three counties making up the Ninth District—Mecklenburg, Iredell, and Lincoln—Martin championed educational improvement, environmental protection, President Nixon's approach to the war in Vietnam, and a conservative approach to managing the nation's finances. He also announced that prominent attorney Bob Bradshaw would serve as chairman of the campaign. "You may safely assume that I intend to use publicity techniques to good advantage," Martin told reporters. "But I also want to assure you that I intend to avoid the razzle-dazzle and keep it as substantive as possible."

During the ensuing months, he did indeed prove himself to be a substantive campaigner. Sometimes, he sounded very much like the lecturing professor he had been at Davidson for 12 years. But there was some razzle-dazzle, too, thanks to the efforts of the consultant he and Bradshaw hired to run the campaign, an innovative Virginia-based Republican strategist named Brad Hays.

A POLITICAL ALTER EGO

An Oklahoma native, Hays first made his mark in politics during Barry Goldwater's 1964 presidential campaign. Then working as an analyst for the chemical giant DuPont in Georgia, Hays was assigned to the company's Savannah River nuclear project just over the border in Aiken, South Carolina. Finding himself with free time on his hands, Hays decided to pursue his interest in conservative politics. He was elected chairman of the Aiken County Republican Party. During the 1964 presidential race, Hays worked tirelessly to boost support for the GOP ticket in the traditionally Democratic state. It was one of six that voted for Goldwater—and Aiken was one of South Carolina's best-performing counties for the Republicans.

Party leaders noticed. They invited Hays to the nation's capital to discuss how to broaden the GOP's appeal in the South. After flying him to Washington, they put him up in a hotel and treated him to a shot of whiskey at the bar. According to his longtime friend and aide Paul Shumaker, such treatment led Hays to think he "might like this politics business." He agreed to come to work as the Republican National Committee's first regional field director, focused on what had been the Democrats' Solid South. His work was critical to Richard Nixon's successes in the region in 1968 and 1972.

Brad Hays "lived life hard and lived a hard life," Shumaker said. Crusty, blunt, and preferring to stay out of the limelight, Hays believed in building campaigns around quantitative data and hard facts, not guesswork and wishful thinking. His focus was on winning elections, not formulating public policy. In style, he couldn't have been more different from Jim Martin, and the two never became close friends. But their strengths proved to be complementary. "Brad was his political alter ego," Shumaker said.

Early in their relationship, Hays figured out that one of Martin's electoral assets was that he looked and acted like a leader. The consultant once assembled a focus group of Charlotte residents to assess their reactions to film footage of Martin making a speech. But someone forgot to turn the sound on. For the first several minutes, the audience only saw the video. After the audio was flipped on, the focus group watched the remainder of the footage. Hays discovered that the participants rated Martin just as positively with the sound off. While it was important that his candidate said the right things, Hays concluded it was also important that as many voters as possible got a good look at him.

A PRIMARY LESSON

On December 20, the same day Martin announced for Congress, rumors swirled in Charlotte that school-board chairman William Poe would not run. He confirmed the rumors a few days later. Belk, Bahakel, and other experienced Democratic candidates also backed off from the race, leaving the way clear for Jim Beatty to seek his party's nomination. Although Charlie Jonas had held the post for two decades and the district had at least a moderate Republican lean, Beatty was confident he'd be competitive for the open seat. The initial signs indicated he might well be right. For one thing, the Democratic state legislature had redrawn the district to exclude Republican-rich Wilkes County, which had previously voted heavily for Jonas. For another, Beatty had been the top vote-getter in all three of his legislative races. Although Martin was the two-time commission chairman in Mecklenburg, where the lion's share of the district's voters resided, he actually trailed the sports hero significantly in name recognition. One early poll gave Beatty 40 percent and Martin only 20 percent, with 40 percent undecided.

Both men faced token primary opposition. On the Republican side, the other candidate was Graem Yates, a marketing consultant who said he was running because Martin was insufficiently conservative. Indeed, Martin's support for the city-county merger and new public hospital had left some Republicans grumbling. A few nursed even older grievances. Shortly after Martin Luther King's assassination in 1968, Martin had sought to calm tensions by stressing the need for local action to address racial disparities. In particular, he criticized discrimination in the marketing and sale of housing. For some longtime residents of the segregated South, it was a bridge too far. Even forward-thinking conservatives on race relations worried that such an idea would lead to excessive and arbitrary government regulation of housing and lending practices.

One day early in the campaign, Martin got word that Lance Inc. CEO Philip Van Every wanted to see him. Martin assumed the prominent business leader was doing him the courtesy of informing him face to face that he and other Lance executives would be supporting Jim Beatty. After a brief meeting involving the company's entire senior management, Van Every excused everyone else, stood up, and towered over Martin, who was seated on a sofa. "Don't I remember that you came out for open housing?" he asked. "Yes, sir," Martin responded. "You still feel that way?" Van Every pressed. "Yes, sir," Martin again replied, assuming the interview was about to end badly for him.

Van Every looked him in the eye. "Well, I'm going to support you," he told a surprised Martin. "I'm going to support you, and my family is going to support you, and everybody I do business with is going to support you." Van Every explained that he was tired of seeing politicians say and do anything just to get elected. "If you are going up to Washington, and if you had caved in to the little bit of pressure I just put on you, I would worry about you," he said. "I won't agree with you all the time, but it won't matter. I trust you."

Van Every was as good as his word. Martin's fledging campaign quickly received $15,000 in donations from Van Every, his family, and business colleagues—the largest single bloc of donors Martin would attract in 1972 (and the equivalent of $85,000 in 2015). Not only did it help validate the campaign, but the episode also reinforced to Martin the lesson that it was more important to do what he thought was right than what might be politically expedient. This was not an argument against being prudent or taking public opinion into account. Throughout his career, Martin was a gradualist who believed in setting long-term goals that could be achieved incrementally by building consensus. What his Van Every interview demonstrated to Martin, however, was that those long-term goals ought to be ambitious and consistent with his fundamental principles, not designed simply as a means of maintaining power and popularity. Politics, he came to realize, was about persuasion, not merely mobilizing those who already agreed with him. Republicans in particular couldn't afford simply to turn out their existing base in a historically Democratic state. That was a recipe for perpetual irrelevance.

The episode had a fascinating coda two years later when Martin was serving in Congress. A lobbyist came to see him about legislation that would exempt fig paste from import duties. It would have had the effect of reducing production costs for snack-food companies. When Martin said he'd take a look at the details of the bill and get back to him, the lobbyist interjected, "You don't need to worry about it. You remember Lance is in your district, and they make fig bars." Martin kept insisting that he'd need to study the issue more thoroughly, and the lobbyist kept insisting there was nothing more to study. So with the lobbyist in the room, Martin called the company and asked to speak to Van Every, who in turn asked to speak to the lobbyist. After several times saying, "Yes, Mr. Van Every," the man hung up the phone and left without saying another word. The tariff reduction ended up passing easily. Martin voted for it because he thought it was good policy, not because he felt obligated to do so.

Van Every wasn't the only local conservative who liked and supported Martin despite having occasional differences with him. Mecklenburg Republicans leaned right on most fiscal, social, and defense issues. So did many Democrats in the county. Indeed, in the May 6, 1972, primaries, Mecklenburg voters opted for the most conservative alternatives—former Alabama governor George Wallace over former North Carolina governor Terry Sanford for the Democratic presidential nomination, for example, and Jim Gardner over North Carolina House minority leader Jim Holshouser for the Republican gubernatorial nomination. Martin was a conservative, too. But his positions were not always predictable. So first during the "pre-primary" period of late 1971 and then into the spring of 1972, he requested private meetings with prominent Republicans and conservative Democrats whose support was still up for grabs. He listed the many views they had in common and explained his reasoning on issues of disagreement. More often than not, the outcome of the conversation was a new donor to, or public endorsement of, the Martin campaign. It was a major reason why so many potential Republican candidates dropped out of the running, leaving little-known Graem Yates as his only primary opponent. It was a tactic Martin used to great effect later in his career.

The results of the primaries were never in doubt. Jim Martin won 15,273 votes, or 80 percent of the Republicans who turned out. In the Democratic primary, Jim Beatty won far more votes (46,041), as well as a higher share (84 percent). Although it was shaping up as a good Republican year, Martin and Hays recognized the stiff challenge Beatty represented. If 1972 was to be the year the GOP finally made a breakout in North Carolina politics, as some observers were beginning to predict, Martin would have to earn his place in that story.

THE GOP'S SURGING FORTUNES

Why were state Republicans so optimistic? They expected a strong tailwind from the Nixon reelection campaign, but that wasn't the only reason. Since 1966, when the party enjoyed its first real electoral successes in urban counties such as Mecklenburg, Republican activists had steadily built an infrastructure for recruiting candidates, setting up professional campaigns, and turning out their vote. For the 1972 cycle, they felt their candidate recruitment had reached a new high. The gubernatorial nominee, Jim Holshouser, was a Davidson graduate and Boone attorney who had served in the North Carolina House since 1962 and as chairman of the state Republican Party since 1966. Because he had been a party builder and legislative leader, Holshouser had more experience and a broader set of political contacts than did Jim Gardner, the 1968 nominee. The primary was highly competitive. Gardner actually led Holshouser by a few hundred votes in the initial vote in May but lost in the runoff. The Republicans still managed to move forward to the fall without a bitter division between the two camps. One reason was that the eastern North Carolina conservatives who tended to favor Gardner over Holshouser were even more enthusiastic about the party's nominee for the United States Senate, broadcaster and former Raleigh city councilman Jesse Helms. They merely shifted their emphasis to the Senate race while still working to turn out voters for the entire GOP ticket. The Holshouser wing of the party did the same thing in the Piedmont and western counties. Helms and Holshouser campaigned together on multiple occasions.

The Republicans' high hopes extended beyond the statewide contests. Their down-ballot prospects looked good, too. Of the four sitting Republicans in the United States House, three of them—Wilmer Mizell, Earl Ruth, and Jim Broyhill—were on the ballot again and favored for reelection. The only open seat they'd be defending was the Ninth District. The Democrats would be defending an open seat as well, in the Triangle-area Fourth District. The incumbent, Nick Galifianakis, was running for the Senate against Helms. The Democratic nominee in the Fourth District was state representative Ike Andrews. Facing him was one of the GOP's promising young recruits, former Gardner aide Jack Hawke. In legislative and local races, Republicans also attracted more competitive candidates than ever before.

The other reason for Republican optimism in 1972 was that the opponents seemed uncharacteristically shaky and disorganized. Democrats were nervous about being on the same ballot with George McGovern, one of the most liberal candidates ever to be nominated for president. They were also deeply divided by a rough-and-tumble primary for governor. Hargrove "Skipper" Bowles, who had served in Terry Sanford's administration and the legislature, ran against Lieutenant Governor and former House speaker Pat Taylor, who enjoyed the support of many allies of incumbent governor Bob Scott. By making effective use of TV ads and other modern tactics, Bowles prevailed. But the result left Taylor feeling beaten up and the Scott faction feeling alienated. There was another Democratic split as well, this one in the Senate race. Galifianakis had defeated ailing incumbent Everett Jordan in the party's primary. Republicans planned—successfully, it turned out—to exploit these divisions among Democrats.

A STATE-OF-THE-ART CAMPAIGN

With strategic direction from Brad Hays, supervision by Bob Bradshaw, and fundraising help from former Mecklenburg GOP chairman Marcus Hickman, the Martin for Congress campaign set up shop in an office on Charlotte's Park Road. It would eventually employ five staffers, including campaign manager Zachary Smith, and spend $122,000 (about $700,000 in 2015 dollars) on broadcast advertising, mailers, signs, and logistical support. That was more than twice the amount Jim Beatty's campaign was able to raise. It wasn't just traditional GOP donors opening their wallets for Martin. Much of Charlotte's Democratic business community, which first had grown comfortable with and then enthusiastically supportive of Charlie Jonas over two decades, ended up in the camp of the Republican successor Jonas endorsed, Martin. Among the city's top bankers, for example, only NCNB vice president Luther Hodges Jr., a former Democratic county chairman, made significant contributions to Beatty. Graeme Keith, executive vice president of First Union National Bank, did Martin another favor. He urged one of his marketing officers, Jim Lofton, to join the congressional campaign. Lofton would work for Martin for the rest of the latter's political career, both on Capitol Hill and in Raleigh.

Local bankers weren't the only business executives to opt for Martin. He also received the lion's share of the campaign donations made by local manufacturers, retailers, professionals, and political action committees representing doctors and business groups. Donald Bryant, a former Charlotte city councilman, chaired a group called Democrats for Martin, which included former state legislator and Eckerd drugstore CEO Ed O'Herron, former Davidson president Grier Martin, former city councilman and NCNB executive vice president Pat Calhoun, and politically active executives from Duke Power, Presbyterian Hospital, and many of the community's other large employers. Several other Democrats on the Charlotte City Council either formally endorsed Martin or publicly praised his leadership on the county commission.

While Martin attracted many right-of-center Democrats, Beatty had a prominent local Republican in his corner: campaign manager Peter Verna, a construction-industry executive and Beatty's one-time football coach. He and Luther Hodges helped organize a "Businessmen for Beatty" group. Still, their quest for donations and endorsements fell far short. So Beatty tried to turn his opponent's crossover support into a liability by describing the race as "a candidate of the people versus a machine," meaning the Charlotte business establishment. The Martin camp responded with humor. At a subsequent campaign rally, Martin's son Jimmy and three of his friends walked onstage with guitars and tambourines to entertain the crowd. They played at other campaign stops and even in the bed of a pickup truck parked in shopping centers. What did they call their band? The Martin Machine.

At the direction of Brad Hays, the Martin team used its resources to run a state-of-the-art campaign. It commissioned large-sample tracking polls, sent out targeted mailings, and produced broadcast ads. It even purchased a Western Union teletype machine to receive daily blasts of news, press releases, and talking points from the Republican Party in Washington. While his congressional campaign certainly was professional, the candidate himself never lost his down-home appeal or pretended to be something he wasn't. There was no personal makeover. Martin's wife remembered one campaign stop in Lincolnton to which Jim drove the family car while wearing red pants and a red, black, and white sports coat. "He looked like a used-car salesman," Dottie said.

A NEW SET OF ISSUES

Although Martin launched his congressional bid by referencing a broad set of issues, the campaign team soon recognized it needed to narrow the focus to four areas of sharp contrast with the Democratic nominee: the conduct of the Vietnam War, the legal treatment of draft evaders, drug laws, and forced busing.

Just before the May 6 primary, Martin and Beatty debated at Central Piedmont Community College. Asked if they would support a recently filed bill that would cut off funding of the war within 90 days, Beatty gave a qualified yes. Martin pounced, arguing that such a move would undercut Nixon's attempts to negotiate a ceasefire in Vietnam on favorable terms. "This nation needs to be behind the president and give him full support," Martin said, "rather than the disunity that is flourishing in Congress right now." He also challenged Beatty's support for "conditional amnesty" for those who had fled the country to avoid conscription. Beatty had suggested that draft evaders be allowed back without criminal penalty to perform some other kind of public service, such as the Peace Corps. Martin disagreed. "They knew what the consequences would be when they left," he said. "They should come back nobly, ask for a hearing, and have the existing laws apply to them."

During the 1971 legislative session, Representative Beatty had introduced a bill to liberalize the state's laws on marijuana. After some revisions in committee, the bill passed both chambers and became law. It made possession of small amounts of marijuana a misdemeanor, punishable by fines and jail time, rather than lengthy imprisonment. It also allowed first-time offenders, typically teens and young adults, to have their records expunged if they committed no additional offenses. Martin described his opponent's position as irresponsible. While Martin said he strongly opposed legalization, he argued that softening penalties, as Beatty suggested, might have even worse consequences by encouraging "experimentation with the drug without providing for any of the government controls over its manufacture and sale that would be provided under legalization."

As for the controversial implementation of cross-district busing, Martin proposed to amend the Constitution to prohibit any state or locality from assigning students to schools on the basis of race. Beatty condemned forced busing as well but stopped short of endorsing a constitutional prohibition. "It has not been clearly determined that an amendment would do what it is intended to do," he said, "and it may do more than it is intended to do. Those things might not be desirable." Martin argued that the solution to racial disparities ought not be imposed by federal judges. It is "my strong belief that the public school system should basically be a local institution," he said.

At every opportunity, Martin praised President Nixon and linked Beatty to McGovern. Beatty knew the connection would be toxic to his campaign and vigorously denied it. He even avoided saying McGovern's name in public, remarking only that his positions weren't the same as those of "the Democratic nominee."

Martin's positions on Vietnam, draft evasion, drug laws, and forced busing were all sincerely held. However, they were also part of a conscious strategy to dispel any public doubts about his political philosophy. Hays, Bradshaw, and other advisors worried that if all voters knew about Martin was that he was a college professor, they might associate him with campus radicals and left-of-center politics. Martin made sure to emphasize that his Ph.D. was in the hard sciences. When local activists questioned the wisdom of building the McGuire Nuclear Station on Lake Norman, for example, Martin criticized their "scare tactics" and argued that nuclear power was both safe and better for the environment than alternative energy sources. He also used his scientific expertise to distinguish between wise environmental policies, such as the antipollution program he helped establish as a county commissioner, and a bill in the United States Senate that would set impossibly low thresholds for emissions into the air or water, at a huge cost to consumers and workers. The idea that sound science and rigorous cost-benefit analysis, not apocalyptic claims and rhetorical excesses, should guide regulatory policy was one to which Martin would return again and again during his career.

SPRINT TO THE FINISH LINE

Because he started the race at a significant disadvantage in name recognition, Martin began holding events and conducting door-to-door campaigning in mid-July, six weeks before the Beatty campaign began its retail operation in earnest. Then it was time to ramp up the razzle-dazzle. On September 19, the Martin campaign bought a half-hour block of time on Charlotte's WBTV. Rather than have the candidate alone speaking directly into the camera, Hays had Martin answer questions from supporters in the studio, as well as those calling in from "campaign coffees" in private homes around the district.

Two days later, Martin appeared with Jonas at a Charlotte rally that drew more than 2,000 people. "I do not know of a man in my time who has offered himself for public office who is more exceptionally qualified than Jim Martin," the retiring congressman told the enthusiastic crowd. Speaking next, Martin again tied himself closely to the president and his strategy in Vietnam. "If you are prepared to vote for President Nixon once, I'm offering you a chance to vote for him twice," he said. "I will support the president, especially in winding down the war and getting a real peace." The event had lighter moments, too. Several speakers told their favorite stories about Jonas. And Martin, cracking a grin, recounted his campaign stop earlier in the day at a bra and girdle factory in Statesville. "They're the ones if you want to talk about the people who really shape and mold this country," he quipped.

Although at a financial disadvantage, the Beatty campaign also went on television in September, using a populist appeal designed to sway the undecided vote. Its most powerful spot began by telling viewers that Beatty grew up so poor that he couldn't afford a bike and had to do his newspaper route by foot. Then it showed a film clip of Beatty's famous record-setting mile run in 1962. "Jim Beatty is running for you," the ad concluded. The same slogan was plastered on the campaign's billboards, signs, and T-shirts. Beatty also tried to avoid letting Martin set the agenda. Instead of devoting his public and media appearances to responding to Martin's attacks on Vietnam, drugs, and forced busing, Beatty preferred to talk about programs for the elderly, job creation, and President Nixon's trial balloon of a national value-added sales tax to help states and localities with education funding. Nixon's proposal would be "the wrong tax on the wrong people at the wrong time for the wrong purpose," Beatty said. Martin originally suggested that Nixon's idea might be worth considering if it could keep local property taxes down—a swap that he and other Mecklenburg leaders had made in the past. But he eventually came out against a national value-added tax on the grounds that it would burden businesses and hamper growth.

About a month before the election, the two candidates met for a debate at the Charlotte Junior Women's Club. Martin talked about foreign policy and the *Swann* case. Beatty warned against creating a "false hope" that a constitutional amendment could halt forced busing. When asked if he endorsed McGovern for president, Beatty "danced around the question with a flair that would do justice to Mohammed Ali," as *Charlotte Observer* reporter Henry Eichel put it. Meanwhile, the Martin campaign went on TV with another ad. It showed the candidate talking to suburban voters standing in front of their homes. "Unfortunately, neighborhoods like this are experiencing crime," Martin said in the ad. "As your candidate for Congress, I've pledged to keep our neighborhoods intact—and to resist forced busing that threatens the very foundations of our country's neighborhood concept."

In early October, a *Charlotte News* poll of Mecklenburg voters showed Jim Beatty leading Jim Martin by 49 percent to 34 percent, with 17 percent undecided. The Martin campaign commissioned its own survey about a week later, conducted by UNC-Charlotte political scientist Schley Lyons. It gave

Martin an 8-point lead, 48 percent to 40 percent. But these polls looked only at Mecklenburg County, where most of the district's voters resided. To many, the conflicting data suggested that the race remained fluid and that many voters were not yet firmly committed. Media commentator John Kilgo reported that "Beatty, the Democrat, is running slightly ahead of Martin in most of the polls taken." Another journalist, E. E. Witherspoon of the *Lexington Dispatch*, predicted that "this race will be close and Beatty is likely to win." Martin himself seemed uncertain about the race. "You know what you're supposed to do when you're ahead, and you know what you've got to do when you're behind," he told reporters. "But when you're dead even, you don't know what to do."

Still, Brad Hays and Bob Bradshaw were confident their strategy was working. They continued to link their candidate tightly to the national ticket. During the last two weeks of the campaign, Vice President Spiro Agnew and President Nixon's son-in-law Edward Cox made campaign stops in Charlotte. So did Harry Dent, the president's special counsel and political advisor, who said that the White House and national Republican Party "have a special interest in Jim Martin." The weekend before Election Day, President Nixon campaigned in Greensboro with Holshouser, Helms, and Martin at his side. The Martin campaign's last flight of TV ads urged voters to help him help Nixon, closing with a photo of the two Republicans shaking hands.

The two largest daily newspapers in the district, the morning *Charlotte Observer* and the evening *Charlotte News*, split their election-eve endorsements. The *Observer* endorsed the Republican Holshouser for governor but recommended Democrat Jim Beatty for Congress. "Mr. Martin has conducted, we think, a bad campaign, one that has turned away many former supporters who are dismayed by the positions he has taken," the newspaper stated. It criticized Martin's opposition to forced busing and his hawkish views on foreign policy, while calling Beatty "a man of compassion as well as one of realism," which "should enable him to better understand the problems of the 'little people' who often feel left out of governmental affairs." On the other hand, the *News* endorsed Democrat Skipper Bowles for governor while urging readers to elect Martin to Congress. The paper noted that Beatty's 1971 drug bill had been substantially rewritten by his legislative colleagues after significant criticism, and that he had often been absent or disengaged from the General Assembly's work. "By contrast," the editorial continued, "James G. Martin has displayed more ability and more dedication in his years in office," arguing that "even his critics find him straightforward and consider him an intelligent student of government."

On November 3, 1972—four days before the elections—the *Charlotte News* published its final poll of Mecklenburg voters. The news was very bad for the Democrats. Nixon's support had grown by 7 points, Galifianakis had gone from leading Helms in Mecklenburg by 23 points to trailing him by 10, and Bowles had gone from leading Holshouser by 16 points to trailing him by 8. As for the Ninth District race, Martin enjoyed the support of 52 percent of Mecklenburg voters versus Beatty's 39 percent.

It was in this context that the two candidates made their closing statements to the voters. Beatty, now desperate, came as close as he ever had to criticizing Martin by name. Discussing his accomplishments in the legislature, Beatty said he had earned his chairmanship of the House's Education Appropriations Subcommittee on his merits. "It was not given to me to better my political career and then taken away from me because I could not get the job done," he said, an obvious dig at the fact that Martin's fellow commissioners had replaced him as chairman the previous December. But the Republican candidate, now seeing victory in his grasp, didn't rise to the bait. Instead, Martin clarified his positions on contentious issues with an eye toward the future. On school desegregation, for example, he explained that opposition to forced busing did not constitute a defense of past segregation. "I believe that it was wrong when I went to school to be transporting students away from a nearby school to a distant school on the basis of race," he said, "just as I think it is wrong now to do that, either to segregate them or to arbitrarily mix them." He also distinguished his support for Nixon's strategy to bring the Vietnam War to a successful end from President Johnson's large-scale deployment of American troops, which Martin argued had taken too much of the responsibility for fighting the Communists away from the Vietnamese themselves. When asked to sum up his vision for America, Martin put it simply: "Maximum freedom—that's what this country is all about."

BREAKTHROUGH AT LAST

After a grueling sprint to the finish, Jim Martin began election night at the Charlotte home of his Davidson fraternity brother Reitzel Snider, who had been the first contributor to Martin's initial campaign for county commission in 1966. With him were Dottie, his children, his parents, and his three brothers. Just after nine o'clock, they drove to the White House Inn, where the local politicos assembled to watch the election returns. The Martin party headed to a reserved eighth-floor suite. On the television, the initial results looked scary. Democratic-leaning precincts reported first, giving Beatty a sizable lead. But Martin and his team were more interested in telltale returns from bellwether precincts. It wasn't long before Marcus Hickman, Martin's chief fundraiser, announced, "Well, boys, we've got ourselves a congressman."

The November 7 general election did indeed produce an electoral triumph for state Republicans. Nixon was reelected easily, winning 49 states and more than two-thirds of the vote in North Carolina. Holshouser edged Bowles with 51 percent to become North Carolina's first GOP governor of the 20th century. Helms became the state's first modern Republican in the Senate, winning an impressive 54 percent of the vote. Of the statewide contests Republicans actively contested, only the office of lieutenant governor eluded their grasp, as Democratic activist and Wilson County attorney Jim Hunt won his first electoral race by a landslide over Republican businessman Johnny Walker. The GOP reelected its incumbent congressmen, gained 19 seats in the state legislature, and took over several more boards of commissioners in traditionally Democratic counties.

And although Jack Hawke fell short in his congressional bid in the Fourth District, Jim Martin's margin of victory over Jim Beatty in the Ninth—59 percent to 41 percent—proved even larger than the final polls had predicted. He hadn't just held Jonas's seat for his party. Martin had clearly established himself as a rising star in North Carolina politics. His next stop would be the nation's capital.

What he didn't know at the time was that one of his first challenges in Washington would involve the self-destruction of the very Republican president who had just won a landslide reelection—and to whom Martin had so closely attached himself during the 1972 campaign.

CHAPTER FOUR

"AT THE DROP OF A RAT"

On June 29, 1972, as Jim Martin pursued his first congressional campaign, Warner Bros. released a politically themed film directed by Michael Ritchie and starring Robert Redford. *The Candidate* depicted the behind-the-scenes machinations that put Redford's character, Bill McKay, into position to defeat an incumbent United States senator from California. At the end of the film, having improbably won the election, McKay turns to his campaign manager and asks, "What do we do now?" The movie's most famous line, it symbolized the extent to which politics had become more about winning than about governing, at least in the minds of the filmmakers and millions of Americans who watched and enjoyed *The Candidate*.

But Jim Martin was never like Bill McKay. He had done his homework. He had a clear sense of what he wanted to accomplish in Congress and how it would affect his young and growing family. A year earlier, Jim had asked not only his wife but also his children what they thought of his plans. The family deliberation continued for several days. "We voted every morning," Dottie said, "and he won every morning around the breakfast table."

Shortly after celebrating Jim's victory, the Martins began making plans. There was never any doubt the family would move to the nation's capital. It was standard practice at the time, and the only way for the family to be together most nights. But Jim and Dottie decided not to sell their house in Davidson until after he won reelection in 1974. Only then would they know for sure they wouldn't be moving back to North Carolina for a while. At that point, they planned to use the proceeds from the sale to build a family home on their lot at Lake Norman.

For their move to the nation's capital, the Martins selected a community in Alexandria, Virginia, where they initially rented and later bought a house. Jimmy and Emily would both graduate from Groveton High School, now West Potomac High. Ben would attend the local elementary school until the family returned to North Carolina in 1984. Although willing and able to play the role of congressional spouse as needed, Dottie devoted most of her time to family and other private pursuits. The Martins joined a local Presbyterian church, where she became an active member. She also earned a real-estate license and worked for several years at a realty firm owned by a friend from North Carolina.

In setting up his new office on Capitol Hill, Martin asked the advice of Brad Hays, Charlie Jonas, and longtime congressman Jim Broyhill, among others. Jim Lofton, who had left First Union bank to work on the congressional campaign, had become a close friend. His background also included stints as a buyer for the Belk department stores and director of civic affairs for the Charlotte Chamber of Commerce. Martin brought Lofton to Washington as administrative assistant. He also retained several staff members who'd worked for Jonas, including Lawrence Bowles, who handled legislative affairs. Charlie Sutton became the congressman's first press secretary but soon moved back to North Carolina to get married and join the Holshouser administration. Paul Jones, who had covered Martin on the county commission as a reporter at Charlotte's WBTV, served as press secretary for most of Martin's time in Congress. Martin's personal secretary, Peggy Barker, came with extensive Washington experience at the National Republican Congressional Committee. She was succeeded by Karen Roberts. Another staff member who later joined Martin's district office in Charlotte, Dottie Fuller, worked for Martin during the rest of his congressional service and then served as his personal secretary after he became governor.

FIRMLY IN THE MINORITY

To be a freshman Republican in the House of Representatives in the early 1970s was to reach the lowest rung of the shortest ladder in Washington. Although the GOP gained 14 seats in 1972, Democrats still enjoyed a 49-seat majority in the chamber they had controlled for all but four years since 1933. The leader of the Republican minority was Gerald Ford, who had represented

A REPUBLICAN CONGRESSMAN CHARTS HIS COURSE IN A DEMOCRATIC CAPITAL.
MARTIN FAMILY PHOTO

Michigan's Fifth District in the House since 1949. He was a smart, principled, and compassionate man whom Martin grew to love and respect. But Ford and other Republican leaders saw no prospect of achieving a majority, particularly after the emerging Watergate scandal began inflicting significant damage on the party. They counseled Martin to carve out a niche for himself and not to have unrealistic expectations.

It wasn't every day that a Princeton-trained scientist got elected to Congress. GOP leaders soon put their new colleague's expertise to good use. Martin was assigned to the Committee on Science and Astronautics (later renamed the Science and Technology Committee), as well as the Committee on Interior and Insular Affairs. Even as a freshman, he began taking the lead on scientific matters. For example, there was increasing concern that aerosol sprays might be contributing to the deterioration of the ozone layer. Martin spoke out in favor of legislation to address the emerging issue as long as it provided for extensive scientific study before the government considered any limits or prohibitions on the sale and use of aerosols. The new congressman also continued the scientific defense of nuclear power he had begun during his days on the county commission.

While he leaned heavily on Broyhill and other veteran Republicans for advice in setting up his office and learning his way around Capitol Hill, Martin kept his own counsel when it came to policy issues and floor votes. He didn't hesitate to take controversial stances on bills, particularly when he saw them as federal intrusion into matters best left to states, local governments, or the private sector. During his first two years in Congress, Martin was the most reliably conservative member of North Carolina's House delegation, earning an average 85 percent rating from the American Conservative Union (freshman senator Jesse Helms got a 98). By comparison, another Republican serving his first term in the House, future Senate majority leader Trent Lott, scored a 91. Martin later described Lott as his "closest personal friend in the House." Another up-and-coming Republican, sophomore Jack Kemp of New York, scored an ACU rating of 77 during the 1973–74 Congress. He also became one of Martin's closest congressional allies and friends.

The bills Martin sponsored during his first term illustrated his priorities. The very first legislation he filed was a resolution to prohibit any government authority, including federal judges, from making student-assignment decisions on the basis of race—clearly a response to the forced-busing controversy still under way in Charlotte-Mecklenburg. Martin also filed bills to strengthen legislative-branch oversight, to limit pay increases for members of Congress, and to require that the federal operating budget always be balanced except in times of war or "grave national emergency."

NO SMOOTH SAILING ON WATERGATE

With few exceptions, GOP candidates running in 1972 had tried to attach themselves to President Nixon's reelection campaign, which as early as May of that year already led George McGovern by nearly 20 points. But few Republicans were as explicit as Jim Martin. Mimicking Nixon's famous "V for victory" salute, he would hold up two fingers while saying that "a vote for Martin is like two votes for Nixon." Because he had worked so hard to tether himself to the president, Martin found himself under tremendous political pressure as the Watergate affair unfolded.

The scandal had its origins during the 1972 campaign with wiretapping

and burglary of the Democratic National Committee headquarters at the Watergate complex. Financial records tied the burglars back to Nixon operatives, including Howard Hunt and G. Gordon Liddy. Even before the presidential race concluded with a landslide victory for Nixon, government investigators and news reporters uncovered evidence of a much broader conspiracy involving Republican activists and Nixon administration officials to gather intelligence on their political enemies. Just a month after the president took his second oath of office, the Senate authorized the creation of a special investigative committee, headed by Senator Sam Ervin of North Carolina. Its televised hearings transfixed the nation during the summer of 1973 and led to revelations of the president's involvement in a cover-up of the scandal. By the end of the year, President Nixon was insisting he was "not a crook." By March 1974, a grand jury in Washington indicted seven of the president's top aides and named Nixon as an unindicted co-conspirator (the prosecutor had advised jurors that a president could not be indicted until after he left office).

Martin did not serve on any House committees with jurisdiction over impeachment. But as a Republican congressman with political ties to the embattled Nixon, he was asked repeatedly to comment on the emerging scandal. Martin chose to say little. Even as late as April 10, 1974, he said he would be "honored" if President Nixon chose to visit Charlotte during the approaching midterm elections. Martin later explained that because the impeachment process put the entire House in the role of a grand jury potentially serving an indictment, he felt it would be inappropriate to offer commentary about the case until he had sufficient sworn testimony to peruse. He would not form conclusions based on rumor or innuendo.

Martin's reticence had political consequences, however. Democrats and newspaper editorialists back home blasted his cautious stance. A group of Davidson College professors landed the most painful blow. They took out a newspaper ad questioning their former colleague's position on Watergate, using words such as *immoral* and *corrupt*. While Martin never expected much political support among the mostly liberal faculty, he was stunned and angry at the attacks on his character. "It hurt my family's feelings toward them, and to some extent toward the college," Martin recalled. The rupture was eventually repaired, although it took awhile.

The final release on July 30, 1974, of withheld transcripts from recorded White House conversations led Martin to end his reticence about the scandal. Assembling a large pile of transcripts, investigative reports, and media clippings, the congressman left his Capitol Hill office and camped out on his 27-foot sailboat, *Wooglin*, which was moored at a marina on the Potomac River. He spread the materials on a small folding table and methodically worked his way through them, drawing up timelines and cross-references. He was aghast at what he saw. He even experienced heart palpitations that led him to consult a physician, who diagnosed Martin with paroxysmal atrial tachycardia, a condition easily aggravated by stress. After finishing his research, he concluded that while Nixon may not have known about the initial Watergate burglary or even the broader conspiracy during the 1972 campaign, the president had violated the law and his oath of office during the ensuing cover-up. On August 6, 1974, Martin joined fellow North Carolina congressman Wilmer Mizell in calling for Nixon's impeachment for obstruction of justice. He continued to insist he had been right to withhold judgment until he had a chance to read and digest all the evidence. "I have now read it," Martin said. "I'm not sure I can digest it."

A SURVIVOR IN THE RUBBLE

There was never any doubt that Martin would run for reelection in 1974—or that Watergate would play a major role in the midterms that year. Early in the cycle, it also became obvious who the congressman's Democratic challenger would be: Milton Short, a lawyer and furniture retailer who had served four terms on the Charlotte City Council.

Although Martin had won election two years earlier by an impressive margin, Short and other local Democrats began the year with high hopes. Longtime senator Sam Ervin was retiring, but Democrats expected North Carolina attorney general Robert Morgan to be his likely replacement—and an excellent running mate for the party's candidates in down-ballot races. They also saw Martin as vulnerable because, in their minds, he had dithered too long before coming out in favor of Nixon's impeachment.

Short did go after Martin on Watergate, but he championed a range of other issues as well. With many voters disenchanted with the war in Vietnam, he accused the incumbent congressman of being too supportive of government secrecy and the defense establishment. He criticized Martin for establishing a "booster club" (the 1970s equivalent of today's super PACs) to solicit private donations to fund activities apart from the congressman's formal campaign, such as trips home from Washington and a district office in Statesville. And at a time of high and rising gas prices, Short alleged that Martin had done nothing to make the country less dependent on oil imports from the Middle East. "Can you think of one thing your congressman has done for you?" Short repeatedly asked the voters in his speeches, interviews, and campaign materials.

While a vigorous campaigner, Short had trouble making his attacks stick. On Watergate, Martin said he had consistently pressed President Nixon to tell everything he knew. When it became clear that the administration had not been forthcoming, Martin said, he voted for subpoena power and funding for the House panel investigating the scandal and later called for the president's impeachment. The congressman defended his booster club as a way to provide additional constituent services without charging the cost to taxpayers. On defense, Martin pointed out that he had voted against a major defense-authorization bill because he thought it spent too much. On gas prices, he noted that he had joined other Republicans and some Democrats to write legislation that would clear the way for more exploration of domestic energy resources,

VICE PRESIDENT GERALD FORD JOINS MARTIN FOR A 1974 FUNDRAISER IN CHARLOTTE. MARTIN FAMILY PHOTO

including shale oil. The Short campaign had "badly distorted my voting record," Martin said at a news conference shortly before the November 5, 1974, general election. He described Short's constant references to disgraced former president Nixon as an attempt to win the "vulture vote."

As it turned out, the 1974 midterms did leave the Republican Party looking a bit like carrion. The Watergate scandal helped produce massive Democratic victories—a 49-seat gain in the United States House, a four-seat gain in the Senate, and a net gain of four governorships. In the North Carolina General Assembly, Republicans went from 50 seats to 10, including only one Republican left standing in the 50-seat Senate. The 1974 election left the GOP holding just 80 of the state's 477 county commission seats. The Democratic wave extended into the state's congressional delegation as well. Of the four Republicans representing North Carolina in the United States House, two—Mizell and Earl Ruth—lost their reelections.

Both Martin and his mentor, Jim Broyhill, survived the carnage, each receiving a bit over 54 percent. It was the lowest vote share Broyhill had won since his initial, narrow victory to his seat in 1962. And for Martin, it was a significant drop from the 59 percent he'd won against Jim Beatty two years earlier. On election night, Martin credited the work of his longtime friend Margaret King in developing his voter-contact plan, what became known as the "Neighbors Program." She had actually chaired the Martin campaign in 1974, the first of four such stints for King during his congressional career. It also helped, however, that Martin had done more than just personally distance himself from a scandal-laden administration in Washington. He had spent his first two years assembling a good staff, building a constituent-service operation, and advancing a policy agenda that played to his strengths as a scientist, educator, and former local official.

During his second term, Martin would begin developing expertise in another critical area: tax policy.

"WE WRITE THE TAXES"

Shortly after his reelection, Martin got a call from Broyhill, who served on the GOP panel that handled committee assignments. "We need somebody on the Ways and Means Committee," Broyhill said. Martin asked if it would be possible to get posted instead to Appropriations, the committee on which Charlie Jonas had long served. Broyhill told him that for the 1975–76 session, GOP leaders had decided to fill their list of committee slots in reverse alphabetic order. If Martin volunteered for Ways and Means, he'd likely get it. But if he waited until Appropriations, he might find himself competing with many other members. Besides, Broyhill advised, Ways and Means was likely to rise in importance in the coming years as politicians and others debated the proper role of tax policy in addressing problems such as stagnant growth and soaring inflation. Martin said yes. Back home, some constituents were puzzled. They didn't know what "Ways and Means" meant. "We write the taxes," Martin explained, prompting some to wonder if he had his "head on right" when he accepted the post.

But Broyhill was right—Martin ended up with a plum assignment. Trent Lott traveled to North Carolina in early 1975 to speak at a GOP fundraiser in Statesville. "We need men like Martin—men to whom we can say 'you lead the way and we will follow,' " Lott said of his close friend sitting at the head table. "The Washington action is in the Ways and Means Committee. There you find the power—and there you find Jim Martin."

Recognizing he had a lot to learn, Martin took a deep dive into fiscal policy. He read voraciously: government reports, committee testimony, research papers from entities such as the American Enterprise Institute and the United States Chamber of Commerce, and tax-policy articles in the *Wall Street Journal*, *National Review*, and other periodicals. His colleague and friend Jack Kemp, while not a member of Ways and Means, had spent the past couple of years schooling himself on tax policy. He suggested reading material and experts for Martin to consult.

It didn't take long for Martin to form some initial conclusions and craft some proposed reforms. Recognizing that the existing payroll and income-tax exclusions for employer-provided health plans were unfair to individuals purchasing health insurance or medical services on their own, Martin filed a bill in February 1975 to offer refundable tax credits to Americans with high out-of-pocket medical expenses. He also came to believe that the punitive treatment of savings and investment was one of the worst features of the tax code. When households received wages and salaries, they paid tax on that stream of income only once. There was no additional layer of taxation on the employer side either, because employee compensation was deductible to the firm. But when households received interest, dividends, or capital gains from investments they purchased with savings, that stream of income was taxed at least twice—once when the saved money was previously taxed as wage or salary income, and then again when the investment yielded a return. If the savings went into stocks or mutual funds, the stream of income was usually subject to the corporate income tax, and thus reduced in value a third time. Finally, if a person died without spending his savings down, his stream of investment income might be hit a fourth time by estate or inheritance taxes layered on top of the income-tax code.

Martin thought the best approach was to address the problem in stages. He filed bills to raise the asset threshold for the estate tax, to limit the double taxation of savings accounts and pension funds, and to expand the ability of Americans to invest in subchapter S corporations, in which profits were distributed directly to shareholders without being subject to a separate corporate tax. He was also one of the first cosponsors of a 1975 bill, the Jobs Creation Act, filed by Jack Kemp. The legislation partially excluded capital gains and household savings from the income tax, reduced the corporate tax rate, and eliminated tax biases against employee stock-ownership plans.

But while Martin believed the federal tax code was a major impediment to capital formation and economic growth, he remained strongly committed to fiscal responsibility and balanced budgets. He was also one of the first cosponsors of another Kemp bill, the Fiscal Integrity Act, to promote transparent and balanced budgets. If tax changes were projected to produce significant reductions in federal revenue, Martin wanted to see them offset by spending cuts. When Ways and Means moved a bill to extend the temporary 1975 tax cut into the 1976 tax year, Martin was one of only six committee members to vote against it. "We've got no business providing a tax cut when we are running such enormous deficits," Martin argued.

On February 20, 1976, he held a news conference to propose a tax-reform model that would broaden the base of the income tax by eliminating many credits, deductions, and exclusions. Martin said he even favored expanding the definition of taxable income to include government transfers such as welfare payments and food stamps, arguing that all Americans should pay some income tax, so they would have some sense of how much the government cost. When asked which government benefits ought to be classified as taxable income, he mentioned Social Security. "Martin Calls for Tax on Social Security Benefits," read the front-page, above-the-fold headline in that afternoon's edition of the *Charlotte News*. The congressman and his staff knew he'd stumbled badly. Martin immediately contacted reporters and explained that he had misstated his intentions. His approach would only tax transfers that "hadn't already been taxed earlier." Because Social Security benefits came out of payroll taxes levied on both workers and employers, they shouldn't be taxed again. The basic principle behind his model, Martin explained, was that "we would tax all income from whatever source," but only one time.

He continued to work on his tax-reform ideas, discussing them with his Ways and Means colleagues as well as Kemp, Lott, and other Republicans who were thinking along similar lines. In the meantime, Martin made headlines for another proposal, this one formally introduced as a bill in early 1976. It was a response to the December 29, 1975, terrorist bombing of New York City's LaGuardia Airport, which killed 11 and seriously injured 74. Coming after a string of other bombings, assassination plots, and hijackings, the LaGuardia bombing prompted Congress to study various ideas for deterring terrorism and upgrading airport security. Martin's bill called for a mandatory sentence of death for anyone convicted of bombing an airport. Characteristically, he came up with a memorable pitch: "If you bomb the hangar, hang the bomber."

MORE PRESIDENTIAL POLITICS

Like Jim Holshouser, Jim Broyhill, and many other Republican office-holders, Martin early on announced his support for Nixon's successor, Gerald Ford, in the 1976 presidential race. Given the likelihood of a tough general-election campaign that fall, Martin didn't think it would be wise for the Republican Party to give up the advantages of nominating an incumbent. However, he was careful to lavish praise on Ford's primary challenger, former California governor Ronald Reagan, whom Martin genuinely respected as a forceful advocate for fiscal restraint, a strong national defense, and other causes they shared. On tax policy in particular, Martin's service on the Ways and Means Committee had moved his thinking closer to Reagan's call for permanent tax-rate reductions and away from Ford's preference for one-time rebates. Still, however nuanced the congressman's decision to endorse Ford may have been, it had the effect of lining him up against Jesse Helms and the senator's political organization, the Congressional Club. They vigorously backed Reagan and sought to make North Carolina's presidential primary on March 23 a critical moment after Ford's initial six victories in Iowa (January 19), New Hampshire (February 24), Massachusetts and Vermont (March 2), Florida (March 9), and Illinois (March 16).

Although Helms liked Ford personally, he did not believe the president would be the strongest Republican nominee in 1976. Moreover, Helms had actually pledged his support to Reagan as early as 1973. While the senator toured North Carolina with Reagan in the final week before the March 23 primary, the Congressional Club paid for the statewide broadcast of a 30-minute ad Reagan had cut for the Barry Goldwater campaign in 1964. The Congressional Club also led a strong get-out-the-vote push for Reagan.

Having taken the North Carolina primary for granted, the Ford campaign suddenly realized it faced a major problem. Three days before the primary, President Ford flew to a campaign appearance in Charlotte that doubled as a fundraising reception for Martin. Ford was effusive in his praise for his one-time House colleague, saying Martin had "demonstrated an outstanding capability to deal with issues forcefully, intelligently, and with a great deal of plain old North Carolina common sense." Naturally, Ford also took the opportunity to make his case for the GOP nomination, arguing that under his leadership the nation was recovering from its economic woes and political troubles. "I hope that I can get some help and assistance next Tuesday," he concluded.

Ford got it from most of the Republicans in the room that day. But it wasn't enough. Reagan won North Carolina with 52 percent of the vote. It rejuvenated his campaign. He went on to win other primaries, keeping the president from clinching the party's nod ahead of the Republican National Convention in Kansas City. Although Ford did attract enough uncommitted delegates to win the nomination on the first ballot, it was by the narrowest of margins. He graciously gave a prime speaking spot to Reagan, who made the most of it with a fantastic address. A national star was born. And the Helms organization in North Carolina could claim a great deal of credit for making it happen.

Martin, Holshouser, and Broyhill weren't in Kansas City to see Reagan overshadow Ford with his "concession" speech. They were not selected as convention delegates. According to Congressional Club leader Tom Ellis, a prominent Raleigh attorney, he and other Reagan supporters had offered to seat the Ford-supporting Republican officeholders in the state's delegation as long as they agreed to support the former California governor for president instead. Reagan had, after all, won the North Carolina primary. The offer was declined. Martin said he felt compelled to honor his longstanding commitment to Ford, his friend and former House leader. The exclusion of a sitting governor and two congressmen from the delegation angered many longtime GOP leaders and activists, particularly in the traditionally Republican Piedmont and mountain counties. But Helms supporters believed they had been magnanimous in victory and focused their efforts on shaping the Republican message for 1976. Their chief representative on the party platform committee in Kansas City was ECU political scientist John East, the former congressional candidate and future United States senator.

ON THE DEFENSIVE—AGAIN

After the devastating blow the Republican Party had taken in North Carolina in 1974, state party leaders expected a rebound in 1976. They were sorely disappointed, having failed to anticipate two important factors. First, the Democrats chose a Southerner, former Georgia governor Jimmy Carter, as their nominee to face President Ford. An evangelical running as a moderate on most issues, Carter returned North Carolina to the Democratic column in 1976, winning 55 percent of the Tar Heel vote on his way to the White House. Second, state Republicans woefully underestimated the personal talents and political appeal of Lieutenant Governor Jim Hunt, the Democratic nominee for governor. He crushed Republican David Flaherty, a former furniture executive and Holshouser cabinet secretary, by 65 percent to 34 percent.

MARTIN, WITH BEN OVER HIS SHOULDER, LISTENS TO HIS PREDECESSOR, CHARLIE JONAS (*RIGHT*) GIVE ADVICE TO THE GOP NOMINEE FOR GOVERNOR IN 1976, DAVE FLAHERTY. MARTIN FAMILY PHOTO

"You can't deny him the credit he deserves," Flaherty said of Hunt during his election-night concession speech. "He did a whale of a job and did it for the whole party, not just himself." Republicans regained no ground in the General Assembly (it was no great accomplishment that they held all 10 of their legislative seats, as these were from the most GOP-friendly districts) and receded even farther at the local level, dropping from 80 out of 477 county commission seats in 1974 to just 46 of 484 after the 1976 election.

It was in this environment that Jim Martin won the closest race of his congressional career. His Democratic opponent for the 1976 general election was Charlotte attorney Arthur Goodman Jr., a former member of the North Carolina House. For many local Democrats, Goodman was not their first choice. Party leaders had initially approached Liz Hair, who by this time chaired the county commission in Mecklenburg. She declined. As the general-election campaign unfolded, Goodman pointed to Jimmy Carter's momentum and signs that Democrats were poised to do well in congressional races. If Washington was about to become an even more Democratic place, he said, that was a good reason for local residents to prefer him over Martin. "A Democratic freshman is going to be able to do more than a Republican, I don't care how many terms he's served," Goodman insisted. He also argued that Martin was too cozy with interest groups. Citing contributions to the Martin campaign by politically active doctors, Goodman emphasized that he favored adopting national health insurance for all. Citing contributions to his opponent from "donors in Texas," Goodman said he favored alternative energy sources. "Mr. Martin seems to favor multinational corporations and monopolistic companies, especially oil companies," he said. "I feel my campaign rests on what is important to the average citizen."

Goodman and other Democrats were particularly caustic in their criticisms of Martin's 1975 vote against the Education for All Handicapped Children Act. It required all public schools receiving federal funds to offer individualized education plans to students with physical and mental disabilities and offered states additional dollars to help fund the necessary services. Martin strongly supported the bill's intention and had championed the needs of disabled students as a county commissioner. But once again, he bristled at heavy-handed federal involvement in what was traditionally a state and local function. When the bill came to the House for its final vote, it passed by a 404–7 margin. Martin was the only North Carolina representative to vote no.

Like Short two years earlier, Goodman struggled to overcome his opponent's organizational and financial advantages. And by his third run for Congress, Martin had developed more than just a strong campaign team and a long list of donors. He had also perfected a message that tied together his interest in nuclear power and other scientific issues, his services on Ways and Means, and his knack for communicating complex ideas with memorable phrases and visual aids. In many of his letters and speeches, for example, Martin argued against federal intrusion into matters best left to states, localities, businesses, and families by citing ridiculous instances of overregulation. One of his favorite examples was a 72-page federal rule requiring warning signs on ladders. "When ascending or descending," the regulation stipulated, "users should face the ladder." It also recommended warnings against consumers placing ladders in front of doors or spilling grease on the rungs. "All of this may seem a little ridiculous to you," Martin said. "But your tax dollars are paying for such trivia." He also offered a spirited defense of his economic views, his stance on military spending, and even his lonely, federalist opposition to legislation such as the Education for All Handicapped Children Act.

It worked. On Election Day, November 2, Martin won 53.5 percent of the vote. His margin of victory would never drop that low again for the remainder of his political career.

A SWEET VICTORY

One factor contributing to Martin's electoral success was his knack for communicating ideas in ways voters could understand and remember. The skill would come in handy during one of the defining moments of his congressional career: his fight to defend sound science against regulators and activists aligned with Ralph Nader, who sought to ban artificial sweeteners as potential carcinogens.

In 1879, a student at Johns Hopkins University in Baltimore had discovered that a synthetic compound derived from coal tar had a sweet taste. The product was soon produced and marketed under the name *saccharin*. After the passage of the Pure Food and Drug Act of 1906, newly empowered regulators began to turn their attention to artificial food additives, particularly those like saccharin that competed with the products of politically influential groups such as sugarcane growers. The first federal efforts to ban saccharin ran up

against an even more powerful interest: President Teddy Roosevelt, who used the product himself. Subsequent efforts also fizzled, particularly during wartime shortages of sugar. Things began to change when new federal policies in the late 1950s gave the Food and Drug Administration more regulatory authority. These included the so-called Delaney Clause, which prohibited the use in food of any product shown to increase the risk of cancer in humans or laboratory animals. During the 1960s and early 1970s, regulators began applying the Delaney "zero-risk" standard to substances that had in the past been generally recognized as safe. Initial toxicological studies found elevated instances of bladder cancer among rats consuming high levels of saccharin. Regulators weren't sure whether it was saccharin itself or impurities that were at work. But in early 1977, a new set of studies concluded that impurities weren't to blame. The FDA responded on March 9, 1977, by recommending a ban on saccharin as a food additive.

As a chemist, Jim Martin had long disliked the Delaney Clause. When it was first enacted, substances were often tested in parts per thousand. As the technology improved, they were detected in parts per million and then parts per billion. Zero-risk standards grew increasingly absurd. Regulators were citing animal studies employing very high concentrations of tested chemicals as a justification for banning even trace amounts. Martin and other scientists disdained this reasoning. Their two main objections became popular talking points: "The dose makes the poison" and "A rat is not a man." In the saccharin studies, for example, the rats were force-fed such high dosages that a person would have to drink 800 cans of diet soda a day to get the same exposure. "Fifty cans of pure water each day would kill most of us," Martin observed, as one would drown. Moreover, animal and human physiology differed in important ways. Epidemiological research among human beings often did not confirm predictions based on animal testing.

Just one day after the FDA's announcement, Martin introduced a House resolution to the effect that the regulatory agency should not attempt to ban saccharin without express authority from Congress. By March 16, he was ready to file a bill to amend the Federal Food, Drug, and Cosmetic Act to deny the FDA such authority. It attracted more than 200 cosponsors. Martin became one of the leaders of a coalition of House and Senate members who sought to, in his words, "bomb the ban" while reforming the Delaney Rule itself. Actually, many in the FDA felt that a zero-risk standard no longer made sense but felt compelled to apply the law in the saccharin case. So the coalition's real adversaries included the sugar industry (for obvious reasons) and Ralph Nader's network of consumer organizations, which saw the saccharin ban as an integral part of their larger campaign to combat man-made carcinogens.

Martin's main antagonist was Sidney Wolfe, a physician and head of Nader's Public Citizen Health Research Group. On April 21, Martin and Wolfe joined FDA deputy commissioner Sherwin Gardner and American Cancer Society expert Frank Rauscher for a panel at the American Enterprise Institute. Martin and Wolfe sparred frequently throughout the event, Wolfe growing increasingly testy at being challenged by a congressman who knew at least as much about chemistry as he did. Asked a question about federal regulation of tobacco, for which the link to cancer and other adverse health effects was far better established, Martin explained the principle succinctly. "I think we can allow people to make judgments for themselves, as they do with regard to smoking," he said. "I choose not to smoke. I choose to use saccharin. I would like to be able to continue to make those choices."

A few weeks later, on May 17, the FDA convened a high-profile set of hearings. By this time, Martin and other opponents had developed a strategy not just for winning the scientific debate but also for illustrating the hardship a saccharin ban would impose. The pharmaceutical industry testified that saccharin was an essential ingredient in more than 600 medicines. Because sugar often couldn't be used to disguise what would otherwise be bitter-tasting drugs, a saccharin ban could lead to many patients not complying with their medical treatments. The coalition also included a large and sympathetic constituency: diabetics. Representing them at the FDA hearing were Chicago Cubs third baseman Ron Santo and other professional athletes with juvenile-onset diabetes, as well as several dozen diabetics who arrived from Atlanta on a train they dubbed the "Sweet Georgia Brown Saccharin Special."

Martin was the first witness to testify at the hearing. Sidney Wolfe also testified. Rhetorically, it was no contest. When Wolfe dismissed the concerns of the doctors and diabetics by calling saccharin a "convenience item" that could be replaced by ginger or grated coconut, the room erupted in derisive giggles. On the other hand, the audience laughed with delight when Martin argued that government should never ban something "at the drop of a rat." He may not have originated the phrase—no one quite recalls who used it first—but Martin certainly popularized it. The FDA hearings were front-page news across the country, and his "at the drop of a rat" quote appeared hundreds of times in newspaper articles and news broadcasts. NBC News even described Martin as "leading the congressional drive" to change the Delaney Clause.

Of course, Martin was still a Republican in a Democratic Congress. The cause needed a high-profile Democratic champion. It got one in Teddy Kennedy, who chaired the Senate Subcommittee on Health and Scientific Research. On June 23, 1977, the Massachusetts senator filed a bill called the Saccharin Study, Labeling and Advertising Act. It called for a two-year moratorium on the FDA's proposed ban, as well as a warning label on products containing saccharin. Six House members—five Democrats and Republican Jim Martin—introduced a companion bill. A blended version later passed both chambers. President Jimmy Carter signed it on November 23, 1977. By working effectively across the aisle and with a diverse set of interest groups, Martin had struck a major blow for consumer choice and scientific rigor while elevating his profile on Capitol Hill as a coalition builder and a go-to member on regulatory matters.

Over time, his position was fully vindicated. The saccharin ban never went into effect. Years later, the FDA formally withdrew it and the National Toxicology Program removed saccharin from its carcinogen report, noting that the conclusions from the rat studies of the 1970s had not been replicated by subsequent research on cancer risk among humans.

WHAT A DIFFERENCE TWO YEARS MAKE

The founder of the American Council on Science and Health, Dr. Elizabeth Whelan, was a Harvard nutritionist and a close ally of Martin's in his attacks on federal overregulation. Just before the 1978 midterms, she wrote a letter to the editor of the *Charlotte News*. "The Council hopes that the United States will succeed both in keeping saccharin and nitrates in food, and in keeping Jim Martin in the House of Representatives."

Naturally, local Democrats disagreed. Teddy Kennedy and Jimmy Carter may have agreed with Martin on the saccharin ban. But he remained a reliably conservative congressman (averaging an 86 ranking from the American Conservative Union over his first three terms) and a fierce critic of the Carter administration and Democrats on Capitol Hill. During one 1978 speech, Martin contrasted President Carter's "open-mouth policy" in the Middle East and other international hot spots with what he considered the more successful diplomacy of the Nixon and Ford administrations. He also criticized Carter's proposal to encourage states to offer same-day voter registration, which Martin said would lead to voter fraud on Election Day, and argued that the United States should combat energy shortages in part by deregulating the natural-gas industry. To get more supply to the market, Martin said, "you've got to allow somebody to get a little rich off discovering it."

As in the previous electoral cycle, local Democrats talked a good game about challenging Martin. Liz Hair said that having a Republican representative from the Ninth District was a "humiliation," and that 1978 would be the time finally to defeat him. But again, she decided not to run. So did other Democrats who held city, county, or legislative offices. Thus, the party pinned its hopes on Charles Maxwell, a farmer who had formerly served in the state Senate and on the North Carolina State Highway Commission under former governor Bob Scott. He endorsed President Carter's energy policies and called for balancing the budget. Like previous Democratic candidates, Maxwell also accused Martin of being beholden to big business and special interests. Hoping to overcome the incumbent's advantages in fundraising and organization, Maxwell proclaimed himself "the people's candidate" and insisted that "to win a contest, all it takes is contact and shoe leather."

Brad Hays and the Martin campaign didn't agree, although the congressman certainly did his share of door-to-door campaigning and public events. Most expected the 1978 cycle to be more congenial to Republicans than the 1974 and 1976 cycles. But Hays, who had finally relocated his political consultancy from Washington to Charlotte the previous year, left nothing to chance. The campaign raised $211,000 (about $757,000 in 2015 dollars) and made extensive use of advertising to reinforce the candidate's major themes of fiscal restraint, regulatory relief for businesses and entrepreneurs, limits on federal intrusion into state and local affairs, and a strong national defense. Margaret King served the second of her four stints as Martin's campaign chairwoman, keeping his events calendar and organizing thousands of volunteers into an effective Neighbors Program for voter mobilization.

Martin also continued to enjoy significant crossover support among Democratic business executives and civic leaders in Charlotte and received the editorial endorsements of both daily newspapers. "Jim Martin went to Congress six years ago, a young man of promise," the *Charlotte News* stated. "Year by year since then, he has fulfilled the promise. He is a diligent and earnest congressman, faithful in constituent service, vigorous in the advancement of the conservative philosophy that he and his district share."

The voters seemed to agree with that assessment. On November 7, 1978, Jim Martin was reelected to his fourth term in the House with 68 percent of the vote. It was the largest margin of victory in his political career.

CHAPTER FIVE

THE REAGAN CHAIN REACTION

I n the four years between his narrow loss of the Republican nomination in 1976 and his election as president in 1980, Ronald Reagan kept himself in the public eye by writing columns, producing radio commentaries, and touring the country to make speeches and raise money for Republican candidates. For the most part, he was simply fine-tuning the conservative message he'd developed as an activist and California governor. But on an issue that would prove critical to his 1980 campaign and subsequent presidency—tax policy—Reagan's message began to shift in both tone and detail. The shift reflected the rise of supply-side economics as an intellectual movement, as well as a national tax revolt that began in Reagan's own state of California in 1978. And it bore the unmistakable imprint of the tax-reform work of Representative Jack Kemp and his closest congressional allies.

One of those allies was Jim Martin. He was among a small group of Republicans on the Ways and Means Committee—including Bill Archer of Texas, Bill Steiger of Wisconsin, Bill Frenzel of Minnesota, John Rousselot of California, Guy Vander Jagt of Michigan, and Phil Crane of Illinois—who worked closely with Kemp on pro-growth tax legislation. Their goals were ambitious. They had come to believe that America's "stagflation"—a painful combination of stagnant growth and high inflation—was partly caused by a federal tax code that punished savers, hampered investment, and discouraged work with its high marginal tax rates. They sought no less than a sweeping rewrite of the nation's fiscal policies.

But they were only a small group of Republicans in an overwhelmingly Democratic House. Moreover, they faced opposition from the White House, initially under Republican Gerald Ford and then under Democrat Jimmy Carter. Nevertheless, the House tax-reform faction did bring some advantages to the debate. For one thing, it was ably served by economists working directly for Kemp, including staff members Paul Craig Roberts and Bruce Bartlett, as well as consultant Norman Ture, who had advised Democratic and Republican policymakers on tax policy since the 1950s. For another, outside economists such as Columbia University professor (and future Nobel laureate) Robert Mundell, Harvard University rising star Martin Feldstein, and Mundell's former student Arthur Laffer were providing intellectual ammunition for the movement, as were President Ford's former treasury secretary, William Simon, *National Review* and *Reason* magazine contributor Alan Reynolds, and writers Robert Bartley and Jude Wanniski on the *Wall Street Journal* editorial page. The Kemp faction also had allies in the Senate, particularly Republicans Paul Fannin of Arizona, William Roth of Delaware, and Jesse Helms of North Carolina.

Perhaps the most surprising and important advantage Kemp's group had, however, was that many Democrats had also become receptive to new ideas on tax policy. They were reading the same economic statistics and opinion polls the Republicans were. During the last months of the Ford administration in 1976, they were happy to blame stagflation on the Republican president. After President Carter took office in 1977, Democrats were now fully in control of the nation's capital—and thus responsible, in the eyes of the public, for the performance of the economy. Many Democrats remembered that President John Kennedy and then–Ways and Means chairman Wilbur Mills (both advised by Norman Ture) had initiated tax-rate reductions during the early 1960s. Senator Lloyd Bentsen of Texas was one JFK acolyte who saw the episode as instructive. Other Democrats on Capitol Hill agreed.

Thus, the tax-reform movement of the mid-1970s was both an emerging school of thought and an increasingly bipartisan political coalition. Like so many other movements throughout history, its popular name came not from an adherent but from a critic, Herbert Stein, who had chaired the Council of Economic Advisors under both Nixon and Ford. Stein commented at a public forum that he didn't care much for the new thinking on tax policy championed by Mundell, Laffer, and the Kemp faction in Congress. He called them "supply-side fiscalists." The term was meant to be derisive, but it actually made sense. The dominant economic thinking of the day, Keynesianism, blamed irrational drops in "aggregate demand" for the onset and severity of recessions. To maintain high and steady consumption in normal times, Keynesians advocated steeply progressive tax rates to transfer income from the wealthy to middle-class and poor households, who would be more likely to spend it, rather than save it. To return the labor market to full employment after recessions, Keynesians proposed higher government spending or temporary tax cuts to juice overall spending (on both investment and consumption), coupled with higher inflation, which would reduce real wages and thus induce businesses to hire more workers.

Proponents of the views Stein was criticizing proudly accepted the term *supply-side economics*. On fiscal policy, they favored reducing the anti-investment bias in the tax code as well as the "tax wedge" between a worker's take-home pay and the total cost of employing the worker, including income and payroll taxes. On monetary policy, supply-siders followed Robert Mundell's lead in advocating a strict focus on maintaining price stability, rather than having the Federal Reserve attempt to manipulate the economy. Low, predictable tax rates and low, predictable inflation would create a policy infrastructure within which workers, employers, investors, and entrepreneurs could make their own decisions based on market signals. The result, supply-siders predicted, would be more labor and capital deployed more productively to create sustained growth in jobs and real incomes. Because take-home pay would rise, more people would enter the labor force. Because after-tax returns to investment would rise, capital would flow from tax shelters, real estate, and overseas into new or expanding American businesses.

The implications for government revenues were complicated. In some situations—when marginal tax rates were extremely high, for example, or when an investor's decision to sell stocks was heavily determined by the tax liability—supply-siders argued that the revenue effects could be neutral or even positive as lower rates were applied to a tax base enlarged by economic growth, asset sales, or the elimination of tax shelters. Apart from such special cases, however, the main argument was that the "dynamic" effect of tax cuts on economic growth, and thus on revenues collected on a larger tax base, would over time offset some of the initial, "static" revenue loss.

Later critics would claim that supply-side economics centered on the claim of tax cuts partially or fully "paying for themselves." That was a gross exaggeration. While some supply-siders did make extravagant claims about revenue effects, most insisted that spending cuts to limit and eventually eliminate deficits were essential. Advocates of marrying tax cuts with spending restraint included Ronald Reagan himself, top Reagan advisors such as Hoover Institution scholar Martin Anderson, and many conservatives on Capitol Hill, including Jim Martin. In any event, supply-side economics was about far more than revenue projections or tax cuts. It encompassed monetary policy, regulatory reform, and even reforming public-assistance programs to induce more welfare recipients into the labor market.

EVOLUTION LEADS TO REVOLUTION

As economists and journalists worked out the details of the new economic strategy, Capitol Hill lawmakers toiled to turn abstract theories into practical legislation. The process actually began in late 1974 with the Savings and Investment Act, introduced in the House by Jack Kemp and in the Senate by Paul Fannin and Jesse Helms. It used exemptions, credits, and accelerated depreciation to reduce the tax bias against both household savings and business investment. The following year, Kemp expanded the bill to add a cut in the corporate income tax and a fix to tax laws covering employee stock-ownership plans. He also changed its name to the Jobs Creation Act. Jim Martin was among its initial cosponsors. Over the ensuing months, lawmakers continued to tinker with the bill's provisions. By mid-1977, it called for an across-the-board 30 percent cut in tax rates on personal income, justified in part as a rollback of the "bracket creep" caused by high inflation. The legislation acquired yet another new name: the Tax Reduction Act. Delaware senator Bill Roth agreed to introduce a companion bill in his chamber as long as the tax cut was phased in over three years.

President Carter and Democratic leaders on Capitol Hill grew increasingly nervous about the Kemp-Roth bill. They tried to scuttle it by projecting preposterous revenue losses, savaging it in the media, and offering their own Revenue Act in early 1978 that would slightly roll back bracket creep while raising the capital-gains tax and eliminating various tax breaks for business. But rank-and-file Democrats as well as Republicans kept signing on to Kemp-Roth. Carter's proposed capital-gains tax hike was especially unpopular among pragmatists of both parties who were enamored with the new technology industry. Silicon Valley executives told Congress that venture capital was already scarce enough. They wanted the anti-investment tax bias alleviated, not worsened. In April 1978, Martin's Ways and Means colleague Bill Steiger proposed an amendment to the president's revenue bill to slash the top tax rate on capital gains from 49 percent to 25 percent. Again, the Carter administration used back-channel maneuvers as well as a threatened veto to try to quash the idea.

In the meantime, however, Kemp-Roth continued to gain momentum. By mid-October, its core element, reductions in marginal tax rates, passed both the House and Senate as amendments to the Revenue Act of 1978. At this point, President Carter and his team knew a major tax cut was inevitable. They chose to threaten a veto unless the Kemp-Roth rate reductions came out. In return, Carter accepted the Steiger amendment's near-halving of the capital-gains rate. The president signed it and the rest of the bill into law. The supply-side revolution had officially begun, three years before the Kemp-Roth model itself became law as the backbone of President Reagan's new fiscal policy.

THE CHEMIST VERSUS THE ECONOMIST

Martin's involvement in the first supply-side victory on taxes actually became an issue in his 1978 congressional race. His opponent, Charles Maxwell, alleged that Martin and other supporters of the capital-gains tax cut were only out to help the wealthy. Campaigning at a hydraulics plant in Charlotte, Martin told the assembled workers that "we need to cut taxes and support the free enterprise system so there will be more real jobs like yours." He pointed out that the Steiger amendment was passed with bipartisan support and argued that the best way to combat inflation (a phenomenon of too many dollars chasing too few goods and services) was to remove government-imposed barriers to supply—that is, to capital formation and economic production.

Maxwell tried as best he could to challenge Martin on economic policy. It wasn't until the 1980 campaign, however, that the issue truly came front and center. As the Republican presidential nominee, Reagan cited the high inflation and weak growth of the previous four years as proof that a different policy mix was needed, one that combined lower marginal tax rates with spending restraint and tighter control of the money supply. In 1979, Martin Anderson had outlined all this for Reagan in a document known as "Policy Memorandum No. 1." It became the core of the campaign's economic message.

Even if Jim Martin hadn't subscribed to what was later called "Reaganomics," he would have had a hard time distancing himself from the candidate at the top of the ticket. As it happened, however, Martin fully subscribed to Reagan's agenda. He had spent much of the 1979–80 session working with Kemp and others to fashion more supply-side bills. These included another version of the Kemp-Roth tax cut, as well as the Spending Limitation Act to impose caps on federal spending: 21 percent of gross domestic product in 1980, then 20 percent in 1981, then 19 percent in 1982, then 18 percent in 1983. Martin also filed several bills of his own to reduce gift taxes, to alleviate the double taxation of investment by broadening subchapter S "pass-through" corporations, and to allow more investors to pay the lower capital-gains tax enacted by the Steiger amendment.

For the 1980 cycle, Democrats decided to go after Congressman Martin aggressively on fiscal issues. They chose a Davidson College economist, Randy Kincaid, as their nominee. Kincaid, whose political experience consisted of four years on the Davidson Town Council, espoused traditionally Keynesian ideas. He savaged Kemp-Roth as a "simplistic" and "doctrinaire" approach that would benefit the wealthy at the expense of everyone else. Martin was a "predictable voice for big business," Kincaid said, who was "not very good at economics." The *Charlotte Observer* sounded a similar theme in its endorsement of Kincaid, arguing that Martin was placing conservative ideology above the needs of the district. The *Charlotte News* also gave Kincaid more credence than it had past Democratic nominees, editorializing that while Martin was "the better choice" in 1980, "the district would also be well-represented by Democratic challenger Randy Kincaid."

Martin always took his general-election opponents seriously, even though his seat had stayed in Republican hands for the better part of three decades. That Kincaid was a fellow academic trained in economics only served to strengthen Martin's respect for his opponent. But that didn't keep him from employing humor to get his points across. When Kincaid argued that federal spending was an anchor of the economy and helped prop up aggregate demand to ensure full employment, Martin quipped that government took in money the way "the alimentary canal of a three-month-old baby" takes in food—"with an insatiable appetite on one end and no sense of responsibility on the other." He blasted Keynesian monetary policies for fueling inflation and argued that a Kemp-Roth approach would combat it by increasing production (through lower tax rates and less double taxation of investment returns) and restraining federal spending (which would result in less borrowing). When Kincaid cited contributions to Martin's campaign by chemical companies to support his charge that the congressman was in the pocket of big business, Martin pointed out that he was, after all, a chemist. "What's wrong with one organic chemist in Congress getting support from other chemists?" he asked. "Am I supposed to get support from liberal economists?"

Kincaid claimed that Martin's close ties to the chemical industry also explained the congressman's behavior during the passage of the Comprehensive Environmental Response, Compensation, and Liability Act of 1980, better known as "Superfund." In response to celebrated pollution cases such as New York's Love Canal, the legislation authorized regulators either to compel responsible parties to clean up hazardous-waste sites or to use the new Superfund to finance the cleanup, with the government later suing the polluters to replenish the fund. In committee, Martin had voted against provisions of the bill. But when it reached the floor, he was one of only a handful of members who made speeches on its behalf (although most ended up voting for Superfund). Kincaid alleged that Martin tried to have it both ways for political gain. But Martin insisted he had opposed only certain details of the bill that inflated its cost, while always agreeing with its overall thrust. "Life's too short to go around destroying another person's reputation," Martin said. "Kincaid knows I'm not dishonest." It was a rare departure from his usually cheerful and even playful demeanor. Throughout his career, Martin reacted angrily whenever his integrity was challenged. He also jealously guarded his reputation on environmental issues. While critical of the shoddy science and environmentalist scare tactics he attributed to the likes of Ralph Nader and Sidney Wolfe, Martin considered himself a conservationist and often reminded audiences of the anti-pollution programs he had initiated in Mecklenburg County.

Once again, the Martin campaign out-raised, outmaneuvered, and out-organized the Democratic opposition. North Carolina Republicans on the ballot in 1980 also benefited from the top of the ticket. While Jimmy Carter had won the state by 11 points in 1976, Ronald Reagan defeated him in North Carolina by 49.3 percent to 47.2 percent, with independent candidate John Anderson winning the remaining share. Reagan's major turnout effort and

PRESIDENT RONALD REAGAN AND VICE PRESIDENT GEORGE BUSH DISCUSS REPUB-LICAN PARTY PROSPECTS WITH CONGRESSMAN JIM MARTIN.
OFFICIAL WHITE HOUSE PHOTO

last-minute surge helped Republican John East narrowly defeat incumbent senator Robert Morgan by slightly more than 10,000 votes. But the Reagan effect wasn't nearly enough to help I. Beverly Lake Jr., the Republican gubernatorial nominee. Governor Jim Hunt won reelection with 62 percent. Republicans did pick up two North Carolina congressional seats—Gene Johnston in the Sixth District and Bill Hendon in the 11th. That reduced the Democratic edge in the delegation to 7–4. North Carolina Republicans also gained 14 state legislators and 29 county commissioners.

As for Martin, he defeated Randy Kincaid by 59 percent to 41 percent. On election night, Martin agreed that his economic platform mirrored Reagan's. "The people know that, and they think that the Republicans can best do something about it," he said. However, unlike some other Republicans in 1980, Martin didn't owe his victory to the success of the Reagan campaign. He'd have won anyway, although less decisively. Now, Jim Martin was primed and ready to help the new president turn a successful election into an enduring Reagan Revolution.

UNEXPECTED DRAMA AND PRAISE

At first, it wasn't clear whether he would be assisting the president as a tax-cutting ally on Ways and Means or as an administration official. During the 1980–81 transition, some Reagan aides began talking up Martin as a possible head of the Environmental Protection Agency. By early January, in fact, media outlets reported that Martin was the frontrunner among five potential candidates. The Reagan camp was divided. Some wanted the pick to rid the EPA of left-wing activists and bring the agency clearly into line with the administration's conservative, pro-growth agenda. Others, however, thought it would be wiser to select "a more middle-of-the-road person" to "improve the agency rather than drastically alter it," as the *Charlotte Observer* put it. Both camps welcomed Martin as a compromise candidate. His battle with the FDA and his frequent comments about nuclear energy, consumer choice, and the overregulation of business were popular with Reagan conservatives. But as a Ph.D. chemist who as a county commissioner had promoted conservation, water quality, and regional land-use planning, he was also acceptable to moderates.

Initially, Martin was open to the EPA idea. He'd actually considered retiring from Congress before the 1980 election, frustrated with his inability to steer public policy in an overwhelmingly Democratic capital. He and Dottie were also interested in moving back to North Carolina. Ultimately, pressure from Charlotte-area Republicans coupled with the prospect of a Reagan presidency had persuaded Martin to seek a fifth term. Now, he was being presented with the opportunity to serve President Reagan directly and to work on the scientific and regulatory issues he'd always found compelling. Some of Martin's friends, including Jim Broyhill, urged him to take the job for precisely this reason. Taking it would also mean a graceful exit from Congress on his own terms. After service in the Reagan administration, Martin could move back to North Carolina with a clear conscience. Although some Republicans fretted about the prospect of winning a special election to fill his congressional seat, Martin believed a nominee such as former Charlotte mayor Ken Harris or Mecklenburg County commissioner Alex McMillan had a good shot of keeping it in Republican hands.

Within days, however, Martin took himself out of the running. He had personal and political reasons. At the time, members of Congress could supplement their incomes with speaking fees. Accepting the job of EPA administrator would likely have resulted in lower pay and less time with his family. More importantly, the situation on Capitol Hill had changed dramatically. Republicans now controlled the Senate for the first time since the early 1950s. In the House, they had won enough new seats to form majority coalitions with "boll weevil" Democrats on issues of mutual interest, including taxes. Martin would no longer have to spend his time on Ways and Means simply battling Democratic tax hikes and proposing alternatives as rhetorical devices. He would finally be in a position to help enact sweeping tax cuts along the lines of Kemp-Roth. The prospect was too attractive to pass up.

The *Charlotte Observer* joined many back home in praising Martin's decision to pass on the job of Reagan's EPA administrator (which eventually went to Colorado attorney and state legislator Anne Gorsuch) in order to stay in Congress. "We feel some uneasiness about the direction the Reagan conservatives might take the country," its liberal editorial board admitted. "But if they're going to be in charge, we're glad one of them is Jim Martin."

TRIUMPH ON TAXES, FRUSTRATION ON SPENDING

As the new Reagan administration began to map out its first-year strategy, some observers speculated the president would back off the ambitious policy mix of tax cuts, budget cuts, defense buildup, deregulation, and tight money he had run on during the campaign. They were mistaken. On February 18, 1981, President Reagan announced his economic plan. On taxes, he called for a Kemp-Roth reduction in personal income taxes of 10 percent a year for three years, married to other reforms such as accelerated depreciation for business expenses (a high priority for supply-side economist Norman Ture, now a top official at the Treasury Department).

It fell to Democrats and Republicans on Capitol Hill to work out the details of a plan that could pass both houses. Again, the debate over what became the Economic Recovery Tax Act of 1981 did not occur along strictly partisan lines. Some of Martin's Democratic colleagues on Ways and Means, including new committee chairman Dan Rostenkowski, voiced support for lower marginal rates and other reforms to induce capital out of tax shelters. Some Republicans, including a few of Reagan's own advisors, preferred smaller tax cuts, stretched over more years, to reduce projected deficits.

Rostenkowski and his Ways and Means staff assembled that final version. Its central feature was a scaled-down version of Kemp-Roth—an average 24 percent reduction in the code's 15 marginal rates, with the top one falling from 70 percent to 50 percent. But the legislation also included accelerated depreciation, the indexation of tax brackets and exemptions to inflation beginning in 1984, and a host of other tax changes originally filed as separate bills. One of those was H.R. 3456, which called for a partial tax exclusion for interest income earned from certificates of deposit. Jim Martin had filed the bill on May 6, 1981. His reasoning was that because the deposits into these accounts were made with after-tax dollars, the subsequent stream of income ought not be subjected to a second round of taxation. By late July, Martin's bill had attracted 81 Republican and 84 Democratic cosponsors, more than enough to guarantee its inclusion in the Economic Recovery Tax Act. Three other provisions of the act also mirrored bills he'd filed. One was an increase in the maximum number of subchapter S corporation shareholders from 15 to 25 (Martin had originally proposed doubling the cap to 30). Another increased the share of gifts exempt from federal tax, a cause he'd championed in a 1979 bill. Still another provision significantly increased eligibility and maximum contributions to individual retirement accounts. Martin had proposed something similar in his Individual Savings and Investment Act of 1981, filed in April.

The final version of the Economic Recovery Tax Act passed both chambers on August 4, 1981, and was signed into law by President Reagan on August 13. The Kemp-Roth cut in marginal rates was the headliner. Another key provision, however, was indexing the code to inflation, which brought an end to the "bracket creep" that amounted to automatic, unlegislated tax hikes. In the short run, at least, the bill represented a dramatic turn to supply-side fiscal policy. It was a major political victory for Reagan. Adherents of Reaganomics saw it as a coup for American households and businesses as well, although its fiscal and economic consequences continued to fuel debate for decades afterward.

By 1983, most of the tax-rate cuts took effect and the tight money policies of the Federal Reserve finally broke the back of hyperinflation. Starting that year, the economy experienced a sizzling recovery. Job creation, income growth, and gross domestic product all surged. Reagan's critics charged, however, that the economy grew despite, rather than because of, his fiscal policies, which they blamed for throwing the budget out of whack. Federal deficits averaged 4.1 percent of GDP from 1981 to 1988, compared to 2.4 percent during the Carter presidency and 1.6 percent during the Nixon-Ford years. (Reagan's deficits held the record as the highest for any president since World War II until Barack Obama took office in 2009. Over the first six years of the latter's administration, deficits averaged 6.9 percent of GDP.)

While Martin voted enthusiastically for the 1981 tax cuts, he was less pleased with what was happening on the spending side of the ledger. Some supply-side commentators and Republican lawmakers indeed downplayed the importance of balanced budgets. Martin never did. In 1982, the federal deficit proved to be bigger than projected, largely because the inflation rate fell to 3.9 percent from the previous year's 8.9 percent. Disinflation reduced both spending and revenue from the baseline, but the revenue effect was larger (as indexation didn't kick in until 1984). In response to the surging deficit, Martin argued for immediate, across-the-board spending cuts, including entitlements and defense. He agreed with Reagan that a military buildup was necessary to ratchet up pressure on the Soviet Union. But Martin suggested that it occur gradually and that not every weapon system the Pentagon wanted was justified. "I'm not one of those who say deficits don't matter," he insisted. "They do matter."

He wasn't the only Republican who felt that way. So did some of Reagan's closest advisors. They urged the president to strike a bargain with Congress in 1982. For every three dollars in budget cuts, the administration would agree to one dollar in higher taxes, primarily in the form of delaying or rescinding business-tax changes in the 1981 bill and jacking up payroll taxes for unemployment insurance and Medicare.

Reluctantly, Reagan agreed, signing the Tax Equity and Fiscal Responsibility Act (TEFRA) on September 3, 1982. It had passed the House by a narrow margin, 226–207. Once again, the vote hadn't followed party lines, with 122 Democrats and 103 Republicans in favor to 118 Democrats and 89 Republicans against. Martin was in the latter camp. He wasn't opposed in principle to trading higher taxes to achieve other goals. He'd done as much as a county commissioner when he endorsed a sales-tax hike to keep property taxes low, and he was about to do so in 1983 by voting for a Social Security rescue plan that both raised payroll taxes and reduced future benefits (by phasing in a higher retirement age). But Martin thought the 1982 TEFRA legislation was a bad deal. It backtracked on accelerated depreciation for business expenses, which he thought critical to stimulating investment (the author of the depreciation reforms, Norman Ture, resigned from the administration in protest of Reagan's decision to sign the bill). TEFRA also hiked the excise tax on cigarettes (which helped explain why nearly all of North Carolina's delegation joined Martin in voting no). Furthermore, Martin had his doubts that Congress would follow through on the promised spending cuts.

He was right. In 1982, the federal government took in $618 billion in receipts and spent $746 billion, yielding a deficit of $128 billion, or 3.9 percent of GDP. By 1985, federal revenue rose to $734 billion (a growth rate of 4.4 percent after inflation), but spending grew even more, to $946 billion (a real growth rate of 11.5 percent). The result was a deficit of $212 billion, or 5 percent of GDP.

AN OPPORTUNITY FOR LEADERSHIP

Other Republicans joined Martin in expressing concern that some of Reagan's agenda, such as spending restraint, had begun to stall on Capitol Hill.

They wanted to see more aggressive action. One dissatisfied Republican, two-term representative Newt Gingrich of Georgia, devised an ambitious plan to file dozens of bills and use the resulting public attention to reframe the policy debate. The strategy could never work as a solo act. So in 1982, he approached other colleagues and eventually GOP leaders in the House to develop and implement it. The core committee of what would later be called the Conservative Opportunity Society was based in the office of House minority whip Trent Lott. Its other members were Jack Kemp of New York, Guy Vander Jagt of Michigan, Dick Cheney of Wyoming, Phil Crane of Illinois, and Jim Martin. The committee's job was to develop strategy and provide oversight of the initiative in the House, in coordination with Senate Republicans and the White House. Meanwhile, Gingrich convened a regular Wednesday group of House conservatives that included Vin Weber, Bob Walker, Judd Gregg, Dan Coats, and many others.

This early stage of Gingrich's Conservative Opportunity Society constituted Martin's first direct involvement in House leadership. He enjoyed it immensely, particularly when called upon to delve deeply into policy matters. The experience served to confirm the decision he'd made in late 1981 to seek another term in the House. "The frustrations that I have felt after being here eight years in the minority . . . have worn off now because we've been successful with two historic reversals—the change from rapidly expanding social programs to slowing that down, and ending rapidly expanding tax rates," Martin explained.

He resolved to run for a position in House leadership. In addition to the top two jobs, minority leader and minority whip, posts were available on three important panels: the House Republican Conference, the House Republican Policy Committee, and the House Republican Research Committee. Martin initially set his sights on replacing California representative Clair Burgener as conference secretary.

But first, of course, he had to win his reelection bid in 1982. By this time, Democrats in the Ninth District felt a bit like Charlie Brown trying to kick the ever-elusive football. They'd tried five times to defeat Martin, hoping that changing demographics and the national tide would produce an upset. They'd failed each time. Still, they had legitimate reasons to believe that 1982 might finally be their moment. The national economy was still in a deep recession. While inflation had begun to moderate, the unemployment rate rose steadily through much of the year. President Reagan's approval rating sank accordingly, dipping into the 30s by the eve of the 1982 elections. Democrats knew the cycle would probably be a good one for the party, so they had little trouble recruiting solid candidates and enthusiastic donors throughout much of the country.

In the Ninth District, however, local Democrats had trouble attracting a well-known candidate. They ultimately turned to Preston Cornelius, an Iredell County farmer and superior-court judge. "I think [Cornelius] potentially could be as strong or stronger than any candidates we've ever had," said Margaret King, who once again chaired Martin's congressional campaign and directed its get-out-the-vote operation.

Cornelius certainly ran a spirited, if woefully underfinanced, campaign. Martin raised the equivalent of $454,000 in 2015 dollars, about nine times what his opponent managed. "He has the money," Cornelius insisted. "I have the people." Like Martin's 1980 opponent, Randy Kincaid, Cornelius sounded populist themes during the campaign. He also accused Martin of being ineffective. "In 10 years, he has introduced over 50 bills in Congress and not one, not the first one, has ever become law," stated one Cornelius campaign ad. "Isn't it time we had a truly effective congressman?" Although some version of this attack might have damaged Martin early in his career, when he was a backbencher in an overwhelmingly Democratic Congress, it fell flat in 1982. By this time, several of Martin's legislative proposals had indeed become law—though often as amendments to or provisions of other bills, which Cornelius and his campaign seemed not to understand. As an active member of Ways and Means, Martin had just helped shaped one of the most consequential bills in modern history, the Economic Recovery Tax Act of 1981. Few voters were willing to believe Cornelius would enjoy more influence in Washington, at least not anytime soon.

Nor did Cornelius appear to win many votes by endorsing a new movement in favor of freezing United States production of nuclear weapons. It gained attention throughout 1982 by organizing protests and initiating referendums. In June, nearly a million people rallied in New York City. States and hundreds of towns and cities placed the nuclear freeze on their ballots for nonbinding votes that fall. Most of these referendums passed, in part because the ballot language was so ambiguous that many voters thought they were endorsing arms-control negotiations with the Soviet Union—which President Reagan and most Republicans also favored—rather than an end to all nuclear-arms production in the United States, including the modernization of the existing nuclear arsenal.

Even before Cornelius endorsed the nuclear freeze, Martin had spent a lot of time studying the issue. He shared Reagan's peace-through-strength philosophy and believed it was important to demonstrate American resolve by expanding the country's military capability and replacing aging weapon systems with new missiles, planes, and submarines. On the campaign trail, Martin enthusiastically supported the president's position on the nuclear freeze even as he criticized Reagan's acquiescence to the TEFRA tax hikes of 1982. Most Republicans who came into the district to campaign for Martin struck the same balance. "There's no way I think we should raise tax rates," Jack Kemp said at an October 19 campaign event in Charlotte. "Martin and Kemp are not going to raise tax rates until we get the economy moving again."

The 1982 midterms were painful for Reagan and his party. Republicans had a net loss of seven governorships, one seat in the Senate, and 26 seats in the House, including those of the North Carolina freshmen elected two years earlier, Gene Johnston and Bill Hendon. The state GOP lost 10 legislators and 31 county commissioners. It wasn't as bad as the party's disastrous 1974 and 1976 cycles. For North Carolina Republicans hoping to sustain their momentum from 1980, however, it was still disappointing. To them, Jim Martin's performance was one of the few bright spots. He defeated Preston Cornelius with 57 percent of the vote. "The people still want to be represented by a fiscal conservative," a cheerful Martin proclaimed on election night. It was a moment Republican leaders and activists throughout the state noted with interest.

A ROLLING STONE HITS ITS MARKEY

Martin entered his sixth (and last) term in the House with three major priorities. He wanted to combat federal deficits with a combination of immediate, across-the-board spending cuts and a phased-in requirement for a balanced budget. He wanted to make sure the nuclear-freeze movement did not imperil President Reagan's ability to negotiate with the Soviets from a position of strength. And he wanted to strengthen the role of sound science in the regulatory process to minimize episodes like the attempted saccharin ban.

To advance these three goals, he was determined to enter House leadership. But Minority Leader Bob Michel, Minority Whip Trent Lott, Republican Conference chairman Jack Kemp, and Republican Policy Committee chairman Dick Cheney all announced plans to stay in their respective roles.

So did Republican Conference secretary Clair Burgener, who had originally planned to step aside.

So Martin turned his attention to the vacant post of chairman of the Republican Research Committee, which would give him the opportunity to study complex issues in detail and supervise the task forces that crafted policy positions and messages for the caucus. He'd also have a seat at the table, alongside his close friends Lott and Kemp, when it came time to devising the GOP's political and legislative strategy. Martin announced plans to seek the post. His candidacy proved so popular that he was elected without opposition.

Martin was under no illusion about the ability of even a brilliantly led 163-member Republican caucus to control the business of a 435-member House. On budget reform and the nuclear freeze, Democrats would make the decisions during the 1983–84 session—and in neither case was there enough Democratic dissent to form a majority coalition with the Republicans.

Instead of seeking legislative victories, then, Martin and other GOP leaders sought rhetorical ones. Throughout 1983 and early 1984, Republicans filed bills to reform the budget process, to bring deficits down over time, and to initiate a constitutional amendment requiring balanced budgets. As Democrats filed their own versions of the same ideas, Republicans made theirs more ambitious. It wasn't until 1985, the year after Martin left Congress, that the legislative bidding war produced an enacted bill, the Gramm-Rudman-Hollings Balanced Budget Act, named after the two Senate Republicans and one Senate Democrat who introduced it. The bill called for automatic spending cuts, or sequestration, if total appropriations for non-entitlement programs exceeded preset thresholds. While hardly a perfect piece of legislation, Gramm-Rudman-Hollings did place downward pressure on federal spending and created the legislative tools that Congress and the Clinton administration would use to bring the federal budget into balance during the late 1990s.

Under Martin's leadership, the Republican Research Committee provided intellectual ammunition on budgetary matters to House members. But it was in the debate over the nuclear freeze that Martin played a more direct role. Just after the 1982 midterms, freeze supporters felt they had momentum. Hundreds of state and local referendums endorsing the idea had just passed. Seizing upon a nuclear-freeze resolution sponsored by Representative Ed Markey of Massachusetts, they decided to push it quickly through the House at the start of the session and then use it to put public pressure on Reagan and the

Republican-led Senate. The resolution was modified in the House Foreign Affairs Committee and got a new name, the Zablocki Resolution, from the committee's chairman, Clement Zablocki of Wisconsin. It was scheduled for the House floor on March 16, 1983. In the meantime, advocates assembled a long list of endorsers, ranging from the Union of Concerned Scientists and the National Education Association to the YMCA and the National Conference of Catholic Bishops. Major newspapers editorialized in favor of the resolution. The stage was set for what freeze proponents hoped would at the very least embarrass President Reagan, if not pave the way for success in the Senate.

The opponents had other ideas. A week before the scheduled floor debate, Jim Martin's Republican Research Committee released a series of issue briefs and talking points stating the case against the nuclear freeze. Everyone knew that Zablocki and Markey had enough votes to pass the resolution. The conservative strategy was to rob its passage of any political value. Republicans and conservative Democrats proposed dozens of amendments and debated the merits of each extensively. According to later reflections by both supporters and opponents of the measure, a key moment came when Congressman Martin rose to offer an amendment to the resolution to prohibit any unilateral end to testing and production of nuclear arms intended to replace weapons already in the United States arsenal.

Although supporters said the freeze was intended to be bilateral, Martin insisted that their own past statements belied the claim. He offered as evidence an October 1982 interview conducted by *Rolling Stone*'s William Greider with Representative Markey, the leader of the nuclear-freeze movement. Greider reported that "the movement's political objective is not simply to pass a congressional resolution urging the president to negotiate a bilateral freeze with the Soviets on all testing, production, and deployment of nuclear weapons systems." Rather, Markey explained to Greider that he and his allies planned to target, delay, and defund as many of Reagan's proposed new weapon systems as they could, including the MX missile and the Trident II submarine. "That is not a bilateral strategy," Martin told House members. "That's a unilateral strategy."

Markey and other nuclear-freeze supporters knew Martin had scored a rhetorical point. After he sat down, they figured that would be the end of it. But a few minutes later, as Markey was defending the resolution, Martin rose and asked if he would yield for a question. If the resolution passed, Martin asked, would the United States be entitled to continue modernizing its arsenal before any negotiations with the Soviet Union were concluded? Markey said yes. Martin pressed the point: "There are some members—and I think that includes the gentleman from Massachusetts—who want to take away each of the bargaining chips from the president." He cited Markey's comments in the *Rolling Stone* article. "The ambush was set," as one freeze proponent later put it. Rising to the bait, Markey tried to defend his prior statements by saying that "everything that we do in this Congress is by its very nature unilateral," and that he reserved the right to try to kill the MX program and other weapons programs regardless of the status of negotiations with the Soviets.

Martin sat down. The damage was done. Markey and Zablocki lost a vote to limit debate and call the question. What they thought would be a one-day consideration and passage of the resolution "ended in confusion when freeze supporters gave contradictory answers to questions about what the resolution meant," reported the *Milwaukee Sentinel*, Zablocki's hometown newspaper.

The debate continued off and on for weeks. Martin proposed four subsequent amendments. One called for essential equivalence between the American and Soviet nuclear arsenals. Another exempted nuclear bombers from the freeze. A third exempted nuclear submarines. These three amendments passed easily, with freeze supporters hoping to end the controversy about unilateral disarmament. But they killed Martin's fourth amendment, to exempt intercontinental ballistic missiles, as nothing would have been left to freeze.

The Zablocki Resolution finally passed the House on May 4, 1983, by a 278–149 vote. It should have been a triumphant moment for the nuclear-freeze movement. Instead, it felt anticlimactic. The *Washington Post* reported that freeze supporters in the House were left "scrambling to place the best possible interpretation on what appeared to be a seriously watered-down result." For his part, Martin described the successful amendments as taking "a lot of the zing out of the anti-Reagan objectives of the freeze movement."

Moreover, during the debate, President Reagan made far more news arguing against the freeze than the resolution itself ever produced. Speaking at a March meeting of the National Association of Evangelicals, Reagan urged the listeners not to follow the lead of other religious groups on the issue. "In your discussions of the nuclear freeze proposals," the president said, "I urge you to beware the temptation of pride—the temptation of blithely declaring yourselves above it all and label both sides equally at fault, to ignore the facts of history and the aggressive impulses of an evil empire, to simply call the arms race a giant misunderstanding and thereby remove yourself from the struggle between right and wrong and good and evil."

Calling America's Cold War rival an "evil empire" proved to be one of the defining moments of Reagan's first term as president. The House's passage of the nuclear-freeze resolution was not.

A CLOSING ARGUMENT ON A SORE SUBJECT

In 1983, Representative James G. Martin received the Charles Lathrop Parsons Award from the American Chemical Society for outstanding public service by an American chemist. It was the first such award ever given to an elected official. Later that year, on September 22, Martin filed his last bill in Congress, the Central Board of Scientific Risk Assessment Act. It authorized the National Academy of Sciences to establish a new board to conduct scientific reviews and evaluations of risk assessments made by federal agencies, particularly in cases in which regulators alleged chronic health hazards. Among the three Republican cosponsors was Judd Gregg, a good friend who would later serve as New Hampshire's governor and United States senator. Among the three Democratic cosponsors was a representative from Tennessee, Al Gore.

After Martin left Congress, his idea continued to attract bipartisan support from the likes of Senators Daniel Patrick Moynihan of New York and Bob Dole of Kansas. In 1994, amendments to a farm bill created the Office of Risk Assessment and Cost-Benefit Analysis within the Department of Agriculture. It had the responsibility to ensure that regulations were "based on sound scientific and economic analysis." That fall, Republicans won historic majorities in both houses of Congress. Working with the Clinton administration, they proceeded to enact several regulatory reforms calling for better risk assessment and applying cost-benefit tests. The most gratifying for Jim Martin was the Food Quality Protection Act of 1996, which essentially repealed the Delaney Clause.

By this time, however, Martin was no longer serving in Congress or any other elective office. Ironically, he was back in Charlotte, overseeing a research laboratory where scientists conducted experiments with test animals—including rats. But that's a tale for a later chapter.

CHAPTER SIX

THE OTHER CAROLINA RACE OF 1984

O n August 12, 1981, Congressman Jim Martin sent a letter to Charlie Gregory, a Republican activist from Raleigh. A couple of weeks earlier, Gregory had written Martin to encourage him to seek the GOP nomination to replace Governor Jim Hunt, who would be term-limited out of office in 1984. In his response, Martin was cordial but firm in dismissing the idea. "Running for governor, and then being governor," he wrote, "would be a job I'd not like and people would sniff that out right away." In addition to observing that candidates from the Charlotte area faced difficulties appealing to voters in the rest of the state, Martin mused that his political talents would be best applied in ways other than running for governor in 1984:

> *It takes two different types in government: one who makes a legislator, another who does better in an administrative or executive capacity. The former has a reflective, intellectualized approach; the latter requires more of a quick decision-making approach. Jimmy Carter would probably have been a great Senator, politics and policies aside. On the other hand, Ronald Reagan is in his element. Because I don't feel I fit well into that executive-type mold, I'd likely not perform in executive office as well as I have come to perform as a legislator. Voters can sense that sort of thing.*

By November 1984, North Carolina voters had formed a different sense of Jim Martin. By a significant margin, they chose him as the state's next governor. And over the next eight years, he had more success translating his personal views into public policy than he had in 12 years as a federal legislator. So all the predictions made in his 1981 letter—that he wouldn't run, that he wouldn't be elected if he did run, and that he would prove ineffective as a chief executive—turned out to be incorrect.

Of course, Martin was happy to be proven wrong.

MOVING ON UP—OR OUT

Gregory's letter wasn't the first time someone had approached Martin about running for governor. As early as 1975, some Republican leaders were already suggesting he enter the GOP primary to succeed Governor Jim Holshouser the following year. Martin "could have the nomination virtually for the asking," wrote Associated Press correspondent Robert Cullen in a November 3, 1975, article. Martin politely but firmly rebuffed these advances, and did so again in 1980.

So what made him change his mind? For one thing, six terms in Congress had taken a personal toll. Between committee meetings, floor debates, constituent service, trips back and forth to North Carolina, and reelection bids every two years, he had little time left to devote to Dottie and his children. "You can put up with that for a while," he said, but eventually the lack of family time became "part of the burden that made it unattractive to live that way." The December 31, 1982, death of his father, the Reverend Arthur Martin, strengthened his desire to move back home, so as to be closer to the rest of his family.

Constantly raising money to replenish the coffers of his campaigns also became a dispiriting grind. Although the Ninth District was friendly territory, Martin still ran a real campaign every two years, both to discourage any primary challengers and to minimize the risk that local or national factors might give Democrats a chance at an upset. Martin later said that running for reelection was like a perpetual treadmill. "Every election, Brad Hays would somehow arrange that it would be about $150,000 in debt at the end of the campaign—the rascal," Martin explained with a chuckle. "It was easy to pay that off. You'd just announce that you were going to run again right after the election." Donors would then give in expectation of another race in two years, erasing the campaign's prior debt but thereby obligating the candidate to follow through on the promise. By 1983, Martin decided he wanted off the treadmill.

His disaffection with serving in Congress didn't end with fundraising responsibilities, however. As a young member in the 1970s, he had welcomed the chance to meet interesting people and work on important issues, even as a Republican in a Democratic House. "You can dig in and work to modify something a little bit," Martin said. "But being in the minority 12 years does not fill you with a sense of opportunity." While he was proud of his role in fashioning successful legislation such as the Reagan tax cuts, much of his congressional career seemed to revolve around stopping bad ideas—such as the saccharin ban and the nuclear freeze—rather than implementing good ones. In short, Martin explained, "I was tired of serving in Congress. I saw no way for the GOP to get a majority. I was looking for a respectable way to end my political career." The end would come in one of two ways. Either Martin would become North Carolina's governor and spend four to eight years in Raleigh, after which he and Dottie would return in triumph to their Lake Norman home, or their move back home would happen right after he lost the 1984 election.

These issues were part of the calculation. But Jim Martin had another reason—the best possible one—to consider the race: he had changed his mind about the office itself. Martin had come to believe he would be a good governor. From his earliest thoughts about politics back in the 1950s, he had seen the development of a conservative philosophy of governance at the state and local level to be a necessary component of any successful resistance to intrusion by the federal government. The intellectual challenge of crafting policy, managing state government, and charting a new course for Republican politics in North Carolina appealed to him. He would no longer be on the sidelines of government, one face among many, hoping to get some playing time before the end of the game. He would be the starting quarterback.

Sometime in early 1983, Dan Hoover, a reporter at the Raleigh *News & Observer*, placed the first in a series of calls asking Martin if he was running for governor. By the second or third call, Martin decided he "ought to think about it and look at it." He began in-depth discussions with Dottie, his brother Joe, Brad Hays, and other confidants. At the suggestion of former congressman and gubernatorial candidate Jim Gardner, Martin then broadened the discussion to include several dozen potential supporters across the state.

To some participants in the conversation, the second route to political retirement Martin had described—the quick one—seemed the more likely. The pessimists had reasons for their low expectations. It wasn't yet clear that

1984 would be a good election year for Republicans. The 1982 cycle had been a tough one, and not just in Washington. Democrats were the clear majority party in state governments nationwide, holding 34 of the 50 governorships and 72 of the nation's 98 partisan legislative chambers. Nor did Martin have any guarantee of help from the top of the ticket in 1984. President Reagan actually began 1983 with his lowest approval rating, 35 percent in the Gallup poll.

The electoral math looked even more challenging within the state. The GOP had elected only a single North Carolina governor in the 20th century, Jim Holshouser, largely because of the Democrats' George McGovern debacle of 1972. Since 1977, Jim Hunt had spent two active terms building one of the South's strongest Democratic parties by uniting Terry Sanford–style progressives with African-Americans, social conservatives in rural counties, and centrist business leaders in and around Charlotte, Greensboro, Raleigh, and other cities. Democrats enjoyed a 102–18 majority in the North Carolina House and a 44–6 majority in the Senate. And in Martin's original stomping ground, county politics, the Democrats continued to reign supreme, controlling 89 of the state's 100 county commissions. The pessimists' concern was not only that North Carolinians, even conservative ones, were used to voting Democrats into state and local offices. Because of the long odds, some Martin advisors argued, it would be difficult for the congressman to attract top-flight talent and raise sufficient funds for a competitive statewide campaign—particularly given the fact, already evident in 1983, that Senator Jesse Helms would draw heavily on Republican resources to overcome the biggest political challenge of his career, a Senate race against Jim Hunt.

But there were also optimists in the Martin camp, including the candidate himself. They had good reasons for their assessment, too. Shortly after the 1982 election, for example, leading indicators began to suggest that the national economy would post stronger growth in 1983 and beyond, thus strengthening Reagan and his party for the 1984 cycle. That's precisely what happened. After several years of inflation-adjusted GDP growth, including a contraction during 1982, the boom began. Real GDP shot up at an annualized rate of 5.1 percent in the first quarter of 1983 and 9.3 percent in the second quarter. As voters gained confidence in the economy, they gained confidence in Reagan's leadership. His approval rating improved through the spring and summer of 1983, and finally broke 50 percent by the end of the year.

Political developments in North Carolina also began to create a scenario in which Martin might hope to emulate the Republicans' surprise 1972 gubernatorial win. In addition to riding a strong reelection wave for President Nixon, Holshouser had benefited from the fact that North Carolina's United States Senate race, between Democratic congressman Nick Galifianakis and Republican Jesse Helms, had diverted some Democratic resources from the governor's race. In 1984, the coming slugfest between Helms and Hunt promised to soak up at least as much Democratic time and money as it would Republican time and money.

More importantly, Holshouser had been able to capitalize on the divisive 1972 Democratic gubernatorial primary between Skipper Bowles and Pat Taylor. The political organization of outgoing governor Bob Scott had endorsed Taylor. In response, Bowles's primary campaign often seemed to aim its fire more at Scott than at Taylor. After Bowles won the Democratic nomination, efforts to repair the fissure failed. Some Scott-Taylor partisans sat out the general election, helping Holshouser by default.

By early 1983, it was clear that the Democratic primary for governor would be crowded. Rufus Edmisten, the eventual nominee, later cited gubernatorial succession as the main cause. Jim Hunt had fought for it and become the first North Carolina governor to serve eight years in the office. Democratic politicians who might have run for governor in 1980 therefore had to wait four more years. "That's why we all ganged up in 1984," said Edmisten, who had served a decade as North Carolina's attorney general. The Democratic field for governor would eventually include Edmisten, Lieutenant Governor Jimmy Green, former Charlotte mayor and state senator Eddie Knox, former state commerce secretary Lauch Faircloth, Insurance Commissioner John Ingram, former state representative Tom Gilmore, and four lesser-known candidates (including Glenn Miller, head of the KKK-offshoot White Patriot Party). As so many Democrats began to signal their interest in the gubernatorial race, Jim Martin and Brad Hays concluded that history might repeat itself in 1984—that a Republican nominee might be able to take advantage of a divisive Democratic primary.

THE PRIMARY THAT NEVER HAPPENED

But first, Martin would have to win the Republican nomination without enduring a divisive primary of his own. Such an outcome was far from guaranteed. Tensions remained between the Piedmont- and western-oriented faction of "traditional" Republicans, headed by Holshouser, and the eastern-oriented faction, headed by Helms and including many former (and current) conservative Democrats. Martin was linked to the Holshouser wing by geography, temperament, and his endorsement of Gerald Ford over Ronald Reagan. Since the 1976 party rupture over the presidential nominee, the leaders of the Congressional Club, Tom Ellis and Carter Wrenn, had sought to dominate Republican politics in the state. In 1980, the top three GOP candidates for statewide office—John East for Senate, Bev Lake for governor, and Bill Cobey for lieutenant governor—were all recruited and managed by the Congressional Club. Only East was victorious. In 1982, Bill Cobey, the former athletic director at UNC–Chapel Hill, sought elective office again, this time as a congressional candidate in the Fourth District. But the 1982 midterms were rough for Republicans. Cobey lost again.

Ever since Hunt's reelection in 1980, GOP leaders had sought to line up a prospect for the next gubernatorial race. When Knox signaled his intention to succeed Hunt, some Republicans even tried to talk another former Charlotte mayor, John Belk, into switching parties and seeking the GOP nomination. Belk declined. By early 1983, the only prominent Republican publicly considering the race was Cass Ballenger, a four-term state senator from Hickory. Pundits also mentioned Jim Martin as a potential candidate, although he had not yet signaled his intentions. They speculated that the Congressional Club might offer up its own candidate as well.

Martin and Hays spent the first few months of the year analyzing the race and identifying prospects for a campaign team. By late summer, they were ready to go public. Some 200 supporters and the state's political reporters were on hand at an August 18 launch event in Charlotte. The time had come, Martin said, "to strike out on a new career with no guarantee of success, but rather the assurance of a grinding, difficult, uphill campaign."

Ellis and Wrenn, far from satisfied with a choice between Ballenger and Martin, began to advance an alternative: Bill Cobey. "They were portraying [Martin] as not being conservative enough," Cobey said later. But a key person didn't agree with Ellis and Wrenn's assessment—Jesse Helms himself. A week after Martin's campaign announcement, Helms spoke at an event in Gastonia. The senator suggested that an ideal ticket for North Carolina Republicans in 1984 would be Martin for governor and Cobey for lieutenant governor.

Recognizing that his top political aides saw things differently, Helms said that Tom Ellis "is one of the finest human beings I know, but Tom does not dictate to me and I do not dictate to Tom. He thinks I'm wrong and I believe that's his privilege."

Indeed, the Congressional Club was still not on board with the idea of a Martin candidacy. In September 1983, it sent out a fundraising letter pitching Cobey for governor and warning that Martin couldn't be elected statewide. Former state GOP chairman Bob Shaw, a Martin supporter, was outraged. "I feel that Mr. Ellis should be reminded that without Sen. Helms . . . the Congressional Club would have difficulty in raising enough money to run a city council race in Turkey, NC," Shaw wrote in a September 17 letter to the *Wilmington Star-News*.

Whether or not the club would proceed with running Cobey despite Helms's stated preference for Martin became a moot point when Cobey, influenced by the senator's comments, asked to see Martin in person. The two met in late September at a Ramada Inn in Burlington. Contrary to what some Helms supporters were saying about Martin, "he was very conservative and I found out at that meeting that he was," Cobey said. He decided to endorse Martin.

Cobey ran for Congress from the Fourth District again in 1984, this time successfully. He would later serve in Martin's cabinet as secretary of what became the Department of Environment, Health, and Natural Resources.

A FLEDGLING CAMPAIGN TAKES FLIGHT

Announcing for governor was one thing. Putting together a winning statewide campaign was quite another. There was no question that Charlotte-based consultant Brad Hays would devise the strategy. But who would execute it?

Over the next few months, Martin and Hays began to put the team in place. It included campaign manager Jack Hawke, Washington-based media consultant Jay Smith, Houston-based pollster Lance Tarrance, longtime Martin advisor Bob Bradshaw, press secretary Max Veale, fundraising director Betty Sue Taylor, campaign scheduler Charlene Crews, and research director Charles Hughes. Not all of them stayed with the campaign through Election Day. Max Veale was replaced by Karen Hayes (later Karen Rotterman), a former professor and Reagan administration official. And Jay Smith was replaced by another D.C.-based media consultant, Don Ringe, who had previously worked on some of Martin's congressional campaigns.

Most of Martin's 1984 campaign team would continue to play key roles in Republican politics for decades afterward.

Hawke's ties to the state party were already deep. A Pennsylvania native, he had come south to attend the Duke University School of Law and ended up serving as executive director of the state GOP in 1965 and on the successful congressional campaign of Jim Gardner in 1966. After two unsuccessful runs for Congress in 1972 and 1974, Hawke worked in the Holshouser administration and then in private business. The Martin campaign rejuvenated his political career. Hawke would serve nearly two years in the Martin administration before becoming state party chairman in 1987 and then a political consultant to, among many others, Governor Pat McCrory.

Bob Bradshaw also chaired the state GOP and then advised dozens of candidates in Mecklenburg County and beyond.

After serving as Governor Martin's communications director, Karen Hayes Rotterman and her husband, Marc, founded a political consulting firm in Raleigh that worked for many local, state, and federal candidates.

Media consultant Don Ringe went on to produce ads for two other statewide candidates, Jim Broyhill and Richard Vinroot.

One of the campaign's key activists in the western part of the state, Asheville-based attorney Bob Orr, was twice appointed by Martin to vacancies on the state court of appeals. The second time, in 1992, voters elected to keep him on the court. He then won two elections to the state supreme court.

Two of the Martin campaign's field representatives in 1984, Paul Shumaker and Nelson Dollar, also became significant players in Republican politics. Shumaker became a campaign strategist for many GOP politicians, including United States senator Richard Burr and two speakers of the North Carolina House, Harold Brubaker and Thom Tillis. After serving in the Martin administration for eight years, Nelson Dollar became a consultant and eventually a powerful state representative from Wake County.

The campaign's director of operations—the person who hired Shumaker, Dollar, and other field representatives, in addition to supervising volunteers and crunching get-out-the-vote data, among other roles—was Art Pope, a young lawyer who later became a state representative and state budget director under Pat McCrory. At the local level, key county chairmen for the campaign included Rocky Mount attorney Jim Trotter, who became Martin's general counsel, and Asheboro attorney Alan Pugh, who served in several administration posts, including secretary of the Department of Crime Control and Public Safety. Another young aide on the 1984 campaign was Thomas Stith, a future Durham city councilman and chief of staff to Governor McCrory.

A statewide gubernatorial campaign would obviously require more campaign cash than Martin had ever raised before. Hays told him victory in 1984 would require raising enough money to run TV ads during the last eight weeks of the race in the Triad, the Triangle, and eastern North Carolina, where the congressman was virtually unknown. So Martin traveled to all 100 counties to meet with potential donors and fundraisers. One of his first trips was to Asheboro, where Alan Pugh chaired the Randolph County GOP and his brother Richard Pugh, a veteran of the Holshouser administration, was also active in party politics. Martin had been the keynote speaker for the county's Lincoln Day Dinner the previous year. He struck the Pugh brothers as brainy and frugal—both assets for a gubernatorial candidate, in their view. Indeed, Alan Pugh recalled that Martin had driven to his 1982 speech in a dilapidated old Ford. Afterward, the congressman mailed an invoice for mileage reimbursement. Alan Pugh sent it along with a note: "Here's the check. If I send you another $100, will you send me the title to that Ford?" Martin impressed the Pughs with his campaign strategy and grasp of issues. Each brother decided to make a $1,000 contribution. They were the second and third donors to the gubernatorial campaign. Martin called it "a good down-payment" and made Richard Pugh one of his campaign cochairs.

There would be many more fundraising meetings and pitches in the months to come. Martin didn't exactly relish the prospect. But win or lose in 1984, he consoled himself, at least he wouldn't have to do it again in two years.

One other trip Martin made shortly after his campaign announcement was to a Holiday Inn in Statesville, where he met with the minority leader of the North Carolina Senate, Cass Ballenger. As he had previously done for Bill Cobey, Martin laid out his political plans and policy agenda for Ballenger, who came away impressed and supportive. Rather than run for governor, Ballenger decided to file for reelection to the state Senate. Two years later, he would win election to Congress to replace Jim Broyhill, whom Governor Martin had appointed to the United States Senate. Ballenger would hold the seat for 18 years, retiring in 2004.

THE DEMOCRATIC DONNYBROOK

Facing only token opposition in the Republican primary, Martin and his team were free to focus on the general election. Not so his potential Democratic rivals. With six major candidates vying for two slots in a runoff primary, the competition was destined to be fierce. Moreover, there were preexisting tensions. Jimmy Green blamed Rufus Edmisten for playing a role in a joint state-federal corruption investigation that had resulted in Green's 1983 trial on bribery charges. Both Lauch Faircloth and Tom Gilmore had served in the Hunt administration and hoped to draw from the governor's base of support. But so did Eddie Knox, who had served as co-manager of Hunt's 1976 gubernatorial campaign and then as chairman of Hunt's Advisory Budget Commission. John Ingram had lost the 1978 Senate race against Jesse Helms and saw the 1984 governor's race as an opportunity for political vindication.

Political observers tended to divide the six major Democratic candidates into halves: the business-oriented centrists (Knox, Faircloth, and Green) and the populists (Edmisten, Gilmore, and Ingram). The division made some sense. Knox drew significant financial support from the Charlotte business community and emphasized economic issues. Faircloth, a successful businessman, led the primary field in large-dollar contributions, most of them from agribusiness executives in eastern North Carolina. First as speaker of the House and then as lieutenant governor, Green had been among the staunchest supporters of business interests in the General Assembly. On the other side of the divide, both Edmisten and Ingram had won repeated statewide elections as self-styled outsiders challenging the power of banks, utilities, insurers, and other big businesses. Gilmore was by far the most consistent progressive in the race, securing the endorsements of the AFL-CIO, the North Carolina Association of Educators, the League of Conservation Voters, the state chapter of the National Organization for Women, the Durham People's Alliance, and several liberal newspapers.

But the dynamics of the Democratic primary were more complex than a simple ideological model could convey. For example, Knox and Gilmore appealed to urban and suburban voters, while Edmisten, Faircloth, Green, and Ingram all emphasized their rural roots. Most actively sought votes among traditionally Democratic constituencies such as public employees and African-Americans. The two frontrunners, Edmisten and Knox, both hailed from the western part of the state. Green and Faircloth frequently pointed that out while speaking in the vote-rich east, their home base. Personal issues even played a role. On the campaign trail, Ingram frequently bragged about his nearly 30 years of happy marriage, a not-so-subtle dig at Knox and Edmisten, both of whom had remarried after divorcing their first wives. One reason North Carolinians should vote for him, Ingram said, was his "family stability."

In Jimmy Green's case, the personal had by 1984 entirely overwhelmed the ideological. He'd spent 16 years in the state House, including a term as speaker, before being elected lieutenant governor in 1976. He fully expected to be the Democratic frontrunner for governor in 1980. But when Jim Hunt obtained the power to succeed himself, Green decided to wait another four years as lieutenant governor. Unexpectedly, he drew a strong primary challenge in 1980 from Carl Stewart, who like Green had been House speaker. Stewart enjoyed the support of many left-leaning Democrats, including part of the Hunt organization. Green won the 1980 Democratic primary with only 51 percent of the vote. It was the biggest scare of his political career to date. Unfortunately for him, his troubles were just beginning. Just as an unofficial Green-for-governor campaign began to crank up in 1981, a bid-rigging scandal netted a Fayetteville highway contractor close to Green. The lieutenant governor admitted that the contractor, bound for prison, had years before given him cash, as well as free paving for one of his tobacco warehouses. Prosecutors in Rufus Edmisten's office found no evidence of a quid pro quo and declined to press charges against Green. But the following year, one of Green's employees was arrested as part of an undercover FBI investigation in Columbus County. Known as "ColCor" (for Columbus Corruption), the probe resulted in many prosecutions of public officials, most of them successful. The Jimmy Green case fell into the unsuccessful category. He was charged with accepting a $2,000 bribe from an undercover FBI agent and agreeing to accept thousands more. The problem faced by the state's special prosecutor, James Blackburn, was that Green had returned the check the following day and alleged that the government had tried "with no success whatsoever to entrap me into breaking the law." The jury saw insufficient evidence for the charges and acquitted Green. But the political damage was done. During the 1984 primary for governor, he repeatedly referred to the state's prosecution as the turning point in the race. "It has been said to me every day of the campaign that 'Jimmy, had you not experienced that ordeal, there would have been half of the people in the race,' " Green told one reporter. " 'You'd have had it in the bag months ago and there would've been no contest.' " True or not, Green believed it—and blamed, among others, Rufus Edmisten.

As for the attorney general, Edmisten mingled economic populism with a conservative political pedigree and a personal reputation for, as the *N&O* put it, "womanizing," "public drinking," and "a penchant for belting out country music at the drop of a hat." A native of Boone, he had first come to public prominence during his 10 years of service in Washington as an aide to Senator Sam Ervin. During the Watergate scandal, when Ervin chaired the investigative committee, Edmisten played a very public role. After the senator announced his retirement in 1974, the Ervin organization encouraged Edmisten to enter electoral politics, which he did by returning to North Carolina to run for the recently vacated job of attorney general. But his wife, Jane, decided to remain in Washington. The two lived apart for years and finally divorced in 1982. By the 1984 campaign, Edmisten was remarried and proudly stating that he had not consumed any alcoholic beverages in more than a year. As one source put it to the *N&O*, "Rufus's skeletons have been out bleaching in the sun for so long that there can't be much meat left to pick."

Edmisten wasn't the only candidate with tangled political roots. Lauch Faircloth, arguably the most conservative Democrat in the primary, had first gotten into politics as a strong supporter of former governors Kerr Scott, Terry Sanford, and Bob Scott—leaders of the party's progressive wing. Despite spending much of the 1960s and 1970s in appointive posts in state government, Faircloth had never run for elective office. Early on, he got some unsolicited advice from Edmisten that it would take $3 million "to get your name known." Faircloth responded to Edmisten that "it's going to cost you $6 million to get yours cleaned up." Throughout the campaign, Faircloth stressed that he was a businessman, not a politician. He knocked Knox, a Wake Forest law graduate, for being a "big-city lawyer" and Edmisten for "spend[ing] his entire life on the public payroll." Faircloth described his own philosophy as "a more fiscally conservative approach to state government and more moderate to liberal on social issues."

Similarly, Eddie Knox melded a right-of-center background with some left-of-center positions. As a college student in 1960, he had been a campus activist for the Sanford campaign, along with his friend Jim Hunt. But in 1964, Knox chose to work as an events coordinator for the gubernatorial campaign of former state judge Dan K. Moore, who successfully threaded the political needle between the primary bids of two other Democratic lawyers, liberal Richardson Preyer and conservative I. Beverly Lake Sr. Tellingly, Knox had chosen the moderate in the Democratic primary, while Hunt (and most of the Sanford organization) worked for the liberal Preyer. After Governor Moore took office in 1965, he put Knox on the state's Board of Alcoholic Beverage Control. Knox stepped down in 1970 to challenge and defeat an incumbent Democratic state senator from Mecklenburg. During his two terms in the General Assembly, he often proposed and voted for conservative legislation. But he also backed the Equal Rights Amendment and introduced a bill to require a permit for carrying a handgun. Neither measure became law. But the gun-control bill did have lasting political consequences for Knox.

EVERY WHICH WAY BUT LOOSE

The 1984 Democratic primary for governor proved an expensive proposition. By the end of April, the six major Democratic candidates had spent $6 million (the equivalent of $13.5 million in 2015 currency). Campaign spending by Faircloth ($2.1 million), Knox ($1.5 million), and Edmisten ($1.2 million) accounted for nearly 80 percent of the total.

At the beginning of 1984, Edmisten was far ahead in public polls, followed in order by Ingram, Knox, Green, and Gilmore. Faircloth was last. By March, however, a *Charlotte Observer* poll put Knox in the lead with 24 percent, Edmisten second with 17 percent, and Faircloth third but still in single digits. Just days before the May 8 primary, another *Observer* poll estimated 24 percent for Knox, 21 percent for Edmisten, and 14 percent for Faircloth, whose massive advertising campaign had paid off.

The race remained highly volatile, however. Nearly a fifth of Democratic primary voters remained undecided. So the candidates sought to make as much news as they could during the final days. Ingram proposed to submit all future tax increases to a public referendum. Edmisten blasted electric utilities for charging deposits to reconnect households after tornados. Gilmore emphasized his support for labor unions and opposition to jetties on the Outer Banks. Green sought state-employee votes by promising to upgrade the state health plan, then sought social-conservative votes by proposing an end to state funding for abortions except in cases of rape, incest, or when the life or health of the mother was at stake.

The candidates' closing arguments went beyond political promises. There were also plenty of attacks—most directed at Eddie Knox, the apparent front-runner. The sharpest one came not from a candidate but from the National Rifle Association. Citing his 1974 gun-control bill and his record as mayor of Charlotte, the NRA sent mailers to 57,000 North Carolina members questioning Knox's support for the Second Amendment. Knox responded with a TV ad in which he defended the rights of hunters but held up a "Saturday-night special" handgun to illustrate the type of firearm used by criminals. "With crime in North Carolina up over 70 percent in the last 10 years," he said in the commercial, "Eddie Knox will not apologize for trying to protect lives." In subsequent comments, a furious Knox blamed Faircloth and especially Edmisten for instigating the NRA mailing, allegations both men denied. Indeed, when the state later brought charges against the NRA for electioneering without registering as a political action committee, Knox said that Edmisten "ought to have been indicted as an accessory." The next flareup involved an anonymous flier distributed to black voters. It attacked Knox's civil-rights record. Again, Knox alleged that Edmisten's campaign was involved.

Although the Knox campaign tried to blunt the attacks, Edmisten appeared to pick up momentum just before the May 8 primary. Relying on sheriffs and other key local politicians, the Edmisten campaign had the best turnout machine. Just a few weeks earlier, such an advantage had seemed unlikely. In March, Edmisten's longtime friend and political strategist, Charlie Smith, had died in a plane crash. Horrified, campaign workers and the candidate himself struggled to get back on track. By the last week of the race, they did. In the primary on May 8, Edmisten led the field with 31 percent of the vote, followed by Knox at 26 percent, Faircloth at 16, Gilmore at 9, and Green and Ingram at 8 percent each. Most of the undecided vote had swung to Edmisten, virtually none to Knox. Edmisten's support was also distributed broadly across the state. He won pluralities in 72 counties, while Knox carried only 15.

Because Edmisten fell far short of a majority, however, the two men would have to settle the matter in a runoff four weeks later, on June 5. Ideology proved to be a poor predictor of how the losing candidates and other constituencies would sort themselves out. The strongest business conservative, Faircloth, endorsed Edmisten, citing the latter's ties to small towns and rural areas. The most liberal candidate, Tom Gilmore, opted to endorse the moderate Knox, who agreed to champion one of Gilmore's causes—open government. Not surprisingly, Jimmy Green also endorsed Knox over Edmisten, as did Ingram.

As for Jim Martin, he won the Republican primary easily over Ruby Hooper, a retired dietician at the state psychiatric hospital in Morganton, thanks in part to the campaign's excellent get-out-the-vote effort, which included a pre-primary mailer sent to GOP voters and featuring both Helms and Martin. So far, developments had fit the Martin campaign's most optimistic scenario. The Democratic primary had been bruising and expensive. Knox, whose Charlotte base overlapped Martin's, had come in second. The adversary the Martin campaign preferred to run against, Edmisten, had topped the balloting. Martin aides guessed that rural Democrats who supported Faircloth or Green might find Martin a more congenial alternative for governor than either Edmisten or Knox. The campaign immediately sent letters to eastern Democrats touting the Republican as "a conservative alternative . . . to Rufus and Eddie." The strategy was hardly a secret. Asked by the *News & Observer* to describe the May 8 primary result, Brad Hays was forthright: "It couldn't have come out better."

THE SCHOOL OF HARD KNOX

As the runoff campaign began, other prominent Democrats made their picks. Edmisten secured the endorsement of former governor Terry Sanford, a longtime friend of Edmisten's recently deceased mentor, Charlie Smith. Former governor Dan K. Moore co-hosted a major fundraiser for Knox. Another Knox supporter was Charlotte mayor Harvey Gantt. By far the most important potential endorsement in the Edmisten-Knox contest, however, would have been that of the Democratic Party's then-undisputed leader, Governor Jim Hunt, who was in the thick of his famous challenge to Jesse Helms. But Hunt stayed neutral. To the Edmisten camp, the governor's decision was unsurprising and welcome. To some in the Knox campaign, including the candidate himself, it was something else entirely: a disappointment, perhaps even a betrayal.

The spirited four-week runoff campaign got under way even as the May 8 results were still coming in. After blasting Edmisten for making the campaign "dirtier than I imagined it would be," Knox lit into the attorney general for presiding over a rise in the state's crime rate and for accepting campaign contributions from out-of-state auto dealers during a dispute about dealership restrictions. Edmisten shot back that Knox's allegations were "the biggest bunch of bull I have ever heard in my life." It was actually the Edmisten campaign that launched the first assault of the runoff with an ad questioning Knox's ties to Charlotte-based Duke Power. While Edmisten quickly pivoted to a mostly positive message, however, Knox continued to press his attacks. At a May 18 rally in Charlotte, he repeated a story that had first cropped up a decade earlier: that while working for Sam Ervin in Washington, Edmisten had failed to pay his North Carolina income taxes.

Later, while campaigning at the home of state senator Jim Richardson, a leader of Charlotte's African-American community, Knox made perhaps the most controversial allegation of all: that Edmisten allies had tried to intimidate black voters who didn't support their candidate. Here's how Knox described the message his black supporters in Wilson allegedly received: "Better not work for that fellow [Knox]. . . . Someone could hurt you." Edmisten responded with exasperation that often flared into anger. He called the allegation of voter intimidation "the most utterly ridiculous, absurd, baseless charge I have ever heard in my life. That's as wild as me saying I'm going to go out here and take a chainsaw and cut down a telephone pole." G. K. Butterfield, a black Edmisten campaign staffer and future judge and congressman, also objected to Knox's allegation. "I know firsthand there was no voter intimidation whatsoever," he told the Associated Press. "I would challenge anyone to produce evidence of such intimidation."

While playing defense when necessary, Edmisten spent much of his time emphasizing Democratic unity and campaigning with Faircloth in eastern North Carolina. He responded quickly to a potential threat to that unity when rumors spread that Hunt's organization was helping Knox in the runoff, rumors based partly on the fact that the manager of Hunt's Senate campaign, Joe Grimsley, had attended a Knox strategy session. Edmisten aides immediately intervened to confirm Hunt's neutrality. When reporters asked Grimsley why he had met with the Knox team, he explained that he'd been asked to describe the Hunt campaign's television buys and schedule so that the Knox campaign could adjust its plans accordingly. While Grimsley restated that the Hunt campaign wasn't choosing sides in the runoff, Knox asserted that members of the Hunt organization wanted to lend their support to him but hadn't been permitted to do so. Whether the product of miscommunication or something else, growing tensions between the Knox and Hunt teams would eventually affect Democratic prospects in both the gubernatorial and Senate races.

Edmisten's call for unity did not faze the Knox campaign. It would spend more than $580,000 on the runoff. Edmisten spent about $500,000. In the final days, both candidates visited black churches, party rallies, and other gatherings of likely runoff voters. Knox trumpeted his endorsements by nearly all metropolitan newspapers in the state and said his mix of legislative, legal, administrative, and political experience was a better fit for the governor's office than Edmisten's background as a Capitol Hill aide and state attorney general. Edmisten reiterated his theme of party unity, arguing that the Knox campaign's aggressive tactics would imperil Democratic chances in the fall. "My mama would love to get Eddie Knox over her knee and give him a good spanking," he quipped. "After half an hour, he'd stop that stuff."

Turnout for the June 5 runoff was much higher than expected. Edmisten won with 52 percent of the vote. He carried 74 of the 100 counties, including most rural areas, while Knox performed strongest in urban counties. A win was a win. But even in its hard-won victory, the Edmisten team saw trouble signs for the fall. The final pre-runoff polls had put the attorney general up 7 to 9 points. But Edmisten won by only 4. Contrary to what happened in the first primary, most of the undecided vote in the runoff had swung to Knox, suggesting that his attacks on Edmisten had potency. The former Charlotte mayor had also made the race surprisingly close in some eastern counties, particularly those in and around the path of the proposed extension of I-40 from Raleigh to Wilmington. The region's long-promised link to the interstate system was a sensitive issue there. After initially sticking with Hunt's position that the extension might take a decade to complete, Knox had by the end of the primary promised to finish I-40 to Wilmington during his first four-year term. Edmisten assured area voters that he supported the project, too, but said it might take longer than that. In the runoff, Knox performed better than expected in New Hanover, Brunswick, Columbus, and nearby counties.

Edmisten aides weren't the only ones who noticed. So did Jim Martin, Bob Bradshaw, and Brad Hays.

CHAPTER SEVEN

DIVISION LEADS TO ADDITION

Republicans got what they wanted in 1984—a long, contentious, and expensive Democratic primary for governor. Nevertheless, Jim Martin seemed to face long odds in the fall. The Gallup survey released just before the Rufus Edmisten–Eddie Knox runoff had also tested both Democratic candidates against Martin. Only 26 percent favored the Republican, while large majorities favored his Democratic opponents (63 percent for Edmisten, 62 percent for Knox). Fewer than half of North Carolina voters even knew who Martin was.

Insiders in both campaigns, however, discounted the early polls. Although Edmisten's advisors were confident their candidate would win the November election, they expected a much more competitive race after Martin introduced himself to voters outside the Charlotte region. Similarly, Hays and the Martin team knew their candidate was very appealing on television and would benefit from strong, well-funded reelection campaigns by President Reagan and Senator Helms.

Furthermore, Edmisten's often-repeated fears about party unity were widely shared among Democrats. Skipper Bowles, whose bitter primary with Pat Taylor had helped set up Jim Holshouser's 1972 win, said that the Edmisten-Knox contest risked a similar outcome. "It is shaping up that way so much that it scares me," Bowles said.

As soon as the runoff results made the news, the Martin campaign began receiving phone calls from disappointed Knox supporters offering to help. The editorial board of the liberal *News & Observer*, a bastion of Democratic Party politics since the late 19th century, urged Knox to say he was "wholeheartedly in support of the Democratic ticket." But it was not to be.

The relationship between the two men, already tense, got rockier on run-off night. Once Knox knew he had lost, he put in a call to Edmisten's Raleigh hotel room to concede and to congratulate him. But Edmisten was still celebrating in the ballroom and missed the call. Later, when reporters asked Knox about giving Edmisten a strong endorsement, he said he would talk to Edmisten "if he wants to talk to me." Later in the evening, the two men finally connected. Edmisten offered to help raise money to retire his opponent's campaign debt, but Knox was noncommittal. He even passed on a proposed meeting with Edmisten and Jim Hunt the following morning.

Knox actually seemed to be angrier with Hunt than with Edmisten, harking back to his previous insistence that the governor had blocked longtime lieutenants such as Secretary of Administration Jane Patterson (originally a Tom Gilmore supporter) and Secretary of Transportation William Roberson (originally a Lauch Faircloth supporter) from helping the Knox campaign while allowing others such as state ABC board chairman Marvin Speight to support and work for Edmisten. "I thought Eddie was an excellent candidate and would have made a good governor," Hunt said later. But he also thought other candidates were viable and attractive. He followed the advice of his political mentor, Bert Bennett, who urged him to remain neutral and focus on winning the Senate race. So Hunt told his cabinet secretaries not to campaign for gubernatorial candidates, although he imposed no similar rule on lower-level appointees such as Speight. For Knox to blame him even in part for his loss to Edmisten came as a surprise, Hunt said. In the days after the runoff, both Edmisten and Hunt spoke with Knox and tried to win his explicit endorsement. The governor offered to hold a joint fundraiser to help pay off Knox's campaign debt. Hunt even sent the Knox campaign a personal check for $1,000.

But Knox was unmoved. He offered neither Democrat his endorsement. Hunt's check was returned. Speaking at a June 27 fundraiser, Knox urged his supporters to make up their own minds. A few days later, the second shoe dropped: Knox's wife, Frances, and brother Charles announced their endorsement of Helms in the Senate race. Then in August, Frances, Charles, and three other brothers of Eddie Knox formally endorsed Martin for governor. The final step came on October 8, when Knox stood next to Reagan, Martin, Helms, and other Republican candidates at a Charlotte rally that attracted 30,000 people. At the event, Knox was announced as the national cochairman of the Democrats for Reagan organization. While Knox never formally endorsed Martin or Helms during the 1984 cycle, the signals weren't hard to interpret. He felt ill-treated and betrayed by the Democratic establishment. "I think I've been pretty gracious to say that I'm going to vote the Democratic ticket when I know that my friends not only did not help me but in instances worked against me," Knox explained.

Martin quickly moved to exploit the Democratic rift and looked for ways to align his campaign messages with those of Knox. But he was choosy. For example, the longtime congressman told reporters he did not consider Edmisten's failure to pay North Carolina taxes while residing in Virginia a pertinent issue. On the other hand, he picked up Knox's theme of using North Carolina's rising crime rate to question the attorney general's effectiveness.

Just after the runoff primary, as Edmisten took a breather in Raleigh, Martin campaigned aggressively in eastern North Carolina and stressed another overlap with Knox: Martin's pledge to complete I-40 from Raleigh to Wilmington within four years. Although he had made the promise before Knox did, Martin decided to give the issue greater prominence when he saw how much it appeared to damage Edmisten in the state's southeastern counties. Indeed, contrary to historical precedent and the advice of aides, Martin stressed that completing I-40 to the coast would be the only highway pledge he'd make. He contrasted his position with the usual tendency of state politicians to promise far more projects across the state than could possibly be completed with the funds available.

Still another overlap of the Knox and Martin campaign messages involved taxes. Unlike most competing states, North Carolina included both business inventories and intangible personal property such as stocks, bonds, and bank accounts in its property-tax base for cities and counties. Fiscal conservatives had long complained that these policies made the state a less-attractive place for executives, investors, and entrepreneurs to locate and create jobs. During the Democratic primary, Edmisten argued that North Carolina couldn't afford to eliminate either tax, given the potential revenue impact on localities. But Knox advocated using a corporate-tax credit to reduce the burden of the inventory tax. That dovetailed nicely with Martin's decision to make tax reduction his top issue. He sought to remind voters of his role in helping craft the 1981 tax cuts, telling Bill Friday, UNC president and host of public television's *North Carolina People*, that "Reaganomics is working better than Tip O'Neil's

'Tiponomics' did prior to that." Martin would eventually call for a phased repeal of the inventory tax, the intangibles tax, and the sales tax on food, first enacted under Governor Terry Sanford.

The tax issue gained prominence just two days after Edmisten's runoff victory when the General Assembly convened for its short session. Democratic and Republican House members introduced a bill to do what Knox had proposed: use corporate tax credits to offset some of the cost of the inventory tax. Meanwhile, Senate president pro tem Craig Lawing and Senate Finance Committee chairman Marshall Rauch tried to repeal the intangibles tax. Proponents of the tax cuts pointed to a projected $600 million budget surplus. The 1984 session was the time, they said, to begin tackling the state's problematic tax code. But Hunt and other party leaders disagreed, preferring to focus on a $300 million plan to raise teacher pay by 15 percent and state-employee pay by 10 percent. Both Martin and Edmisten came to the Legislative Building to lobby lawmakers—Martin for the tax cuts, Edmisten against them. The inventory and intangibles taxes "are two of the greatest handicaps that North Carolina imposes on itself," Martin said, adding that they had a particularly pernicious effect on economic growth in border and rural counties. But the arguments of Hunt and Edmisten prevailed. The inventory-tax bill died first, never making it out of committee. The intangibles-tax bill passed the Senate but was so substantially amended by the House that the resulting tax relief, $2 million a year, was trivial. Lawing rejected the House version as "the crumbs that fall from the table" and didn't even bother to form a conference committee to attempt to reconcile the bills.

So Hunt and Edmisten got the policy they wanted—a big spending increase for Democratic-leaning constituencies during an election year. Martin, however, got the issue of tax relief. It became central to his campaign.

ON THE HUNT FOR JESSIECRATS

The 1984 legislative session revealed more than just a policy disagreement about the state tax burden. It also offered further evidence of tensions within the Democratic Party. Jimmy Green was serving his last session as lieutenant governor and did little to boost Edmisten's political position. In fact, while Edmisten and his wife were vacationing, a Senate committee eliminated state funding for a victims' compensation program that the attorney general had strongly supported. Edmisten also came out strongly for a proposed statewide ban on the sale of phosphate detergents. But in the waning hours of the 1984 session, one of Green's allies killed the bill in committee, citing its potential cost to North Carolina households. Conservative-leaning Democratic senators no doubt had genuine concerns about state spending and regulatory burdens. But tweaking Edmisten was a welcome side benefit.

As Martin and his campaign team sought to court conservative Democrats, eastern counties became a major focus. In his first two statewide victories, Senator Helms had drawn a sizable crossover vote among these "Jessiecrats" by emphasizing shared values. The Martin team's strategy for winning the governor's race was somewhat different. It counted on strong showings in urban counties such as Mecklenburg, Wake, Guilford, and Forsyth, where Helms campaigns didn't fare as well. This was a natural fit for Martin, who'd won elections in Mecklenburg since 1966 and whose message and priorities were attractive to suburban voters. However, the strategy also counted on cutting into Democratic margins in the east. So the campaign recruited prominent Knox, Green, and Faircloth supporters from the region to endorse Martin. Both sides understood the stakes. "My trouble up to the last day of my campaign for governor," Edmisten later admitted, "was that I was still trying to woo over Eddie Knox supporters and Jimmy Green supporters."

Martin's first coup came in early July when Monroe Waters, who had run Knox's eastern campaign efforts from Greenville, gave the Republican nominee his support. Over the next few weeks, Martin announced additional Democratic supporters, including Wesley Ives, a Knox campaign veteran who had once served as executive director of the state Democratic Party. By Election Day, nearly 200 former campaign staffers or county managers for Knox, Faircloth, or Green would endorse Martin for governor. But explicit endorsements from the candidates themselves proved more challenging. Faircloth had already endorsed Edmisten, and Green was carefully coy.

Despite their tempestuous relationship, Edmisten tried repeatedly through the summer and early autumn to bring Green back into the party fold. Days before a September 22 fundraiser, the lieutenant governor was still withholding his endorsement. "I'm interested to see who is going to help" in retiring his campaign debt, Green said. In fact, several of Edmisten's major donors attended the fundraiser. A few days later, Green served as master of ceremonies at the annual Emerald Isle fish fry of Marvin Speight, a top fundraiser for

Edmisten. "Jimmy Green is a staunch Democrat," Speight explained. "He is not leaving the Democratic Party. He is not that upset. He is not the type of fellow who is going to abandon ship."

But behind the scenes, the Martin campaign was working furiously either to secure Green's nod or at least to keep him neutral. Arlene Pulley, Green's longtime aide and campaign manager, was a central figure. Shortly after Edmisten won the runoff, Green asked Pulley to appear on his behalf at a party unity event. She did so but returned to tell Green that she couldn't bring herself to support Edmisten. Later, Martin called Pulley to see if she would cross over. She declined to work directly for the Martin campaign. But quietly, Pulley recruited former Green supporters to assist Martin.

A telling moment came on October 20, when Martin visited Green's hometown of Clarkton to attend its annual Tobacco Festival. Martin tactfully sat behind Green at the viewing stand, and the two chatted throughout the event. Martin told Green that he appreciated the latter's public neutrality in the governor's race, as well as the support of many of Green's campaign staffers and political allies. Green then invited Martin to stop by his house for coffee. Although the conversation was largely personal rather than political, it began a relationship that culminated in Green's joining the Martin administration as a government-affairs consultant. Arlene Pulley also came to work for Martin, first on his transition team and then in the governor's office. She later won election as a Republican to a Wake County House seat.

ON THE ROAD WITH PROFESSOR MARTIN

Between the party primaries and the fall homestretch, the Martin campaign proved adept not only at seizing opportunities but also at mitigating mistakes. Most were minor, the result of Republicans still struggling to build a truly statewide political organization. Although Martin was a skilled and experienced campaigner, running for governor was another thing entirely. Reporters were more aggressive and skeptical than those he'd dealt with as a county commissioner and congressman. Martin also felt obligated to stay in Washington when the House was in session, meaning that he was mostly a Thursday-to-Sunday campaigner, not a full-timer. When he was on the trail, Martin's staff fretted that he still had a tendency to speak over the heads of his audience—to answer "What time is it?" by explaining how to build a watch.

The travel burden was alleviated by the presence of an increasingly effective surrogate: Martin's wife, Dottie. Although she had mostly stayed out of the limelight during his congressional campaigns, Dottie came to enjoy meeting average voters and made a positive impression on audiences.

But most of the burden fell on the candidate himself. It took its toll. Staffers began to check behind Martin to make sure he didn't leave his briefcase at events and learned to reserve quiet spaces for the candidate to collect his thoughts after traveling. They knew that long hours on the road sometimes made Martin tired and testy. On one memorable occasion in September, press aide Karen Hayes got an early-morning call at the Raleigh campaign office. It was Martin. "Do you know where I am?" he asked. "Not right this minute, congressman," she replied, "but I know where you are supposed to be very shortly." Martin explained that he was at that location, the North Raleigh Hilton, for a campaign speech. "Do you want to know how I got here?" he asked. "I hitchhiked." The campaign driver had failed to pick him up at his hotel, so Congressman Jim Martin, campaigning to become governor of North Carolina, had thumbed a ride to his speech.

An earlier and more serious challenge for the Martin team had led to the hiring of Karen Hayes in the first place. On July 6, campaign press secretary Max Veale was arrested in Raleigh on a charge of soliciting prostitution. Veale, a former *Charlotte News* reporter, said he had been driving around downtown looking for a fellow Martin campaign staffer when he came across two women standing on the street corner. Veale insisted he stopped only to ask directions, but one of the women—an undercover police officer—said he asked her price for performing sexual favors. After his arrest, Veale was let go from the campaign, replaced by Hayes. But his role in the 1984 campaign wasn't over just yet.

THE CONVENTIONS OF NATIONALIZED POLITICS

While Edmisten and Martin positioned themselves for the general election, most of the public attention was directed elsewhere. Ronald Reagan was running for reelection. Expecting the president's strong showing in North Carolina to produce a coattail effect, the state GOP fielded dozens of candidates for Congress, the state legislature, county commissions, and offices that had often been ceded to Democrats in the past. Most importantly, the Helms-Hunt Senate race was on its way to becoming one of America's most expensive, compelling, and controversial political contests. Both the Edmisten and Martin campaigns had to adjust their strategies accordingly. They resigned themselves to the fact that their campaigns would have to compete for media and public attention with those of many other candidates. And they had to figure out whether and how to integrate their messages with the rest of their parties' tickets.

For Edmisten, the strategy was to link himself to Hunt while distancing himself from Walter Mondale, the Democratic presidential nominee. When the Democratic National Convention convened on July 16 in San Francisco, Hunt and Edmisten were on hand to serve as cochairs of the North Carolina delegation. But Hunt declined an invitation to fill a prime speaking slot, and Edmisten also did his best to keep a low profile. A few weeks later, on August 8, Mondale made a campaign stop in Asheville. He was welcomed to the state by Commissioner of Agriculture Jim Graham and Lacy Thornburg, the party's nominee to replace Edmisten as attorney general. Neither North Carolina's Democratic governor nor the man running to replace him was present. Edmisten later admitted that his campaign had scheduled an event in Boone as an excuse not to be on hand for Mondale's speech.

On August 20, the Republican National Convention began its four-day run in Dallas. While Edmisten downplayed his connection to Mondale, Jim Martin tied himself to Reagan. Still, Martin stayed only one day at the convention. Instead, he spent most of the week making stops on his "Jim Martin Listens" tour, a concept Jack Hawke devised to earn media coverage outside the Charlotte market. In virtually every speech and media interview during the tour, Martin made frequent allusions to the president, trumpeting his congressional votes in favor of Reagan's tax cuts, regulatory reforms, and other policies. "If Ronald Reagan wins and Jim Martin wins, North Carolina wins," he proclaimed.

The theme got a strong reinforcement just after Labor Day, when the Martin campaign began its long-planned blitz of statewide advertising. Although the first Martin TV ad was a simple biographical piece, the congressman talking directly to the camera about his career in county government and Congress, a second wave of ads emphasized his ties to President Reagan, including a spot picturing Martin with the president. Subsequent TV ads featured the candidate promising fiscal restraint ("As your governor I'll cut taxes we don't need and give that money back to you") and a new war on drug trafficking ("We've got to stop the dope out there before it finds its way in here"). A separate flight of radio ads turned up the heat on Edmisten, featuring man-on-the-street interviews that questioned the Democrat's competence and knowledge of state issues. In total, the campaign bought more than $500,000 worth of broadcast ads in September and early October, following the $30,000 worth in August on billboards and barn signs to set up the broadcast ads' messages and taglines.

A Gallup poll in mid-September brought Martin's opportunity—and Edmisten's challenge—into stark relief. It showed Reagan with 62 percent of the vote in North Carolina. In the governor's race, the poll found Edmisten leading Martin by 51 percent to 39 percent. That represented a 12-point drop for Edmisten and a 13-point gain for Martin from the previous Gallup poll, taken just after the Democratic runoff. A separate *Charlotte Observer* poll taken at roughly the same time found exactly the same Edmisten lead: 51–39.

His Democratic opponent still enjoyed a double-digit lead, but Martin had the momentum. Not surprisingly, he continued to attach himself to Reagan's campaign organization and message at every opportunity, while Edmisten continued efforts to distance himself from Mondale. At the massive October 8 rally in Charlotte at which Knox was named cochairman of Democrats for Reagan, Martin contrasted the crowded podium and 30,000 attendees to the previous, lightly attended August appearance by Walter Mondale in Asheville, an event from which Edmisten and Hunt had been absent. "They had a unity rally and no one came," Martin quipped.

THE EDMISTEN COUNTERATTACK

While recognizing the drag of the national ticket on his campaign, Edmisten remained upbeat about his chances. After all, he was still polling above the 50 percent mark, and North Carolina was still overwhelmingly Democratic in registration. Although the Martin campaign had enough money for statewide media buys, both sides knew the Democrats would still win the fundraising war. Through Election Day, the Martin campaign would raise and spend a total of $3.1 million, or about $7 million in 2015 dollars. Edmisten would spend $4.5 million, about $10.2 million in 2015 dollars. The two nominees together spent about six dollars per registered voter—which made the Martin-Edmisten race the second-most-expensive gubernatorial race in North Carolina history, when adjusted for inflation and population growth. (The most expensive would be Martin's reelection bid against Lieutenant Governor Bob Jordan in 1988, which cost $7.41 per registered voter. The 2012 race between Republican Pat McCrory and Democrat Walter Dalton, by comparison, cost only $2.41 per registered voter.)

Outside Edmisten's inner circle, Democratic activists were optimistic to the point of being cocky. Paul Shumaker, then a field rep for Martin, was working a county fair one afternoon and heard an Edmisten staffer casually discuss the job he expected to get in the coming Democratic administration. Within the inner circle, Edmisten and his team thought they had a surefire way to hold down Martin's numbers among Reagan Democrats and rural voters: by emphasizing the congressman's connections to big-business interests and the city with which they were most often associated, Charlotte. After all, the Democratic adversary Edmisten had just bested, Knox, had blamed "the Mecklenburg thing" as one of the reasons for his loss. Edmisten agreed with this critique. He saw Martin as vulnerable to the same dynamic. "I knew that big business was for him because big business does not traditionally care much for the attorney general," Edmisten later explained. "Since I was already tagged as a semi-populist, I thought, 'Why not go ahead and run as one?' " Another part of his populism strategy was to refer to his opponent as "Professor Martin."

Rising utility prices had proven to be a powerful issue in the Democratic primary, so Edmisten sought to use them in the general election. On the stump, he found increasingly colorful language to describe the contrast. Jim Martin "jumps 20 feet high every time the utility companies say so," Edmisten declared during a campaign stop in Burlington. "I jump 100 feet for the ordinary citizen." On September 23, his campaign launched a statewide ad buy criticizing Martin's congressional record on telephone rates, energy policy, and other issues. The following day, Edmisten held a press conference in front of Duke Power's Charlotte headquarters. He promised to place new limits on electric rates. "When faced with a choice between the special interests and the people of our state," Edmisten said, "[Martin] has sided with the special interests every time." Martin defended his congressional record but devoted most of his response to deriding Edmisten's "demagogic attacks on the utility companies." With the benefit of hindsight, Edmisten said later that holding the press conference at Duke Power had been a mistake. It insulted the company's thousands of (mostly Democratic) employees, many of whom jeered at him from the windows. Edmisten signs posted on utility poles across the state began, perhaps not so mysteriously, to fall to the ground. As for Martin, he responded this way: "I'm for big business—and for small business, and every business in between. Rufus doesn't understand, but business is where jobs come from."

Another line of attack focused on environmental issues. Despite his record in Mecklenburg County, and despite having been considered to head the EPA, Martin's critics said his congressional votes on regulation made him a foe of the environment. The Edmisten campaign pointed out that during Martin's time in Washington, the League of Conservation Voters had given him lower-than-average scores in its annual ratings. One vote got particular attention: Martin's support for the bill making it a federal responsibility to dispose of nuclear waste. The North Carolina delegation had voted unanimously for the measure, Martin replied, so if Edmisten had been a congressman and voted against it, "he would have been voting with the most liberal members of the Congress."

Although the two men sparred on a variety of issues, Edmisten and his allies aimed most of their punches at Martin's proposal to cut North Carolina's taxes on business inventories, intangible assets, and food. At first, Martin proposed to phase in the elimination of the food tax by starting with an exemption for North Carolinians over the age of 65. By late October, however, he argued that, given healthy growth in state revenue, the tax should go away for everyone by 1986. He further proposed to repeal the intangibles tax in 1985 and the inventory tax by 1988, using state reimbursements to prevent localities from taking a revenue hit. By his calculations, Martin said, the tax cuts would still give legislators enough money to fund necessary programs, award annual pay raises to teachers and state employees, and preserve a healthy General Fund balance. Ending North Carolina's punitive tax treatment of inventories and intangibles would attract new investment and create jobs, Martin promised. "There are two basic approaches to government and the role that it plays in our lives," Martin said. "At the heart of the argument is the question of fewer taxes or more growth in government."

Edmisten increasingly attacked Martin's tax ideas. He called them "a wild, off-the-wall gimmick," "pure economic hocus-pocus," and "tax breaks for the rich" that would "repeal every tax that produces the money for educational excellence." The liberal editorial board of the *N&O* piled on, describing Martin as a "candidate for the rich" who would cut taxes at the expense of valuable government services. House speaker Liston Ramsey said that Martin "has been in Washington too long. A lot of that voodoo economics has rubbed off on him." In a fundraising letter, Edmisten cited the tax issue as one of many that linked Martin to "narrow-minded extremists, special interests, and radical policies" from outside the state. Still, Edmisten recognized his potential vulnerability on the issue, particularly because he was on the ballot with Mondale, who had promised to raise taxes if elected. So by late October, Edmisten shifted his position to favor a repeal of the taxes—but at a far more gradual pace than Martin was proposing. As a means of neutralizing the issue, however, Edmisten's pivot would prove to be too little, too late.

A final clash involved social policy. Both out of conviction and in the interest of broadening the Republican Party, Martin campaigned aggressively for the votes of black North Carolinians. He spoke before prominent African-American organizations, including the state NAACP convention, and even set a goal that at least 2 percent of state contracts would be awarded to minority-owned companies during a Martin administration. Edmisten shot back that Martin had voted against the Martin Luther King Jr. holiday and for bills to amend the Voting Rights Act. Edmisten also warned that Martin's election would threaten abortion rights.

Other Democrats tried to link Martin more explicitly to Republican politicians specializing in social issues, especially Jesse Helms. In 1984, future congressman David Price was chairman of the state Democratic Party. Helms and Martin shared "rather similar records" and political ideologies, Price told a reporter for the *Lexington Dispatch*. "People don't think of [Martin] that way because he's articulate and very urban in appearance." If Price's goal was to trick Martin into creating tensions with the Republican Party, the canny congressman didn't fall for it. "I am basically conservative," Martin said, so he and Senator Helms were "in agreement more often than not. It doesn't bother me for Chairman Price to say that I'm conservative, because North Carolina is primarily a conservative state."

Just as during his previous campaigns, Martin focused mainly on the fiscal and operational issues of government. But he didn't shy away from social issues when asked about them. He restated his opposition to the Equal Rights Amendment and taxpayer financing of abortion. On September 28, a group of conservative ministers endorsed Martin over Edmisten, saying the congressman had "strong religious and moral ties."

Despite launching these varied lines of attack against Martin's positions, Edmisten did not attempt to make the 1984 gubernatorial election into a starkly ideological choice in the manner Hunt did in the Senate race and Mondale did (whether intentionally or accidentally) in the presidential race. In fact, some of the Democrat's marketing budget was devoted to muddying the ideological waters. One statewide Edmisten ad described him as "a North Carolina kind of conservative" in the mold of his former boss, Sam Ervin.

ANOTHER DEBATE ABOUT DEBATING

Just as he had rebuffed Knox's call for multiple debates during the Democratic runoff, Edmisten said no to Martin's proposal of a series of televised debates. Frontrunners typically see more risk than reward in debates, and Edmisten had a healthy respect for Martin's speaking skills. During one of the few appearances they had previously made together, Martin used a characteristic tactic to rattle him. While Edmisten was speaking, Martin would appear to be taking notes. Actually, he was filling out a report card that gave Edmisten letter grades on content, style, and delivery. Then Martin would slip the card to Edmisten after he sat down. Both men got a laugh out of it, but it also served to increase Edmisten's respect for Martin as a formidable opponent. "He was a superb candidate, cool, and rolled with the punches," Edmisten said later.

His reticence to debate Martin was strengthened on August 28, when the two faced off before the North Carolina Highway Users Conference in Raleigh. Edmisten hadn't planned on it. He agreed to participate in the event with the understanding that Senator Helms would be on the podium with him. Upon arrival, he discovered otherwise. With TV cameras rolling, Martin challenged Edmisten's handling of the state's recent bid-rigging scandal and his refusal to make the completion of I-40 to Wilmington the state's top road-construction priority. He also took a jab at Edmisten's reticence to debate him. "You have to be a very powerful group," Martin told the audience, "to get both me and my opponent in the same room at the same time." In a technique reminiscent of his congressional use of stacks of paper to depict federal overregulation, Martin held up a book of highway projects and began tearing pages from it, illustrating existing projects the state would have to forgo to fund all of Edmisten's newly promised road projects. Following the joint appearance, the two men exited the room without exchanging pleasantries or even handshakes.

After this experience, some friends advised Edmisten to refuse future debates altogether. But others, including his brother David, disagreed. "You can't totally ignore a man who asks for a debate," he said. "You get more negative press by ignoring the debate than by going ahead with a small number, either one or two." This argument prevailed. The two campaigns agreed to a single live debate on Sunday, September 30. It was sponsored by the North Carolina Association of Broadcasters and appeared on radio and television stations across the state. (One additional television program pitted Martin and Edmisten against each other, but it wasn't a formal, live debate. The two major-party candidates, plus Libertarian candidate Fritz Prochnaw, separately recorded answers to questions from public-television host Dick Hatch.)

The September 30 debate didn't break much new ground. But for North Carolinians who might have been more closely following the Reagan-Mondale and Helms-Hunt races, it restated and clarified the distinctions between the two gubernatorial candidates. Edmisten pressed home his charge that Martin was too friendly to big business. In particular, he rapped the congressman for supporting a policy called "Construction Work in Progress" (CWIP), which allowed utilities to bill customers for the cost of new power plants while they were still being built, rather than waiting until completion to begin recovering costs. Martin defended the policy. By allowing utilities to bill throughout the construction process, he argued, CWIP reduced the need to borrow large sums up front at high interest rates, thus saving rate payers money in the long run. Martin also blamed utility rate hikes in part on "heavy environmental costs on the production of coal and oil and nuclear power" that "have to be borne by you, the consumers," returning to one of his familiar campaign themes about the overregulation of business.

Edmisten also tried to capitalize on Martin's promise to complete I-40 to Wilmington in four years by suggesting that such a priority would harm residents waiting for roads in other parts of the state. That gave Martin the opportunity to contrast what he called "the politics of illusion" with "the politics of integrity." By promising more highway construction than highway revenues could finance, Edmisten and previous gubernatorial candidates had broken trust with the voters, he said. But he also defended the I-40 project to voters elsewhere in the state by arguing that its completion would reduce shipping time and cost for products bound for the state port at Wilmington. (Later, Martin said voters were better off with candidates who pledged too little than with those who pledged too much. "Would you rather have unpaved promises or unpromised paving?" he often asked.)

On fiscal policy, Martin restated his economic-development case for eliminating inventory and intangibles taxes. Edmisten denied that the state's tax burden was high enough to deter economic growth and argued that raising teacher pay would be a better way to use surplus dollars. He also questioned Martin's advocacy of merit pay, rather than across-the-board increases for teachers. Observing that he had spent 12 years as a classroom instructor at Davidson, Martin insisted that raising teacher pay would be a priority of his, but that the compensation system needed reform. He pointed with approval to the design of a new "Career Ladder" pilot program in the Charlotte-Mecklenburg Schools. "I want to change the policy whereby, in the past, we have provided the same pay for every teacher" regardless of performance, he said. The issue would prove to be one of the most contentious of his tenure as governor.

THE TIPPING POINT

After 12 years, Brad Hays knew his candidate. He knew Martin would perform well on camera. A single debate was unlikely to determine the outcome of the election, however. All along, Hays counted on a strong get-out-the-vote effort to ensure GOP turnout, coupled with TV advertising in the last weeks of the campaign to put Martin over the top with Democratic crossover voters. As the campaign approached its final weeks, the effects of the ads were unmistakable. Both camps could see it in their internal polls. For Martin, the magic moment came about two weeks out. After a long day of appearances, he returned to his Lake Norman home with several campaign aides and family members. A phone call came in from Hays. The campaign's tracking poll for the first time showed the two candidates in a statistical tie. "We got him!" Martin exclaimed. But he and his team chose not to publicize the poll. They didn't want to seem overconfident—after all, nothing was guaranteed in politics. They still had to get their vote out.

In past cycles, North Carolina Democrats had often overwhelmed their Republican rivals with precinct-level organization. In 1984, they sought to hammer their advantage home with a single, coordinated campaign to get out the vote for Hunt, Edmisten, and other candidates using checklists, buses, vans, and even babysitters for stay-at-home moms. But Republicans, particularly those in the Martin campaign, were determined not to cede the ground game in 1984. One of campaign manager Jack Hawke's key duties was to work with Margaret King and operations director Art Pope to establish a statewide version of the Neighbors Program to mobilize the party base with phone calls and door-to-door canvassing by volunteers walking their own streets and contacting their own neighbors. Although operating separately, the Helms campaign complemented the program with a series of automated phone calls to Republican-leaning households featuring Reagan, Helms, and stock-car racer Richard Petty.

On the Democratic side, Edmisten made a last-ditch attempt to bring the fractious party together. "It's sort of like a family feud," he told a Mocksville audience. "You may fight a little bit, and then you make up and get back together and you're stronger." At a subsequent campaign stop in Greenville, Edmisten argued that conservative-leaning Democrats wouldn't accomplish much by electing a Republican governor to serve with a Democratic legislature. The last such governor, Jim Holshouser, had done little more during his term than conduct "guided tours of the governor's mansion," he joked.

But Edmisten's public bravado didn't reflect the campaign's increasingly worried mood. Other Democratic candidates were struggling, too. Harrison Hickman, a North Carolinian who became a prominent Democratic consultant, put it this way to the *N&O*: "I have visions of 1972 dancing in my head. There is clearly a national movement toward Reagan." Edmisten feared the coming Republican tide would roll over him. Two weeks before Election Day, his own internal poll showed Mondale collapsing and Martin surging to only a 5-point deficit. Even before the two candidates' poll tracks crossed a week later, Edmisten said, "I knew it was gone."

Martin planned to use the analogy of converging tracks as his closing argument. At Jack Hawke's instigation, the campaign had months earlier arranged to lease a diesel train and three cars for about $28,000. On October 22, it launched an old-fashioned whistle-stop tour of 17 cities. Martin, family members, campaign staff, reporters, and high-dollar donors rode the train from

Asheville to Charlotte, then on through the Piedmont to Raleigh, Goldsboro, and eastern North Carolina. The Edmisten campaign sneered. "We feel like we can cover more ground traveling by airplane," said Richard Carlton, the Democrat's campaign manager. But the train tour wasn't about miles traveled. It was about creating photo opportunities and exciting GOP activists. At the kickoff in Asheville, Martin promised he would be "a tax-cutting governor because I believe that will help to strengthen the state's economy." In Lexington, he emphasized the point. "Couldn't you hear that engine as we were pulling in here saying 'cut those taxes, cut those taxes'?" he asked. "When we're leaving here, it's going to say 'I knew he could, I knew he could.'" In Goldsboro, Martin said that "President Reagan has got America on the right track, just as we've got our campaign on the right track."

As an attention-grabbing device, the tour got off to a promising start. Staffers used hand-held tape recorders to capture audio of Martin speaking on the train, then sent the clips via phone lines to radio stations serving future stops. Local newspapers usually covered the tour, although sometimes the resulting stories didn't make the top of the fold. When the train reached Durham on October 24, however, a huge crowd of reporters, cameramen, and spectators was waiting. Martin and his staff thought their whistle-stop tour was about to have a big payoff.

But that's not why the crowd was there. What followed was one of the strangest episodes of the 1984 campaign.

THE PURLOINED LETTER

After multiple attacks on his character during the Democratic primary, Edmisten braced himself for similarly rough treatment from Republicans in the fall. In fact, some campaign aides even conducted opposition research on Martin in an attempt to prepare a possible counterattack. The result didn't make the Democrats feel any better. "To be frank about it," Edmisten said later, "they couldn't find anything" in Martin's past to use against him.

By mid-October, with no character attacks launched from the Martin camp, Edmisten started to believe perhaps the worst was behind him. Then his campaign received a partial copy of a letter on Martin campaign stationery that referred to Edmisten's alleged "boozing," "womanizing," and consorting with "gamblers and dopers." Although the Democrats had only the first page of a letter purportedly aimed at Guilford County Republicans, they assumed the rest of the letter was equally explosive—and intended to make statewide news. Rather than take a wait-and-see approach, Edmisten decided to step forward and seize control of the story. Standing with his wife, Linda, before a packed October 24 press conference at the Democratic Party headquarters in Raleigh, Edmisten brandished the letter and angrily disputed what he called a "smut sheet" from the Republican campaign. "Mr. Martin has become personal and dirty," Edmisten said. "He has lied on the political questions and hurt my family and my wife on a very personal level." The Edmisten campaign didn't stop with a press conference. Over the next few days, it ran a new statewide TV ad that accused Martin of "character assassination" by citing the letter and a separate public comment from Wake County GOP chairman Ernie Pearson about Edmisten's being "a drunk."

Although Pearson did make that remark—Martin publicly condemned it and asked him not to repeat it—Martin denied any knowledge of the letter, which he called "garbage" and "a fake." He asked Brad Hays to investigate whether or not any Republican activists or voters had actually received it. None had. The campaign released signed statements from its Guilford County chairman and volunteers stating they had no knowledge of it.

Over the next several days, Martin expressed sympathy for the Edmistens and speculated that whoever had concocted the letter might actually have intended to hurt Martin, by implying that he would resort to smear tactics to win a race. Privately, Martin suspected that the Edmisten campaign might itself be responsible. This idea originated with his brother Joe, who had written his master's thesis about Robert Penn Warren's novel *All the King's Men* and in the process learned a great deal about Huey Long, the Louisiana politician who inspired its plot. On many occasions, Edmisten had proclaimed Harry Williams's award-winning biography of Huey Long to be his second-favorite book (after the Bible). The Martins concluded that fabricating a personal attack attributable to one's opponent in order to generate public sympathy for oneself—a "reverse smear" similar to one of the fictional events in *All the King's Men*—was just the kind of tactic Huey Long, or an admirer of Huey Long, might employ.

But they were mistaken about the source of the letter. Years after the episode, former Martin campaign press spokesman Max Veale came forward to admit he had concocted the letter using stationery he took home as he left the campaign in July. In fact, Veale—who had since returned to the political world in roles that included a stint on Representative Cass Ballenger's congressional staff—contacted then–secretary of state Rufus Edmisten in 1992, asked for a meeting, and apologized in person for the trick. While Veale later claimed he was simply playing a "joke" on Daniel Hoover, a former *N&O* reporter who served as the Edmisten campaign's press secretary, both gubernatorial candidates came to believe Veale had intended a sort of "bank shot," a way to strike both of them at the same time. Martin would later use a different sports analogy. He likened Veale's actions to a bowler trying to pick up a 7–10 split.

As it happened, the ball managed to hit only one of the intended pins, the Democratic one—and then only because Edmisten chose to move himself into the ball's path. Because there was no evidence the letter had ever been mass-produced and mailed, its contents wouldn't have seen the light of day had the Edmisten campaign not chosen to hold a press conference. That created several rounds of press coverage devoted to Edmisten's personal life, at a time when he could least afford the distraction—during the final days of the campaign. By contrast, after its initial disavowals, the Martin campaign directed its attention elsewhere. The strategy, Jack Hawke explained, was "to make sure the message gets out that nobody is circulating that stuff except Rufus Edmisten."

The candidate himself complied with this strategy most of the time, but his wit occasionally got the best of him. Just days before the election, Martin was in Asheboro for a speech. As a high-school band played "Yankee Doodle Dandy," the former tuba player appeared before the crowd, accepted the baton, and conducted for a few bars. Turning to the assembled reporters, Martin quipped, "I wonder if they can play 'I'm gonna sit right down and write myself a letter—and make believe it came from you'?"

"TO BUILD A BROADER BASE"

The day before Halloween, what both campaigns knew in private became very public: Jim Martin had overtaken Rufus Edmisten. The *Charlotte Observer* reported the results of its latest statewide survey. Martin led with 47 percent. Edmisten was at only 41 percent. A few days later, Gallup delivered similar news via several media clients: the Republican was now in the lead. Support for Martin had soared by 23 points to 49 percent since the May primaries. Support for Edmisten had dropped by 19 points to 44 percent. Gallup's key finding was that Republican-leaning North Carolinians were more likely to turn out than Democratic-leaning ones, a probable result of President Reagan's strength in the state and Senator Helms's momentum in the homestretch. Among all registered voters, Martin and Edmisten were tied at 46 percent. But among likely voters, and with undecided voters equally allocated between the two candidates, the final Gallup poll predicted a 53–47 victory for the Republican. In the end, Martin would beat that spread.

On November 5, the day before Election Day, the two candidates boarded planes to hopscotch the state's media markets with airport press conferences. Their parting shots reflected the message that each campaign thought would work best to sway late-deciding voters. Edmisten attacked Martin's tax-cut plan as fiscally risky and doomed to die in a Democratic legislature. "It's a gimmick and he knows it's a gimmick," Edmisten told reporters. "He doesn't believe in that any more than I'm an astronaut in space." Martin defended his tax plan while stressing his outreach to former Faircloth, Knox, and Green supporters in the east. His campaign even placed an ad in the *Wilmington Morning Star* and other regional newspapers charging that "Rufus doesn't give a hoot about eastern North Carolina."

For what they hoped would be Martin's election-night victory celebration, the campaign chose the Raleigh Hilton Inn, on Hillsborough Street near North Carolina State University. Later renamed the Brownstone Hotel, it was the same place Holshouser had celebrated his victory in 1972. While Martin supporters gathered in the ballroom, the candidate and his top aides remained in an eighth-floor suite to watch the returns come in. In another room, leaders of the Democrats for Martin group held their own hopeful vigil. Meanwhile, the Edmisten campaign set up shop on the east side of town at the Raleigh Inn on New Bern Avenue. Although the public polls predicted otherwise, many Edmisten supporters remained convinced their man would prevail. Some wore buttons that read, "I Was There At the Raleigh Inn Nov. 6 When Rufus Was Elected." (These buttons became collectibles. In late 2013, one sold on eBay for $27.84.)

Although the 1984 campaign for North Carolina governor had many twists and turns, there was little drama on election night. At 7:30, when the polls closed in most of the state, ABC News immediately cited exit polls and called the race for Jim Martin. The crowd at the Raleigh Hilton erupted in cheers. The crowd at the Raleigh Inn muttered in disbelief. Asked for comment,

Edmisten's press secretary, Daniel Hoover, merely responded, "It's 7:31."

The news for Democrats got no better as the night wore on. Ronald Reagan was reelected in a landslide. Jesse Helms, whom Democratic activists across the country loved to hate, bested Jim Hunt, the party's rising star. Shortly after the media's projection that Martin had won, Dottie appeared before the jubilant Republicans to raucous cheers. Two hours later, around 10, Jim entered the ballroom. "I knew that if you brought me this far, I couldn't mess it up in the last few weeks," he said. As it turned out, Martin's margin of victory—54 percent to Edmisten's 45 percent—was even larger than Democrats had feared. Martin's vote total of just over 1.2 million was about 138,000 votes fewer than President Reagan received in North Carolina but 51,000 more than the number who voted to reelect Senator Helms. Since GOP registrations totaled only 500,000 voters, more Democrats than Republicans had voted for Martin.

Not all Democratic activists were disappointed with the outcome, of course. The ones at the Hilton Inn—the Martin supporters—were pleased. They got even more excited when Eddie Knox showed up at their hotel suite. Many of the men in the room were wearing Knox campaign buttons on one lapel and Martin buttons on the other. Although Knox had not formally endorsed Martin, he basked in the moment and even sang a bit of the old hymn "I've Been Redeemed." At two in the morning, when Martin held his first news conference as governor-elect, Knox slipped into the back behind the gaggle of reporters, who immediately took notice. The two men later met privately amid speculation that Knox might be asked to serve in the Martin administration. That never happened, but the two remained cordial for many years afterward.

As for Rufus Edmisten, he harbored no ill will toward Martin. Four years after losing the gubernatorial election, Edmisten made a comeback as the Democratic nominee to replace longtime secretary of state Thad Eure. He won the job at the same time Governor Martin was winning reelection. The two men worked together on issues of mutual concern, including a commission on securities regulation, and enjoyed a laugh or two at each other's expense.

Much later, Edmisten looked back at the 1984 race with a mixture of regret and jovial self-deprecation. "I wished I'd whipped him," he said of Martin. "But if I had become governor, I'd probably just be getting out of the federal penitentiary because of the people I had around me."

CHAPTER EIGHT

GOVERNING BY TWISTS AND TURNS

The world's top-selling puzzle game isn't Scrabble or Sudoku. It is the Rubik's Cube, invented by Hungarian professor Ernő Rubik in 1974. It hit the world market in 1980 and quickly became one of the most popular diversions of all time. It was still in its heyday in 1984 when Jim Martin began his successful run for governor. To him, however, it wasn't a diversion at all. It was a teaching tool.

As a professor, Martin had always been on the lookout for good visual aids to impart scientific concepts. His interest carried over into politics. Much as he had once used teetering stacks of paper to illustrate the growth of federal regulation, Martin by 1984 saw the Rubik's Cube as a useful prop for introducing himself and his unique background to audiences outside his Charlotte-area congressional district. At the beginning of his stump speech, Martin would show a scrambled cube to the audience. Sometimes, he said it signified the complexity of North Carolina's economy. Sometimes, he said it represented the jumble that was state government in Raleigh. Then, as Martin continued his speech, he would seem absent-mindedly to twist and turn the cube without looking down. At just the right moment, the former chemistry professor would raise the solved cube, each side a single color, and proclaim that if state leaders were thoughtful and diligent, they could get "it"—the economy or state government—"back into shape."

Having won the 1984 gubernatorial race by a surprisingly healthy margin, Martin now had some real-world puzzles to solve. How would he transform a successful campaign into an effective government as a Republican in a Democratic town? How would he reconcile his stated opposition to partisan hiring in

THE GOVERNOR-ELECT
DANCES WITH DOTTIE AT
THE INAUGURAL BALL ON
JANUARY 4, 1985.
MARTIN FAMILY PHOTO

government with the need for like-minded officials to carry out his programs? And how would he convince skeptical Democrats to enact the centerpiece of his electoral platform, the largest tax cut in North Carolina history, when he had few personal ties to the General Assembly and no veto power?

FROM JIM TO JIM

While challenging, these were still the best kinds of political puzzles to solve. They arose from success. After their failures in the 1984 elections, many North Carolina Democrats were despondent and flummoxed. Jim Hunt had lost to Jesse Helms. President Reagan was reelected by a landslide. The state GOP picked up three seats in the United States House—Bill Cobey in the Fourth District, Howard Coble in the Sixth, and Bill Hendon (again) in the 11th—giving the party five of the state's 11 seats. Alex McMillan narrowly defeated Democrat D. G. Martin (son of former Davidson College president Grier Martin) to keep Jim Martin's congressional seat in Republican hands. Republicans more than doubled their state-legislative seats (to 49 from 24) and the county commissions they controlled (to 23 from 11). For most Democrats, however, the bitterest pill to swallow was the loss of the state's chief executive. Although the institutional powers of North Carolina's governor were weak by national standards, the office nevertheless served as the hub of state government. It produced budget proposals and implemented legislation. It hired and fired thousands of state employees and vendors. It made thousands of additional appointments, often coveted ones, to unpaid positions on state boards and commissions. It was the most visible political job in Raleigh. Now, it belonged to a Republican congressman from Charlotte.

The transition process began just hours after the election, when Martin reviewed a plan drawn up by his brother Joe. It called for quick action on several fronts. On Wednesday morning, the governor-elect met with the man who was now the de facto leader of the state's Democrats, Lieutenant Governor–elect Bob Jordan, for what Martin called a "candid conversation." On Wednesday afternoon, he met with Governor Hunt to discuss the transition and the status of the budget outline being assembled by Hunt's staff. Between meetings, Martin held press conferences to define his administration's agenda. He argued that his nearly 200,000-vote margin was proof that North Carolinians favored his proposed reductions in inventory, intangibles, and sales taxes. "They want a tax cut," he said. "They want some relief." At the same time, however, he signaled that he might be willing to work with legislators on crafting a tax package they could support. "You know how legislation works," he told reporters. "You start here, try this, try that, and hope that you come out at the place you intend." Martin also restated his pledges to improve education through merit pay for teachers and not to engage in excessive political patronage.

Democratic leaders responded warily. House speaker Liston Ramsey said after the election that he hoped to find "middle ground" on budget and tax issues. Bob Jordan warned that "it's one thing to cut taxes. It's another thing to decide what you are going to cut out when you cut taxes." Hunt, who was about to become a private citizen for the first time since 1972, offered the most specific comments, largely skeptical. "We're coming into a period where we're going to see if people are going to be responsible," he said of the incoming Martin administration. While he questioned whether or not cutting taxes would do much to boost the economy, Hunt also allowed that the state's revenue growth might allow for tax reduction "with the possibility that it would not hurt the schools, roads, and new industry." But he still championed "public investments," meaning government spending, as the main driver of economic growth.

While maintaining his distance from Martin on policy matters, Hunt sought to ensure that the transfer of power wasn't rocky. He tapped longtime aide Jane Patterson to work on the transition. Hunt met with Martin on several occasions. Although he had "admired [Martin] from afar" as a college professor and congressman, Hunt later said their personal conversations made him appreciate the value of having someone trained as a scientist in the office of governor. Science was "not just about theory—you have to prove that it works," Hunt observed. He was also impressed by Martin's immediate willingness to shoulder the responsibilities of the office. During their transition meetings, Hunt offered to take the hit for what promised to be an unpopular decision about a disposal site for low-level radioactive waste. "If you want me to go ahead and do it before you come in, I will," Hunt told Martin. The Republican declined the offer. "I'll handle that one," he said. For his part, Martin appreciated Hunt's insights on how to balance the demands of being governor with the duties to his wife and children. In particular, he followed Hunt's advice by keeping Sundays largely free from work appointments. The Martins even ended up at the same Raleigh church, White Memorial Presbyterian on Oberlin Road, that the Hunts had attended during their tenure in the capital city.

Despite public statements of mutual respect from Martin and Hunt, there were tensions. Shortly before leaving office, Hunt made more than 200 appointments to state boards and commissions, including new posts for former Democratic officeholders, liberal activists, Hunt's campaign manager, his personal secretary, and other office staff. While last-minute personnel moves by outgoing administrations were hardly novel, Martin and his aides were surprised by something else: the discovery a few weeks after taking office of a tap on the phone line coming into the governor's office in the Executive Mansion on Blount Street. The wire led to a house a couple of blocks away. Personnel from the State Bureau of Investigation and others agencies were never able to determine how long the tap had been in place or who had installed it. For all the Martin team knew, it could have been there for many years, without Hunt's knowledge or approval. But the unsolved mystery didn't exactly strengthen the level of trust between officials of the new Republican administration and their Democratic predecessors.

BUILDING A CABINET

Within days of the election, Joe Martin, Bob Bradshaw, Margaret King, and other members of the governor-elect's inner circle moved quickly to establish a 25-member transition staff at the Legislative Office Building. Its director was Phil Kirk, a former Republican legislator and Jim Broyhill aide who had served as a cabinet secretary and chief of staff to Governor Holshouser. The team also included Patric Dorsey, a New Bern Republican with close ties to the Congressional Club. She had just run unsuccessfully against longtime Democratic secretary of state Thad Eure. Her job during the transition was to plan Martin's January 5 inauguration and related events. Both Dorsey and Kirk would end up in the new governor's cabinet, Dorsey as secretary at the Department of Cultural Resources and Kirk heading the same department he'd led under Holshouser, Human Resources. The other top departmental jobs in the new Martin administration went to

- Jim Harrington, secretary of the Department of Transportation. A Cary developer, Harrington had served Holshouser, too, as head of Natural and Economic Resources. While Martin's initial focus on taxes and education kept Harrington out of the limelight, he later moved to center stage and proved to be one of the administration's most creative and energetic leaders, helping to fashion what became the Highway Trust Fund bill of 1989.
- Grace Rohrer, secretary of the Department of Administration, which encompassed a wide range of agencies and functions, including personnel and facility management. Another Holshouser veteran, Rohrer had played a key role in Republican politics in 1972 when state party chairman Frank Rouse decided to endorse Gardner over Holshouser in the gubernatorial primary. As the Republicans' vice chairman, Rohrer had stepped in after the controversy to run the party for the remainder of the cycle. A historian by training, she then served as head of the Department of Art, Culture, and History under Holshouser—the first woman ever in the cabinet of a North Carolina governor.
- Howard Haworth, secretary of the Department of Commerce. The chairman of Drexel Heritage Furniture Company in Morganton,

Haworth opted not to take a state salary as commerce secretary, just as the previous secretary under Governor Hunt had done. He soon retired from Drexel Heritage, where he had started as a sales trainee, to devote his full attention to his cabinet service, in which he proved an energetic and successful business recruiter. Haworth would later serve as Martin's appointed chairman of the state Board of Education, playing a key role strengthening local control and flexibility in education policy.

- Thomas Rhodes, secretary of the Department of Natural Resources and Community Development. A six-term veteran of the state House from Wilmington, Rhodes headed a sprawling department that supervised environmental regulation and the state park system, among other functions. The governor counted on Rhodes's legislative experience and knowledge to serve the administration in handling these issues, although Martin often kept his own counsel on scientific matters.

- Helen Powers, secretary of the Department of Revenue. A Democrat and former executive at NCNB and the Bank of Asheville, Powers had supported the Martin campaign and agreed with cutting intangibles and inventory taxes to encourage economic development. When the governor-elect approached her about joining his cabinet, Powers described it as a "bombshell" because she had "never aspired to political office." She was the first woman to head the department.

- Joe Dean, secretary of the Department of Crime Control and Public Safety. A former army officer and policeman, Dean had made his reputation as a federal prosecutor during the 1970s. He then worked as an attorney in private practice. Martin hired Dean in part because of the latter's good relationships with county sheriffs, district attorneys, and law-enforcement personnel across the state. Dean headed the department for nearly all of Martin's eight years in office before resigning to become the Republican nominee for attorney general in 1992.

- Aaron Johnson, secretary of the Department of Correction. A former Fayetteville city councilman and minister, Johnson was the only black member of the cabinet. His job proved one of the hardest in the administration, as a surge in the prison population strained capacity. The department had also long been rife with political patronage. As Johnson tried to root it out, he drew media attention, much of it unfavorable.

One of Martin's most important recruits was C. C. "Cliff" Cameron, the retired chairman of First Union National Bank in Charlotte, as executive assistant for budget and management—or the commonly used title, state budget director. For one thing, Cameron was one of North Carolina's best-known and most-respected business leaders, having just finished a term as chairman of the state's chamber of commerce, North Carolina Citizens for Business and Industry (NCCBI). For another, he was a Democrat, as was his chief deputy, Marvin Dorman. In fact, Cameron had served on the Advisory Budget Commission as a Hunt appointee. As for Dorman, he was keeping the same job, deputy budget director, he'd held in the Hunt administration. While both men were respected across the aisle, their appointments gave some Republicans pause. Cameron would be chiefly responsible for crafting the new administration's budget proposals, including tax cuts. The state's top elected Democrats, Bob Jordan and Liston Ramsey, praised the selection of Cameron and Dorman as ensuring a smooth transition from the old administration. That's precisely what concerned some GOP leaders and activists. They had worked to elect Martin as an agent of change, not continuity.

Cameron took the job as budget director with only nominal compensation, mostly in the form of rent for a Raleigh apartment. He had known Martin since the latter's days on the Mecklenburg commission and had supported his campaigns for Congress. Now, Cameron wanted to do his part to ensure that Martin succeeded as governor. But he also took the job out of a sense of duty to North Carolina. He believed the new governor's policy of tax cuts and fiscal restraint would boost the economy. Describing Hunt as a "populist-type governor," Cameron contrasted him with Martin, whom he described as "more business-oriented, supportive of business, very conservative in all phases."

The transition team made some progress in filling the next tier of state jobs as well, although it took several months for the administration to hire its full complement of deputy secretaries, assistant secretaries, and agency heads. Once again, many had previously served in the Holshouser administration. Others had experience working on Capitol Hill for Martin or other

Republican congressmen, or had been early supporters of Martin's gubernatorial campaign, such as Asheboro attorney Alan Pugh, who became a deputy secretary at the Department of Administration, and his brother Richard Pugh, who was appointed to the state Board of Transportation. Other notable hires were former aides to, or allies of, the Democrats whom Rufus Edmisten had defeated in the 1984 gubernatorial primary. For example, Eddie Knox's brother Charles, a Charlotte attorney, was tapped to chair Alcoholic Beverage Control. Elizabeth Drury, a lawyer who'd worked in the Knox campaign, volunteered for the Martin campaign. She joined the governor's staff. Monroe Waters, who helped run Knox's campaign in eastern North Carolina, became director of adult probation and parole at the Department of Correction. Arlene Pulley and Bill Franklin, who had worked for Jimmy Green, became Martin's director of citizen affairs and director of intergovernmental relations, respectively. Green himself joined the team as head of a new bipartisan Government Relations Advisory Council. Its purpose was to help push Martin's tax cuts and other policies through the heavily Democratic legislature. Green would remain a paid advisor to Martin for most of his administration.

When filling out his management ranks, Martin decided to expand on his predecessor's efforts to hire African-Americans. Hunt had sought to appoint at least one black assistant secretary of each department. Most of these appointees, however, had titles such as "assistant secretary for minority affairs." Martin saw the practice as a positive step but overly narrow. He resolved to maintain the goal, even if it meant retaining staff members who were registered Democrats, while expanding their portfolios beyond serving as ombudsmen or diversity officers. For example, Lew Myers, a Democrat, became the Department of Commerce's assistant secretary for small business. Another African-American, Henry McCoy, was promoted as an assistant secretary at the Department of Administration. (He would later change parties and serve in the North Carolina Senate as a Republican.)

A REDESIGNED OFFICE IN RELOCATED DIGS

In addition to assembling a cabinet, Martin and the transition team had some immediate decisions to make about how the governor's office would be staffed and managed. Two things were obvious from the start. First, Martin's

THREE PARTICIPANTS IN THE 1985 BLACKBERRY FARM SUMMIT: PENNSYLVANIA GOV-
ERNOR DICK THORNBURGH, GOVERNOR JIM MARTIN, AND TENNESSEE GOVERNOR
LAMAR ALEXANDER
OFFICIAL STATE PHOTO

core staff would include Jim Lofton, upon whom he had relied for his 12 years
on Capitol Hill, and key personnel from his gubernatorial campaign, including campaign manager Jack Hawke, communications director Karen Hayes,
scheduler Charlene Crews, and research director Charles Hughes. Dottie
Fuller, a longtime secretary for the congressman, would also remain at his side
in Raleigh. Second, Martin did not want a single chief of staff to control information flow and access to him. Also, as had been done during the Holshouser
administration, the governor's office would be moved from its traditional location in the State Capitol to the Administration Building, where Martin would
have enough room to work in proximity with all his key staff members. It was
also the site of what would become regular Thursday press conferences, held
weekly during legislative sessions and at least biweekly during the rest of his
tenure, during which Martin answered reporters' questions and advanced the
administration's key messages. Although Hunt had done something similar,
Martin's press conferences were more focused and part of a broader strategy,
including a statewide newspaper column and regular TV interviews with stations outside Raleigh, for leveraging his communication skills to offset the
institutional advantages of the legislature. "We're a Republican administration

facing an overwhelming Democratic majority," Hawke explained. "The success of our legislative package as well as our administrative actions depends on how the public perceives them."

Lofton became the governor's executive assistant and staff director. His wife, Sarah, became executive assistant to First Lady Dottie Martin. Hawke's formal title in the governor's office was special assistant for policy. In practice, he was Martin's top political aide, serving as a liaison to Republican activists, donors, and officeholders. Jim Trotter became the top lawyer in the office. Crews became director of project development. John Higgins, an experienced administrator recently retired from the United States Navy, became the governor's top advisor on state personnel issues. Higgins was actually a liberal Democrat, but Martin had come to know him personally—his son Jim Jr. was married to Higgins's daughter Patricia—and respected his judgment. Other aides in the governor's office included senior education advisor Lee Monroe, a former executive vice president of historically black Shaw University, and K-12 education advisor Gene Baker, a former school principal who had been the Republican candidate against state superintendent of public instruction Craig Phillips in 1984. Wilma Sherrill, a veteran of Congressman Billy Hendon's campaign who would later serve in the state House, handled job placements. I. Beverly Lake Jr., the former Democratic legislator who had won the Republican nomination for governor in 1980, became legislative liaison, assisted by attorney Bernie Harrell. Among the younger staffers in the office were two former Martin campaign workers, Art Pope and Thomas Stith, who would play far more significant roles in future Republican governments. Pope, a Duke law graduate, was hired as special counsel for state boards, commissions, and agencies. Stith, a graduate of North Carolina Central University, became minority affairs advisor.

Charlie Hughes and Karen Hayes continued their roles from the campaign, as directors of research and communications, respectively. Hayes then advised Martin in the search for a press secretary. They decided to offer the job to Tim Pittman, a former reporter at the Greensboro *News & Record* and the *Fayetteville Observer*. Although Pittman was not yet a Republican, he said yes to the job because Martin impressed him with his philosophical approach to government and detailed knowledge of policy issues. As for Paul Jones, Martin's longtime congressional press secretary, he ended up joining the administration elsewhere, as director of the Governor's Highway Safety Program. A former receptionist and case worker from Martin's congressional office, Lisa Keith, later joined Jones.

One of Martin's closest advisors, however, was never destined to stay in Raleigh. Although Joe Martin had played major roles in both the 1984 campaign and the transition—recruiting and supervising talent, drafting speeches and statements, and offering candid advice—he had always planned to return to Charlotte. While fiercely loyal to his older brother, Joe didn't share his partisan or philosophical leanings. And he wanted to return to his job as vice president of NCNB under his friend Hugh McColl. But Joe would continue to advise the governor on a regular basis, playing a key role in shaping his operational and personnel decisions. Together with Charlotte businessman and longtime state Board of Transportation member Seddon "Rusty" Goode, another of Jim's longtime confidants, Joe would also continue to help direct the governor's political action committee, which financed political trips and other partisan activities that could not properly be arranged and funded out of the governor's office in Raleigh.

Similarly, neither campaign strategist Brad Hays nor campaign chairman Bob Bradshaw had any interest in joining the administration or relocating to Raleigh. Hays remained in Charlotte, regularly advising the governor by phone as well as during regular trips to the capital. As for Bradshaw, he was Martin's choice to succeed David Flaherty as chairman of the North Carolina Republican Party. Flaherty had joined the administration as head of the Employment Security Commission. There was some initial pushback about the pick from Republican activists, who questioned Bradshaw's professional and personal relationships with top Democrats, including Lieutenant Governor Bob Jordan. But Bradshaw proved a popular choice. He had longstanding ties to both the western, Martin–Holshouser wing of the party and the eastern, Helms–Congressional Club wing. His presence helped tamp down tensions between the two factions, at least at first.

SETTING THE TONE FROM THE START

Inaugural festivities began on January 4 with a private event at the North Carolina Museum of Art. Some 300 dignitaries braved a cold rain to attend the late-afternoon affair. Then the group departed for North Carolina State University's Reynolds Coliseum, where 8,000 guests awaited at the Inaugural

Ball, a charity event sponsored by the Junior League of Raleigh. The bipartisan crowd danced to music from the North Carolina School of the Arts Jazz Ensemble and thrilled to performances by the North Carolina Theatre, folk singer Mike Cross, and the North Carolina Symphony, which played the "Sleeping Beauty Waltz" for Jim and Dottie Martin's first dance.

The orchestra in which the governor-elect had once played, the Charlotte Symphony, performed the following day at his swearing-in ceremony. The frigid Inauguration Day began with a prayer breakfast honoring the newly elected governor and lieutenant governor. Martin told the audience that "we must pray as if it is entirely up to the Lord, which it is, and then work as if it's entirely up to us, which it is!"

Martin, Jordan, and other elected officials then proceeded to the swearing-in ceremony in front of the Archives and History Building. The new governor's 18-minute inauguration address was carefully crafted to restate the major themes of his successful campaign while also calling for bipartisanship and respectful dialogue. "North Carolina has prospered through a blend of rivalry and unity," he began, referring to sectional divides, political debates, and competition among businesses and sports teams. "Yet we have reached our greatest achievements when called to a unity of purpose." During his administration, Martin said, that common purpose would be economic development. "I believe deeply in our system of private enterprise, based on traditional principles of self-reliance," he said. "I believe the most powerful economic force for maximizing the greatest good for the greatest number is the art of investing one's own resources, at the risk of losing it all, in the hope of realizing a profitable return and thereby creating jobs for others." To promote enterprise and growth, Martin recommended "strategic tax reforms to remove unique taxes that impose a competitive disadvantage on North Carolina businesses and workers," as well as improved education, including "better pay for better teachers." In his conclusion, he quoted a sermon his late father, Arthur Martin, had given at a family reunion decades before. "Our future grows out of our past," the Reverend Martin had said. His son then observed that, "with its problems, its opportunities, and its challengers, the future calls us together."

The festivities didn't end at the inaugural ceremony. That evening, the Martins attended a large party at the Raleigh Civic Center, where the governor encountered the Smoky Mountain British Brass Band and stopped to do a bit of conducting.

The next day, a Sunday, Martin and his family went to church at Raleigh's First Presbyterian. During the service, its 60-member choir performed some of Martin's own arrangements, including a benediction from the book of Jude he had set to music for his father's funeral. Later in the day, the Martins held a public reception at what would become their new home, the Executive Mansion. Some 4,500 people made their way through the residence over the course of the afternoon and early evening.

As it turned out, the first couple wasn't able to occupy the mansion for the first six weeks because it was being repainted. Their younger son, Ben, was the first family member to spend the night there—or at least to try to. Ben and a friend asked to sleep among the draped furniture and half-painted walls. It must have seemed a great adventure to the two seventh-graders. But it turned out to be creepier than they thought. A few hours later, the boys sheepishly returned to the Martins' temporary quarters across the street.

When the family members finally moved in, they found the historic building bearing a new coat of paint but still in great need of repairs and updates. Dottie threw herself enthusiastically into the task, with Jim helping her solicit donations from North Carolina's many furniture and home-furnishings companies for both the mansion and the Administration Building, where the governor and his key aides would be based. Dottie also went out of her way to decorate the mansion as a showplace for all the state's governors, rather than simply a home for the Martin family. For example, she learned of a formal portrait of former Democratic governor Dan K. Moore's wife, Jeanelle. Dottie had it brought out of the state archives, cleaned up, and displayed prominently in the mansion. She even invited the Moore family to view the unveiling of the portrait and served them cookies made from Jeanelle's own recipe, published decades earlier when she had been first lady.

Both Martins made good first impressions in what was still a Democratic town. The governor's inauguration speech, for example, drew praise from prominent Democrats such as state treasurer Harlan Boyles and state superintendent of public instruction Craig Phillips. But as his successor was about to take the oath of office, Jim Hunt couldn't resist confiding his concerns about Martin's policy ideas to a newspaper reporter. "I think the legislature is going to move forward for strong economic growth, for improved education and for training our people," Hunt said. "The question is, are we going to stay committed to the progress in education or are we going to drop back?" Jack Hawke had a ready response. "If there's too much partisan attempt to hinder what the governor's going to do, it's going to backfire and people will resent it," since "they voted for what Jim Martin wants to do," he said.

STATE DEMOCRATS SEEK TO REGROUP

As if its electoral losses in 1984 weren't bad enough, the North Carolina Democratic Party suffered another black eye in late January when Republican Larry Etheridge of Wilson, running on Martin's tax-cut message, won a special election to a North Carolina House seat.

Democrats quickly sought to recover their footing and rebuild their brand. Some leaders argued that the party needed to strike a balance between cooperating with Martin on some issues while challenging him on others. Most Democratic activists, however, were more inclined to an aggressive approach. Prominent Raleigh defense attorney Wade Smith became the new chairman of the party. Raleigh attorney Ed Turlington became executive director. John Bennett, the son of Jim Hunt's political patron, Bert Bennett, became the party's full-time fundraising consultant. The party also hired its first "youth coordinator," Harry Kaplan.

Together with Lieutenant Governor Bob Jordan, they launched a "Democrats Forward" task force that commissioned polls, held focus groups, and convened public meetings across the state. The state party also helped the Democratic leaders of the legislature sharpen their communication skills and set up a Democratic Legislative Campaign Committee to begin raising money for the next election. Their efforts drew notice from the Democratic Leadership Council, a new national association of party activists and politicians that counseled moderation as an effective response to Republican gains. DLC leaders and rising Democratic stars such as Representative Richard Gephardt of Missouri, Senator Sam Nunn of Georgia, Senator Joe Biden of Delaware, and Governor Chuck Robb of Virginia trekked to North Carolina to offer ideas and compare notes.

Republicans had their own aspirations for 1985, hoping to build on their momentum while preparing for what history suggested might be a tougher election cycle in 1986. They knew that the parties of reelected presidents typically lost ground in their final midterms, a phenomenon called the "six-year itch." To buck this trend, the state GOP embarked on several initiatives. One was the immediate recruitment of legislative candidates for targeted races. "Our number one goal is to maintain what we've got" in the General Assembly, explained Representative Harold Brubaker of Asheboro, who a decade later would become North Carolina's first Republican House speaker in modern times. "Our number two goal is to add something to it." Another initiative was Operation Switch, a publicity campaign and advertising blitz designed to recruit Democratic politicians, civic leaders, and average voters with conservative views to join the Republican Party. Its leader in North Carolina was J. T. Knott, a former Democratic county commissioner in Wake County. Democratic commissioners and mayors in several other communities joined Knott in publicly changing their registrations.

The state's most prominent party-switcher, however, was former gubernatorial candidate Eddie Knox, who made his journey to the Republican Party official on May 30. Thousands of Democrats statewide followed suit. By the end of 1985, the share of North Carolina voters registered Republican had risen by more than a percentage point. The process continued throughout Martin's tenure as governor. The Republican share of North Carolina's registered voters reached 32 percent in 1992, up from 26 percent in 1984. During the previous eight years, from 1976 to 1984, the GOP share had risen only 2 points. (After 1992, the trend trailed off. Indeed, registered Republicans still make up slightly less than a third of the state's electorate, while the Democratic share has fallen dramatically, voters registering as unaffiliated making up the fastest-growing group.)

THE TAX BATTLE BEGINS

North Carolina's new Republican governor was clearly committed to following through on his policy agenda. It was just as clear that the Democratic leaders of the General Assembly would resist it. For example, they telegraphed that they would propose tax plans of their own, structured quite differently. House speaker Liston Ramsey floated the idea of slashing the lowest income-tax rate. Lieutenant Governor Bob Jordan advocated tax relief aimed at low-income households, such as ending intangibles taxes for checking accounts and CDs but not stocks and bonds. "You would be helping people who need it the most," he said. Another powerful lawmaker, Senator Ken Royall of Durham, introduced two tax bills early in the 1985 session. One would repeal the state's inheritance tax. Representative Billy Watkins, a top lieutenant to Ramsey who filed an identical bill in the House, called the inheritance tax "truly double-taxation" and "the most burdensome, most detested tax in the state." Senator Royall's other revenue bill would raise the state sales tax by half a percent to fund local school construction, while partially offsetting the effects by giving income-tax credits to low-income North Carolinians and ditching the intangibles tax on bank accounts. Other Democratic bills filed in the first days of the session offered different versions of the same tax swap, while Representatives Joe Mavretic of Tarboro and Dan Blue of Raleigh—both future speakers of the House—introduced separate bills to reduce or eliminate the sales tax on food.

As he prepared to make his debut on the state legislative stage, Martin reaffirmed his priority: reducing taxes on business inventories, investments, and food. He also announced the creation of the Governor's Efficiency Study Commission, a panel of business leaders and management experts charged with scouring the state budget for savings to transfer to other fiscal priorities, including tax relief. Retired NCNB chairman Tom Storrs served as chairman and Raleigh businessman Greg Poole as vice chairman. Meanwhile, Martin tried to allay the concerns of cities and counties that they would lose revenues from a repeal of local inventory and intangibles taxes. But he ruled out an idea some Democratic lawmakers had proposed for replacing the revenue stream to localities: instituting a state-run lottery. Martin called it "a tax on the weak" that "bleeds money from a lot of people who need it." As for his own tax policies, Martin argued that their benefits wouldn't be limited to those who paid inventory or intangibles taxes because "people who are unemployed have low income by virtue of the fact that they don't have a job." Making the state's tax climate for business more attractive would "build a stronger economic base in their part of the state," resulting in higher employment and wages. Martin made the same case to a chamber of commerce meeting shortly before the start of the legislative session. "I don't mean to preach to the choir," he told the assembled business leaders, "but I've found that choirs need to hum together once in a while and find out where the downbeat is."

When Martin gave his first State of the State address to the General Assembly on February 28, however, his choir—the 50 Republican lawmakers—made up less than 30 percent of the audience. His task was to convince Democrats to support a new Republican governor's proposals, including his signature plan to phase out taxes on food, intangibles, and business inventories (in the latter case by using state income-tax credits to offset business property taxes paid to localities). The package had a projected fiscal impact of $328 million over the first two years, reaching nearly $500 million a year when fully implemented (the equivalent of $1.1 billion in 2015 dollars). Martin reminded Democratic lawmakers that many of them had previously expressed an interest in reducing or eliminating these taxes. He expressed "a sincere commitment to work honorably and cooperatively with you" while respecting "your jurisdiction and prerogatives." His proposals were bold, but Martin presented them as endorsed by the voters in 1984 and as consistent with continued improvement in education and other public services. Beyond his fiscal agenda, the governor used his State of the State address to advance a broader message of reform. He called for openness in government and a gubernatorial veto. The latter was a cause he hadn't advocated during the 1984 campaign but had already come to believe was a necessary check on the institutional power of the General Assembly.

DIFFERENCES ON EDUCATION

The tax debate between state Democrats and Republicans occurred within a broader context partially determined by second-term initiatives from former governor Hunt. One of them was the Basic Education Program (BEP). It created a new curriculum, minimum standards for teaching time and student promotion, a funding floor that gave more resources to poor districts, and thousands of new staff positions to reduce class sizes, offer new courses, and provide more non-teaching personnel such as counselors and support staff. Students who failed to reach the 25th percentile on state tests or supplemental local tests would be required to attend summer remedial classes or repeat their grade. The program was intended to increase education spending by about 32 percent over eight years, reaching $670 million in annual impact by 1992–93.

Martin endorsed many of the principles of the BEP. But he expressed caution about the size, scope, and cost of the program as originally proposed. Martin argued that it was overly prescriptive, limiting the flexibility of local districts and putting too much money into non-teaching positions and services outside the academic core. He acted on these beliefs in his first budget plan by proposing $185 million—about half of what Hunt had recommended—to begin implementing the BEP and other education initiatives over the 1985–86 and 1986–87 fiscal years. While adding non-teaching positions to public schools might be worthwhile at some point, he said, "I don't think it outranks the desirability of a tax cut." Craig Phillips blasted Martin's position on the BEP, describing it as "take care of the classroom and to hell with all the rest."

Martin also argued for gradualism on another education initiative, the Career Ladder program. Based on four classroom evaluations per year, teachers were eligible for an initial 5 percent pay bump for a basic performance rating and then a 10 percent bump for a higher rating the second year. During its 1984 session, the General Assembly had authorized Career Ladder pilots in 16 school districts for the 1985–86 school year and then a statewide expansion in 1986–87. Ever since his days on the Mecklenburg commission, Martin had touted the idea of paying teachers in part on the basis of performance, rather than just seniority or credentials. While highly supportive of the Career Ladder initiative, he suggested at a meeting of the North Carolina School Boards Association that the testing period be extended at least another year before considering whether or not to expand the program statewide. "It would be a serious mistake to impose on ourselves a schedule that would put a plan in place before we can be sure that it would work," he told the assembled superintendents and school-board members. They welcomed his announcement. But Martin still believed strongly in performance pay, a position that put him at odds with much of the education establishment, especially the North Carolina Association of Educators, the state affiliate of the nation's largest teachers' union, the National Education Association.

He also differed with the education establishment on another of its emerging priorities: state involvement in preschool programs. Superintendent Phillips and some Democratic lawmakers wanted to create new programs serving three- and four-year-olds. As early as the mid-1960s, Martin had supported the addition of kindergartens as a means of getting children ready to learn reading and other fundamental skills by the end of first grade. But when it came to further expansion of the state's early-childhood efforts, he urged a focus on the disadvantaged, whose challenging home environments put them at serious risk of academic failure. He also preferred that the sector remain mostly private. "It is not only not a priority of mine to provide for day care statewide at state expense on state property for three- and four-year-olds," Martin explained, "but it is something that I do not support."

THE EXECUTIVE VERSUS
THE LEGISLATURE

Democratic resistance to the new Martin administration was hardly limited to philosophical disagreements about taxes and education. Ramsey, Jordan, and other leaders of the party were also committed to preserving and even expanding the Democratic-controlled legislature's prerogatives while seeking to constrain the new Republican governor's powers and prospects. For example, Hunt and previous governors had staffed departments and agencies with personal loyalists and Democratic activists. While Martin had campaigned against the misuse of political patronage, he always reserved the right to replace key staffers—such as deputy secretaries, directors, managers, and others who made or carried out major public policies—with individuals who shared the new administration's views. As the governor and his cabinet secretaries began making these personnel changes, however, Democrats cried foul. Legislative leaders threatened to eliminate state funding for positions left vacant at the end of the Hunt administration. Some even proposed moving programs and agencies from the control of Martin's cabinet to Democratic-run departments such as Justice, Agriculture, Labor, and the courts. Representative Peggy Stamey, a Wake County Democrat, filed legislation to limit the governor's ability to designate state employees as "exempt" from the State Personnel Act, and thus subject to employment at will. Perhaps not coincidentally, her husband had lost his job as assistant commissioner of the Division of Motor Vehicles when Martin took office.

Some of the Democrats replaced by Republican appointees chose not to go quietly. Larry Wheeler, deputy secretary at Cultural Resources, alleged as he left that under Patric Dorsey the department's programs were being "given a religious focus," and that Dorsey disliked avant-garde art. In March, state prison director Rae McNamara chose a legislative hearing as the setting for resigning in protest after the administration replaced several other correction officials. Martin explained that the department had been "highly politicized" in the past, with officials pressuring subordinates to give money to Democratic candidates. "Of course there is a right" to contribute voluntarily to campaigns, he said, "but there's no right to compel others to do so." In a similar incident, the governor terminated the employment of DMV official J. G. Wilson Jr., who had sent a fundraising letter for the Edmisten campaign to hundreds of his employees. "I don't feel that I did anything wrong," Wilson insisted.

Democratic leaders repeatedly attacked Martin on the issue. Few were mollified by the governor's decision to place or retain Democrats in state agencies such as the Board of Education, his issuance of an executive order that nearly halved the number of exempt positions, or his observation that fewer than 1 percent of state employees had been replaced during the transition. At the same time, to the extent Martin tried to signal bipartisanship by putting Democrats in his administration, his actions drew criticism from Republicans long shut out of power and job opportunities in state government. Representative Ray Warren, an outspoken GOP member from Mecklenburg County, complained that "Gov. Martin seems to be appointing the same kind of people [Jim] Hunt would have appointed. We didn't work that hard [in the campaign] for that to happen."

Democrats contested not just who should staff departments but also how much power the executive branch should have. Early in the 1985 session, Representative Billy Watkins filed a bill to amend the state's Administrative Procedures Act to use administrative-law judges appointed by the General Assembly, not the governor, to adjudicate regulatory disputes. Another House bill, filed by up-and-coming Lee County representative Dennis Wicker, also drew significant attention. It called for a referendum on a constitutional amendment to repeal gubernatorial succession. Just eight years earlier, lawmakers friendly to Hunt had approved a referendum to allow him to run for a second term in 1980. Now, the sentiment on Jones Street had changed. By early March, Wicker's bill to hold a repeal referendum in 1986 had already passed the House by a 102–15 margin. A few weeks later, it passed the Senate by 38–12. If enacted, the amendment would not have prohibited Martin from running for reelection in 1988. But it would have kept any future governor—whom some Democrats feared might also be Republican—from serving two terms. Separately, the legislature approved other measures designed to rein in Martin, including limits on the governor's control over the state Board of Elections.

With the General Assembly attempting to limit the new governor's influence at every turn, it came as no surprise that lawmakers gave a cool greeting to Martin's call for a gubernatorial veto. An initial version, filed by Republican senator Wendell Sawyer of Guilford County, would have authorized a referendum to give governors a veto that could be overridden by a two-thirds vote of the legislature. Despite support from editorial boards, civic groups, and all five previous governors (four Democrats and one Republican), the idea quickly lost steam. A Senate committee killed the bill in a voice vote on March 28. House Republicans then filed their own bill, which softened the override requirement to a three-fifths vote. It fared little better.

The legislature's assault on executive power drew criticism from prominent opinion leaders and Democrats outside the General Assembly, including a group called the Committee on Constitutional Integrity, which counted former senator Sam Ervin among its leaders. While many Democrats expressed their concerns in philosophical terms, others were worried that even if their party regained the governorship in 1988, the powers of the office would be permanently weakened in the meantime. The man seen as most likely to pay that price, Lieutenant Governor Bob Jordan, reached the same conclusion. He decided to kill two House bills limiting Martin's appointment power over Council of State and judicial offices. But he endorsed or allowed to pass other encroachments on gubernatorial authority, including a version of Watkins's rewrite of the Administrative Procedures Act.

Although Martin lacked the formal power to defend himself against many of these measures, he did win one high-profile skirmish with the Democrats. It concerned his personal security. Previous governors had relied primarily on agents from the State Bureau of Investigation. Given the proximity of the security detail to the governor and his key aides, however, Martin thought it awkward for the detail to consist of SBI agents answerable to Democratic attorney general Lacy Thornburg and SBI director Robert Morgan, a former United States senator. The discovery shortly after the Martins moved into the Executive Mansion that one of the phone lines had been bugged did nothing to allay the governor's concerns. He preferred to rely on Highway Patrol troopers, who answered to his own secretary of crime control, Joe Dean. While Thornburg voiced no objection to the shift, Democrats in the legislature blasted it.

FIGHTING FOR HIS AGENDA

From the start, Martin and his team knew they'd have to take their case for tax cuts and other policies over the heads of Democratic lawmakers to influential interest groups and the general public. The board and staff of NCCBI, the state's chamber of commerce, largely consisted of Democrats. But they readily endorsed the governor's call for repealing inventory and intangibles taxes. When it came to the foundations of sustained economic growth, NCCBI president Ivie Clayton observed, "the thing missing in North Carolina is capital. Headquarters [of companies] don't come here because we tax capital." The organization pointed out that while the state had enjoyed industrial expansion, it didn't fare as well in business starts—even in the much-vaunted Research Triangle Park, which lagged similar employment centers in Massachusetts, California, and Texas in attracting venture capital to new enterprises in part because those states didn't tax investment as heavily. The case for repeal went beyond business concerns, however. "We get plenty of retirees in North Carolina, but we don't get any rich ones because when you combine our intangibles tax and income tax, they are taxed at 12 percent," Clayton said. "That's kind of sadistic." Other business groups and corporate executives took up the call as well. For example, textile giant Burlington Industries disclosed that it had recently built a distribution center in Virginia to avoid North Carolina's inventory tax.

In mid-March, Martin launched a statewide public-information campaign for his tax plan with press conferences in Raleigh, Charlotte, High Point, Fayetteville, Greenville, and Asheville. His Charlotte-based PAC followed up with mass mailings and radio spots, while Martin devoted the first of his new series of newspaper columns to extolling the potential benefits for workers in the form of more jobs and higher wages. The Republican National Committee weighed in with radio ads of its own featuring GOP legislators touting the benefits of Martin's proposed tax cuts and state budget. While the governor and his supporters made the public case for reform, they held back from introducing their tax plan as legislation, hoping to attract Democratic cosponsors for the bill. They waited in vain. None stepped forward. Thus, it wasn't until early April that companion bills from Minority Leaders William Redman in the Senate and Betsy Cochrane in the House put the Martin tax plan formally on the table.

It quickly became evident why Democrats had spurned invitations to cosponsor Martin's bill. Behind the scenes, legislative leaders were working on a tax bill of their own, which debuted on April 16. It packaged elements from a variety of Democratic ideas, including Liston Ramsey's proposed cut in the state's lowest income-tax rate, Billy Watkins's proposed repeal of the inheritance tax, Ken Royall's proposed elimination of intangibles tax on bank accounts, and Dan Blue's proposed elimination of sales tax on items purchased with food stamps. There was also a small reduction in the inventory tax. In total, the final version of the bill offered $147 million in tax relief by the second fiscal year of the budget biennium, 1986–87, or a little more than half the $258 million called for in Martin's plan. By the fourth year, 1988–89, the annual fiscal impact of the House bill was $219 million, versus Martin's $489 million. "We have accepted the governor's premise that there should be tax relief," said Representative George Miller, whose House Finance Subcommittee had worked out the sprawling package.

Two days later, on April 18, the bill went to the House floor. The drama heightened when Martin entered the gallery, something governors rarely did. Accompanied by Dottie, Martin had come to the Legislative Building to speak at a public hearing in favor of a gubernatorial veto. He decided to watch the debate on the House tax bill. After repeated Republican amendments to insert Martin's tax cuts were defeated on party-line votes, the bill passed with unanimous support. Republicans couldn't afford to vote against what was still a significant reduction in North Carolina's taxes. They hoped their more-ambitious approach would fare better in the Senate.

Initially, they had reason to be optimistic. Leading Senate Democrats had expressed disappointment about the House tax bill, particularly the small size of its tax cut on business inventories. They had also promised to give Martin's plan more serious consideration in committee. But as April passed to May, Republican optimism faded. Rather than endorse a full phase-out of the inventory tax, the Senate Finance Committee embraced the idea of marrying a partial statewide tax cut with a constitutional amendment to allow localities to ditch the remaining inventory tax if they wished.

As Senate leaders huddled to craft their own tax package, Martin met with Jordan and personally lobbied Democratic senators to think bigger. He told them that even if they didn't phase out taxes on inventories and food, he would still be willing to endorse their plan if it repealed taxes on intangibles. His budget director, Cliff Cameron, explained that when it came to alleviating the tax burden on investment, repealing the intangibles tax "will do a lot more good for North Carolina" than the House bill's elimination of the inheritance tax, given that the former would affect far more taxpayers.

On May 13, the American Legislative Exchange Council, a nationwide association of conservative state lawmakers, held a meeting in Raleigh. Both

Martin and Jordan addressed the gathering, which attracted a number of Democratic and Republican lawmakers. The governor said he would "continue to build alliances" to get a deal on tax cuts. Jordan later told reporters that he was "hopeful that we can work out a compromise to fund Democratic programs" while also cutting taxes.

Over the next two weeks, whatever sentiment there was in the Senate to outbid the House and come closer to Martin's original marker on tax reduction began to evaporate. For one thing, Democratic leaders in both chambers came to believe it would be politically unwise to give the new Republican governor a victory. But members also got nervous about tax collections. Preliminary estimates by the General Assembly's fiscal staff suggested that revenue growth over the coming 1985–87 budget biennium might not be as strong as previously forecast.

On June 4, Senate leaders unveiled a scaled-down plan. In dollar amount, it differed only modestly from the House bill: $167 million in the first full fiscal year of implementation, 1986–87 (the House had offered $147 million) and $223 million by 1988–89 (the House figure was $219 million). But the Senate came Martin's way a bit on the details, including larger cuts in inventory and intangibles taxes. Although disappointed with the Senate version, the governor endorsed it during the subsequent negotiations. Legislative lobbyist Bev Lake said it "improves substantially on the House package."

After some delay, House and Senate negotiators began working on a compromise tax bill in late June. At their first meeting, the legislature's fiscal aides once again sounded a warning about weakening economic growth, which they feared would crimp revenue collections. The governor's budget office sharply dissented. Martin alleged that top Democrats were artificially deflating the revenue forecasts in order to justify smaller tax cuts. "They've been throwing up these smoke screens all year," he said. "They want to be able to spend more money." Martin pointed out that despite a $640 million budget surplus in 1984, lawmakers had declined to cut taxes that year. "They spent every nickel of it," he argued. "They want to do the same thing this year. They haven't gotten the message yet." At the same time, however, Democratic leaders charged that it was Martin who was politicizing the tax dispute, rather than crafting sound policy. They pointed to comments by Cliff Cameron about the perilous condition of the Highway Fund, which had far more road projects in the queue than dedicated revenues from gas taxes and other fees. Even as the Martin administration argued for larger General Fund tax cuts, Cameron had allowed that "I think it's inevitable we're going to have to increase gasoline taxes." Because the state was then transferring some General Fund dollars into the ailing Highway Fund, Democrats contended they were being put in a political box—that either they'd be attacked in the next election for failing to cut business and sales taxes or they'd be blamed for higher gas taxes if the fiscal pressure of large General Fund tax cuts resulted in fewer transfers to the Highway Fund.

The Martin administration dismissed the charge that it was playing politics. In fact, the governor had never taken a general no-tax pledge. He had from the start held open the possibility that the users of North Carolina's highways might have to pay more, in gas or car taxes, in response to the squeeze placed on the system by escalating travel demands on the one hand and increasing fuel efficiency on the other (which had the effect of reducing revenue collected per mile traveled).

Martin had also not ruled out an idea some Democrats advocated: letting local governments raise sales taxes to fund school construction. Assuming a binary choice between higher property taxes and higher sales taxes, Martin had since his county-commission days viewed the latter option as less burdensome on the economy. His case for his 1985 tax-cut package was that the inventory and intangibles taxes were themselves highly burdensome on the economy, while cutting the sales tax on food and drugs would extend the immediate benefits of tax reduction to low-income families.

Still, while Martin and other Republicans believed in the merits of their position, they repeatedly forecast dire political consequences for the Democrats if the legislature failed to enact significant General Fund tax relief. To underline the point, Martin did a barnstorming tour of the state on July 2, holding press conferences in each media market. "Every indication is that the people of North Carolina are with me" on tax cuts, the governor said. "They are backing me on this. They are not backing that little, small band of leaders, mostly in the House, who are trying to scuttle it."

Even as Martin's plane jumped from airport to airport however, Democratic leaders were striking a new deal. "Whether he flies around the state, sits in his mansion, or sits in his office, we're going to do what we think best for the state of North Carolina," House Appropriations Committee chairman Billy Watkins said defiantly.

The legislative deal essentially split the differences between the two chambers on inventory and intangibles taxes while retaining a number of smaller tax cuts, including a spousal exemption from inheritance taxes. The final package was even smaller in fiscal impact than the earlier House and Senate bills: $123 million in 1986–87 and $170 million in 1988–89. That worked out to roughly half what Martin had sought by the second year and only one-third of the governor's target by the fourth year.

WIN, LOSE, OR DRAW?

Did Jim Martin win or lose the biggest political battle of his first year in office, the tussle about taxes? A case could be made either way.

Despite his best efforts, the 1985 tax bill was closer to what the House wanted, and much smaller in magnitude—3 percent of the General Fund when fully implemented—than he wanted. Democrats had rejected his private prodding for larger cuts and spurned his public pronouncements about the political consequences. They were still firmly in control of the General Assembly and hoped to make sizable gains in the next election. "I was rebuffed right from the start" by the Democrats, who had "been in majority power for so long that they didn't know how to behave," Martin later reflected.

As for Republican legislators, many privately grumbled they had not been adequately consulted or effectively deployed by a still-green Martin administration. The frustration wasn't limited to the tax debate. Republicans were disappointed with other legislative outcomes, too. A budget provision that Martin, most Republicans, and some conservative Democrats had supported to slash spending on abortions didn't make it into the budget bill, for example, although the abortion fund did shrink and women were disallowed from using it more than once a year. The governor's attempt to reshape the Basic Education Program to focus more on core teaching staff and academic subjects didn't come to much either. The two-year budget devoted more than $200 million to the BEP, its elements only modestly changed from the original proposal. Overall, the state budget enacted by the Democratic legislature authorized a 13 percent increase in General Fund spending for the 1985–86 fiscal year, far more than Martin had recommended and more than three times the combined rates of inflation (2.7 percent) and population growth (1.3 percent).

Another of the governor's airport-to-airport publicity blitzes, this one advocating veto power, had also failed to put sufficient pressure on House

Democrats. They nixed a veto bill in late April. In fact, they brushed aside most of the governor's objections and weakened the power of his office. In addition to using a rewritten Administrative Procedures Act to limit his regulatory authority, state lawmakers curtailed Martin's ability to transfer and manage state funds within budget codes, weakened his influence over state licensing and governance panels, limited the administration's ability to hire private counsel rather than having to rely on Democratic attorney general Lacy Thornburg, and restricted the number of exempt positions Martin could fill with Republicans or friendly Democrats. Another legislative assault on his turf was the creation of a new panel, the North Carolina Commission on Jobs and the Economy, to devise an economic-development strategy in competition with the Department of Commerce. It reported to Bob Jordan, not Martin, and its executive director was Billy Ray Hall, a Hunt administration veteran. Then, at the tail end of the 1985 session, Democrats slipped through perhaps their most brazen attempt to deal the governor and his Republican Party a body blow. They authorized a May 1986 referendum to move all of North Carolina's state and local elections to odd-numbered years—an attempt to insulate state Democrats from the consequences of being on general-election ballots with liberal Democratic presidential candidates such as Walter Mondale. This referendum would be followed by another in November 1986 on reinstating a one-term limit for governors.

Despite these missed opportunities and setbacks, a case could also be made that Jim Martin had done better than expected in his first year as a Republican governor in a Democratic capital. During the 1984 campaign, he had made big tax cuts the centerpiece of his message. His decisive victory on Election Day proved to have real consequences. During previous sessions, Democrats had talked about alleviating the tax burden on investment and job creation but done little. In 1985, they enacted one of the largest state tax cuts in the country—as well as the single largest tax cut in North Carolina history to that time. Martin took, and deserved, much of the credit for this outcome, even though he had pressed for more. "It's a start," he told reporters. "We'll go on from there."

Indeed, Martin had reason to believe he was framing the tax issue well for future action. As the 1985 session wound down, he ramped up criticism of the pork-barrel accounts that leaders used to reward loyal lawmakers, discipline wayward ones, and protect Democrats in competitive districts. Martin's budget office insisted that lawmakers not deliver pork-barrel checks and sent questionnaires to hundreds of recipient organizations asking for details about what they did and how they planned to spend their subsidies. Jim Trotter even announced the administration might challenge the constitutionality of some grants. Democratic lawmakers and staffers were livid. But they couldn't afford to raise a ruckus about defending their pork-barrel spending, not after citing budget constraints to justify adopting smaller tax cuts than Martin had sought.

Similarly, while the governor had not gotten his way on reshaping the BEP or enacting veto power, his public comments and campaign-style tactics elevated both issues and articulated clear messages that future Republican candidates and lawmakers could use to their advantage. In fact, both of these causes championed by Martin would eventually be successful—the first in 1989, when the General Assembly decentralized education funding with Senate Bill 2, and the second in 1996, when a Republican-led House and a Democratic Senate finally approved a constitutional amendment to give North Carolina's governor a veto.

As for encroachments on the power of the governor, the Martin administration saw the 1985 session as only the beginning of what promised to be a lengthy struggle. "The one essential, unmistakable characteristic of the North Carolina General Assembly is an incredible concentration of power," Martin told reporters after the session concluded. "Of the 170 legislators, six or so . . . hold the power and decide who can do what, especially in the House. On most major issues, the other 164 might just as well stay home." In the coming years, the governor would return to this theme repeatedly, steadily gaining support even among Democrats for the idea of reforming and decentralizing power in the General Assembly.

Martin's strategy of taking his case for reform directly to the people was heavily influenced by his experience in Washington. As a House member, he had watched President Carter flail helplessly despite having strong Democratic majorities in Congress. Then he watched President Reagan achieve significant legislative success by using the bully pulpit to forge bipartisan coalitions, despite the resistance of Capitol Hill leaders such as Tip O'Neill. Martin consciously emulated Reagan—even to the point of calling House speaker Liston Ramsey "Tip" in his stump speeches, seemingly by accident, and then correcting himself in what proved to be a guaranteed laugh line. When it came to cultivating public opinion, the strategy worked well. In a *Charlotte Observer*

poll taken near the end of the 1985 legislative session, 64 percent of North Carolinians said they had a favorable impression of Martin and 54 percent said he was doing an excellent or good job. The Democratic-run legislature fared far worse, with 31 percent rating its performance excellent or good and 52 percent rating it fair or poor. Solid majorities supported Martin's positions on a gubernatorial veto and other issues.

When it came to advancing his ideas and delivering on his campaign promises, the governor believed he had made real progress in his first year and that fundamental change in Raleigh could happen only over time. Nevertheless, he and his closest advisors concluded that they needed more legislative wins to strengthen the governor's position for reelection in 1988. One experienced hand in Republican circles, former Holshouser confidant Gene Anderson, agreed wholeheartedly. "They have two ball games going on at once—the political ball game and the governmental ball game," Anderson said of the Martin administration. "They have the political ball game in order. Where they have a problem is in the governmental ball game."

Martin agreed. To win more games in the 1986 and 1987 seasons, his team needed a shake-up.

CHAPTER NINE

FINDING A FORMULA FOR SUCCESS

About a month after the North Carolina General Assembly wrapped up its 1985 session on July 18, Governor Jim Martin and 25 of his top aides left the capital city for the Pine Needles Lodge and Country Club in Southern Pines. It wasn't a vacation. It was a working retreat, much like the gathering of Republican reformers and strategists Martin had attended a few weeks earlier at Blackberry Farm in the Tennessee mountains.

At the Blackberry meeting in July, the topic had been how to translate the GOP's national successes into enduring Republican gains down the ballot. At the Pine Needles retreat in August, Martin and his cabinet secretaries, agency heads, and personal staff had a more immediate goal: achieving greater success in the state legislature.

The problem wasn't just the obvious partisan gap between a Republican governor and a Democratic General Assembly. During the 1984 campaign, Martin had focused on a few big issues, including tax cuts to create jobs and merit pay to encourage excellent teaching. He'd largely stuck to his campaign priorities during his first year in office. Now, the administration needed to develop and promote a broader agenda of reform—not only because the state needed it but also because it would strengthen Martin's position. Introducing more initiatives in more areas would give him opportunities to build alliances with rank-and-file lawmakers, making it harder for Democratic leaders to keep their caucuses whipped into constant opposition. And with more ideas on the table, Martin would have more ways to negotiate deals to advance his main priorities, including further tax relief.

In truth, it would have been impossible for the Martin administration to propose and advance a broader agenda during its first year. The timing precluded it. Well into the 1985 legislative session, cabinet secretaries were still staffing up and learning their way around. Staffers in the governor's office had also been climbing a steep learning curve. Some lacked experience in state government. Others weren't sure at first where their responsibilities and authority stopped. As for Martin himself, it took time to recognize that a management approach appropriate to a congressional office might not serve him well in his new job. Although he had entrusted key staff members such as Cliff Cameron and Jim Trotter with significant authority in their own spheres, he remained involved in much of the day-to-day operations. Martin's desire to make every decision, attend every meeting, and sign every non-trivial piece of correspondence was commendable. But all too often, it meant that those decisions, meetings, and letters got delayed or deferred. Another early call, for Martin to work out of the Administration Building rather than the State Capitol so he could be closer to his staff, had exacerbated the situation. He was too involved in minutia and too little deployed in selling the administration's message to lawmakers, opinion leaders, and the general public.

Some among Martin's circle outside government had more specific concerns. Back in Charlotte, Joe Martin watched with alarm the early partisan fights about board appointments and state jobs, believing them to be inconsistent with the governor's campaign message on political patronage. As early as March, Joe warned his brother against what he called "arrogantly partisan" actions by Jack Hawke and other aides. First Citizens Bank chairman Lewis "Snow" Holding, a conservative Democrat whom the governor was trying to woo to the GOP, recommended Hawke be placed in a job "where he can't hurt you."

Joe had frequently butted heads with Hawke during the 1984 campaign, at one point even packing his bags and leaving the Raleigh campaign office to return home to Charlotte. But many of Martin's other confidants also thought he needed a staff shake-up. They advised the governor to replace his current arrangement of four senior staff reporting directly to him—executive assistant Jim Lofton, special counsel Jim Trotter, budget director Cliff Cameron, and political aide Hawke—with a more hierarchical structure. Martin continued to resist the idea of having a true chief of staff. But he recognized the need to clarify responsibilities and delegate more authority.

GOVERNOR MARTIN ANNOUNCES HIS APPOINTMENT OF RHODA BILLINGS AS CHIEF JUSTICE OF THE NORTH CAROLINA SUPREME COURT ON JULY 31, 1986.
OFFICIAL STATE PHOTO

Thus, there were both strategic and tactical matters to address. At the strategic level, the Martin administration needed a plan for setting the policy agenda. At the same time, it needed to adjust its tactics, and in some cases its tacticians, to implement the strategy. During the August 1985 retreat in Southern Pines, Martin and his team focused primarily on the strategic piece. All nine cabinet secretaries were present, along with deputy budget director Marvin Dorman (Cameron was out of the country) and Martin's top legal, policy, government-relations, and communication staffers. They agreed to spend the next few months developing specific initiatives on education, transportation, welfare, crime, and other policies.

Separately, Martin decided to relocate the governor's office back to the State Capitol and to reshuffle his staff. In early September, he sent Hawke to the Department of Administration to head up the Office of Policy and Planning, a post made vacant when the former director, Lynn Muchmore, left to become an assistant secretary in the Department of Natural Resources and Community Development. Two months later, Martin appointed legislative lobbyist Bev Lake to a superior-court judgeship and replaced him with Ward Purrington, a former Republican legislator who enjoyed strong relationships with members of both parties. Jim Lofton, the only top aide to follow Martin from Jones Street to the State Capitol, assumed some of the tasks Hawke had performed, such as supervising the research and communications staff. To fulfill the more political role Hawke had played, Martin turned to Alan Pugh, brought over from the Department of Administration. Pugh's job was to make sure the governor's supporters inside and outside government felt valued and consulted. That wasn't to say they should expect to get their way all the time. As Brad Hays explained it to Pugh, "The biggest part of your job is to protect the governor from his friends." Pugh would report to special counsel Jim Trotter, who like Lofton gained responsibilities from the staff shake-up. Trotter's ties to eastern North Carolina Republicans and conservative intellectuals were especially valuable to the administration. He had worked on Jim Gardner's congressional and gubernatorial campaigns in 1966, 1968, and 1972 and subsequently had grown close to Jesse Helms, John East, and key supporters of the Congressional Club. Trotter's brother-in-law, Vermont Royster, was a longtime editor and columnist for the *Wall Street Journal*. Trotter's cousin was popular essayist and novelist Tom Wolfe.

A STRATEGY FOR REFORM

Within Martin's inner circle, Trotter was especially enthusiastic about laying out a broader policy agenda for 1986 and beyond, on issues ranging from education and transportation to ensuring a proper separation of powers among the legislative, executive, and judicial branches. "If [Martin] can accomplish meaningful steps in those areas—and he can make good appointments—in my book he will have had a successful administration," Trotter said after the staff changes.

Even though North Carolina's economy was growing at a brisk pace, the state had no shortage of challenges to overcome. Rising crime rates and longer sentences put extreme pressure on state prison capacity. Population growth left urban and suburban areas struggling to keep up with demand for new schools, roads, and infrastructure. At the same time, some rural areas were lagging as the traditional triad of North Carolina manufacturing—furniture and wood products, textiles and apparel, and tobacco products—felt the effects of international competition and technological change.

During late 1985 and early 1986, administration officials studied these issues in depth and produced both rhetorical approaches and specific policies to pursue through the remainder of Martin's term. Here were the main priorities:

- **Transportation needs.** During his 1984 gubernatorial campaign, Martin made one specific commitment on transportation: completing I-40 from Raleigh to Wilmington. Beyond that, the governor had talked only in general terms about the growing state's transportation needs and how the lack of interstate-quality road access was a particular impediment in rural areas.

  To devise the administration's approach to these issues, Jim Harrington urged DOT officials not to dwell on past mistakes or engage in partisan blame but instead to focus on hard numbers and creative thinking. In 1981, during a previous DOT cash crunch, Governor Jim Hunt had gotten the General Assembly to enact a three-cents-per-gallon increase in the motor-fuels tax. Nevertheless, increases in average fuel efficiency led to lower-than-anticipated revenue collections per mile traveled, despite an overall rise in motorists and vehicles. Shortly after the 1985 session, Martin publicly endorsed Harrington's prediction that additional revenues might be needed. Many Republican lawmakers and conservative activists balked at the idea. They had opposed Hunt's tax hike four years earlier and thought Martin's talk about gas taxes conflicted with the administration's overall message on tax relief. On the other hand, they agreed that North Carolina's inadequate road system demanded attention.

  Transportation officials spent much of 1985 and early 1986 tackling the problem. Harrington formed a task force to set priorities and vet funding options. Among its members were legislative leaders and other Democrats. In urban areas alone, DOT estimated nearly $3 billion in immediate highway needs and $2 billion more in work scheduled through the year 2000. At current revenue estimates, officials projected it would take more than 50 years to complete the listed projects. Adding rural needs into the mix widened the gap. Martin's charge to his team, however, was not simply to accept the existing priority list and compute how high gas taxes would have to rise to pay for it. He stressed that any tax increase would have to be a "last resort." Harrington's task force ultimately concluded that North Carolina needed to spend at least $200 million a year more on roads. To pay for it, members suggested a mixture of gas or car taxes and bond issues, as well as a transfer of programs such as driver education and the Highway Patrol from the Highway Fund to the General Fund, which would free up more driving-related revenues to be spent on roads. The Highway Patrol transfer was one idea Hunt had recommended to Martin during their 1984 transition talks.

At the same time, Harrington, Martin, and United States secretary of transportation Elizabeth Dole (a North Carolina native and future senator) made it clear that the state could not count on additional federal funds to meet its transportation needs. In fact, at a National Governors Association meeting, Martin harked back to one of his longstanding positions as a congressman: fiscal federalism. He endorsed a plan proposed by Governors Lamar Alexander of Tennessee and Robert Orr of Indiana to end Washington's involvement in road funding outside the interstate system and to eliminate most of the federal tax on motor fuels. States would raise their own taxes as needed to shoulder their own responsibilities.

• **Education reform**. During the 1985 session, the legislature agreed that the Career Ladder pilots for teacher compensation in 16 school districts ought to be evaluated carefully before taking the program statewide. But most lawmakers shrugged off the governor's suggestion that the state's other major school-reform initiative, the Basic Education Program, be focused more on classroom needs and pared down in both cost to taxpayers and constraints on local districts. As Martin and his team reflected on the 1985 session and strategized about future ones, they concluded that the governor was more likely to win an argument for expanding local control and flexibility than he was to win an argument for rewriting the BEP itself.

Martin also needed to restate his strong support for paying teachers according to performance. He did so at a late-1985 appearance before the North Carolina School Boards Association.

He proposed raising teachers' starting pay, providing subsidized loans to encourage college students to pursue teaching, offering additional financial incentives to attract teachers to difficult-to-staff schools and subjects, and using student scores on standardized tests both to identify high-performing teachers and schools for possible bonuses and to flag low-performing teachers for more training. A teacher whose students routinely failed to meet achievement benchmarks "should welcome such an effort by the system to help salvage or rebuild his or her chosen career," Martin told the audience. During subsequent speeches and press conferences, the governor argued that funding the Career Ladder's eventual expansion should be a higher priority than funding non-teaching positions in the BEP.

Recycling a successful tactic from his Mecklenburg commission days, Martin placed greater emphasis on his stated goal of increasing the percentage of General Fund spending devoted to public schools. That share had sometimes declined during Hunt's tenure. Martin made sure his budget team pursued a different course. So even when the Democratic legislature outspent his recommended budget levels, Martin could correctly argue that his budgets consistently made K-12 education a top priority. The strategy worked. Expenditures on elementary and secondary education rose from 44.8 percent of the General Fund in 1985–86 to 46.5 percent in 1988–89, the last fiscal year of his first term.

• **The prison crisis**. When Governor Martin took office in 1985, North Carolina was, like other states, experiencing a marked rise in both reported crimes and prison population. Five years earlier, in 1980, a group of inmates had filed a suit alleging prison overcrowding so severe it violated their civil rights. While the statewide system incarcerated 17,500 offenders, it could house only 13,000 according to federal standards. In July 1985, state officials and the plaintiffs signed a settlement that eliminated triple-bunking and mandated other costly improvements in some prisons. Martin and legislative leaders concluded it was only a matter of time until the same requirements were imposed on the rest of the system. It fell to Secretary of Corrections Aaron Johnson and Martin's policy staff to come up with a long-term strategy for addressing the problem without breaking the bank.

By early 1986, the plan was ready. It called for major sentencing changes to alleviate pressure on the system, including expanded use of intensive probation, electronically monitored house arrest, and other means of diverting offenders from prison. Even so, the plan proposed $200 million in additional spending to add approximately 10,000 new prison beds, some of them in new private facilities to be operated on contract with the state.

- **Fiscal policy**. The governor resolved to continue his push to eliminate taxes on business inventories, intangible property, and food. But he concluded that he would need to be both patient and flexible to accomplish his goal. Faced with the possibility that deficit-reduction efforts in Washington might crimp federal funding for states and localities, he realized that proposing additional tax cuts during the 1986 session of the General Assembly would be futile. Martin went farther than that, in fact, endorsing a bill authorizing another half-cent local-option sales tax. The bill had originally been filed during the 1985 session and went nowhere. Backers planned to try again in 1986. To the extent that counties used sales-tax revenue rather than higher property taxes to replace lost federal funds or to meet growing demands for schools and other facilities, that would be less damaging to local economies, Martin reasoned. He also hoped, however, that endorsing the bill's passage in 1986 might improve the chances of enacting his preferred state tax cuts in the future by strengthening his ties to key lawmakers and signaling his willingness to negotiate.

Democratic legislators and local government officials indeed welcomed Martin's endorsement of a higher local-option sales tax. But some Republicans were disappointed and angry. They thought he was damaging the party's tax-cutting brand and giving too much ground to the Democrats. Liberal-leaning editorialists at the Greensboro *News & Record* and the Raleigh *News & Observer* praised the governor's position—which, of course, served to convince his GOP critics they were right to be concerned—but the newspapers couldn't resist tweaking Martin for the apparent contradiction on tax policy. Even Lieutenant Governor Bob Jordan got into the act. "It's interesting to see now those people who were cutting taxes seem to be changing their mind," he told a gathering of Democratic donors in early 1986. "We're not going to let them forget that."

Despite criticism from foes and disaffection among allies, Martin defended his position as philosophically consistent and politically practical, calling it "not a change of direction at all." He still planned to renew his call for more cuts in inventory, intangibles, and food taxes in future legislative sessions. To do so, however, he needed to identify more fiscal space in the state budget.

That was the job of his Governor's Efficiency Study Commission, a 73-member panel of business executives and community leaders who spent much of 1985 developing a list of 414 recommendations. The commission estimated in a late-September report that the proposals would save the state nearly $250 million a year. Democratic officeholders and even Martin's agency heads pushed back on some of the recommendations. One of them, phasing out state funding for the North Carolina Symphony and the North Carolina Museum of Art, proved especially controversial. The governor eventually disavowed the idea of fully privatizing the two institutions, although the share of their budgets derived from private sources did subsequently rise. But the administration immediately began implementing dozens of the commission's other recommendations on purchasing practices, contracting with private vendors, charging user fees for some services, and reforming state operations.

- **Emerging environmental issues**. When Governor Martin took office in early 1985, two waste-disposal issues were simmering.

One involved low-level radioactive waste. Over the previous two decades, the construction of nuclear plants and the proliferation of medical diagnostic and treatment technologies employing radiation had created a dilemma: how best to dispose of irradiated items such as testing materials, tools, and protective clothing. These weren't spent fuel rods. They didn't pose a large health or safety risk. But the material also couldn't be tossed into general-purpose landfills. Officials turned to incineration as a solution. It proved challenging to get the public to accept the presence of incinerators near their communities, however, regardless of what scientific risk analysis showed. And even after incineration, the resulting ash had to be disposed of somewhere. The only site in the region accepting low-level radioactive waste, in Barnwell, South Carolina, was scheduled to close by 1992. North Carolina was one of eight states in a regional compact to locate a new disposal site by that date.

Low-level radioactive material wasn't the state's only waste-disposal headache. Another was the increasing volume of hazardous waste produced by manufacturers and other businesses. During the 1970s and early 1980s, private firms had tried repeatedly to build hazardous-waste incinerators in North Carolina, only to be stymied by permitting delays and local protests. In 1984, the General Assembly responded by creating the Hazardous Waste Treatment Commission. Its job was to identify potential sites for a large-scale incinerator and to develop strategies—such as careful risk abatement and financial incentives—for convincing communities to accept it.

During the first few months of Martin's tenure as governor, both waste-disposal disputes continued to escalate. A Kentucky-based company announced plans to build a low-level radioactive-waste incinerator in southeastern North Carolina. Similarly, two private firms proposed to build hazardous-waste incinerators, one near Greensboro and the other near Laurinburg. If successful, these projects would make a state-directed incinerator project unnecessary. It would be "far better," Secretary of Commerce Howard Haworth told other state officials, "if the private sector [would] be the owner and operator of hazardous waste treatment facilities." But environmental activists and neighborhood groups blocked each private-sector project.

Martin increasingly found the opponents' tactics and rhetoric irresponsible and shrill. A 1985 law to require more public disclosure of chemicals stored at plants and warehouses rubbed him the wrong way as well. The entire drift of the debate reminded him of the scientific illiteracy he had observed in Washington during the 1970s among federal bureaucrats and Naderite pressure groups. Rather than cater to "a small group of people who want to create a chemophobia," Martin said, the public interest would be "best served by a program of how you handle what's there."

In addition to devising strategies for addressing transportation, education, taxes, and the environment, Martin and his top aides prepared positions on a variety of other issues. One was welfare reform. When Martin took office, eight North Carolina counties had introduced work requirements for receiving cash assistance or food stamps. That number quickly rose to 11 by late 1985, with Secretary of Human Resources Phil Kirk recommending that the "workfare" approach reach half the state's counties by 1987. On another controversial issue, the administration continued to press for more restrictions on tax-funded abortions, including a requirement of parental consent for minors seeking to use the state abortion fund.

SETTING THE POLITICAL STAGE

Just after the 1985 legislative session, the Jim Martin Committee began soliciting funds to help Republican legislative candidates the following year. As long as Democrats enjoyed large majorities in both chambers, Martin knew, the ability of any Republican governor to advance his policy agenda would be severely constrained. In the short run, however, the governor's plate contained two political matters that had nothing to do with the legislature.

Early August brought the retirement of Earl Vaughn, an associate justice of the North Carolina Supreme Court who was battling lung cancer. Under the state constitution, it was Martin's responsibility to pick a replacement justice, who would then stand for election in 1986. One candidate for the seat was Wake County's Donald Smith, the state's only Republican then serving as a superior-court judge. Another was Francis Parker, a prominent Charlotte attorney. Martin's legislative lobbyist, Bev Lake, also wanted the job. But Martin ultimately decided to appoint another leading contender, Rhoda Billings, who chaired North Carolina's Parole Commission. Billings had been a district-court judge, a private-practice attorney, and a professor at the Wake

Forest University School of Law. She was only the second woman to serve on the state's highest court.

Just days after Martin announced his appointment of Billings in early September, ailing senator John East announced he would not seek reelection to a second term in 1986. The Congressional Club had powered East's narrow Senate victory in 1980. Its top leaders, Tom Ellis and Carter Wrenn, were keen to keep the seat in the hands of a Republican aligned with Jesse Helms. After all, it was the Congressional Club that had elected East in 1980, they reasoned, not the traditional Republican wing. On the same day East announced his plans not to seek reelection, the Congressional Club endorsed the Senate candidacy of David Funderburk, a Campbell University professor and former United States ambassador to Romania. Representative Jim Broyhill, Martin's mentor in Congress, soon expressed his interest in the GOP nomination as well. Although the two Republican factions had worked cooperatively during the 1984 campaign, and although early interactions between Funderburk and Broyhill were respectful, both sides recognized more than half a year before the May 1986 primary that they were headed for an intra-party contest that, in intensity and bitterness, might well exceed their mid-1970s confrontations.

Despite his longstanding ties to Broyhill, Martin sought to maintain formal neutrality. In November 1985, he told a group of Republican donors that the party was poised to fare well in 1986 and beyond, but only "if we can maintain our cool, if we can be generous toward each other." By that time, however, the Funderburk campaign had already begun aggressively attacking Broyhill's congressional record. And many of Martin's political operatives and supporters, including Brad Hays, had already gravitated to the Broyhill camp. Others would soon follow, including three cabinet secretaries. Joe Martin, head of the Jim Martin Committee, sent a letter to the group's county chairmen giving them the formal go-ahead to pick sides in the Funderburk-Broyhill race and other GOP primaries, after which they would be invited to rejoin the Jim Martin Committee. Then Joe promptly stepped down himself to join the Broyhill campaign's steering committee. (His replacement was Rusty Goode.)

While Hays and his team worked on the Broyhill campaign, they never took their eyes off the main prize: the Executive Mansion. Martin was popular, and North Carolinians generally felt good about the trajectory of the state's economy and government. But Democrats still had a built-in advantage in statewide elections, and probable nominee Bob Jordan had a strong base among business donors and interest groups. He would be a formidable adversary in 1988. So Hays decided to treat the 1986 midterm election as a dry run for a Martin reelection bid. By deploying the governor as a fundraiser and prominent surrogate for candidates across the state, Hays hoped to strengthen Martin's ties to donors and activists while sharpening his stump speech and trying out new messages.

Paul Shumaker, a field rep for the 1984 campaign, had gotten his start in politics as a congressional intern for Broyhill. Naturally, when Broyhill announced his bid for the Senate, Shumaker agreed to work on his campaign. So when state GOP chairman Bob Bradshaw subsequently offered him the job of running the party's statewide campaigns for the legislature and other offices in 1986—essentially the "mini-Martin" effort Hays had in mind—Shumaker said he was unavailable. A few hours later, Hays called him. "I thought I trained you better," he said. Shumaker got the message and accepted Bradshaw's offer. Over the ensuing months, he and other GOP staffers would raise and spend hundreds of thousands of dollars to run television and radio ads, stage political rallies, and keep Martin front and center throughout the election cycle as the chief campaign asset for the Republican Party's down-ballot races.

To succeed, they would have to keep converting conservative Democrats into reliable GOP voters, if not registered Republicans. Martin had furthered the cause with Operation Switch. He followed up in late 1985 by tapping Eddie Knox, newly reregistered as a Republican, to lead a statewide effort to defeat a constitutional amendment shifting North Carolina's elections to odd-numbered years. At the end of the 1985 session, Democrats approved a May 6, 1986, referendum on the change. It was a transparent bid to hurt Republicans—so much so that Jordan, Ramsey, and other Democratic leaders grew embarrassed and began distancing themselves from it as the referendum approached. Voters ended up overwhelmingly rejecting what Knox and the governor derisively called the "Perpetual Elections Amendment."

Martin's political interests extended beyond the next election and the borders of the state. Inspired by the Blackberry Farm summit, he relished the opportunity to help Republicans gain a foothold in other state and local governments. In September 1985, Martin traveled to Miami to assume the chairmanship of the Southern Governors' Association. In December, he journeyed to Delaware for a follow-up to the Blackberry Farm session. Republican participants discussed how best to craft and market conservative ideas on education, transportation, and other issues. The chairman of the Republican Governors Association, Dick Thornburgh, told the gathering that the party could pick up eight or more governorships during the 1986 midterms if its candidates ran on a practical platform for extending the Reagan Revolution to the states.

Privately, state Republicans had low expectations for the 1986 cycle in North Carolina. Many thought simply holding on to most of their recent gains in the General Assembly would constitute a successful "six-year itch" election. What they were really hoping and preparing for was another strong Republican cycle in 1988, when Martin and the GOP presidential candidate (presumably Vice President George H. W. Bush) would be on the ballot. Party chairman Bob Bradshaw set a goal of controlling at least one legislative chamber by 1990. Others embraced the goal, noting that it didn't necessarily require electing 61 Republicans to the House or 26 to the Senate. "When parties become evenly matched, party lines start breaking down and you get bipartisan coalitions," state representative Ray Warren observed in late 1985. "If we came within 10 seats, Republicans and disenchanted Democrats could elect another speaker." Warren's words would prove prophetic. (Ironically, he later left the Republican Party and became a Democrat and gay-rights activist.)

MARTIN VERSUS THE GENERAL ASSEMBLY: ROUND TWO

By early 1986, the governor was ready to announce his new policy agenda for the coming short session, as well as the long one in 1987. His chosen means was a live speech on public television and nine commercial stations across North Carolina on January 25. Speaking from his desk in the State Capitol, Martin reviewed the successes of his initial year in office, such as lowering the tax burden and raising the share of General Fund spending devoted to education. He devoted most of the address, however, to his new initiatives on prison overcrowding, highway construction, water and sewer projects, and teacher pay. Martin described 1985 as "a year of transition, and a year of testing, and a very busy year just getting organized and building a new leadership team for state government." He promised to make 1986 the "Year of the Family," a theme that tied together his various proposals on education, crime, and the economy. "Strengthened by [our state's] greater resources, guided by respect for its traditional values, steadfast to its commitment to economic liberty and human dignity for all," the governor concluded, "let us go forward in 1986, confident of what we can make of North Carolina: truly one united state."

After the TV broadcast, Martin went on the road to deliver essentially the same speech to civic groups, chambers of commerce, and other audiences. The process culminated with the May 14, 1986, release of the governor's budget recommendations. They included $203 million for expansion in prison capacity over 10 years (with four of the new institutions to be privately run) and a $220 million-per-year "Roads to the Future" plan, to be funded both by transferring the Highway Patrol and driver education to the General Fund and by hiking the state's motor-fuels tax to 15 cents a gallon, up from 12.5 cents. For the coming 1986–87 fiscal year, Martin also recommended more budget savings, reforms of the pork-barrel process, tuition increases for public colleges and universities, and a 3.2 percent pay raise for most teachers and state employees, along with extra funds to boost the pay of starting teachers and to reward others for "meritorious classroom performance."

Although the governor described his proposals as compromises between the prevailing positions of Democrats and Republicans, he was hardly surprised when legislative leaders attacked them. "Transfers, as far as I am concerned, are out" to free up Highway Fund dollars for road construction, said Aaron Plyler, the powerful cochairman of Senate Appropriations. Bob Jordan and Liston Ramsey criticized the idea of private prisons and said Martin's pay raises for public employees were too small. Tony Rand, another Senate Appropriations cochair, ridiculed the governor's road-funding plan and other budget proposals for having been "involved in a rather bad wreck."

The 1986 legislative session got under way on June 5. In addition to acting on Martin's proposals, lawmakers were expected to consider more taxing authority for local governments and other matters. But transportation funding and the state budget dominated the session. The Senate decided on a bigger gas-tax increase than Martin sought but agreed to his transfer of driver education to the General Fund (while refusing to do the same for the Highway Patrol). Ramsey and House leaders balked at first but finally agreed to the deal, which hiked the motor-fuels tax to 14 cents at retail and put another 3 percent tax on the wholesale price. On the state budget, the General Assembly settled on much higher pay hikes, 6.5 percent for teachers and 6 percent for most state employees, while agreeing to some of Martin's spending reductions and tuition hikes. As expected, lawmakers gave North Carolina localities the authority to levy another half-cent sales tax to offset the loss of federal revenue-sharing funds, although they softened the impact by repealing the tax on household property. Perhaps unexpectedly, they made some changes to the pork-barrel process, tacitly agreeing with the governor that it should be more formal and transparent.

Martin didn't make much progress on prison construction. But overall, he counted the 1986 session a success. Some of his critics agreed. The *News & Observer* dinged Jordan and Ramsey for going along with Martin on transferring driver education to the General Fund and for abolishing the household property tax, which the paper described as a nod to the governor's tax-reform agenda.

In October, just before the elections, Martin announced that his administration had adopted 300 of the 414 recommendations from his Governor's Efficiency Study Commission, saving tens of millions of dollars. To implement the rest of the ideas, he said, meant "continuing to arm-wrestle, stare down, and cajole" the recalcitrant Democrats. It was an issue he hoped would help GOP candidates.

The prospect of competitive General Assembly races in the fall wasn't the only political drama to play out during the tail end of the 1986 legislative session. Martin found himself with two momentous appointments to make. On June 21, Joseph Branch, the Democratic chief justice of the North Carolina Supreme Court, announced he would retire on September 1, about a year before reaching his mandatory retirement age of 72. The sitting justice with the most years of service on the court was Jim Exum. Democrats immediately urged Martin to appoint Exum as chief justice, citing the fact that previous governors had followed seniority in filling the job. Then, on June 29, a week after Branch's retirement announcement, John East committed suicide. Suffering from debilitating medical conditions that had already prompted his announced retirement from the Senate, East used a running car in his garage to asphyxiate himself. It fell to Martin to appoint someone to fill the remaining six months of East's term.

Most observers expected the governor to pick Jim Broyhill, who a few weeks earlier had defeated David Funderburk in the contentious GOP primary for East's seat. But Congressional Club leaders preferred that Martin pick a caretaker—perhaps the late senator's widow, Priscilla East, as a gesture of deference to the family and to Republicans who had backed Funderburk. On July 3, however, Martin confirmed that Broyhill would indeed fill the seat. Brad Hays and other GOP strategists hoped the move would bolster Broyhill's campaign against the Democratic nominee, Terry Sanford, who had maintained a modest but consistent lead in recent polls. It didn't work, as Sanford would go on to defeat Broyhill. Congressional Club leaders, having first lost the Senate primary, thus sustained another political bruise. They began devising plans to wrest back control of the state Republican Party.

Meanwhile, the governor and his aides continued to consider their options for replacing Joseph Branch. The newly appointed chief justice would stand for election in November. Rhoda Billings, whom Martin had appointed in 1985 as the court's first Republican member in more than 80 years, was already scheduled to be on the ballot in November to defend her seat against Democratic nominee John Webb, a sitting judge on the court of appeals. If the governor chose to elevate Billings to chief justice, that would create another vacancy on the court for a Republican justice, who would then face the voters in November as an incumbent (however brief the term of service). Some GOP strategists believed Billings would have a better shot at winning an election for the higher-profile office of chief justice. She felt so, too.

During the first two weeks of July, Democrats ramped up public pressure on the governor to appoint Jim Exum. Party leaders formally nominated Exum as the Democratic candidate for the chief-justice election in November. Exum then urged Martin to "follow precedent" by appointing him to the post in the meantime, warning that failing to do so "would plunge the chief justice's succession into the arena of partisan politics." If anything, however, the public pressure made Martin resentful and less likely to pick Exum, whom Republicans and some conservative Democrats already disdained as the court's most liberal justice. While the governor still believed that reforming judicial selection through constitutional amendment was a worthy goal, he wasn't going to sacrifice possible GOP gains in the meantime.

On July 31, Martin appointed Billings as chief justice. To fill her vacant post of associate justice, he picked Charlotte attorney Francis Parker. To fill the seat Exum would soon vacate to run for chief justice, Martin picked former superior-court judge Robert Browning.

One other judicial seat remained to be filled, on the court of appeals. It was being vacated by Willis Whichard, the Democratic candidate against

Browning for the Exum seat on the North Carolina Supreme Court. To fill this post, Martin turned to 39-year-old Asheville attorney Bob Orr.

MORE COMPETING PLANS

While state Republicans and Democrats prepped for the 1986 elections, advisors to Martin and Jordan were looking past November to the main event: the gubernatorial race of 1988. Despite his prominent position as lieutenant governor and North Carolina's traditional Democratic leanings, Jordan knew the race would be challenging. Martin was popular. And the state was posting strong economic growth. Voters would need a reason to reject their incumbent governor. If the good times continued, how could Jordan and Democrats persuade North Carolinians to toss out the incumbent?

The answer, they concluded, was to focus on rural areas where growth was comparatively weak. The North Carolina Commission on Jobs and Economic Growth was tasked with developing Jordan's economic-development strategy. A parallel effort led by Secretary of Commerce Howard Haworth spent much of 1985 and 1986 producing the Martin administration's own plan, called North Carolina's Blueprint for Economic Development. It was no accident that the main elements of both competing plans went public during the same week, Martin announcing his blueprint at an August 27, 1986, press conference and Jordan's panel releasing its main recommendations during public meetings on August 28 and 29.

The two plans weren't far different in broad themes. Both called for better roads and schools. Both emphasized the potential benefits not just of attracting new, large employers but also strengthening the competitive position of traditional industries and fostering entrepreneurs. There were critical differences in details, however. To improve the quality of the workforce, the Martin plan called for merit pay for teachers and a greater focus on vocational education. The Jordan plan put a greater emphasis on funding the BEP. To boost growth in rural areas, the Martin plan restated the case for eliminating the inventory and intangibles taxes while endorsing low-interest loans to rural communities to improve their water and sewer systems. The Jordan plan recommended a much more extensive array of grants, loans, and targeted tax breaks for individual businesses in economically distressed counties, as well as a new private but government-subsidized entity to administer many of them: a Center for Rural Economic Development. Haworth noted that the Martin administration had studied similar ideas but rejected them as "somewhat liberal, sometimes bordering on the socialistic." Martin's tax policies were designed to reduce costs for all businesses, Haworth explained. "They aren't tax credits and they're not giveaways" aimed at struggling companies that "have weak financial circumstances and therefore need more help from us in order to survive," he said. The governor added that subsidy programs would put him and future state leaders in the position of deciding which companies got breaks and which didn't. "That could lead to political decisions and we should avoid getting into that kind of pork barrel," Martin argued.

The governor and lieutenant governor continued to spar about economic-development policy throughout 1986. Martin insisted the best way to promote economic development in rural areas was to improve the quality of basic services such as roads, schools, and water systems while making the state's overall tax system more competitive.

It was a theme he also championed as chairman of the Southern Governors' Association. As the host of its August 1986 meeting in Charlotte, Martin made the fate of the region's rural counties and traditional industries a focus of discussion. Later that month, he headed to South Carolina for a National Governors Association meeting devoted to similar topics. For Martin, the debate about economic development didn't have implications just for upcoming elections and the 1987 legislative session. He believed that for GOP candidates for state and local offices to become truly competitive, they would need a distinctively Republican approach to expanding economic opportunity, one consistent with the party's principles and relevant to the practical concerns of businesses and communities.

BEATING THE MIDTERM SPREAD

For the 1986 cycle, the North Carolina Republican Party fielded its largest slate of candidates ever for a midterm election—five for supreme court, three for court of appeals, nominees for 132 of the state's 170 legislative seats, and hundreds of additional nominees for county commission, sheriff, and other local offices. It helped that Martin and state GOP chairman Bob Bradshaw had tapped Frank Rouse, a former Republican chairman himself, to lead a special candidate-recruitment task force. The party also deployed a larger, more professional, and better-funded campaign organization than Republicans had ever managed to muster for a midterm. As Brad Hays had planned all along, the organization kept media consultant Don Ringe and Martin's field staff and volunteers in place and engaged with North Carolina voters.

Stumping for other candidates gave Martin valuable practice campaigning as an incumbent governor. It wasn't quite like running as a county commissioner or congressman. Hays would later tell a story that illustrated the difference. On several occasions when Martin was running for reelection to his seat in the United States House, Hays had urged him to go beyond shaking hands, to give hugs and kiss babies. But it wasn't Martin's style. He declined. During the 1986 cycle, however, Hays glanced at the *Charlotte Observer* one morning and saw a picture of Martin kissing a little girl on the cheek. He called the governor. "I thought you didn't kiss babies," Hays said. "I don't," Martin replied, "but governors do."

Hays and other Republicans weren't fooling themselves. Party leaders knew that the Democrats' continued advantages in voter registration, campaign cash, and grass-roots organization would make it difficult for Republicans in a non-presidential year. After making spectacular advances in North Carolina in 1984, they were prepared to be satisfied with holding most of those gains in 1986, with the expectation of making another leap forward in 1988. Republicans weren't simply playing an expectations game, purposefully downplaying their chances in order to catch their opponents unaware or spin whatever happened in November as a moral victory. Outside observers agreed with their assessment. *News & Observer* reporter Rob Christensen wrote two weeks before the 1986 elections that the legislative races offered Democrats "a chance to regain some of the party's lost strength." Without Ronald Reagan on the ballot, he reported, "the conventional wisdom is that Democrats will pick up a few seats." He quoted David Olson, a political scientist at UNC-Greensboro, who said that if Republicans lost no more than five seats in the General Assembly, "they will be doing very well indeed." Ed Turlington, executive director of the state Democratic Party, predicted a net gain of five to 10 seats, and perhaps more if the cycle proved to be particularly pro-Democratic.

As Election Day approached, the two sides poured tens of thousands of dollars into last-minute radio spots, newspaper ads, and get-out-the-vote efforts. When the smoke cleared, the 1986 election cycle produced the expected Democratic gains in many places but also some surprises. Nationally, the "six-year itch" factor yielded congressional losses for President Reagan's Republicans—eight seats in the United States Senate and five in the House, including those of North Carolina Republicans Bill Cobey and Bill Hendon. At the same time, however, GOP candidates scored impressive victories in other races. Most notably, Republicans had a net gain of eight governorships, including Jim Martin's friend Carroll Campbell in South Carolina, Guy Hunt in Alabama, Bob Martinez in Florida, and Bill Clements in Texas. The work Martin, Campbell, and others had begun at Blackberry Farm to strengthen the Republican brand for down-ballot races had already begun to pay off. Even the GOP's loss of five seats in the House was less than historical precedent would have predicted.

Similarly, the results of the 1986 elections in Martin's own state were mixed and not at all dismaying to Republicans. Their greatest disappointment was Jim Broyhill's loss to Terry Sanford, by 3.6 points. Billings and the other Republican candidates for the appellate courts also fell short, winning an average of 45 percent of the vote. But it was the Democrats who fell short of expectations in General Assembly races, netting just two seats each in the Senate and House. Several endangered Republican freshmen managed to hold their seats against tough, well-funded challengers. Liston Ramsey couldn't disguise his disappointment. "I was hoping we could pick up more Democrats, but I think President Reagan's trips into [North Carolina] strengthened those Republican candidates," he said. "Reagan's name won't be on the ballot in 1988 and it will be a good Democratic year." At the local level, North Carolina Republicans didn't just manage to protect recent advances but added to them, gaining 41 county-commission seats—even more than the 37 they'd netted in 1984. The GOP now controlled 31 of the state's 100 county commissions and 19 of its county sheriff offices, both record levels of power in local government for the state's minority party.

PREPPING FOR THE NEXT SESSION

The hard-fought elections of 1986 produced Democratic gains. But Republicans outperformed expectations. Martin and his political team felt good about what they had accomplished. The governor had expanded his donor base and sharpened his message. The public clearly liked what it saw—a Greensboro *News & Record* poll in early 1987 found that 63 percent of North Carolinians described Martin's job performance as "excellent" or "good." Martin's efforts to help Republican candidates for state and local offices had elevated his political profile outside North Carolina as well. Martin had joined Tennessee governor Lamar Alexander and other politicians to form the Southern Republican Exchange to facilitate policy formulation and discussion. Shortly after the 1986 elections, Martin announced he would host the next Southern Republican Exchange conference in Raleigh in early 1987. He also moderated a Republican Governors Association panel examining the election results.

Martin was emerging as one of the national Republican Party's leading voices on state government. But as a precursor to the 1987 legislative session in North Carolina, his personal involvement in the 1986 elections didn't seem as beneficial, at least at first. Democrats whom Martin had targeted on the campaign trail were not exactly members of his fan club. Ramsey said he and other legislators felt insulted by attacks on their policies and operation of the General Assembly. The governor "recruited people to run here in order to try to eliminate me," Senator Aaron Plyler complained. "Why would a governor try to do that and still expect to work with the legislature and try to get his programs through?"

In Martin's view, the notion that he had alienated legislators with his political activity was based on a fallacious assumption: that he hadn't tried persuading them with argument and charm. He was willing to meet them halfway. He was willing to be patient to achieve his goals. But a Democratic Party firmly entrenched in power on Jones Street would never be willing to accommodate the ideas of a Republican governor, he believed. Instead, Democrats needed to perceive a real risk of losing elections if they stymied his reforms. Picking up seats in 1986 would have sent that message clearly. But Martin figured that Republicans' better-than-expected results in a tough national environment would give the Democrats pause and leave some open to working with him on key issues—or at least unwilling to be corralled by the "supersub," a group of powerful House and Senate leaders who often met in secret to finalize budgets and work out other deals. Sometimes called the "Gang of Eight," the supersub consisted of Lieutenant Governor Bob Jordan and Harold Hardison, Tony Rand, and Ken Royall from the Senate, plus Speaker Liston Ramsey and Billy Watkins, Martin Nesbitt, and Bob Etheridge from the House. The Martin camp had noticed a few Democratic legislators such as Representative Harry Payne of New Hanover rebelling against the leadership during the 1986 session on both procedural and policy grounds. It hoped the trend would continue.

Jordan was among the Democrats who winced every time Martin called them out for running the legislature unfairly. He had enough political experience to recognize a potential vulnerability. So Jordan's team embarked on a political strategy of its own. On one hand, the lieutenant governor would champion the cause of opening up legislative proceedings to more public scrutiny. On the other hand, he and surrogates would begin a concerted campaign of attacks on Martin's job performance. Ed Turlington, executive director of the state Democratic Party, became the lieutenant governor's chief of staff, joining an office that included policy advisor Laura Bingham and communications director Brenda Summers. To replace Turlington at the state party, Jordan brought in Ken Eudy, a former journalist with a facility for one-liners. Eudy, who had covered Martin as a reporter in Charlotte, began issuing a series of sharply worded statements. "I knew he had a thin skin," Eudy said later, "and I felt that if I needled him constantly enough that he would melt down." The state Democratic Party's new tack got Martin's attention. He took to calling Eudy a "media star." But he rarely rose to the bait or lost his cool.

As the governor geared up for the 1987 session, he made important staff changes of his own. Raleigh businessman Claude Pope, who had chaired the governor's economic development board, became commerce secretary. His predecessor, Howard Haworth, vacated the post in preparation for being named to the state Board of Education, of which he later became chairman. To replace Pope as chairman of the economic development board, Martin turned to Jim Broyhill. Other Republican officeholders or candidates who lost their races in 1986 joined the administration as well. Bill Cobey became deputy secretary at the Department of Transportation. Former state representative Tommy Harrelson, the unsuccessful Republican nominee against Charlie Rose in the Seventh District, also became a deputy secretary at DOT. Another former House member, George Robinson, joined DOT as assistant deputy secretary after losing the GOP primary to replace Broyhill in the 10th District.

The biggest change of all came a few weeks after the 1987 session began, when Phil Kirk left Human Resources to fill a new position as Martin's chief of staff. The governor had long resisted the idea. But his closest confidants were adamant. Brad Hays was among the most forceful advocates. So was Phil

Kirk himself, although he actually turned Martin down twice before finally accepting the job (he hadn't wanted to leave Human Resources). "The almost universal advice from business leaders, privately from the leaders of the efficiency commission, my brother, my wife, and all my executive staff was in the direction of having a chief of staff," the governor said. Martin later explained that the fact Kirk had performed a similar role for Holshouser made the idea easier to accept.

Kirk's job switch set off a round of other staff changes. Employment Security Commission chairman David Flaherty took over at Human Resources, which he had headed under Holshouser. Meanwhile, because the new chief of staff assumed some of the responsibilities Jim Lofton had handled, the latter left the governor's office to head the Department of Administration, replacing Grace Rohrer. She then moved into the governor's office as the director of policy and planning. Two aides already serving in the office, Jim Trotter and Ward Purrington, received broader portfolios. Trotter also got a new title, general counsel. Purrington was promoted to special assistant and director of legislative relations, now treated as a cabinet-level post. Kirk also brought in a deputy chief of staff, Nancy Temple, who had worked for him at Human Resources.

It was as if Martin, the chemist, had gone into his laboratory, devised a new set of ratios and procedures, and emerged with yet another formula for operating North Carolina's state government. Would it be a formula for success? The governor's latest staff reorganization would get its first test during the 1987 session as he once again sparred with legislative leaders. His first political confrontation of the new year, however, would not be with the Democrats.

A BRUISING POLITICAL BOUT— WITH REPUBLICANS

While Martin and his team saw the North Carolina GOP as surpassing expectations in the 1986 elections, the leaders of the Congressional Club thought otherwise. Tom Ellis and Carter Wrenn considered Broyhill's Senate campaign lackluster. They thought a more conservative candidate such as Funderburk would have been more successful by drawing a clearer ideological contrast with Sanford. At the state level, they were troubled by Martin's endorsement of the gas-tax hike and thought the GOP might have actually gained seats had legislators and the governor been more consistently conservative on taxes and other issues. More generally, the Congressional Club had dominated Republican politics in North Carolina during much of the 1970s and early 1980s from its base in Raleigh and points east. Martin's election in 1984 had made a traditional Republican from the west the state party's de facto leader. His selection of the widely respected Bob Bradshaw as state GOP chairman in 1985 had soothed tensions for a time. But after Broyhill's defeat, Ellis, Wrenn, and other Congressional Club leaders decided to take action. On December 6, 1986, some 300 activists met at the Raleigh Civic Center to vent their frustrations and strategize about how to "reassert the voice of conservatives in the party." Martin and Bradshaw were taken aback by the fervor of their critics. "As party chairman I have not excluded anyone from party affairs," Bradshaw said. "Not only am I not anti-conservative, I *am* a conservative."

The battle continued over the successor to Bradshaw, who wanted to step down in early 1987. Martin planned by February to pick an interim chairman, who would then stand for election at the Republican Party's state convention in May. He publicly floated the names of several candidates he thought might please both camps, including former Helms aide and state senator Hamilton Horton, Lenoir County GOP chairman P. C. Barwick, and Gastonia businessman and fundraiser J. A. Dalpiaz. But Ellis and Wrenn shot down each— even Dalpiaz, the very man who had served as the Congressional Club's floor manager for Ronald Reagan at the 1976 state convention and blocked Ford supporters Martin, Holshouser, and Broyhill from attending the RNC.

Instead, Ellis and Wrenn offered their own candidate, Barry McCarty, a professor at Roanoke Bible College in Elizabeth City and Martin's appointee as chairman of the state Social Services Commission. They also convinced Senator Helms to intervene in the dispute with a public call to rotate the chairmanship between west and east every two years.

In subsequent private meetings in December and January, Martin tried to reach a consensus with Helms and the leaders of the Congressional Club about the chairmanship, to no avail. Ellis and Wrenn had decided to strengthen their activist network to capture control of county parties not only for the purpose of electing delegates to the state convention in 1987, but also to exercise more control over recruitment, fundraising, and get-out-the-vote efforts for

candidates all the way down the ballot. The prospect of a competitive primary for president in 1988 was particularly compelling to Congressional Club leaders, who cherished their role in delivering the state to Reagan in 1976. They hoped to be in a similar position in 1988. Running McCarty for state GOP chairman was a central element of the strategy.

Meanwhile, Brad Hays and other Martin advisors suggested another potential replacement for Bradshaw: Jack Hawke. Since his days working on Jim Gardner's campaigns in the 1960s, Hawke had staked himself out as a clear conservative. Once again, however, Ellis and Wrenn rejected the idea. Martin concluded he had no alternative but to put his own man in the job and see that he won election outright at the May convention. Even so, he chose diplomatic, even self-deprecating language to explain the decision. "I would rather avoid spending a lot of political energies on that kind of dispute," Martin told the *N&O*. "But I don't know if I am going to be skillful and gifted enough in avoiding that." Of all his potential choices, Hawke was the most enthusiastic about taking the job and fighting for it. So Martin picked him, and the state party's executive committee confirmed the choice on January 31, 1987.

The governor's team immediately went to work. While Hays and the political staff began recruiting delegates for county conventions, Hawke traveled from one GOP meeting to another to win support. He described the

Republican Party as "North Carolina's conservative voice" and promised a unified effort to reelect Martin in 1988 and Helms in 1990, both of whom would boost the GOP's down-ballot candidates. "If we pull together on the things that unite us, we can win," Hawke told Republicans in Wilmington. "We can not only become part of the two-party system in North Carolina. We can become the dominant party."

Helms initially told reporters he "had not proposed anybody" for the chairmanship and wouldn't do so in the future. By late February, however, the senator changed his mind. He publicly endorsed McCarty at a Congressional Club fundraiser in Raleigh, although the senator was also careful to praise Hawke. Congressional Club activists pushed their candidate at every opportunity. They also ramped up attacks on what they labeled the "country club Republicans" who opposed McCarty. The governor's team answered the charge with chuckles rather than protests, noting that both Ellis and Wrenn were members of Raleigh country clubs, while Hawke had never belonged to one. Throughout the battle over the chairmanship, Martin succeeded in staying above the fray. He backed Hawke but carefully avoided making personal attacks on his adversaries. He was looking ahead to 1988 and remembering the Democrats' fatal disunity in 1972 and 1984.

The race for GOP chairman played out long before the state convention in May. Beginning with precinct meetings in February and then county conventions in March and April, the Hawke and McCarty factions fought for control of local parties and delegations. From the start, it was apparent that the governor's organization had the upper hand—and not just in the traditionally Republican counties of the Piedmont and west. Hawke supporters dominated conventions in such eastern counties as Onslow, Pender, Carteret, and Nash. Congressional Club leaders began pinning their hopes on victories in populous urban areas, particularly their home base of Wake County, where McCarty supporter Tony Maupin was county chairman.

But Wake was also home to many traditional Republicans and GOP officials serving in the governor's administration. They put up their own candidate for county chairman, attorney Arch Allen. When nearly a thousand Republican activists gathered at the state fairgrounds for the March 24 county convention, the stage was set for a testy confrontation. Raleigh attorney Chuck Neely, a McCarty supporter and law partner of Tom Ellis, served as convention chairman. Cherie Poucher, a Hawke supporter, served as secretary of the county party. After counting noses, the Hawke faction knew it had the majority and tried to hasten the proceedings. Not surprisingly, the McCarty faction tried to slow things down, hoping pro-Hawke delegates would be the first to leave. Eventually, Neely was ousted as convention chairman by Glen Downs, a Hawke supporter (and future top aide to Lieutenant Governor Jim Gardner and Congressman Walter Jones). Arch Allen was elected county chairman. Hawke supporters dominated the delegates elected to the state convention.

Although county-by-county efforts continued for several more weeks, the outcome in Wake was widely viewed as the clincher. Martin would get the party chairman he wanted. Now, he wanted something else: to move past the dispute as quickly as possible. He and his aides began a series of conversations and initiatives to close the intra-party divide. With the help of go-between Jack Bailey, a Rocky Mount businessman with ties to both Helms and Martin, the effort culminated in a private meeting Martin convened just before the May 30 state convention in Asheville. The meeting included Hawke, McCarty, and their respective campaign teams, including Ellis and Wrenn. They discussed convention details, party operations, and campaign strategies for 1988.

As the state convention began, McCarty formally withdrew. Martin and Helms stood together on the stage in a show of solidarity. Helms later described the tone of the convention as encouraging and remarked that many Hawke supporters and Martin loyalists had gone out of their way to shake his hand or give him a hug.

The factional dispute wasn't quite over yet. But Martin's strategy of focusing on Republican victories in 1988 was successful. Strikingly, it didn't take long for the various players in the drama to renew their political ties. Some former combatants, such as Wake GOP chairman Arch Allen and future state representative Chuck Neely, went on to form lasting friendships. Martin had several subsequent meetings with the Helms organization about joint campaign efforts in 1988, including a lengthy strategy session with Ellis and Wrenn just before the governor formally announced his reelection bid on January 4. He appointed former United States attorney Sam Currin, a former Helms aide, to a superior-court judgeship in Wake County. Helms's son-in-law John Stuart was promoted to a new job in the Martin administration. Ellis ended up hosting a fundraiser for Martin's reelection campaign in his Raleigh home. And in 1989, when Jack Hawke sought reelection as state chairman, Ellis and Wrenn supported the move.

Once again, the governor had emerged from a difficult political battle with both a hard-won victory and a reservoir of good will.

MARTINS IN THE MANSION

As the governor learned to deal with often-combative Democrats, sometimes-restive Republicans, and the other pressures of his office, his single greatest asset may well have been the first lady. Dottie was a gracious hostess, a kind friend, a keen judge of character, and a source of strength. Ever since his days as a college professor and county commissioner, Martin had been a hard worker. Still, his responsibilities were now far greater than even his congressional work load. His days began early and ended late. "The governor carried a big briefcase full of work home every night," Phil Kirk later recalled. Unlike Jim Hunt, however, Martin generally avoided calling his agency heads or staff members late at night or early in the morning. He made sure to reserve plenty of family time for Dottie and the children. They enjoyed getting away on the weekends and scheduling vacations when they could, particularly if sailing was part of the itinerary.

Work habits weren't the only difference between Hunt and Martin. The two families had separate approaches to inhabiting the Executive Mansion. The *News & Observer*'s Rob Christensen described the Martins' tenure in 1987: "Grilled salmon with dilled beurre blanc has replaced the Hunts' chicken-and-rice dinners. Liquor is being served after eight dry years, and the governor's long black Fleetwood limousine is taken out of the garage more often."

At first, Dottie had concerns about how she and the family would adapt to living in the mansion. "It couldn't have been any more different than what I expected," she later remarked. "It was an incredible experience." Dottie particularly enjoyed getting to know the mansion staff, including the prison inmates who helped maintain the building and tend the gardens. One early acquaintance was a marine captain incarcerated for shooting the man he had caught with his wife. When the governor was asked if he was afraid of having such a man in proximity, he replied, "Not as long as I don't mess with his wife." The marine later became maître d' at an exclusive country club.

The Martins were proud of how many inmates were able to turn their lives around after working at the mansion. They also enjoyed entertaining guests, whether political friends or foes of the governor, young Ben Martin's friends from school, or celebrities such as Barbara Bush and Arnold Schwarzenegger. On one memorable occasion, Bob Hope and his wife, Dolores, stopped at the mansion for a reception after the comedian's visit to entertain the troops at Fort Bragg. Dottie hosted the small gathering on the porch and arranged for glasses of sherry to be served. "I am Dolores Hope—with an *o*," announced one of the guests of honor, "and I would like a vodka tonic." Dottie made sure she got one.

The first lady's responsibilities extended far beyond the mansion. Dottie received countless invitations to make presentations and attend ceremonies. She accepted many of them. "I got to where I enjoyed doing stuff that I didn't think I might," she recalled. During her travels around the state, Dottie took the opportunity to promote two causes near to her heart. One was a program called Parent to Parent that helped families combat drug and alcohol abuse. The other began when Dottie read in the *Wall Street Journal* about a Texas program that encouraged the planting of wildflowers along highway medians and interchanges. She wrote a note to Jim Harrington at DOT asking how to adopt a more expansive version. The result was North Carolina's much-praised wildflower program, which uses revenue from the sale of vanity license plates and volunteer labor to beautify major highways from the mountains to the coast.

TESTING THE NEW FORMULA

The 1987 legislative session put to the test everything the governor had done since mid-1985 to build an effective administrative team, to craft a broad policy agenda, and to strengthen his political hand against his likely 1988 re-election foe, Bob Jordan. Martin now had a chief of staff, several new secretaries and deputy secretaries, and specific legislative goals across a range of controversial issues.

On January 28, 1987, Martin signaled his main priorities in his state budget plan. It proposed to expand the Career Ladder program statewide by the fall of 1988, to give a 4.5 percent average pay increase to state employees and teachers, to put $38 million more into building public and private prison capacity, to use $6 million to expand the administration's workfare program statewide, and to fund 84 percent of the $426 million originally slated for the Basic Education Program over the 1987–89 biennium while providing school districts more flexibility in spending the money. Recognizing the strain put on local infrastructure by North Carolina's burgeoning population, Martin also proposed that the state issue $1.5 billion in bonds to create a school-construction fund, from which counties could borrow at a low interest rate. He recommended another revolving-loan fund of $120 million for local water and sewer projects.

While advancing most of Martin's goals, the budget didn't propose any additional action on inventory and intangibles taxes. The governor and his aides decided to place the initial focus on K-12 education, where they thought they had a better chance of winning over Democratic legislators. They hadn't given up on taxes, however. The previous year, President Reagan and Congress had enacted sweeping tax reforms that broadened the base of the federal income tax while lowering the marginal rates. A legislative panel estimated that adjusting North Carolina's tax laws to the federal code's lower deduction amounts would hike state revenues by tens of millions of dollars. Martin hoped that as the revenue estimates firmed up later in the session, they'd come in on the high side, thus giving him an opening to propose offsetting cuts in inventory or intangibles taxes. Separately, the governor proposed a cut in another tax affecting the business climate: the payroll tax that funded unemployment-insurance benefits. Betsy Justus, head of the Employment Security Commission, advised Martin that a low jobless rate and steady funding of the UI trust fund in the past meant that North Carolina could cut the payroll tax by $50 million a year while maintaining current benefits and even setting up a separate state emergency fund.

Once again, Democratic leaders in the legislature greeted the administration's plans with skepticism. They criticized the pay raises and BEP expansions as inadequate and the Career Ladder expansion as premature. But neither the lieutenant governor nor the speaker of the House was as dismissive as two years earlier. Jordan, for example, questioned the details of Martin's loan funds for local schools and water systems, not the general concept, and ended up proposing a $2 billion plan that Martin praised as similar to his own $1.6 billion package of bonds and appropriations. Legislative leaders chose to offer no clear statements about their budget priorities until after the April 15 filing deadline for income taxes. A fiscal item that couldn't wait, however, was the governor's proposed cut in UI payroll taxes. After a few weeks of discussion, the General

Assembly passed it on March 16 to meet a deadline for applying the lower tax rate to employers for the 1987 tax year.

One leading legislator, Billy Watkins, chose not to wait for the revenue numbers before responding to Martin's budget. He quickly announced his own fiscal priority: a one-cent hike in the state sales tax to fund school construction. He argued that raising taxes was a better solution than issuing bonds. Jordan carefully distanced his tax stance from that of Watkins, who had begun making noises about challenging the lieutenant governor in the 1988 Democratic primary for governor. Instead, Jordan talked up a bill to give an income-tax credit for business investments in economically distressed counties, one of the ideas advanced by his rural development task force. The annual fiscal impact of $12 million, he said, would be "more than offset by the new and additional corporate tax revenues that will come from the business development that was stimulated by our targeted investment tax credits." Jordan's rhetoric demonstrated how much Martin's consistent advocacy of tax reduction as economic-development policy had shifted the terms of the debate in North Carolina, although the governor still favored broad tax relief over the kind of targeted incentives Jordan and the Senate were proposing.

When the post–April 15 revenue figures came in higher than expected, Martin seized the opportunity to restate his case against inventory and intangibles taxes. The concept of balancing the state budget, he said, should include "a balancing between excess resources and the taxpayers." He revised his budget plan to include a $40 million cut in the intangibles tax. Democratic leaders initially rebuffed him. The House approved its sales-tax hike on May 14. The Senate had already approved the investment tax credits and was heading to a vote on the $2 billion bond package for schools and other local infrastructure. Things seemed headed for an impasse. Who would blink first?

It would be Bob Jordan and the Senate. By early June, they backed off their bond proposal and offered the House a compromise to fund $2.9 billion in school construction over 10 years with pay-as-you-go appropriations, rather than new debt. The move prompted Martin to criticize Jordan's leadership ability. State GOP chairman Jack Hawke was characteristically more pointed, calling the lieutenant governor a "wimp." On taxes, however, Jordan and state senators had actually gotten more ambitious since the start of the session. Rather than simply adjusting the state tax code to the new federal code and pocketing the revenue windfall, they crafted a sweeping measure to establish a flat-rate personal income tax of 7 percent, to raise the corporate income-tax rate to 7 percent from 6 percent, and to abolish inventory and intangibles taxes entirely, as Martin had long advocated. Legislative leaders then began a weeks-long negotiation process to resolve their differences. The House offered to drop its sales-tax hike in favor of an income-tax surcharge. The Senate didn't bite. Meanwhile, Martin continued to defend his original school-bond plan and called the legislative alternatives "rinky-dink."

Finally, in early July, legislative leaders announced a deal. It retained the Senate's hike in the corporate tax rate (the first since 1933) and dedicated the extra revenues to school construction. It also eliminated a reimbursement to retailers for the cost of collecting sales taxes and fully repealed the inventory tax. The net effect was a tax increase of nearly $100 million a year, prompting Martin and nearly all Republican legislators to oppose the deal. The repeal of the inventory tax, however, was still a vindication of Martin's longtime position. And some business leaders, including First Union National Bank president John Georgius, saw its repeal as a bigger economic plus than the corporate tax hike would be an economic minus.

Politically, the outcome worked to Martin's advantage. He could say that legislators had followed his lead on the inventory tax (and the previously approved $50 million-a-year cut in the payroll tax) while criticizing their actions on the corporate rate. "We'll be glad to hang the high-tax label around their necks," Phil Kirk said on the eve of the Senate's passage of the deal.

HITS, MISSES, AND A LOW BLOW

As the General Assembly passed other bills and crafted the final budget, the governor won on some points and fell short on others.

Lawmakers approved some but not all of the money Martin sought for prison construction and slightly outbid him with average 5 percent pay raises for public employees. They rebuffed his proposals to restrict the state's abortion fund and to implement performance pay for teachers statewide, although they did appropriate funds to maintain the 16 Career Ladder pilots. Overall, the share of General Fund spending devoted to public schools went up, as Martin had argued for, while the share devoted to higher education went down. Another initiative the governor had championed, toughening North Carolina's laws combating drunk driving, failed to gain traction in the legislature, as did the expansion of workfare and another attempt to give the governor veto power. On economic development, lawmakers enacted Jordan's investment tax credits for distressed communities and created what became the Rural Economic Development Center to administer programs and grants outside the control of the Martin administration. (Hunt administration veteran Billy Ray Hall was hired to run the new state-funded nonprofit.) But on low-level radioactive waste, lawmakers sided with Martin against the idea of withdrawing from the eight-state regional compact after North Carolina was selected to build a disposal facility. Instead, lawmakers set up an authority to find a site.

The governor chalked up another partial victory during the 1987 session on the issue of budget transparency. After Martin's caustic attacks on pork-barrel spending and the Gang of Eight's secret budget writing, Democratic leaders responded by opening up the budget process a bit. They held public meetings of the supersub and required that members file individual bills for local earmarks. There were still secret negotiations. The legislature still ladled out pork. But there was more disclosure. Jordan and the Senate leadership were much more enthusiastic about the procedural changes than were Ramsey, Watkins, and House leaders. Jordan was looking ahead to 1988 and seeking to remove a rhetorical arrow from Martin's quiver.

As the session dragged on into late July, with House and Senate negotiators working out the final details of the budget and other matters, Democrats were presented with an opportunity not just to deplete the Republican governor's stock of political ammunition but also to wound him directly. Martin had long planned to leave August 1 for a two-week sailing vacation with his family in the Virgin Islands. No one had expected the session to last that long. With his departure date fast approaching, Martin asked Jordan if there was any reason to delay or cancel the trip. The governor explained that postponing it would bump the family up against his son Ben's return to school and the work schedule of his daughter, Emily, in Atlanta, and that he planned to hold a ticket reservation in case he needed to return to Raleigh on short notice. The lieutenant governor assured Martin that the arrangement would be fine, and that he wouldn't make the governor's absence a political issue. So the Martins kept their vacation date.

What happened next can at best be described as miscommunication among the Democrats, and at worst as a political ambush. The news media (predictably,

THE MARTIN FAMILY SAILBOAT, *GENESIS*, WAS A 1979 ALAJUELA 33 (A CUTTER-RIGGED DOUBLE-ENDER) THAT CAME FULLY EQUIPPED WITH A DINGHY (NICK-NAMED "EXODUS"), A GALLEY ("LA VICTUALS"), A HEAD ("NUMBERS"), AND AN ENGINE COMPARTMENT ("DIESELROOMINY"). MARTIN FAMILY PHOTO

in light of an earlier incident when the governor had joined Hardee's chairman Jack Laughery on a flight to watch the Kentucky Derby while the legislature tried to help Burlington Industries fend off a hostile takeover) played up the image of Martin sailing in the Caribbean as the General Assembly worked long hours to conclude the session. Asked to comment about Martin's sailing trip, Jordan made no effort to defend the governor or relate their prior conversation. And Ken Eudy jumped at the chance to savage the governor. "How do you know he's been on vacation?" he quipped to reporters on August 10. "He's been on vacation for the last two and a half years."

A day later, an annoyed Martin cut his trip short and flew home. "He shouldn't have made the promise" not to exploit the vacation for political purposes, Martin later said of Jordan. It damaged the personal relationship between the two men. But the episode didn't end up "doing a whole lot of harm" in the long run, Martin observed, eyes twinkling. "I mean, he got beat."

CHAPTER TEN

"BETTER SCHOOLS, BETTER ROADS, BETTER JOBS"

The outcome of the 1988 gubernatorial race was not a foregone conclusion. But it was never much in doubt that Governor Jim Martin and Lieutenant Governor Bob Jordan would face off in the race. The two politicians had sparred and jockeyed for position virtually since Martin's inauguration. So as strategists for the two campaigns planned their formal announcements for early 1988, the question was, how could they maximize news coverage of what was, essentially, not news?

The Martin team decided to emphasize both his status as an incumbent governor and his role as an outsider in a political system long controlled by Democrats. On the morning of January 4, 1988, Martin addressed a crowd of 400 supporters at the State Capitol. He referred to his first State of the State address, in which he had called for unity and cooperation across the political spectrum. "The response from all over North Carolina was positive and encouraging and hopeful," Martin said. "But from the General Assembly leadership, it was underwhelming, at times insulting, arrogant, disrespectful." Despite constant opposition from what he called "the legislative dictatorship" on Jones Street, the state had experienced rapid economic growth and job creation during his first three years in office. After his speech, the governor proceeded down Fayetteville Street to the state Board of Elections to file for reelection, accompanied by the crowd chanting, "Four more years."

Knowing Martin would seek to portray his Democratic opponent as one of those dictatorial legislators, the Jordan team decided on a different tack: emphasizing the lieutenant governor's business background and rural roots. The announcement strategy had four stages. First, on the same Monday that Martin filed for office in Raleigh, Jordan would give an announcement speech at his family's lumber business in Mount Gilead. Next, legislative leaders would hold a news conference on Wednesday responding to Martin's expected attacks—but without Jordan in the camera shot. On Thursday, Jordan would make another campaign announcement in Greenville, aimed at rural voters in the east. Then, on Friday, the lieutenant governor would drive one of his own Jordan Lumber and Supply trucks from Mount Gilead to Raleigh to submit papers and pay his filing fee. A stunt? Of course. But a potentially effective one.

The Democrats' strategy began well enough. Most media outlets paired Martin's Raleigh announcement with Jordan's Mount Gilead speech. Standing on a flatbed trailer in his warehouse, Jordan told 200 supporters that, "in every sense of the word, Jim Martin has been a sitting governor. In every sense of the word, Bob Jordan will be a working governor. Sitting governors like Jim Martin tend to hatch the future. Working governors like Luther Hodges, Terry Sanford, Jim Hunt, and Bob Jordan forge the future." The lieutenant governor repeated his accusations that his opponent had been missing in action during key moments, including the family vacation Martin had taken at the tail end of the 1987 session. Jordan said that "the fight to secure a future of opportunity and hope for our people is not being waged on Millionaire's Row at the Kentucky Derby or on a sailboat in the Caribbean."

But the rest of Jordan's week didn't exactly go as planned. When Democratic legislators launched their counterattack on Martin's tenure in office, the rhetoric went over the top. "I've been here three years, about as long as [Martin] has," said Representative Sam Hunt of Alamance County. "I can't think of a single initiative that he has had. That man is as weak as pond water. And you can print that." Since everyone knew Martin had indeed proposed legislative initiatives—Democratic lawmakers had spent much of the past three sessions either criticizing or modifying them—the attack didn't ring true.

The next problem was meteorological, not rhetorical. A massive snowstorm hit North Carolina on January 7, forcing Jordan to cancel his Greenville speech and reschedule his planned January 8 caravan to Raleigh. So it wasn't until the following Tuesday, January 12, that he left his warehouse driving an 18-wheeler full of pine boards to the capital. An entourage of supporters and reporters trailed in two buses and more than a dozen cars. After parking his truck in front of the Department of Transportation, he admitted to reporters that the event was "a little hokey" but insisted it illustrated an important difference between the two candidates. "As we round the corner and head into the 1990s," Jordan said, "North Carolina doesn't need a governor who is content to be a passenger or a back-seat driver. It needs a governor who is in the driver's seat, with his hands on the wheel, his feet on the pedals, and his eye on the road ahead of us." But if the trip was meant to underline Jordan's blue-collar appeal, its conclusion didn't quite work. The candidate emerged from the truck wearing a green suede jacket and a necktie. Much later, Jordan's official biographer, longtime capital reporter Ned Cline, wrote that the gimmick just didn't fit the candidate. Jordan's supporters "agreed the truck was fine, and the jacket was fine," Cline related. "But the two images didn't fit together."

THE CHALLENGER'S CHALLENGES

While Jordan's announcement week did not prove a triumph of political theatrics, the Democratic candidate and his team knew they needed to take some risks to win. Martin was an experienced, effective campaigner with high favorability ratings from the public. North Carolina's economy had added more than 300,000 net new jobs since Martin's inauguration, pushing the unemployment rate down from 6.5 percent in January 1985 to 4.2 percent in December 1987. Although North Carolina had little experience with gubernatorial reelections—Jim Hunt was the only two-term winner to date—the history of such races elsewhere suggested that a likable incumbent presiding over a growing economy would always begin as the favorite.

On the other hand, when the Jordan team began planning for the 1988 race, the national political environment looked at least neutral, if not favorable. Ronald Reagan was nearing the end of his second term. Despite being personally popular, he had lost face during the Iran-Contra affair and watched his party lose the Senate in 1986. The early polling on 1988 suggested a wide-open general election for president, which was why a full slate of credible candidates lined up for the major-party nominations. The eventual GOP pick, Vice President George H. W. Bush, had to overcome serious campaigns by Senator Bob Dole of Kansas, Representative Jack Kemp of New York, former governor Pete du Pont of Delaware, and televangelist Pat Robertson. Meanwhile, state Democrats considered such potential nominees as Massachusetts governor

Michael Dukakis, former senator Gary Hart of Colorado, Senator Al Gore of Tennessee, and Representative Dick Gephardt of Missouri as far more competitive in North Carolina than Walter Mondale had been in 1984—and thus less of a potential drag on the state Democratic ticket.

Moreover, Jordan was hardly an electoral novice lacking substantial political resources. Before his election to the state Senate in 1976, Jordan had spent 15 years as one of the state university system's key leaders, first as a trustee of the six-campus Consolidated University of North Carolina and then, after the creation of the 16-campus UNC system, as a member of its new Board of Governors. Jordan had also served on the Mount Gilead Town Council for 11 years. These experiences armed him with a deep knowledge of government and a statewide network of contacts with deep political roots, deep pockets, or both. As a state senator and lieutenant governor, he had proven his ability to convert these assets into votes, influence, and campaign contributions. He wisely gave his gubernatorial campaign an early start, commencing shortly after the 1986 midterm elections to recruit staffers, donors, and activists. During 1987, his campaign raised $1.1 million, nearly keeping pace with the incumbent governor's $1.4 million. The lieutenant governor counted business leaders across the state—including Charlotte executives who had contributed to Martin's prior campaigns—among his supporters. In short, Bob Jordan was not the state Democratic Party's sacrificial lamb in 1988. His was a serious campaign waged to win, not merely to place.

With the benefit of hindsight, many observers have deemed Jordan's scenario for victory unrealistic. Although early polls suggested the eventual Democratic presidential nominee, Dukakis, might compete effectively in North Carolina, Bush ended up winning the state with 58 percent. It was a landslide, albeit not quite as large as Reagan's 62–38 walloping of Mondale in the state four years earlier. However, it's erroneous to assume that presidential politics would trump everything else. Even in 1988, Bush's strong showing at the top of the ticket didn't guarantee Republican success down the ballot. In Indiana, for example, Bush beat Dukakis by a 60–40 margin, yet the state's secretary of state, Evan Bayh, became the first Indiana Democrat in 20 years to be elected governor. Ticket-splitters had, and would continue to have, a long history in North Carolina as well. For example, even as George W. Bush won 56 percent of the vote in North Carolina for president in both 2000 and 2004, Democrat Mike Easley was elected and reelected governor.

More to the point, public polls several times during North Carolina's 1988 gubernatorial campaign put Jordan within striking distance of victory. Martin emerged the winner in the end. But his victory wasn't inevitable, or handed to him by Bush and the national GOP. Martin and his team had to earn it.

BOTH SIDES STRESS UNITY

The composition of Martin's campaign team had changed since the 1984 race. Brad Hays was still in charge of the war room in Charlotte, and senior advisors such as Bob Bradshaw, Margaret King, and Joe Martin continued to offer support. Don Ringe produced the broadcast ads again, and Lance Tarrance did the survey research. Tim Pittman left the governor's office to serve as chief spokesman for the campaign. His replacement as press secretary to the governor was Jim Sughrue, who'd done press work for the Department of Transportation. Kevin Brown, a former Broyhill aide and state DOT official, came on board as campaign manager. Jack Hawke, who'd done that job in 1984, was now the state chairman of the Republican Party. Paul Shumaker, who had worked on the day-to-day operations of the 1986 trial run from his post at the state party, performed similar work for the 1988 reelection campaign. There were several new faces at the campaign office. For example, Dawn Lowder, a fundraiser for the state party, became finance director. She and the campaign relied on a strong network of business executives—including longtime Martin friend Rusty Goode of Charlotte and finance chairman Charlie Shelton of Winston-Salem—to give and raise significant sums for the reelection effort.

As he'd done four years earlier, Martin moved quickly to unify state Republicans behind his campaign. Given the tensions with the Congressional Club that had burst into open conflict over Hawke's election in 1987, his concerns were reasonable. As it turned out, however, Martin had two important things going for him in this regard. First, he had an excellent emissary in Bob Bradshaw, who remained a respected figure in both camps. Second, there was no obvious point of contention, at least not at the start of the 1988 election cycle. North Carolina had no Senate race that year. The Congressional Club was focused primarily on the battle for the GOP presidential nomination, in which its leaders joined many Martin allies in supporting the governor's longtime friend Jack Kemp, and on the upcoming reelection campaign for Jesse Helms in 1990, to which Martin had already pledged his wholehearted support.

It wasn't until March that the wounds began to fester. By then, Kemp's presidential aspirations had fizzled. Some conservative activists and Congressional Club leaders transferred their allegiance to Pat Robertson. But when North Carolina held its presidential primary on March 8 as part of a Super Tuesday set of regional contests, Bush won 29 of the state's 54 delegate slots. The Robertson organization immediately sought to dominate the precinct meetings and conventions that would select the delegates. The 29 Bush delegates would be obligated to vote for their candidate on the first ballot, after which they'd be free to transfer their support, presumably to Robertson, if subsequent ballots were required. Naturally, Bush supporters in North Carolina were determined not to let that happen. Many were also Martin loyalists.

The resulting contests had the potential to spark another GOP conflagration. At two of the 11 district meetings to select delegates, Robertson supporters outmaneuvered the Bush organization and seized control. At three others, however, the Robertson faction found itself outgunned and left in a huff to elect its own slate. The most boisterous confrontation occurred at the Fourth District convention in Louisburg on April 31, when conservative activists loudly complained of rules violations by pro-Bush presiding officers. Some Robertson supporters actually stormed the stage and tried to take over the meeting. Law-enforcement officers had to break up the resulting fracas. Ellis and other conservative leaders responded with restraint, and Martin made calls to both sides in an attempt to resolve the disputes. He also used humor to defuse the situation. After watching a professional wrestling match at Raleigh's Dorton Arena with his son Ben, the governor said he had checked to see if any of the wrestlers were available to "maintain order" at the upcoming state GOP convention. Unfortunately, he said, "they're booked that night."

In the end, the issue didn't reopen the wounds from 1987. Neither did the prospect of a competitive GOP primary for lieutenant governor. With Martin's encouragement, former congressman Jim Gardner announced in late 1987 that he would run for the office. Most Republican legislators and local officials quickly embraced Gardner's candidacy. That left another candidate for the nomination, state representative Bill Boyd of Randolph County, on the outside looking in. Boyd had solid ties with the Congressional Club and the emerging Pat Robertson organization. Again, however, the tussle between Gardner and Boyd didn't erupt into a broader intra-party fight. Gardner had represented eastern North Carolina in Congress and was credited by all sides as an early party builder. He easily won the nomination for lieutenant governor.

Democrats had their own worries about party unity. Although Jordan had been the presumptive nominee for governor for years, not all Democrats welcomed the prospect. During the 1987 session, Liston Ramsey's right-hand man, Billy Watkins, publicly talked up a potential run for governor. So did William Carl, co-owner of the Raleigh-based Golden Corral restaurant chain, and state auditor Ed Renfrow. Even longtime Commissioner of Agriculture Jim Graham floated a trial balloon about seeking the nomination. A horrified Jordan team saw history repeating itself. While his personal relationship with Watkins was rocky at best, Jordan stayed in constant contact with other House leaders and Democratic power brokers around the state. He also met privately with Carl, Renfrow, and Graham. By early May 1987, Carl withdrew his name from consideration and backed Jordan. Graham let his trial balloon quietly deflate. Renfrow actively pursued the idea for several months before backing out.

That left Watkins as the only potential primary challenger. His unofficial campaign over the course of 1987 never caught fire. Even Ramsey was careful to clarify that his public praise of his friend did not constitute a formal endorsement. There was certainly no love lost between the two camps. Watkins angrily accused state Democratic chairman James Van Hecke of using party resources to promote Jordan's candidacy. In response, some in the Jordan camp threatened to run a primary challenger in Watkins's House district. Shrugging off the threat, Watkins continued to insist that the gubernatorial nomination ought to be a competitive campaign, rather than a coronation. Most North Carolina Democrats were inclined to disagree, however. They wanted to defeat Martin. Unifying early behind Jordan seemed the best way to do that. By late November, Watkins bowed to the inevitable. He even repeated the reasoning other Democrats had offered him, that "to repeat the mistakes of 1984" with a divisive primary would pave the way for Martin's reelection.

Jordan's inner circle included longtime Democratic stalwarts as well as interesting new faces. Future White House chief of staff and University of North Carolina president Erskine Bowles, the son of 1972 gubernatorial nominee Skipper Bowles, began his service as Jordan's state finance chairman in early 1987, and was later assisted on the campaign staff by Laura Davis. Van Hecke, the party chairman, was a Greensboro public-relations manager. He and Ken Eudy kept up a barrage of attacks against Martin through 1987 and 1988. Chapel Hill–based media consultant Michael McClister produced Jordan's broadcast ads. Harrison Hickman, who had previously worked for Jim Hunt and Terry Sanford, handled the polling. On the campaign itself, Jordan's executive assistant, John Crumpler, left the lieutenant governor's office to become campaign manager. Randy Johnston, a former party staffer who had worked on Democratic congressional campaigns, served as political director. Phil Wells, a former reporter at WECT-TV in Wilmington, became press secretary. Two former workers on Lauch Faircloth's 1984 gubernatorial campaign, John Talton and Cynthia Simmons, became campaign treasurer and events coordinator, respectively.

ORIGIN OF A CATCHPHRASE

While actively preparing for reelection, Jim Martin continued to work with former Tennessee governor Lamar Alexander, newly elected South Carolina governor Carroll Campbell, and other friends to rebrand Republicans as an effective governing party at the state and local level. Martin helped lead

Southern Republican Exchange meetings and offered advice to numerous GOP candidates.

A surprisingly competitive mayoral race in Charlotte in late 1987 gave him a chance to advance both causes—his reelection bid and local party building. Incumbent Democratic mayor Harvey Gantt, one of the South's most prominent black politicians, faced Republican Sue Myrick, a former member of the city council. Myrick made traffic congestion one of her key campaign themes. Many of Martin's longtime allies in Mecklenburg politics pitched in to help. A few days before the November 3 election, the governor came to Charlotte for a campaign appearance with Myrick. She defeated Gantt by a narrow margin. The victory demonstrated the GOP's effective organization in the state's most populous county and gave a lift to Republicans across North Carolina.

During the same month he stepped in to boost Myrick's campaign, October 1987, the governor joined his leadership team for a strategy session at Raleigh's Peace College. Much like their retreats in Southern Pines in 1985 and at Meredith College in 1986, the Peace College meeting afforded them an opportunity to set priorities. To complement his longstanding commitments to expanding performance pay for teachers and improving infrastructure, Martin added new initiatives on coastal development and senior citizens. Still, the core of his agenda continued to be education, transportation, and pro-growth tax policies. During his first term, the governor had discussed each of these issues at great length, using a variety of phrases to bundle them into a single message. As far as can be determined, it was in a media interview in late 1987 that Martin first used the phrase that would define his reelection campaign. He was explaining to Associated Press reporter John Flesher how he had gone about picking the issues he championed during his first three legislative sessions. "If you look at the historic responsibilities of governors," Martin said, "it's to strengthen the quality of life in our state through better schools, better roads, and better jobs. I and my administration have a strong record on that."

For months afterward, "better schools," "better roads," and "better jobs" cropped up occasionally in the governor's other interviews and off-the-cuff remarks. It was much later, at an event in North Wilkesboro, when they reached official status. As campaign aide Paul Shumaker told the story, Martin arrived at the event thinking it was a fundraiser, only to learn it was a full-fledged rally with hundreds of supporters expecting to hear a campaign speech. The governor quickly huddled with spokesman Tim Pittman to come up with one, using bits and pieces of the talks he'd already been making. What resulted was one of Martin's best-received speeches. The loudest applause came when he promised to continue working for "better schools, better roads, and better jobs." The first two made the third possible, he explained, while better jobs would in turn help produce revenue to pay for more school and road improvements. The audience loved the turn of phrase. So did Martin, who immediately asked if the campaign could have it printed on a banner for future events.

"Get him a banner," Brad Hays told Shumaker. "Hell, get two of them!"

A BATTLE OF COMPETING NARRATIVES

Jordan had only token opposition in the Democratic primary, and Martin had no opposition at all. Still, both men spent the 1988 primary season on the campaign trail perfecting their general-election messages. While most observers respected the lieutenant governor's legislative achievements and leadership ability, they thought Martin possessed superior skill at communicating.

The gap was clearly evident as the campaign unfolded. The first Martin-Jordan debate occurred on January 22, 1988, just a couple of weeks after the two men formally entered their respective primaries. At a forum put on by the state press association at Chapel Hill's Carolina Inn, Martin asked if Jordan was trying to present "a neo-macho image" by driving a truck to Raleigh to file for office. "I just wanted to give you an easy question," the governor added as the audience guffawed. Later, when Jordan repeated the now-familiar Democratic line about a "sitting governor," Martin mugged for the crowd and moved his eyes up and down, calling attention to the fact that Jordan was also sitting. Again, the journalists broke out in laughter.

Recognizing the problem, Jordan worked with a speech coach and pressed his staff to write punchier, more memorable lines. Longtime Hunt aide Gary Pearce also pitched in to help Jordan prep for subsequent debates. Over time, the lieutenant governor's performance improved. But the Democrats' strategy for defeating Martin never hinged on winning formal debates or sound-bite exchanges. Their goal was to act early to frame the media narrative for the race, laying the groundwork for a barrage of attack ads to come later. The Republicans knew this, of course, and sought to establish an alternate narrative.

In Jordan's telling, the General Assembly had made major strides over the past three years, while the "do-nothing governor" spent his time criticizing and politicking from the sidelines. In Martin's telling, he had managed to set much of the legislative agenda—pro-growth tax cuts in 1985, highway funding in 1986, and school construction and tax policy again in 1987—despite being a Republican governor without veto power in what was still an overwhelmingly Democratic capital. His core message was to link his policies and leadership to North Carolina's robust economic growth. Since Martin's inauguration, North Carolina's per capita income had grown by an average annual rate of 6.5 percent, faster than the nation's 5.5 percent and the Southeast's 5.8 percent. Job creation also far exceeded regional and national benchmarks. "Let's keep a good thing going" became one of the governor's signature lines during speeches and media appearances. It was also the theme of the campaign's initial flight of TV ads, which ran during the statewide broadcast of the ACC basketball tournament in mid-March. "Take a look around," Martin invited viewers in the ad, mentioning the favorable statistics on job growth, education, and new industries ranging "from turkeys to high tech."

A separate event in early 1988 gave the governor another chance to tout his record on jobs. It involved the largest employer in western North Carolina, the Champion International paper mill on the Pigeon River in Canton. For years, Tennessee residents who lived downriver from the mill had complained about discolored water, pollution, and fish kills. They blamed the chemicals Champion used to bleach its wood pulp. In 1983, Tennessee and the EPA filed suit. The case finally reached the United States Supreme Court in 1987. It ruled that in cases in which two states disagreed over quality standards for common bodies of water, the EPA could intervene.

It was now up to the two governors, Martin in North Carolina and Democrat Ned McWhorter of Tennessee, to work out a compromise. Martin decided to travel to Nashville on January 14 to meet with McWhorter. On the way, the former chemistry professor stopped in Canton and used Mason jars to take samples of water upstream and downstream from the plant. With thousands of jobs at stake—both in Canton and in affected communities on both sides of the border—Martin publicly urged McWhorter to join him in balancing the need for tighter standards with economic realities. Holding up the two jars, he pointed out that the water upstream from the Champion plant was itself discolored, due to natural causes, though it wasn't as dark as the sample

MARTIN ADDRESSES A CROWD IN FRONT OF NORTH CAROLINA MUSEUM OF HISTORY. OFFICIAL STATE PHOTO

taken downstream. "Is that difference enough to shut down $160 million in economic impact in that area?" Martin asked.

On March 9, 1988, the two governors announced a deal. Tennessee agreed to a less-aggressive standard on the river's color, and Champion agreed to $200 million in upgrades at the mill to reduce its environmental footprint. Martin was widely credited for helping resolve the controversy.

Jordan and his team knew they couldn't win without crafting an effective response to Martin's message on jobs and the economy. They chose to emphasize the gap between urban and rural areas. Jordan argued that Martin's economic policies were too passive and unfocused. Rural communities needed immediate state help, he said, in the form of grants, loans, and targeted tax incentives. "We're going to have to use government," Jordan had told a gathering of business executives in Pinehurst in early 1987, with Martin looking on. "The government is going to have to help create some jobs."

The debate resumed at the Emerging Issues Forum, an annual event created by Jim Hunt and held at North Carolina State University. With Jordan and future Democratic presidential nominee Michael Dukakis also present, Martin agreed that government did indeed have a critical role to play in economic development—but mostly as a provider of public services at an economical cost. For the state to attempt to steer investment capital to specific counties or companies would be to inject politics where it didn't belong. "Government should not play the role of making business decisions," Martin said. The debate continued throughout 1987 and into early 1988.

Jordan's first major proposal as an announced candidate for governor was to replace North Carolina's Department of Commerce with a public-private partnership. The lieutenant governor argued that it would be able to act more nimbly to recruit prospects and would do a better job of advertising the state's business climate. As evidence that a new approach was needed, Jordan pointed to specific employers that had either downsized or left the state, citing the closing of the American Tobacco Company in Durham and the relocation of RJR Nabisco's corporate headquarters from Winston-Salem to Atlanta. He also noted projects the state had failed to attract, such as a Mack Truck plant that ended up in South Carolina and a computer-chip research consortium, Sematech, that went to Texas. Later, Democrats also assailed Martin for failing to win a major federal project, the Superconducting Super Collider. North Carolina had been one of several states angling for the $4.4 billion project, offering hundreds of millions of dollars' worth of land, infrastructure, and other inducements if Washington would put the particle accelerator on a rural site near Oxford. Texas ultimately landed this project as well (although it was only partially completed when Congress pulled the plug in 1993). Rather than doing the real work of economic development, the lieutenant governor insisted, Martin preferred to make speeches and take credit for the work of others. "The most dangerous place to be in North Carolina is between the governor and a television camera," quipped Brenda Summers, Jordan's communications director.

The governor called Jordan's proposed replacement for the Department of Commerce "an incredibly dumb and dangerous idea" and denied that North Carolina was falling short in economic competition. New jobs from start-ups or expansions had more than made up for jobs lost from companies that downsized or departed during his tenure, Martin pointed out. He described Jordan and other critics as "bad news bearers" whose claims wouldn't fool the state's increasingly optimistic voters. He also cited major projects that had come to North Carolina during his first term, such as a Sara Lee bakery in Tarboro, and touted the results of trade missions he'd made to European and Pacific Rim countries. Martin had in his first three years taken as many business-recruitment trips as Jim Hunt had in eight years.

Interestingly, the governor never let the spirited defense of his record shade into denial of lingering or emerging economic challenges. "The biggest concern I have is that, after such a long steady period of economic growth, that we may be in for a recession next year or soon after," Martin said in late 1987. "Nobody believes we've repealed the downturns in business cycles." He argued that the policies implemented during his first term hadn't just encouraged growth but would also help cushion the blow if North Carolina followed the rest of the nation into a downturn.

SETTING UP OTHER ATTACKS

To advance another line of attack against Martin—that he was insufficiently committed to school improvement—Democrats didn't just issue statements. In early April, the Jordan campaign launched its first major ad buy of the 1988 campaign. While listing his legislative accomplishments, the spot portrayed the lieutenant governor presiding over the state Senate. But it also took a shot at Martin for his initial opposition to full funding for the Basic Education Program in 1985 and his opposition to the 1987 tax hike for school construction. As expected, the Jordan campaign also sought to capitalize on Martin's decision to go on a family vacation near the end of the 1987 session. The lieutenant governor and a host of surrogates made constant references to the episode. James Van Hecke, for example, dismissed the governor's influence in Raleigh by saying, "It's a little tough to convince folks that he was having an impact across the sea." In mid-December 1987, Ken Eudy arranged to have a seat cushion gift-wrapped and sent to the governor's office as a Christmas present, suggesting it could be used on sailboats, at the Kentucky Derby, or on a golf cart. "When he is not sailing the Caribbean," one fundraising letter under Jordan's signature stated, "Martin is spending virtually full time flying around the state—cutting ribbons, speaking at road dedications and taking credit for new industries that were recruited by Democratic administrations."

Martin freely admitted that his style differed from the frenetic approach of his predecessor, Hunt, whom Martin described as "involved in 1,000 issues" during his eight-year tenure. "I don't think anybody can productively lead that many crusades," he said. "I think you productively lead five or six at a time." The governor also rebuffed criticism of his relationship with legislative leaders.

Despite his initial efforts to cultivate them with regular meetings and social gatherings, they had treated him as a Republican interloper and worked from the beginning to make him a one-termer. Martin admitted he had been taken aback by the vehemence of the Democrats' opposition at the beginning of his term. During campaign seasons, he later reflected, he'd come to "expect the opposition to give as good as they got, and you wanted them to receive as good as they sent." But he wasn't accustomed to that dynamic after elections were over. During his past service in county government and Congress, "people tended to find ways to work together with bipartisan coalitions for this, that, and the other," Martin said.

Still another line of attack was to turn Martin's 1984 rhetoric about political patronage against him. In March and April, Democratic officials and legislators held multiple press conferences to press home the charge that the governor had been hypocritical about the issue, citing the administration's decision to hire three Republican congressional candidates who lost their races in 1986, as well as alleged instances of firing foes and hiring supporters to replace them. Beginning with the 1984–85 transition and periodically after that, some state employees with unaffiliated or Democratic registrations had claimed they were mistreated, passed over for promotion, or even terminated for political reasons. Democrats also criticized Martin for hiring Jimmy Green as a consultant and tapping Charles Knox to chair Alcoholic Beverage Control.

Bobby Stott and two other Democrats let go from managerial jobs in state government filed lawsuits for wrongful termination. Melinda Lawrence, a Raleigh attorney who would later serve as executive director of the left-wing North Carolina Justice Center, represented the three plaintiffs in what became a consolidated case. Among other exhibits, the plaintiffs cited a series of memos prepared for the incoming Martin administration in 1984 by Arlene Pulley, the former Green aide who later became the head of Martin's Office of Citizen Affairs. The Pulley memos identified three dozen state employees who had actively supported Rufus Edmisten and thus could not be relied on to serve the new Republican governor, according to Pulley. But the crux of the legal case was what actually happened, not what was discussed. Attorney General Lacy Thornburg, a Democrat, was charged with defending the governor. In prepping for the case, attorneys in Thornburg's office conducted a comprehensive review of recent hiring decisions. Among the top 152 jobs in state government, the review found, the Hunt administration had employed

151 Democrats, one Republican, and no unaffiliated voters. The Martin administration, by contrast, employed 66 Democrats, 64 Republicans, and 22 independents. Moreover, the Democrats in top jobs had supported a range of gubernatorial candidates including Edmisten during the 1984 cycle. The hit on Martin's hiring practices was, in short, quite a stretch. But the Jordan campaign still hoped it would dent the governor's reputation and give it an opening. (After dragging on for many years and reaching the federal appeals court, the *Stott v. Martin* case concluded in 1992 with a dismissal of all claims.)

ONE HOLIDAY AND TWO ERRORS

Few expected that one of the most contentious issues of the Martin-Jordan campaign would involve a state holiday honoring the birthday of Dr. Martin Luther King Jr. But that's what happened. The issue had its origins during the 1987 session, when Representatives Dan Blue and Ray Warren filed a bill to make the third Monday in January a paid holiday for state workers. While careful to praise King's record of leadership, Martin came out against Blue's bill, just as he had as a congressman opposed the 1983 bill creating the federal holiday. Because King was first and foremost a minister, Martin had argued, it would be more appropriate to commemorate his work on a Sunday, rather than a workday. And because King had led a movement to open up opportunities for employment and economic progress, giving workers a holiday in his honor didn't fit the bill. "Martin Luther King was crusading for days on, not days off," Martin said.

Jordan approached the issue with what proved to be self-defeating caution. He had previously endorsed the idea of designating a holiday in King's name, as long as it didn't disrupt the operations of state government. Blue's bill followed that course. It capped the total number of paid state holidays at 11. In years when Christmas fell on a Friday, Saturday, Sunday, or Monday (those years in which at least one of the state's three days off for Christmas fell on a weekend) the number of state holidays would rise from 10 to 11. But in other years, the new King holiday would have to replace an existing one. Blue's bill left it up to the state Personnel Commission to pick another day to be supplanted. It passed overwhelmingly.

That didn't end the controversy, however. The state then surveyed public employees to ask which existing holiday they wanted to give up and to suggest that if they wanted to make the King holiday optional, they still had time to lobby their legislators to rescind the law. Most respondents said they preferred the holiday be optional. When Blue and other Democratic lawmakers cried foul, Martin officials argued that the General Assembly had ducked the toughest call—which existing holiday it would replace—and foisted it on the administration.

After a cordial meeting with the civil-rights leader's widow, Coretta Scott King, Martin sought to tamp down the controversy by endorsing her suggestion that North Carolina create a new committee to organize commemorations of King's birthday. He created the commission by executive order in September 1987. A month later, his personnel office announced its decision: in years Christmas fell on a Tuesday, Wednesday, or Thursday, the addition of the King holiday would result in state employees working either Christmas Eve or the day after Christmas. Martin's next step took everyone by surprise, except for Brad Hays and the campaign team. The governor asked Jordan to serve on the new MLK holiday commission as its chairman. Fearing a trap, Jordan declined the invitation. But refusing the offer was itself the trap. The lieutenant governor fell right in.

Jordan's second error came during a March 17, 1988, speech to a meeting of black newspaper publishers. Despite the obvious presence of a UNC Center for Public Television crew, Jordan told the audience he "couldn't get elected without the white redneck vote in eastern North Carolina," so he couldn't be forthcoming about his potential agenda as governor. "I am not going to come out with programs that will defeat me, no matter how I stand on that program, because I want to get elected," Jordan continued. "There may be programs that you believe in and I believe in that will not be campaign issues, because if they are, I won't be governor." Chris Fitzsimon, the public TV reporter in the room, turned to his cameraman and joked, "If the camera isn't rolling, you're a dead man." Fitzsimon then approached Jordan after the speech to ask for clarification of the lieutenant governor's remarks. Amazingly, Jordan repeated the gist of them. Together with his transparently political decision not to serve on the MLK commission, Jordan's comments made him look shifty and unprincipled on matters of race. The Martin campaign pounced. "It sounds like something Jimmy the Greek might say," the governor said a day after Jordan's remarks came to light. That would hardly be the end of the matter, however.

The previous month, Martin had been faced with a racially tinged controversy of his own, albeit not of his making. On February 1, two armed Indian activists had stormed into the offices of the Lumberton *Robesonian* newspaper. Eddie Hatcher and Timothy Jacobs took the office workers hostage and demanded the state investigate their allegations of rampant corruption, racism, and cocaine trafficking within the law-enforcement agencies of Robeson County. While Martin aides didn't want to reward an act of terrorism with any substantive concessions, they also sought to resolve the 10-hour standoff without bloodshed. Hatcher and Jacobs finally gave themselves up when the governor agreed to have a task force look into the allegations. The two were convicted on state kidnapping and weapons charges but were acquitted in a separate federal trial just before the 1988 election. Hatcher later committed two murders in an unrelated incident and received life in prison, where he died of natural causes in 2009.

CONVENTIONS AND THE CONVENTIONAL WISDOM

North Carolina Democrats never had any illusions that defeating Martin would be easy. But many also never bought into the conventional wisdom that the governor was destined for reelection. Still, the first two independent polls of the race shook their confidence. A *Charlotte Observer* poll in February showed Martin with 54 percent of the vote and Jordan with 38 percent. A *News & Observer* poll in early March put Martin at 56 percent and Jordan at only 25 percent. Some Democratic donors and activists began to panic. In reality, neither campaign gave the survey results much credence. Both polls screened for North Carolinians likely to vote in the upcoming presidential primaries, thus producing Republican-leaning samples. The governor himself labeled the results "virtually impossible."

Much more promising for the Democrats was the next *Charlotte Observer* poll, released on June 4, the same day Martin was scheduled to address the state Republican convention in Raleigh. It surveyed all registered voters and found 47 percent for Jordan and 46 percent for Martin. At the same time, the poll found far stronger job-approval numbers for the governor (58 percent of respondents rated his performance either excellent or good, up from 52 percent in 1986) than for the General Assembly (34 percent). Thus, the explanation for the tighter race lay more in Jordan's gaining name recognition and support across the state than in the governor's becoming less popular. Now, it was the Republicans' turn to panic, but most didn't. Martin told reporters that while his own private polling still showed him ahead, it had also detected Jordan's momentum. "We expect the race to get close," he said, "and it may be that it's already close."

At the state GOP convention, Martin repeated his campaign themes: that North Carolina's economy was on a roll, that he had successfully set the legislative agenda despite being a Republican governor in a Democratic town, and that Jordan and other Democrats were far more interested in defeating him than in working together.

Two weeks later, at the state Democratic convention in Raleigh, the lieutenant governor didn't disagree. "He accuses me of opposing him in the legislature," Jordan said of Martin. "He is right. I plead guilty." He and other speakers sounded a strikingly populist message, in part to reinforce the attacks on Martin's work ethic and absence from the concluding days of the 1987 session. "We're organized, we're unified, and come November, the country-club Republicans will have more time to play croquet and go yachting," shouted Senator Tony Rand, the Democrat running against Jim Gardner for lieutenant governor.

THE LEGISLATIVE SESSION INTERVENES

Both sides continued to spar on taxes, education, transportation, and the economy in advance of the General Assembly's 1988 short session, which began in June. Martin proposed a $450 million highway bond issue, in part to fund a new "intrastate" system of four-lane roads envisioned by a study commission led by Democratic senator Bill Goldston. Another major Martin initiative was to merge state regulatory and conservation agencies to produce a new department, what would become Environment, Health, and Natural Resources. Legislative leaders quickly telegraphed that they wouldn't consider either the highway bond or the departmental reorganization, decisions the governor chalked up to their unwillingness to give him policy victories in an election year. Of course, that meant they ended up giving him effective campaign issues.

About a month before the session began, Martin proposed adjustments to the 1988–89 state budget. They included a 4.5 percent average pay raise for public employees, a new elder-care initiative, a pilot preschool program for at-risk four-year-olds, and a partial restoration of the tax credit retailers had lost in 1987 for reimbursing the costs of collecting sales taxes. He also recommended a change in the formula for allocating corporate income taxes. Instead of equally weighting a corporation's real property, employment, and sales in the state, Martin proposed to double-weight the sales factor—which would have the effect of reducing the corporate tax burden on manufacturers and other companies with significant facilities and payrolls in the state. The change had been requested by RJR Nabisco, which was considering the construction of a bakery in Garner. The governor insisted any such change be applied to all corporations. The two proposed tax cuts totaled $37 million a year.

On the eve of the session, however, the administration amended its budget plan to reflect lower-than-expected tax revenues. Although such adjustments were hardly rare, legislative leaders jumped at the chance to attack Martin for initially proposing "Washington-style deficit spending," as Jordan put it.

While the administration may have had a shaky start, it was the legislature that ended the session with few accomplishments and bad optics. Jordan and Rand, for example, tried to win points with the voters by pledging to abolish the pork-barrel spending Martin had consistently criticized. But when the House refused to go along, the Senate just ladled out the pork again. Jordan and Rand also promised to open up the budget process further, only to participate in an unannounced supersub meeting to finalize a budget deal.

BACK ON THE TRAIL

On June 25, Martin and Jordan met for their second debate, at a bar association convention in Myrtle Beach. Martin dubbed the lieutenant governor "Not Now Bob" for refusing to advance the governor's highway bond and state reorganization proposals during the 1988 session, and opened with a jab at one of Jordan's worst moments. "I'm here to ask you for your vote regardless of your race, creed, or the color of your neck," he told the audience. Jordan apologized for his "redneck" remark and repeated his charge that Martin had been a "sitting governor." Responding to the governor's call for continuity during

MARTIN CAMPAIGNS WITH NASCAR LEGEND RICHARD PETTY. MARTIN FAMILY PHOTO

North Carolina's strong economic performance, Jordan allowed that "things are going good, but good is not good enough. We can be and should be great."

During July and August, the two candidates continued to make public appearances, give speeches, and prep for the campaign homestretch after Labor Day. The national party conventions—the Democratic gathering in Atlanta in mid-July and the Republican gathering in New Orleans in mid-August—reinforced one of Martin's advantages. He welcomed the opportunity to tie his reelection bid to George Bush, while Jordan tended not to link himself too tightly to Michael Dukakis. A Mason-Dixon poll taken after the Democratic National Convention found that the gubernatorial race continued to be close, with Martin at 46 percent and Jordan at 42. Again, the conventional wisdom that the governor was destined for reelection was questionable. It was a real race. Neither side could afford to let up. And neither was immune to the stresses of a competitive statewide campaign.

In the Jordan campaign, for example, there was growing tension between Michael McClister and Harrison Hickman. The latter was used to offering his clients not just insights into public opinion but also messaging suggestions for reaching undecided voters. But what may have worked for Sanford and Hunt didn't work for Jordan. Hickman was dismissed. Still, McClister proved to have a rocky relationship with the campaign and candidate. Jordan passed on some of his advertising ideas. For a time, the campaign drew on the skills of yet another outside consultant, one who would rise to national prominence four years later: James Carville.

On the Republican side, Martin was an old hand at campaigning by this time, yet he was hardly immune to the strains of being on the trail. At the direction of Brad Hays, the campaign developed a standard operating procedure. Martin arrived about 15 minutes before each campaign event and left about 15 minutes before the crowd. He would always have access to a holding room where he could gather himself before a speech and make phone calls to handle pressing state business. The campaign would provide him with briefing papers of 10 to 12 pages, which the governor would typically read in the car. Afterward, he often asked staffers to quiz him on the contents. Eventually, Martin boiled his chief themes down to sentences on an index card. They came in categories: "Crises" for tough issues he'd handled, "Buffalo" for business recruitment projects, "Successes" for the main achievements during his first term.

Throughout the campaign, the governor kept in constant contact with his brain trust in Charlotte. Brad Hays came to Raleigh at least once a week, often working long hours and pushing his body to the limit. On one occasion, Hays entered the governor's office dripping blood, his shirt covered in shards of glass. He had been sideswiped by a dump truck while crossing Jones Street. On another occasion, Hays joined the Raleigh campaign staff for an early-morning meeting. Hard work, hard living, and the stress of the campaign had taken their toll. He had a heart attack while meeting with the governor. Still, he asked to be taken back to his hotel to sleep it off. When Martin ordered he go to the hospital instead, Hays threatened to have the driver fired. Fortunately for him, the threat was ignored. Hays later underwent quadruple-bypass surgery.

THE ATTACK ADS BEGIN

The relentless focus of Brad Hays may not have been good for his health. But its value to Martin became evident just before Labor Day, when the campaign launched the first in a series of ads challenging Jordan's job performance and veracity. Perhaps the most surprising twist was a spot aired on radio stations with large black audiences. It went after the lieutenant governor for refusing Martin's invitation to chair the MLK holiday commission. Set in a fictitious barbershop named Smitty's, the ad portrayed the barber and his customers talking about the controversy. "I wonder what Bob Jordan has got against Martin Luther King?" one of the characters asked. The campaign insisted the ad posed a legitimate question about Jordan's lack of candor. It also described the ad as part of a broader effort to reach out to black voters. The Jordan campaign and prominent African-American leaders were outraged. Representative Dan Blue, then chairman of the legislative black caucus, said the spot showed Martin "doesn't mind stooping to any depth to confuse the voters." The lieutenant governor called the commercial "a cheap shot" and "a mistake" that would hurt Martin more than Jordan.

The Jordan campaign soon launched attack ads of its own. They were designed to advance the message that, in the lieutenant governor's words, Martin had run "a lazy government" that was not up to the needs of a growing state. One ad cited the events of 1985 to suggest the governor was against the BEP. Another purported to show Martin sailing in the Caribbean and playing golf while the legislature was working in Raleigh. Still another listed the legislature's 1987 ban of phosphate detergents as one of Jordan's signature accomplishments, noting that Martin had said he would have vetoed the measure if he could. By far the most talked-about commercial, however, used footage of four chimpanzees to lampoon Martin's 1988–89 budget, which the administration had later revised due to lower-than-projected revenues. Wearing shirts and ties, the chimps were shown making phone calls, using an adding machine, and tossing papers into the air. Set up with a circuslike drum roll, the ad was a funny vehicle for delivering a serious message about the Martin team's alleged incompetence. At press conferences, Jordan used a series of scripted quips to push the same message. "If this administration were a TV series, it would be called 'Bloopers, Blunders, and Practical Jokes,' " Jordan said at a Democratic function. "If incompetence were an Olympic event, the administration would have a lock on the gold."

Hays and the campaign were ready for the attacks. On education, they observed that school spending had risen as a share of the state budget during Martin's term, as it had not during the previous six administrations. They also pointed out that Martin had prioritized "better pay for better teachers" over hiring for non-teaching positions in public schools. On the environment, the governor explained that the stringent water-quality standards his administration had implemented were a better way to combat pollution than banning household use of phosphate-based detergents, although he allowed that the ban might be seen as an "interim device" until the standards went into effect. Less diplomatically, the Martin campaign observed that one of Jordan's own companies had been fined $5,000 for running afoul of environmental regulations. Hays even had an ad produced and in the can that used footage of one of Jordan's timber crews harvesting trees. But he ultimately decided it was not needed.

The Martin campaign did pull the trigger on three other commercials targeting Jordan. One of them, like the chimp ad, opted for the funny bone over the jugular. It had a rotund good-old-boy actor talking to the camera about budget priorities and then slipping through a revolving bookcase to attend a secret meeting—only to show Jordan's picture hanging on the wall. Martin consultant Don Ringe had done a similar spot for Carroll Campbell's successful gubernatorial race in South Carolina two years earlier. Another zinger showed footage of Jordan's "redneck" remark from the spring and described him as "another double-talking, liberal politician who will say anything to get your vote." The third spot depicted Jordan as switching positions on open meetings and other issues, for political advantage. "Bob Jordan can't seem to make up his mind," the ad concluded. "But you can. Martin for governor."

While the campaigns exchanged blows over the airwaves, the candidates continued busy schedules of speeches, rallies, and press availabilities. It was at such an event in Wrightsville Beach on September 17 that the lieutenant governor launched perhaps his most caustic assault, charging that Martin and his top officials had abused their power through the awarding of state jobs and contracts. Speaking to state members of the Associated Press, Jordan cited the wrongful-termination lawsuits by Democratic state employees, decried the decision to hire several spouses of senior Martin administration officials, and called the governor's hiring of Jimmy Green a "payoff" for implicitly supporting the Martin campaign in 1984. The Jordan campaign followed up the lieutenant governor's comments with a statewide TV ad blasting the "$329 a day" Green had received as an advisor to the governor. Martin was insulted and angered by Jordan's questioning his personal integrity. Speaking to the same group a day after the lieutenant governor, Martin termed the charges a "smear" and vowed revenge. "I am going to get even with him," he told the astonished reporters. "Because on November 8, he is going to be whipped. He will probably say that is unethical, but that's the way I will get even with him . . . [by] crush[ing] him on November 8."

It may have been no coincidence that just before Jordan lobbed his ethics charges at Martin on September 17, the *Charlotte Observer* came out with its latest poll. Martin now led Jordan 51 percent to 43 percent. A few days later, on September 22, the *N&O* published its own survey, in which Martin led 47 to 36. The trend was also evident in the campaigns' internal polls. Republican fortunes were rising in general in North Carolina and elsewhere as the Dukakis presidential campaign began to flag. But it wasn't just that. In the *N&O* survey, 63 percent rated Martin's job performance as excellent or good, a level of approval the newspaper's pollster termed "unbelievable" and "very high for somebody who's been in office for four years."

Given the situation, one might have expected the challenger to peg his hopes on getting the incumbent to commit a gaffe during a televised debate. But the Jordan campaign was wary. The two men had made just three joint appearances so far in the campaign, including a September 7 meeting of a transportation group in Raleigh. None was recorded for broadcast. Recognizing his potential vulnerability in such a format, Jordan agreed to only one televised debate: a North Carolina Association of Broadcasters event on October 29 at Winston-Salem's Benton Convention Center. Jordan was probably right not to bet the farm on debates. While his performance at the Winston-Salem forum was solid, Martin got in most of the evening's best lines. Referring to the controversy about Jordan's "redneck" comment, for example, he said he thought the lieutenant governor "ought to tell us what that hidden agenda is."

As in 1984, Martin's campaign strategy relied heavily on appeals to conservative Democrats and independents. Although there was no divisive primary in 1988 to exploit for crossover votes, the Martin team still had plenty of assets to deploy for the effort. One was the governor's positive message, his appeal to North Carolina voters to "keep a good thing going." Throughout 1988, the state's economy continued to add jobs at a rapid clip—more than 100,000 positions during the first nine months of the year, for a net increase of roughly 400,000 jobs since his inauguration. *Judge me by results*, Martin was saying, *not by my party registration*. Furthermore, Jordan's strident criticism of Green didn't hurt the Martin effort in the eastern counties, where the former lieutenant governor still enjoyed significant support. Immensely helpful to Martin's appeal to eastern Democrats was that he made sure to have the last leg of I-40 to Wilmington under construction by the end of his first term.

MAKING THE FINAL TURN

About two weeks before the November 8 general election, the *Charlotte Observer* published its latest survey results: 51 percent for Martin to 40 percent for Jordan. Another new survey, from Mason-Dixon, also had Martin above the 50 percent mark. While taking nothing for granted, the governor began transitioning to a broader message of Republican unity and down-ballot success. State Republicans hadn't overlooked their other electoral opportunities for 1988. They fielded fewer legislative candidates than in 1986, but those candidates were for the most part better campaigners and fundraisers. Republicans also had a large slate of candidates for judicial and county offices. When President Reagan made a campaign stop in Raleigh on October 21, Martin took the opportunity to talk up the entire GOP ticket, including lieutenant governor candidate Jim Gardner. He amended his campaign slogan to "Better schools, better roads, better jobs—and a better lieutenant governor!"

He did the same thing a few days later when the campaign restaged one of its attention-getting tactics from the 1984 campaign: a three-day whistle-stop train tour of 22 cities from Asheville to Morehead City. Martin mentioned Gardner and a list of local candidates at every stop, citing the recent news that the number of registered Republicans in North Carolina exceeded one million for the first time. "We're charging to the finish line with all the power that a locomotive can give us," he said. At a later rally in Greensboro, he argued that sending more Republicans to the General Assembly would tell Democrats to "stop the obstruction," facilitating more bipartisan cooperation. More visibly relaxed on the campaign trail than he had been just weeks earlier, Martin even joked about some of Jordan's most biting attacks on him, including the ethics charges and the chimp ad. "You want to see me do my back flips?" he asked a Wilmington audience. "If he beats me with a bunch of apes, I don't deserve to be governor."

For his part, Jordan spent the last weeks of the 1988 campaign urging Democratic activists to ignore the polls. "Forget about what you see in the newspapers and what you see on television," Jordan told a Pender County crowd. "This race is ours to win if we get the people out to vote." Jordan, Tony Rand, and other Democratic candidates focused their efforts on counties in the east and urban areas that traditionally leaned Democratic, hoping to mobilize a last-minute surge of support. Jordan even put more of his own money into his campaign, which would end up spending $6.7 million (the equivalent of $13.3 million in 2015 currency), significantly more than the Martin campaign spent.

It wasn't enough. On Election Day, Martin won 55 percent of the vote to Jordan's 45 percent. As in 1984, Martin's decisive victory reflected a combination of strong support in traditionally Republican counties in the Piedmont and west; victories in the crucial urban-battleground counties of Mecklenburg, Guilford, Forsyth, Wake, Buncombe, and New Hanover; and significant reductions in his opponent's margins in traditionally Democratic counties in the east.

Other Republicans on the North Carolina ballot did well, too. In the lieutenant governor's race, Jim Gardner edged Tony Rand with 51 percent of the vote. Republicans picked up 13 legislative seats, many in previously Democratic strongholds in urban counties, giving them 59 of the 170 seats—the highest total the GOP had yet reached in the century. The party also captured 33 of the state's 100 county commissions, again a historic high. And for the first time, Republicans managed to crack the Democratic monopoly on statewide judicial races by electing Bob Orr to the North Carolina Court of Appeals and Howard E. "Howdy" Manning Jr. to the superior court in Wake County (until 1996, superior-court contests were statewide partisan elections).

Why did Martin win? Observers pointed to many factors—the Bush campaign for president, the health of North Carolina's economy, the dissension within the Jordan campaign. Ultimately, however, the race was a clash of candidates. Martin proved the better one. He was more polished, more disciplined, less prone to error. Moreover, Jordan was a respected public servant with significant legislative experience, but as the challenger in the race, it was his job to make the case against the incumbent, not just to say what he would do as governor. It was a role for which he proved ill suited. Even if it had fit him better, the attacks Jordan was tasked to deliver lacked the ring of truth. North Carolinians had watched Martin do his job for four years. They didn't see him as lazy, boastful, or unprincipled. They saw him as an effective leader. And they rewarded him with four more years on the job.

CHAPTER ELEVEN

A NEW COMBINATION OF ELEMENTS

The day after the 1988 elections, two Democratic state representatives, Dave Diamont and Donald Dawkins, met at a Laurinburg restaurant to commiserate over lunch. Jim Martin had been reelected. Jim Gardner would be lieutenant governor. Republicans had gained 13 seats in the General Assembly—the largest such GOP gain in the nation—including 10 seats in the House. Diamont and Dawkins were among a clutch of House Democrats who had long criticized four-term speaker Liston Ramsey and his lieutenant Billy Watkins for ruling the chamber with an iron fist. The Democratic dissidents saw the GOP's victories in 1988 as both a consequence of Ramsey's style of leadership and a potential remedy. By ruling imperiously and constraining policy innovation, they argued, Ramsey had given Republicans valuable election issues. At the same time, however, having 46 Republicans in the chamber presented the dissidents with an opportunity. If the GOP caucus held together, it would take only 15 Democrats to join them to elect a new speaker and reform the process.

A few days after their lunch, Diamont and Dawkins met again, this time in Asheboro, where they were joined by fellow Democratic representatives Dan DeVane, Pete Hasty, and Sam Hunt. A third meeting just before Thanksgiving brought 14 dissident Democrats together—already close to the magic number needed. Once they decided to approach the Republicans about forming a coalition, they called the governor's office to ask how best to proceed.

The day before Christmas, a delegation consisting of DeVane, Hunt, and Walter Jones Jr. (the future Republican congressman) met with Jim Martin. The governor was intrigued, to say the least. He encouraged the dissidents to continue recruiting Democratic support and to come up with a candidate for speaker whom Republican lawmakers could embrace. That candidate proved to be Representative Joe Mavretic of Edgecombe County, who had repeatedly clashed with Watkins. He'd even tried right after the 1988 elections to convince Ramsey to make a change. After Ramsey refused, Mavretic had begun drawing up his own plans for how a reformed House would operate. He concluded that it was essential to "get rid of Watkins" as the gatekeeper in the House, and that "the only way to do that was to get rid of Liston."

His plans for legislative reform weren't his only selling point as a prospective speaker. Mavretic enjoyed a close friendship with Representative Johnathan Rhyne of Lincoln County, whom Republicans had picked as minority leader to replace Betsy Cochrane, newly elected to the Senate. Mavretic's wife had attended law school with Rhyne and his wife. Mavretic knew he could trust Rhyne. So the elements of the plan were in place.

On December 30, 1988, Mavretic, DeVane, Jones, and Hunt met at the Executive Mansion with Martin, legislative lobbyist Ward Purrington, Rhyne, and Charles Cromer, the minority whip. Rhyne pledged the support of the Republican caucus in return for fair consideration of its bills, proportional representation on committees, and Republican chairs of some subcommittees. Mavretic pledged to bring more than enough Democrats to the coalition. Martin offered general advice but was careful not to intervene in the details of the agreement. His case for replacing the incumbent speaker, after all, was that "nobody should have [Ramsey's] kind of power to dictate how a freely elected member of the General Assembly could vote." He was hardly going to suggest the governor ought to do the same thing.

DEMOCRATS REACT TO REPUBLICAN GAINS

The dissension among House Democrats was part of a larger story. Trouble had been brewing within the state party for years. Discontent about overly dictatorial leadership at the General Assembly was one factor. Another was demographics. As blacks became an increasingly critical element of the party's electoral coalition, for example, African-American leaders pointed out that party leadership posts were not reflective of the change. Other Democratic

officeholders and activists had a different complaint: that outgoing chairman James Van Hecke had been too closely tied to Bob Jordan. They wanted the next group of party leaders not to be beholden to any one politician—including former governor Jim Hunt, who was already the subject of rumors about a potential rematch with Senator Jesse Helms in 1990 or a gubernatorial run in 1992. More generally, Democratic leaders were frustrated by the opposing party's historic gains in state and local offices in 1988. Without changes in both Democratic strategy and governance, they feared, the GOP tide would keep rising.

At the General Assembly, the initial public drama after the 1988 elections centered on what role Senate Democrats would allow the new Republican lieutenant governor to play. Powers such as assembling Senate committees and assigning bills were written into legislative rules, not the state constitution. Gardner argued that the voters had chosen to place a Republican in charge of the North Carolina Senate. Democrats saw things differently. They had a 37–13 majority and were entitled to organize the chamber and carry out their policy priorities. In truth, Martin and other Republicans never expected Gardner to retain the powers that Democratic lieutenant governors had enjoyed. They hoped for the best in the Senate but knew that the real action on expanding Republican influence lay with the secret negotiations under way in the House.

Once Ramsey caught wind of the impending coup, he and other Democratic leaders tried to head it off. Watkins offered to resign as chairman of House Appropriations. The speaker called some of the 20 dissenters now committed to Mavretic. Bob Jordan, House speaker pro tem Jack Hunt, and even Senator Terry Sanford called others. None would budge.

Just days before the election for speaker on January 11, 1989, Watkins approached Martin with a proposal. If the governor would help unravel the Mavretic coalition, Watkins promised to deliver House support for a gubernatorial veto and other administration priorities. "They offered me some very attractive proposals," Martin said, "like I could write my own ticket." Still, he declined. He put his faith in the plans he'd seen from the Mavretic coalition, not the promises of those who had opposed and criticized him for four years.

When it came to a vote, all 20 of the Democratic dissenters joined 45 of the 46 Republicans (GOP representative Monroe Buchanan abstained) to elect Mavretic as speaker. Among those Democrats voting to overthrow Ramsey were Harry Payne, a future commissioner of labor, and Roy Cooper, a future attorney general. As for the Ramsey supporters, their emotions ran the gamut from stunned to livid. "They have virtually destroyed the Democratic Party," Watkins said of the dissenters. He and other former Ramsey lieutenants formed what they called the "Kennel Club" to hurl opprobrium at Mavretic and his allies.

LOOKING FOR "MORE BEYOND"

A few days earlier, on January 7, Jim Martin had taken his second oath of office as governor of North Carolina before thousands of shivering spectators. The previous evening, Jim and Dottie had delighted the audience at the Inaugural Ball with a dance to the song "Memory" from the eight-year-old Broadway musical *Cats*. At the inauguration ceremony, Martin made a much earlier cultural reference. Before the voyages of Christopher Columbus, the Spanish crown had stamped the Latin phrase *"Ne Plus Ultra"* on its coins. The motto, "No More Beyond" in English, had a double meaning. It suggested that no lands lay to the west beyond the Spanish peninsula. It also suggested that no country was greater than Spain. After the discovery of the New World, Spanish rulers changed the motto to "More Beyond" to reflect their broadening horizons. Martin suggested that the phrase aptly described what he had in mind for North Carolina:

> *There are new challenges for us to face, along with unfinished business from the past. There is, indeed, a brighter future for North Carolina. Today, let us rededicate ourselves to fulfill that destiny for our state. Let us accept the responsibility to work together for better schools, better roads, better jobs, better environment, and for better quality of life for our people. Plus Ultra. For there is truly more beyond.*

Martin had reasons to feel confident about the prospects for bipartisan cooperation in the General Assembly. His old rivals Liston Ramsey and Bob Jordan were no longer in charge. Joe Mavretic had become speaker, thanks to Republican votes. The new Senate president pro tem, Henson Barnes of Goldsboro, was considered a fiscal conservative. And even though his office was significantly weakened, Lieutenant Governor Jim Gardner would also be a helpful ally.

Changes were afoot within the governor's team as well. Secretary of Commerce Claude Pope, suffering from the cancer that would soon take his life, resigned a few weeks after the inauguration. Martin picked his former congressional colleague Jim Broyhill as Pope's replacement. Another cabinet member, Thomas Rhodes, decided to leave the Department of Natural Resources and Community Development. His replacement was former congressman Bill Cobey. Also heading to a post at Natural Resources was Nancy Temple, who'd served as deputy chief of staff and previously in campaign jobs for former United States representative Gene Johnston and the Reagan-Bush team. Kevin Brown, manager of Martin's 1988 campaign, replaced Temple as deputy to Phil Kirk. There was turnover in the press shop, too. Communications director Karen Rotterman became an assistant secretary at Human Resources, after which she worked at Glaxo and in a consulting firm with her husband, Marc Rotterman. The governor's press secretary, Jim Sughrue, left to return to the Department of Transportation. Tim Pittman, who'd left the governor's office to work on the reelection campaign, now returned as communications director. His first deputy was David Prather, moving over from Transportation, to be followed by Nancy Pekarek. Another aide in the governor's office, research director Charlie Hughes, departed when Martin appointed him to the North Carolina Utilities Commission. And Dawn Lowder, who'd raised money for the 1988 reelection campaign, became director of citizen affairs as Arlene Pulley headed to the North Carolina Parole Commission.

PLANNING AN AMBITIOUS AGENDA

How could the Martin administration turn its political momentum into policy achievements? On November 9, 1988, just a day after his reelection, the governor met with his (sleep-deprived) staff members at the mansion for what turned into a seven-hour strategy session. The discussion continued off and on for the next several weeks. Harking back to the priorities they'd set in 1985, Martin and his team analyzed what they'd managed to accomplish and what opportunities the new political and legislative environment in Raleigh might afford them.

The newly reelected governor also consulted with his peers in other states, journeying to Florida in early December for the fifth meeting of the Southern Republican Exchange. After that, it was on to Kansas City for a meeting of the Council of State Governments, of which Martin was serving as president. At these events, he shared his experience of running on a "better schools, better roads, better jobs" theme and sought advice from other governors and legislators about how best to deliver on it.

On January 17, 1989, the governor went to the Legislative Building to give his third State of the State address. He summarized the administration's post-reelection review and described an ambitious agenda for his second term. As before, Martin would emphasize six major bundles of issues:

- **Transportation needs**. The legislature's vote in 1986 to raise the gas tax and transfer the cost of driver education from the Highway Fund to the General Fund had reduced the gap between North Carolina's long-term road needs and projected revenues. Two years later, however, legislative leaders had rejected Martin's proposal for a $450 million highway bond. Instead, they proposed a study. Unlike many such panels, designed merely for show or to give lawmakers cover to kill a measure they didn't like, the Highway Study Commission was taken seriously from the start. Key lawmakers and Martin confidants such as Rusty Goode served on it. Secretary of Transportation Jim Harrington supported its work. The architecture of the emerging plan included three core elements: (1) "strategic corridors," also known as the intrastate system, to put a four-lane highway within 10 miles of more than 90 percent of the state's population; (2) urban bypasses and loops around Charlotte, Greensboro, and other major cities to duplicate the functions of Raleigh's Beltline; and (3) "critical connectors" to link rural areas to the interstate and intrastate networks. Everyone recognized that the plan required far more revenue than current taxes could generate. The commission worked through 1988 to prepare a report for the 1989 legislative session.

- **Education reform**. Martin had long described the Basic Education Program as overly rigid, prescriptive, and formulaic. Over the first four years of its implementation, many Democratic lawmakers, civic leaders, and even education officials came to share that view. In 1988, the two-year-old Public School Forum of North Carolina had convened a broad range of policymakers, educators, and business executives to discuss an offer of more autonomy for local districts in exchange for compliance with a new, more rigorous set of accountability measures. Martin's education advisor, Lee Monroe, and his state school-board chairman, Howard Haworth, played a key role in the deliberations. One of Ramsey's former lieutenants, Bob Etheridge, ran for state superintendent of public instruction in 1988 on a similar platform and endorsed the forum's report, as did former governor Hunt. During his State of the State address, Martin observed that "a rising consensus" now favored "a greater degree of accountability at all levels of school leadership, with an emphasis on results," as well as "local flexibility in the management of state programs, even the BEP."

Martin also thought the Career Ladder approach to merit pay had proven its worth and was ready for statewide adoption. For this position, he had less support across the aisle. The North Carolina Association of Educators (NCAE) had spent much of the past four years criticizing the Career Ladder and publicizing teacher surveys showing opposition to the program. Martin and other proponents responded forcefully to the claims made by the NCAE, which the governor took to calling the "Negative Campaign against Evaluation." They noted that where the Career Ladder had been in place the longest, educators and parents tended to support it. The program "can and should be implemented statewide," said one participating principal from Edenton. "The extra income means someone knows you're working hard—someone cares enough to raise your salary," explained a teacher from Burlington. Even the head of Burlington's NCAE chapter, Linda Bryant, raved about the program. "I've seen the biggest improvement in teaching in the last three years—more than I've seen in the 22 years I've been teaching," she said, adding that the Career Ladder was "not a failure here at all." All 16 superintendents in the pilot districts endorsed taking the program statewide.

On another controversial education issue, school choice, it was Martin who had shifted his position over time. As a gubernatorial candidate in 1984, he had expressed caution about giving parents more authority to choose the public schools their children attended. He worried that such a policy might exacerbate racial imbalances. But after studying open-enrollment plans and other programs in Massachusetts, New York, Minnesota, and other states, Martin concluded that with the proper safeguards school choice would help drive education reform by using competitive pressure and fostering innovations such as "career education" high schools in partnership with community colleges. Choice "imposes the ultimate test of accountability on a school system: to meet the needs of the students," Martin said in his State of the State speech.

- **Prison capacity**. Despite the additional funds for facility construction and alternative sentences Martin had secured from the General Assembly during his first term, the state's prisons were still bursting at the seams. Much of the system was under the jurisdiction of federal courts and subject to strict capacity limits. The governor and Secretary of Corrections Aaron Johnson warned that both a crash program of additional construction and long-term changes in sentencing and prison management would be needed. Their goal was a system with a capacity of 18,000 at 50 square feet per inmate. As of early 1989, the capacity at that ratio was only 14,750.

- **Fiscal policy.** Operating parallel to the legislature's study commission on highways was the Tax Fairness Study Committee, chaired by Senator Marshall Rauch. It spent the latter half of 1988 crafting a set of tax-code changes to enhance compliance and reduce the tax burden on low-income households. Unlike most states with income taxes, North Carolina had not updated its code to offset the effects of bracket creep, either by raising the income thresholds to reduce the share of households paying higher rates or at least indexing the state's tax brackets to future inflation. Compared to other state tax codes, North Carolina's system imposed relatively high burdens on households with below-average incomes.

  Martin welcomed the legislature's work on tax compliance and fairness. He also hoped eventually to return to two of his original tax-policy goals: fully eliminating the intangibles tax and the sales tax on food and nonprescription drugs. But as the governor and his budget aides began preparing for the 1989 legislative session, they quickly realized any such plans would have to wait. Already evident were the fiscal effects of the economic slowdown that would turn into a recession the following year. Revenue was still growing midway through the 1988–89 fiscal year, but not as robustly as in the past. In December, Martin suggested that his budget might respond to tighter fiscal constraints by funding only half of the scheduled $113 million installment of the BEP. His trial balloon drew furious fire from Democratic lawmakers. So Martin and his team went back to the drawing board.

- **Environmental issues.** The disputes about how to handle low-level radioactive waste and hazardous waste had simmered throughout Martin's first term. During the 1988 session, lawmakers had blocked the search for a hazardous-waste incinerator site, prompting South Carolina to ban imports of North Carolina waste. That wasn't the only pressure to find a solution. Under federal law, states with no ability to treat or dispose of their waste were at risk of losing Superfund money for cleaning up hazardous sites. Meanwhile, North Carolina had drawn the short straw in an eight-state compact on low-level radioactive waste and agreed to build a new facility by 1993 to replace South Carolina's Barnwell disposal site.

- **Government reform**. Martin was determined to make another try for a gubernatorial veto. Although open to other constitutional or procedural changes to preserve the balance between the executive and legislative branches, the governor argued that a veto amendment be placed on the ballot as a separate measure.

On another matter, judicial selection, Martin continued to favor appointments rather than partisan elections for the appellate courts. One version of the idea had the governor filling vacancies on these courts, after which the appointed judges would stand for retention elections. Another proposal had the governor picking appellate judges for four-year terms, subject to legislative confirmation, after which they would be reconfirmed for eight-year terms by the Judicial Standards Commission.

PROPOSING A BUDGET, THEN ANOTHER ONE

On the same day the newly reelected governor gave his State of the State address, he also released his spending plan for the 1989–91 budget biennium. Intent on taking the Career Ladder program statewide without picking a costly fight over BEP installment, Martin chose to include both in his budget, offsetting the fiscal impact by phasing in both across-the-board and merit-based pay raises for teachers and state employees. Instead of taking effect at the start of the 1989–90 fiscal year in July, the pay hikes would begin the following April. The governor argued that fiscal restraint was the right way to pay for the Career Ladder expansion alongside the BEP. "Some may suggest that taxes be increased," Martin told the assembled lawmakers during his State of the State address. "That might have to be considered in the future if we find a chronic slowdown in revenue growth, but nobody forecasts that grim a picture. So instead I see one year in which we will have to tighten our belts to make room for some urgent improvements, while deferring others." His other recommendations included hikes in college and university tuition and a 78 percent reduction in the state's abortion fund. On the expansion side, Martin included $150 million over two years to increase prison capacity and the use of alternative sentencing, $20 million for increased monitoring of air and water quality, and $2 million to begin early-childhood education for four-year-olds considered at-risk.

The governor considered his plan a reasonable response to the state's policy needs and fiscal conditions. He also assumed his recent reelection, GOP gains in the legislature, and the rise of the Mavretic coalition would provide enough political momentum to make his budget stick. What he didn't foresee was how disappointed public employees would be about any delay in their pay raises, or how aggressively the NCAE and the State Employees Association of North Carolina (SEANC) would seize the opportunity to deal a blow to the Republican who had just defeated their favored candidate in the gubernatorial race. The NCAE blasted the Career Ladder expansion and insisted that all teachers receive immediate pay raises, even if it required higher taxes. It reminded Martin that during his reelection campaign, he had called for raising North Carolina's average teacher salary to the national average by 1992 (although Martin had not specified how the goal would be measured and had later suggested that raises be tied to higher student performance). When the governor visited Hickory to meet with several hundred school leaders and educators, NCAE members booed and mocked him as he tried to answer their questions. They did the same thing during a protest in front of the Executive Mansion in Raleigh. The organization began planning an even larger rally in the capital for early February. In the General Assembly, Martin's approach drew strong support only from GOP lawmakers and the lieutenant governor. Even the House Republicans' Democratic coalition partners were cool to it. Mavretic was openly critical, demanding that "the individuals who campaigned in the executive branch on better education and better schools"—meaning Martin and Gardner—"put their money where their mouth is."

Some of the governor's aides were panicked by the blowback and urged Martin to rethink his position. The governor did indeed do so. But panic wasn't the reason. Instead, he thought he saw the outlines of a grand bargain to give his second-term agenda a huge boost. The NCAE and the SEANC wanted

MARTIN SHARES A SMOKE AND A LAUGH WITH LONGTIME AGRICULTURE COMMISSIONER JIM GRAHAM. MARTIN FAMILY PHOTO

pay raises. Democrats wanted more revenue for education and other programs. Martin and his Republican allies wanted merit pay for teachers and action on the one tax plank from the 1984 campaign platform that the General Assembly had yet to act on, the food tax. So on February 9, the eve of the NCAE rally, Martin called for an "education summit" to bring together legislators, administration officials, and school leaders to discuss the issue.

Over the next several weeks, the governor huddled with aides and ran budget numbers on his personal computer. By early March, he was ready to announce a new plan based on a one-cent increase in the state sales tax, which was estimated to bring in $510 million a year. Some of the revenue would pay for the full installment of the BEP, across-the-board raises for teachers and state employees, and statewide implementation of merit pay. The remaining revenue would be used to cut the state sales tax on food by 75 percent.

However grand the bargain looked on paper—or on Martin's computer screen—the reality proved quite different. The NCAE disliked merit pay more than it liked the idea of immediate pay raises. Many Republican lawmakers disliked tax increases more than they liked merit pay. Left-leaning organizations and editorial boards excoriated Martin for proposing a "regressive" sales-tax hike, rather than raising income taxes. As for the Democrats, they were suspicious. Wasn't this the same governor who had recently campaigned against Jordan and Democratic legislators for raising taxes too much? They feared Martin was drawing them into a political trap.

Even given these divisions and misgivings, something like the governor's grand bargain might have been feasible under different circumstances. But even as he was working out the details of his proposal, the legislature's study commission on highway needs released its report. It soon became the basis of legislation crafted by Representative Sam Hunt and Senator Bill Goldston, with the substantial involvement of Secretary of Transportation Jim Harrington. Combining the original concept of intrastates, urban loops, and rural connectors with more money for streets in the cities and secondary-road paving in rural areas (both needed to attract sufficient votes), the plan called for a 12-year, $8.6 billion program, to be funded by a 5.25-cents-per-gallon hike in the gas tax (a 33 percent increase) and a new title-transfer fee on automobiles, later changed to a 3 percent sales tax on cars, termed a "highway user fee." Martin enthusiastically supported the plan, which promised to put the extra revenue in a new Highway Trust Fund, and urged his fellow Republicans to follow suit. Some refused. Others were willing to go along because of the manifest need for more roads and the fact that gas and car taxes were akin to user fees. But now the governor was asking them to add a sales-tax increase for the General Fund on top of what amounted to $700 million a year in higher gas and car taxes when fully implemented.

A REVOLT, BUT NO REVOLUTION

It was a bridge too far for Republicans such as Wake County freshman Skip Stam, a future House minority leader and speaker pro tem. "I don't think the road tax would hurt us," Stam explained. "But a General Fund tax increase when there's no attempt made to cut out low-priority budget items would hurt us. Two in one year is too much." Some powerful Democrats including Senate leader Henson Barnes weren't inclined to go along either. He vowed to fund high-priority needs without tax increases. That in turn angered Mavretic and other House Democrats, who had agreed to take the lead on the Highway

Trust Fund bill and its required tax hikes in exchange for the Senate's taking the lead on tax increases for the General Fund. As for the Republicans, some members—including Minority Leaders Johnathan Rhyne in the House and Larry Cobb in the Senate—felt duty-bound to support Martin's proposal.

But on March 15, a group of 28 House Republicans endorsed an alternative budget from Larry Etheridge of Wilson County, Trip Sizemore of Guilford County, Robert Grady of Onslow County, and Art Pope of Wake County. Their plan funded the governor's merit-pay expansion and other priorities without raising taxes. It offered $639 million in budget savings, including both across-the-board cuts by agency as well as specific recommendations such as forgoing the scheduled increment of BEP funding. It proposed to use some of the savings to offset the cost of shifting the Highway Patrol to the General Fund, thus allowing more spending on roads without higher gas or car taxes.

As the Republicans developed their alternative budget, they made sure to keep Martin informed. He was diplomatic. He told them he agreed with many of their suggestions but thought Democratic legislators would never go along with them. He persuaded 12 of the 28 Republican representatives to agree to support some tax increases if the Democrats spurned their alternative. But the rest said no. Martin later hosted a steak dinner at the Executive Mansion for the GOP legislators who endorsed his sales-tax proposal. Representative Pope was one of those not invited. Asked if the governor was applying subtle pressure to bring more Republicans on board, Pope replied, "I don't think there is anything subtle about it."

While the disagreement over taxes was tricky, it never threatened the North Carolina Republican Party's newfound unity. Indeed, Martin spent the first several months of his second term strengthening the ties that bound the party. In mid-May, he and former governor Jim Holshouser joined the Congressional Club for a Raleigh dinner to raise money for a Helms reelection bid. One of the speakers was Tom Fetzer, a longtime Congressional Club activist and recent congressional candidate who would soon join the Martin administration as an assistant secretary at the Department of Transportation. Surveying the constellation of GOP stars, Fetzer (himself a future party chairman and Raleigh mayor) publicly joked with Holshouser, who was sporting a small bandage on his forehead, that if a dozen years earlier "somebody had seen you sitting at the head table with Jim Gardner and Tom Ellis, they would have thought that scar on the front of your head was a frontal lobotomy."

A few days later, Republicans gathered in Winston-Salem for their state convention, where Jack Hawke was unanimously reelected for another two years as chairman. Martin, Hawke, Brad Hays, and the rest of the political team also began preparing for what they expected to be another challenging midterm election in 1990. As in 1986, they talked publicly about the possibility of making gains in legislative and judicial seats, while privately hoping just to hold on to most of the historic gains they'd achieved in 1988.

As for Martin's controversial sales-tax hike, he kept trying to convince skeptics that it was the best answer to a difficult question. It did draw support from some education officials, from local school boards, and from North Carolina Citizens for Business and Industry. But with the Republican caucus divided, the Senate showing no interest, and the teachers' association continuing to reject Career Ladder expansion at any price, Martin saw the prospects of a grand bargain disappear. "I am not proposing to raise taxes just to spend more money," Martin said in response to NCAE activists wearing "Dump the Ladder" T-shirts. "If that's what it comes down to, then I'm going to disown it."

Meanwhile, the Senate modified the Highway Trust Fund bill to replace the revenue lost to the General Fund from converting the prior sales tax on cars to the new highway use tax. The move in effect transferred nearly $170 million a year from the road-building program to the General Fund, which Senator Marshall Rauch described as an alternative to Martin's proposed sales-tax hike to fund pay raises. Senators termed it a temporary expedient, to expire in two years, but the governor strenuously disagreed. He predicted their "highway robbery" would prove a lasting drain on the Highway Trust Fund. (Martin was right—the transfer stayed in place for two decades.)

WINS AS WELL AS LOSSES

The governor lost some fights during the 1989 session. However, his administration still played a critical role in a major accomplishment: the Highway Trust Fund bill, finally enacted as a $9 billion package. Furthermore, even the manner in which his sales-tax-for-merit-pay proposal went down to defeat actually lent momentum to another Martin priority: adding flexibility and accountability to the state's education programs.

As the House Appropriations Committee was considering Martin's plan,

Representative Martin Nesbitt proposed an alternative approach that would allow school districts either to adopt the Career Ladder or develop their own plans for spending state money on better teaching and higher performance. It wasn't a new idea. At the beginning of the 1989 session, Senator Richard Conder had filed a bill entitled the School Improvement and Accountability Act. Initially little more than a list of aspirations, the legislation—popularly known by its number, Senate Bill 2—really took shape in late April, as Henson Barnes and other Senate leaders sought to chart a middle course between Martin's Career Ladder expansion and the NCAE's obstructionism. The legislation called for a new, state-designed set of standardized tests for students in grades three through 12, as well as the publication of a set of "report cards" for each school district showing comparative data that would "take into account demographic, economic, and other factors that have been shown to affect student performance." In return, school districts would receive more autonomy to spend state dollars as they wished. The flexibility would extend to teacher compensation and merit pay.

As lawmakers continued to refine Senate Bill 2 during June and July, the relevant provisions grew more specific. Both the governor and the teachers' association endorsed the compromise. Districts could pattern their pay plans after the Career Ladder pilots, a separate pilot program called Lead Teacher, a plan from another state, or a system of their own design for differentiating pay by duties and performance. In a nod to NCAE pressure, the bill called for each local pay plan to be subject to approval not just from elected school boards but also from a majority of teachers and administrators. Although Martin didn't agree with all the details, he eagerly embraced Senate Bill 2 as embodying his longstanding positions. To encourage participation in the differentiated-pay piece, the bill called for a 7 percent funding increase for participating districts, phased in over four years. By championing the Career Ladder, the governor helped ensure performance pay would become a statewide option (although shortages of funds and continued opposition by the NCAE proved to be impediments to its growth).

Senate Bill 2 wasn't the only legislative outcome to the governor's liking from the 1989 session. Lawmakers enacted the Tax Fairness Act, which simplified the state income-tax code by tying it to the federal code and adjusted the brackets to eliminate income-tax liability for 700,000 low-income families and to reduce it for 1.4 million more, while raising the burden on 1.1 million households with higher incomes. Just as Martin had helped combat bracket creep in the federal tax code during his Washington days, he welcomed the 1989 tax reform as rolling back years of bracket creep at the state level, although he would have liked to see the bill also index the state code to inflation (that came later, after Republicans won control of the North Carolina House in 1994). The legislature also changed the tax treatment of S corporations to make them truly pass-through entities—another cause Martin had championed in Congress—thus reducing the double taxation of business income in the state by $85 million a year.

The governor made progress on other issues as well. In the House, Mavretic abolished the old pork-barrel system. The General Assembly approved Martin's reorganization of state resource and regulatory agencies, creating a new Department of Environment, Health, and Natural Resources with Bill Cobey as its secretary and renaming Commerce as the Department of Economic and Community Development. The legislature also agreed to slash the state abortion fund nearly as much as the governor had proposed. The reason wasn't just budgetary. Some key Democrats, including recently elected state party chairman Lawrence Davis, believed the party should moderate its position on abortion by limiting taxpayer funding and requiring parental consent. As for the thorny issue of waste disposal, Martin had early in the session issued an executive order requiring industries to reduce their production of hazardous waste, a move he hoped would soften opposition to building a new treatment plant. Along with pressure from industries blocked by South Carolina from transporting waste there, it helped break the legislative logjam. The General Assembly agreed to restart the process for choosing a hazardous-waste disposal site.

On August 13, the 1989 session creaked to a close. In the end, the General Assembly decided to do precisely what Martin had suggested, amid Democratic catcalls, eight months earlier: defer a significant portion of scheduled BEP funding. The legislature also adopted his proposed tuition hikes.

The Martin administration had accomplished much of the policy agenda it set out at the beginning of the year (although its longtime quests for veto power and judicial-selection reform had again come to naught, the House and Senate disagreeing on the details of each). But the process wasn't always pretty. After raucous protests from NCAE members, constant attacks by Democratic leaders and newspaper editorialists, and opposition to his tax proposals from members of his own party, Martin was fatigued and frustrated. Although the new House coalition had led to fairer consideration of his proposals, Martin's reelection had produced no political honeymoon in Raleigh. He had also opened the door to General Fund tax increases, a precedent Democrats would later use to their advantage. And the closing months of 1989 would bring further political headaches.

DEALING WITH THREE STORMS

As had become standard practice during the governor's first term, Martin and his top advisors left town a month after the conclusion of the legislative session to review the outcome and strategize about the future. Meeting September 7 and 8 at the Pine Needles Resort in Southern Pines, they were joined by Lieutenant Governor Jim Gardner, whom the governor had put in charge of a new task force to combat drug abuse. The crime rate and the state's continuing problems with prison capacity were among the main topics of conversation, along with plans to encourage school districts to use the autonomy they'd received under Senate Bill 2. The team also discussed the challenges of implementing the state's new road-building program—a task that fell to Jim Harrington's deputy, Tommy Harrelson, who would soon replace Harrington as secretary at DOT.

A week after the Southern Pines session, Martin journeyed to Delaware for a meeting of the Southern Governors' Association, where he touted the Highway Trust Fund and Senate Bill 2 as examples of bipartisan efforts to build the infrastructure and education assets needed for economic competitiveness.

As Martin's team planned its policy course for 1990 and beyond, the governor's chief of staff, Phil Kirk, was pursuing a different course—the opportunity to lead North Carolina Citizens for Business and Industry. He interviewed for the job in October and left the administration shortly thereafter. Martin soon replaced him with Kirk's former deputy, Nancy Temple, who became the first woman to serve as a chief of staff to a North Carolina governor. Kevin Brown remained deputy chief of staff under Temple for a time, then joined DOT as assistant secretary. His replacement was Meredith Smith. Events conspired to deny the governor's team any downtime to adjust to all these transitions.

The first storm to hit was a natural one. On September 21, 1989, Hurricane

Hugo struck land near Charleston, South Carolina, and passed through Charlotte and other Piedmont communities. It was a powerful storm, wreaking havoc from the coast to the foothills. The property damage in North Carolina reached $1 billion. Throughout October and into early November, Martin and his aides struggled to identify funds to cover the state's share of federal emergency assistance, as well as the cost of repairing damage to state facilities. The administration suggested tapping reserves for the state health plan, but the idea was shot down by the Council of State, which included all ten statewide elected officials (eight of whom were Democrats). Instead, the panel opted to use salary money reverted to the state treasury from vacant positions, a decision that reduced the state's budget cushion against unforeseen revenue woes.

The second storm was a political one. After the General Assembly allowed the search for a hazardous-waste disposal site to resume, Martin immediately began negotiations with nearby states to come up with a regional solution. The clock was ticking. If by October 17, 1989, a state failed to demonstrate a plan to the EPA for treating its hazardous waste, it risked losing Superfund money. During the late summer and early fall, Martin and the other governors hammered out a compact, similar to the one on low-level radioactive waste, to share the responsibility for handling hazardous waste by burying, treating, recycling, or burning it. North Carolina's contribution to the compact would be to have a hazardous-waste incinerator up and running by 1994. But even as the October 17 deadline approached, one of the two states with existing disposal sites, Alabama, was holding out for faster action by other compact states. Martin delayed a planned trade mission to Asia in order to lobby his fellow Republican, Alabama governor Guy Hunt, to relent. Under pressure from his own Democratic legislature and citing the North Carolina legislature's previous opposition to a site, Hunt said no. Instead, Alabama, South Carolina, Tennessee, and Kentucky formed their own compact. Martin was forced to sweeten his offer: North Carolina's incinerator would be bigger, would be completed by 1991 instead of 1994, and would be accompanied by facilities for recycling solvents and burying ash. After additional weeks of tiring negotiations, the other four states finally admitted North Carolina into the compact. In a special session, the General Assembly ratified the deal.

On November 6, yet another kind of political storm hit the Martin administration. The Raleigh *News & Observer* reported that while serving as the governor's research director during Martin's first term, Charlie Hughes had

FORMER TRANSPORTATION SECRETARY JIM HARRINGTON (*LEFT*) JOINS GOVERNOR MARTIN AND SECRETARY OF TRANSPORTATION TOMMY HARRELSON TO CELEBRATE THE COMPLETION OF THE FINAL MILES OF I-40 TO WILMINGTON.
OFFICIAL STATE PHOTO

compiled files on Bob Jordan and hundreds of other legislators, party officials, and politicians. The files contained newspaper clippings and other printed materials. Hughes was a state-funded employee, yet some of the material on Jordan had occasionally been shared with Brad Hays and others during the reelection campaign. From the start, Martin rejected the notion that the activities of the research office constituted an improper political use of taxpayer resources. "It was a legitimate function of the administration to keep the governor informed and to have a source of information about the positions taken by the leader of the loyal opposition in the legislature," Martin said, although he allowed that "there may have been some times when Charlie was writing that he got maybe a little more florid and partisan than he needed to be." Martin's opponent saw things differently. While admitting the Martin campaign's access to the files did not likely affect the outcome of the 1988 race, Jordan insisted the Republican reimburse the state for the cost of maintaining and sharing the files. "If you don't call him on it this time," Jordan said of the governor, "if and when he runs for the Senate, he'll do the same thing again."

Jordan was referring to the frequently circulated rumor that Martin was angling to run against Senator Terry Sanford in 1992. Political wags had discussed the scenario for years. Representative Sam Hunt even commissioned a statewide poll in April 1989 to test the potential matchup, finding a 20-point lead for Martin. In reality, the governor had never seriously considered the idea. Neither Jim nor Dottie wished to leave North Carolina to live in the nation's capital again. Indeed, in late 1989, with three years of residence in the Executive Mansion still ahead of them, the Martins were already looking forward to the day when they could return to their beloved Lake Norman home for good. But the possibility that Martin might be running for another office was seen as a political asset. And when Martin expressed doubts about a future race, many simply didn't believe him. Even Jesse Helms joked about it at a fundraiser in early 1990, claiming the two had struck a deal. "If I run for the Senate this year, he'll run for the Senate in 1992," Helms told the cheering audience. "Is that all right?"

DAMAGE CONTROL GOES AWRY

The day after the Charlie Hughes story broke, Martin, Hays, Phil Kirk, and Hughes's replacement as research director, Paul Shumaker, met to go over the files in question. While most of the material was indeed innocuous—the kind of files most press offices and staff assistants routinely kept—they also discovered some memos with political comments (often written in the margins), plus some draft campaign slogans. They left the files intact in case there was an investigation. Just two days after the meeting, Nancy Temple replaced Kirk as chief of staff. Shortly afterward, Shumaker left the research office to run a nonprofit and was replaced by Don Beason, who'd been a cabinet secretary under Holshouser and a legislative lobbyist for Martin.

At first, top Democrats responded to the story with caution. State Democratic chairman Lawrence Davis demanded an external review, and state auditor Ed Renfrow asked to see the material Hughes had compiled. But Attorney General Lacy Thornburg's office released a statement indicating that the practice was probably not illegal, and Senate leader Henson Barnes indicated the legislature wouldn't get involved unless it was more than an isolated incident.

By the end of November, however, Renfrow announced that his preliminary review had become a full audit. As analysts from the state auditor's office began scrutinizing phone records, they flagged 651 phone calls made from the governor's office to various organizations and consultants involved in the 1988 reelection campaign. The Martin administration conceded that 23 of the calls were inappropriate, most of them placed by media producer Don Ringe and other contractors as they checked in with their offices back home while visiting the governor in Raleigh. The total cost to the state for the 23 calls was just $15.35, which the Martin campaign immediately reimbursed.

But when Renfrow released his audit report on February 20, 1990, it listed all the remaining calls as questionable as well, while describing Hughes's compilation of the clipping files as "political activity going on within the research office." On the Tuesday the report came out, Jim Martin was sick in bed with a throat infection. The governor's office issued a statement in which Martin thanked the state auditor for "being fair as well as thorough in his review" but described some of what Hughes had done as little more than "inappropriate notes in margins" of legitimate reports. The administration also insisted that most of what Renfrow labeled as "questionable" phone calls were placed for legitimate reasons to Brad Hays, who not only ran the 1988 reelection bid but also advised Martin on administrative and policy issues unrelated to campaign operations.

The audit was embarrassing. What happened next was calamitous. On Tuesday, the day the audit was released, Democratic reactions ranged from mild criticism to mocking complaints about being left off Martin's "enemies list." On Wednesday, however, Davis demanded that the Martin campaign reimburse the state for the entire annual cost of the research office, $200,000, while Attorney General Lacy Thornburg announced plans to confer with Wake County district attorney Colon Willoughby about a potential criminal investigation into misuse of state property. Still in bed with his throat infection, for which he was taking antibiotics and prescription cough medicine, Martin "had all that time to stew" about Renfrow's audit, as Temple put it. He then grew infuriated when he read the statements of Davis and Thornburg early on Thursday morning, February 22. Originally planning to hold a press conference on Friday, when he hoped to be fully recovered, Martin told his staff to reschedule the event for later on Thursday morning. Temple and Tim Pittman recommended against it, citing his ill health as well as the need to let the story die down. The governor insisted. Ever since his days on the Mecklenburg commission, he had jealously protected his reputation and responded angrily to accusations of dishonesty or impropriety. Martin was determined to set the record straight, forcefully and immediately. "At that point," Pittman said later, "the train was rolling down the tracks—and there was no stopping it."

The resulting 90-minute press conference on the morning of February 22, 1990, was memorable, to say the least. Hoarse, visibly fatigued, red-faced, and sweating profusely, the governor said that anyone serving in political office needed to keep information handy about the past statements and positions of politicians with whom he interacted. "There's a distinction between political activity, broadly defined, and the special variety of political activity that's called election campaigning," Martin argued, insisting that the vast majority of what Hughes had done fell into the former category. Martin said he resented being "threatened" by the attorney general with a criminal investigation. The governor invited Thornburg, Davis, Renfrow, and Willoughby to come to the press conference themselves and even stopped several times to ask if anyone was on the way. Martin's aides tried repeatedly to bring the event to a close. Don Beason slipped a note to the governor reporting that someone had seen Thornburg leaving the attorney general's office. Beason suggested Martin take a break to see if Thornburg showed up. The governor refused. "I'm having a good time," he said. Then Pittman handed Martin another note, suggesting he wrap up the press conference. Instead of doing so, Martin read the note to the reporters. "Tim tells me that I don't look good," he said, "Y'all are recording this, so we'll be sure everybody knows it." When the governor finally brought his comments to a close, he circled back to the rumors about a potential Senate race with Terry Sanford. "Ask the people of North Carolina if they understand now why I've lost interest in any other political office," Martin instructed the press. He then left the room with Dottie at his side.

Not surprisingly, news coverage of the press conference was damaging. But it could have been worse. Although some TV stations ran unflattering footage of Martin rambling or wiping his brow, others were more circumspect. WRAL-TV in Raleigh even decided against reporting Martin's comment about having lost interest in future political campaigns. "I thought it was incumbent upon us not to say it," since the governor was obviously sick and incoherent, reporter Chris Fitzsimon explained at the time.

Nevertheless, the damage was bad enough. Temple, Pittman, and other staff sought to keep it from getting worse. Having consulted by phone with Hays, they decided to encourage Martin to leave Saturday morning to attend a National Governors Association meeting in Washington. But the governor had returned to his sickbed after the press conference and stayed there through Friday. He didn't feel up to traveling—and was in no mood to let the matter rest anyway, particularly after the *N&O* editorial board weighed in on Saturday morning. "Fellow citizens who have suffered with the flu bug or other sicknesses going around this year hope that Governor Martin is feeling better," the editorial began charitably, but then added that neither illness nor the effects of medication could excuse what happened. "The governor got up on the wrong side of his bed of pain," the editorial continued. "Had he stayed there, he wouldn't have fallen on his face by rapping the attorney general for simply doing his job." It concluded by recommending that the next time Martin got sick, he should "take two aspirin and don't call a press conference in the morning."

The governor didn't read the editorial the way others did, as garden-variety criticism mixed with cheeky humor. Still recuperating, Martin saw it as a cheap shot—the latest in a long series of attacks by the capital city's pro-Democratic newspaper. An earlier *N&O* story reporting that Thornburg had dropped the idea of a criminal probe of the matter hadn't mollified Martin either. "I still believe the attorney general went too far in threatening me with an SBI investigation," the governor was quoted as saying.

But he wasn't done talking to the *N&O*—not by a long shot. Later that Saturday morning, Martin went to the newspaper's offices a few blocks away to hand-deliver a letter to editor Claude Sitton, who oversaw both the news and editorial sides of the operation. In it, Martin castigated the *N&O* for running a follow-up story suggesting his shaky performance during the press conference was the result of taking strong cough medicine, calling it "wicked for you to print such a false attempt at amateur psychoanalysis." He then confirmed what he'd said at the end of the press conference—that he wouldn't be running for Senate. "I have lost interest in any other political office," Martin wrote in the letter. "It's too brutal for me." Instead, the governor said he would focus on recruiting and coaching Republican candidates. He also vowed to "root you [the *N&O* under Claude Sitton] and Lacy Thornburg out of North Carolina politics, along with any Democrats who take delight in your mischief."

After receiving Martin's letter, Sitton asked the governor if he'd be willing to sit down for an interview. Martin agreed. Rob Christensen, one of the reporters who had been covering the story for the newspaper, was in Greensboro at the time. He hurried back to Raleigh to conduct the Saturday-afternoon interview. Martin took the opportunity to expound further on the points raised in his letter. For example, he argued that Thornburg's treatment of him was comparable to Rufus Edmisten's decision as attorney general to pursue corruption charges against Green. Back then, he asserted, Edmisten "couldn't get to be governor if Jimmy Green was the favorite" in the 1984 Democratic primary. The governor also showed Christensen one of the gifts he'd received from the public after his Thursday press conference: a book of poetry. He then read the same passage from John Dryden's poem "Johnnie Armstrong's Last Goodnight" that Ronald Reagan had cited in 1976 after losing the GOP presidential nomination to Gerald Ford: "Fight on, my merry men all/I'm a little wounded, but I am not slain/I will lay me down for to bleed a while/And then I'll rise and fight with you again."

Looking back many years later, Martin said he still thought he was right to respond to the research-office audit by explicitly ruling out a Senate run in 1992. Although it risked making him more of a lame duck, Martin argued that it removed any political motivation for Democrats to exaggerate small mistakes into big scandals or minor disagreements into major conflicts. But he admitted he did his staff members a disservice by not delaying the Thursday press conference as they suggested, by not telling them what he was planning to say, and by not consulting them about his subsequent visit to the *N&O*. Whatever his intentions in holding the press conference and penning his subsequent "political retirement" letter, the execution went awry due to a "fevered mind" and "the effects of the strong medicine that I'd taken," Martin said.

THE RECESSION STARTS TO BITE

Fiscal analysts from both the executive and legislative branches were nervous about the revenue projections used to craft the new spending plans for 1989–90 and 1990–91. They were right to be. The national slowdown in economic growth would tip into a full-fledged recession by mid-1990. As of January 1990, state revenues were running $100 million below projections. The gap grew to $200 million, then $400 million. Budget director Cliff Cameron responded by continuing a hiring freeze and ordering across-the-board spending cuts for most state agencies. The administration also withheld some income-tax refund checks. Despite the cash crunch, Martin telegraphed that his proposed adjustments to the 1990–91 budget wouldn't include a tax increase, given that lawmakers had rejected his sales-tax proposal in 1989. "If they couldn't get together in a non-election year," he said, "I couldn't see them doing anything in an election year."

By May, annual revenues were projected to fall more than $500 million short of expectations for 1989–90 and $340 million short for 1990–91. (In 2015 dollars, those figures would be $900 million and $610 million, respectively.) To resolve the immediate problem, the Martin administration cut spending further and essentially pushed current expenses into the next fiscal year by tapping reserves and shifting the pay date for teachers and state employees from June 29 to July 2. The real question, then, became how to balance the 1990–91 budget. Martin proposed hundreds of millions of dollars in reductions from the baseline, including $182 million less for public schools, $83 million less for public colleges and universities, $59 million less for Medicaid and other public-assistance programs, and $23 million less for prisons. State spending for most functions would still grow, albeit not as fast as called for in the biennial budget passed in 1989.

Democrats complained about the governor's initial proposal but ended up following a similar course. Shortly after the legislature convened in late May, the Senate Appropriations Committee approved hundreds of millions of dollars of budget savings, including a reduction of local tax reimbursements and a deferral of most of the scheduled installment of the BEP. While proposing to accelerate the scheduled payment of income and sales taxes, Senate leaders again expressed little interest in raising tax rates. Joe Mavretic and leading Democrats in the House were more open to the idea. They got no help from their coalition partners. The House Republican caucus, more unified than it had been in 1989, released a no-tax-hike budget plan of its own that cut spending by an average of 4.7 percent while preserving funds for the Career Ladder pilots and local tax reimbursements.

Even as GOP lawmakers lent support to Martin's initial plan, however, the governor was rethinking it. In early June, the Standard & Poor's rating agency announced that it was reviewing North Carolina's AAA bond rating in light of the state's revenue woes. Martin called a meeting with House and Senate leaders to suggest that "a modest revenue increase" might be needed to reassure rating agencies. Mavretic then asked what "modest" meant. "As little as possible," offered Senate Appropriations Committee chairman Ken Royall. The speaker of the House was unimpressed. "I didn't want to go to the ballet tonight, so I am watching the tap dancing now," Mavretic replied. He recommended that the state raise at least $150 million in annual revenues, perhaps from expanding the sales tax or levying higher excises.

On June 15, a coalition of five groups—the North Carolina Association of County Commissioners, the North Carolina League of Municipalities, the North Carolina School Boards Association, the Public School Forum, and NCCBI—issued a joint call for the General Assembly to raise taxes. Phil Kirk, now the president of NCCBI, said the business group would support a one-cent hike in the sales tax but not higher taxes on corporate income, inventories, intangibles, or cigarettes. Several local chambers of commerce joined the call for tax hikes. But the Senate shrugged them off and passed its no-tax-hike budget on June 18, 1990.

Once again, the governor saw the opportunity to strike a bargain. He asked to address a joint session of the General Assembly on June 21. Martin proposed that the House accept the Senate's approach for the 1990–91 budget in return for a pledge to raise taxes by $529 million during the 1991 session. The response from Democrats ranged from noncommittal to suspicious. The Republican response was a near-unanimous no. The lieutenant governor and other Republicans had actually spent the previous evening and much of the morning before the joint session trying to talk Martin out of proposing the deal. Senator Don Kincaid, who would replace Larry Cobb as minority leader after the latter was appointed to the North Carolina Utilities Commission, opposed the governor's proposal outright. The best Representative Johnathan Rhyne could say was that it was "courageous." Representative Trip Sizemore, the minority whip, called it "the worst alternative available" and said it "does us a disservice."

Martin later said he was surprised at the resolute opposition of Republicans who had earlier expressed openness to new taxes. As for the Democrats, once Standard & Poor's reaffirmed the state's AAA bond rating in late June, any chance of their agreeing to Martin's bargain in an election year went away. It also didn't help that at the same time Martin was asking North Carolina Republicans to bend on taxes, President George Bush announced that he would break the "no new taxes" pledge he had made during the 1988 campaign in order to strike a budget deal with Congress. Bush's flip-flop infuriated the GOP base. Martin had not taken a tax pledge, so he wasn't going back on his word. But Republicans weren't about to do something in Raleigh that looked anything like what was going on in Washington.

The budget deal passed on July 27. It was not truly austere. General Fund spending was authorized at $8.1 billion, up $715 million from 1989–90. Although $237 million of that amount was really an accounting change—local tax reimbursements became an on-budget appropriation, rather than an off-budget revenue earmark—the remaining General Fund appropriation still represented a 6.5 percent increase over the previous year and was 74 percent higher than the 1984–85 budget, representing growth far faster than the increase of population and inflation during the period. Still, the administration and the legislature had originally budgeted for more.

Although the main focus of the 1990 session was balancing the budget, lawmakers did address a few other issues. One was infant mortality. In late 1989, a federal report had estimated North Carolina's infant mortality rate at 12.7 deaths for every 1,000 live births in 1988, up sharply from 11.9 the previous year. It was the highest rate among the 50 states. Martin immediately formed a task force to devise a response. It wasn't the first time the administration had worked on the issue. Academic studies suggested that a lack of sufficient prenatal care was a causal factor. At the administration's urging, lawmakers had in 1987 expanded Medicaid coverage to more expectant mothers. The following year, Secretary of Human Resources David Flaherty recommended raising the eligibility threshold for pregnant women to 185 percent of poverty-level income. The General Assembly went partway there during the 1989 session by raising the threshold to 150 percent of poverty (although Martin had not included that step in his original 1989–90 budget). But now there was a new sense of urgency on all sides. The governor's infant-mortality task force released its recommendations in early 1990. The General Assembly acted on them during the 1990 session, raising the Medicaid threshold to 180 percent of poverty. Although the infant-mortality rate dropped significantly to 11.6 deaths per 1,000 in 1989—that is, before either the 1989 or 1990 policy changes could have been responsible—it continued to drop for years afterward, often faster than the national average.

The 1990–91 budget also included $85 million to build more prison capacity, to sentence more nonviolent offenders to electronic house arrest and intensive probation, and to contract with a private firm to build a 500-bed facility for drug and alcohol offenders. Separately, the legislature voted to put a referendum on the fall ballot to approve $200 million in prison bonds. Martin wanted

GOVERNOR MARTIN CONGRATULATES DUKE UNIVERSITY BASKETBALL COACH MIKE KRZYZEWSKI AND MEMBERS OF THE NATIONAL CHAMPIONSHIP TEAM OF 1991.
OFFICIAL STATE PHOTO

more. Although the legislature had upped the limit on prison admissions in mid-1989 and then again during a one-day special session in early 1990, the system repeatedly bumped up against the cap. The governor was determined to alleviate the pressure to parole criminals before serving a significant percentage of their sentences. He assembled a 20-person task force headed by North Carolina Supreme Court justice Burley Mitchell to build a consensus. While enjoying the support of law enforcement and some lawmakers, the administration's plan was simply too large to fit into a recessionary state budget. By the final weeks of the 1990 session, the governor forged a bipartisan compromise to get started on the problem, although some Democratic legislators authorized the $200 million bond referendum only reluctantly and didn't campaign for it in the fall.

On another priority for the governor, veto power, the 1990 session proved as disappointing as the 1989 one. He opened the door to a structural change Democratic House members requested in exchange—four-year legislative terms—but what they really wanted was to move the election date for the elongated legislative terms and for governor and Council of State offices to the midterm cycle rather than the presidential cycle, a move they thought would hurt the GOP. Martin and Republican lawmakers agreed with the potential effect, and thus disagreed with the proposal. A later effort to authorize a referendum on the veto, gubernatorial appointment of judges, and other reforms passed one House committee but never made it to the floor for a vote.

CRITICISM FROM A DIFFERENT DIRECTION

The conclusion of the 1990 session certainly didn't bring an end to concerns about the budget. To apply a long-term perspective, the legislature created the Economic Future Study Commission to conduct an in-depth study of the state's fiscal needs, revenue capacity, and economic prospects. Martin's appointees to the panel included Phil Kirk, Bob Bradshaw, UNC–Chapel Hill professor Jack Kasarda, Senator Betsy Cochrane, Representative Art Pope, and Betsy Justus, who had recently replaced Helen Powers as head of the Department of Revenue. Other legislative, business, and civic leaders populated the commission. It held meetings through the rest of 1990 and early 1991.

In addition to budget woes, Martin spent the summer and fall of 1990 struggling with the lingering controversies over waste disposal. To satisfy North Carolina's obligation under the new hazardous-waste compact, a state commission had renewed its search for a potential incinerator site. By May, it had narrowed the field to a Granville County site and another on the Iredell-Rowan county line. Many North Carolinians living near the sites resisted the decision. Some protested by physically obstructing access to them, preventing state officials from conducting the necessary soil tests. Local judges also imposed temporary restraining orders. In response, the governor approved rule changes in early August to allow commission director Darrell Hinnant to continue the process without the soil testing. That led to other lawsuits and injunctions. Opposition to the incinerator grew intensely personal. In Granville County, hundreds of opponents staged boisterous rallies and even hanged the governor in effigy. At an October rally in Butner, protesters held up signs bearing such slogans as "Dump Toxic Jim" and "Hitler marched innocent people into an incinerator—Martin and Hinnant want to bring an incinerator to innocent people." In Iredell County, the location of the Martins' home on Lake Norman, the opposition was intense as well, albeit less grotesque. NASCAR's Dale Earnhardt was among the opponents. One Statesville activist called Martin a "lame-brained, lame-duck Republican governor." A local musical group, the Southland Ramblers, recorded a protest song, "The Ballad of Jim's Incinerator," set to the tune of the theme from *The Beverly Hillbillies.* One verse went like this:

> *Jim went out of state and joined a compact.*
> *He thought he could fool us and we couldn't react.*
> *He thought we were country clods, maybe even fools.*
> *But he can't even beat us by changing the rules.*

On December 4, 1990, the commission chose the Granville site. Because it was on state-owned land, however, the Council of State would have to approve it. A week later, the council nixed the idea by a 7–2 vote, with Martin and Gardner outvoted by the Democratic members. South Carolina and Alabama immediately took steps to ban hazardous-waste shipments into their states from North Carolina. The governor was furious. "I sort of feel like the Little Red Hen," Martin said. "Who's going to help me plant my wheat? Who's going to help me bake my bread? Turkey Lurkey said he doesn't want to have any part of it. Goosey Loosey, he's not going to do it."

Meanwhile, another panel, the North Carolina Low-Level Radioactive Waste Management Authority, continued its own search for a suitable location for the burial facility the state was obligated to build under a separate multistate compact. The authority zeroed in on two sites: one in Richmond County and the other on the Wake-Chatham line. Local opposition brought the process to a grinding halt. In July 1990, the authority announced that North Carolina couldn't meet its 1993 deadline, saying that the radioactive waste facility would cost twice as much as originally estimated and wouldn't be completed until 1995.

Martin was frustrated by the constant delays and contentious debate. As a scientist, he had carefully weighed the options and concluded that building the two facilities minimized both the economic costs and environmental risks.

Martin blamed the same sort of environmental extremists he'd battled as a congressman for "fanning the flames." They must have known it was important to dispose of wastes responsibly, he concluded, "but they could get membership and money by opposing it, and they did."

MIXED RESULTS IN THE MIDTERMS

The many policy disputes of 1990 played out against the background of upcoming midterm elections. Martin, Jack Hawke, and other Republicans were determined to recruit another solid slate of candidates, particularly as they grew increasingly optimistic that Senator Jesse Helms would be reelected by a margin large enough to provide a top-of-the-ticket boost. Why were they optimistic? Because Democratic heavyweights kept bowing out of the race. One was former UNC president Bill Friday. Another was Jim Hunt. After initially considering a rematch with Helms, Hunt decided against it after a conversation with Tennessee senator Al Gore. "I don't know a single senator who is happy," Gore told Hunt, who concluded that Washington wasn't for him. That left former Charlotte mayor Harvey Gantt and District Attorney Mike Easley of Southport as the leading Democratic prospects. That field heartened the Republicans. So did the party's successes in the 1989 municipal elections, which included the reelection of Republican mayor Sue Myrick in Charlotte and the election of black Republican Frank Turner to the Raleigh City Council.

To challenge Chief Justice Jim Exum in 1990, the GOP turned to Wake County Superior Court judge Howard Manning Jr. Bev Lake also filed for a seat on the North Carolina Supreme Court, as did former United States attorney Sam Currin, a Helms protégé. Allyson Duncan, an African-American Republican and North Carolina Central University law professor whom Martin had appointed to fill a vacancy on the court of appeals, sought the voters' blessing to stay in her job. At the legislative level, Republicans focused first on protecting the 13 seats they had gained in 1988 and then on a dozen other competitive seats held by Democrats. The GOP's best pickup opportunities were in the Senate. Its goal was to hold enough seats in both chambers to influence what promised to be tough budget negotiations during 1991, and to have at least some say in drawing the congressional and legislative maps after the 1990 census and reapportionment.

But would the governor be the kind of political asset for Republicans in 1990 that he had been during the midterms four years earlier? The circumstances were different. State budget woes, the research-office controversy, the waste-site sagas, and the recession had taken their toll on Martin's political capital. His job-approval ratings had often stayed above 60 percent during his first term but had dropped into the 50s by the end of 1989. On some surveys, the numbers kept dropping. One N&O/WRAL poll on the eve of the 1990 general election had just 42 percent of North Carolina voters giving him an excellent or good job rating, versus 51 percent who said it was fair or poor. Martin's own internal poll put his personal favorability rating at 58 percent and his job-approval rating at 51 percent. Whatever the measure, Martin remained far more popular than his rivals in the General Assembly, whose job performance was rated excellent or good by only 20 percent in the N&O/WRAL poll.

One advantage the party had in 1990 was unity. The tensions that flared during the Broyhill-Funderburk primary in 1986 and the state chairmanship race in 1987 had largely disappeared. Indeed, the governor offered to aid the Helms reelection campaign any way he could, and even suggested the idea for an ad featuring the powerful image of a lone man standing in front of a line of Chinese tanks during the 1989 protests in Beijing. Martin actually appeared in the spot, holding up a photo of the scene in Tiananmen Square. "America needs leaders with the courage to stand up for what's right regardless of what the liberal critics say," the governor told viewers. "For 18 years, Senator Jesse Helms has stood up for us, for North Carolina, for America. On November 6, he needs us to stand up for him."

Martin traveled across the state to campaign for Helms and the party's other candidates. He particularly went after Jim Exum and other "liberal Democratic judges" who would "profess to uphold the law regarding the death penalty while undermining it on the slimmest of technicalities." Heading to some of his campaign stops in a van sporting "Just say NO to the N and O" bumper stickers, Martin credited the Democratic-Republican coalition in the House for the needed reforms in that chamber, and urged voters to bring about the same outcome in the Senate by electing more Republicans to it. He also campaigned forcefully for the $200 million prison bond on the ballot, despite lackluster support from Democrats and editorial opposition from major newspapers.

Following the normal pattern, the 1990 midterms produced a net loss for the party controlling the White House. But the national Democratic gains were comparatively modest—eight seats in the House, just one in the Senate, and no net change in governorships. North Carolina, in particular, had a mixed outcome. Helms won a competitive race against Gantt, and Republicans actually narrowed their gap with Democrats in the United States House delegation to 7–4 when Charles Taylor won the 11th District. In the General Assembly, Republicans lost seven seats in the House but defeated two powerful Democratic senators, Marshall Rauch and Ollie Harris. That left them with 53 members in the 170-seat General Assembly—the second-highest total of the 20th century thus far. The GOP actually netted 14 county-commission seats across the state. In the statewide judicial races, however, Republicans fell short—although in Bev Lake's supreme-court race the margin was so slender that it went to a recount. Martin did succeed in getting voters to approve the $200 million prison bond. All in all, he told reporters, the results of the 1990 elections confirmed that "for many years North Carolina has been a conservative state." Although GOP candidates were massively outspent, they had proven competitive in the judicial races and maintained substantial numbers in the General Assembly, Martin pointed out, showing that the party had come a long way from its mid-1970s trough.

During the spring primaries, Speaker Joe Mavretic and 13 of his 19 allies in the House coalition had faced Democratic challengers. His faction won all but three of the contests. But even before the general election, it became clear that Mavretic would have a hard time winning a second term as speaker. The long list of would-be successors represented a variety of regions and ideologies. Just a week after the November elections, Mavretic threw his support behind Wake County representative Dan Blue, who became the first black leader of a Southern legislative chamber in modern history.

A CALL TO AVOID
ROCKS AND SHOALS

In the weeks after the 1990 midterms, the budget situation worsened. By late November, Cliff Cameron was projecting a $261 million hole in the 1990–91 budget and as much as $1 billion less revenue than projected for the 1991–92 fiscal year. Martin expected the coming legislative session to be a challenging one, particularly now that Republicans would no longer be part of a governing coalition in the House. The bad revenue news promised to make the session the roughest his team had yet faced—and one it would have to face without Cameron, who announced he would leave the budget office at the end of 1990. His deputy, Marvin Dorman, replaced him.

After spending New Year's in Asheville with his family, the governor convened another of the strategy sessions he'd come to like. It began on January 3 at the North Carolina Museum of Art in Raleigh. With his top aides and cabinet secretaries on hand, Martin stressed that budget cuts, not expansion plans, would be the order of the day. He also told them he would not offer another grand bargain predicated on a large tax increase. For one thing, the two previous attempts had failed to gain traction. For another, the recession had proven to be deeper than originally thought. Martin concluded that anything like the one-cent hike in sales tax he'd pitched in 1989 would hurt North Carolina's already weakened economy. If he determined more revenue was needed, Martin said, any proposed hike would be relatively modest. Lieutenant Governor Jim Gardner staked out a position to the governor's right, arguing that no tax increase at all should be considered during the 1991 session. House minority leader Johnathan Rhyne publicly agreed with Gardner.

Martin's argument against new spending had one notable exception. A few months earlier, he'd heard a pitch about a new economic-development idea from Jack Kasarda, a UNC–Chapel Hill professor whom Martin had appointed to the Economic Future Study Commission. Having studied the rise of just-in-time manufacturing and other developments in shipping and distribution, Kasarda developed a concept for combining an air-cargo airport and other transportation infrastructure with industrial sites. Later acquiring the name Global TransPark, the project would allow companies to ship components or partially completed goods into their facilities, finish production, and then ship them out to their final destinations. Martin embraced Kasarda's concept and planned to seek legislative approval to pick a site for a project featuring a two-mile runway, 5,000 acres of developable land, and a price tag of $250 million in federal, state, and private funds.

As the governor prepared to propose a budget for the 1991–93 biennium, he restated an old argument about school-funding priorities. "Statewide, we're not seeing much improvement in anything that can be attributed to the Basic Education Program," Martin said at a December 13 meeting of the county commissioners' association. "It's a way to spend a lot more money doing the same thing we've been doing."

On January 11, 1991, Martin convened a summit of legislators, business executives, educators, and hundreds of other leaders to discuss the status of school reform. Asked to rank the state's education initiatives in order of funding priority, the participants put Senate Bill 2—including optional merit-pay plans—at the top of the list, followed by teacher-salary increases and workforce training programs. The BEP came in fourth.

In his last State of the State address, delivered to the General Assembly on January 31, the governor cited these findings and other evidence to justify forgoing any new funds for the BEP and instead spending $69 million on implementing Senate Bill 2. He also urged state and local policymakers to move forward with "the ultimate accountability" in education, by giving North Carolina parents the ability to choose among public schools. He insisted that a top-down model was the wrong approach. "There are many shrill voices today calling for massive increases in spending for schools, as if throwing more money is the path to excellence in education," Martin said. "It isn't. We already tried that. It didn't work." Instead, under a system combining local flexibility, independent testing, and parental choice, school districts could make more of their own decisions and then be held accountable for the results. The governor's remarks were forceful and dramatic. "Martin changes focus of education debate," declared one newspaper headline.

Shifting the funding focus away from the BEP was only one of several major steps the governor recommended to balance the biennial budget while funding the administration's highest priorities, which included $100 million for workforce training, a $33 million early-childhood program for at-risk preschoolers he called Uplift Day Care, and the debt service on a proposed $355 million bond to construct new education, water, sewer, and mental-health facilities. As expected, Martin declined to endorse a tax increase at the state level. Instead, he suggested the state revisit the arrangement it had made with counties and municipalities when repealing the inventory tax and reducing the intangibles tax. Rather than sending them a scheduled annual reimbursement of $242 million for the lost revenue, Martin proposed applying the funds to the state budget and giving localities the option of raising their sales tax by a half-penny. In effect, this would still be a tax hike to benefit the state coffers, albeit not nearly as large a one as he'd pitched in 1989 or 1990. The North Carolina

Association of County Commissioners and the North Carolina League of Municipalities endorsed Martin's idea, in part because it would give localities more money in the long run (since the reimbursement payments were fixed but the tax-hike proceeds would grow over time). Among the budget savings the governor recommended were cuts in school administration, the abortion fund, and state funding for private organizations such as the Microelectronics Center (created in 1980 to provide supercomputing and, later, networking services to UNC campuses and other institutions), along with tuition hikes and higher patient cost-sharing in the state employee health plan. As a longer-term solution to fiscal imbalances, Martin praised a bipartisan bill from Senator Bill Goldston and Representative Art Pope that would limit spending for each fiscal year to the amount of General Fund revenue collected during the previous calendar year, essentially eliminating the risk of unforeseen cash-flow problems during a fiscal year. Annual surpluses of revenue over expenditures would be used to build a large reserve to cover the cost of actual or figurative rainy days.

While the governor's proposals on education and the budget received the lion's share of attention, his final State of the State speech also reiterated his calls for appointed appellate judges and the gubernatorial veto. That North Carolina remained the only state without the veto "should be an embarrassment to you," Martin told the General Assembly. He also gave the legislators two new proposals to consider during the 1991 session: the aforementioned air-cargo and manufacturing project and the Mountain Area Planning System, which would protect watersheds and other natural resources across 24 western counties in the same manner that the Coastal Area Management Act had already done for 22 eastern counties. Using an extended analogy from one of his favorite pastimes, Martin urged lawmakers to address the many challenges facing the state in 1991 with calm consideration of the substantive issues:

> *You would understand my approach if you've ever tried to bring a small sailboat through a convulsive inlet in a storm. With dangers on all sides, you must be prepared and disciplined if you're to avoid the rocks and shoals. You must not panic, or try extreme maneuvers, or try to run too fast, lest you broach. Rather, you must keep a firm hand on the helm and know the warning signs, and steer very carefully, always mindful that your objective is not to fly, or drive it aground, but to come through safely to the other side.*

GOVERNOR PROPOSES,
LEGISLATURE DISPOSES

During the 1989 and 1990 sessions, Martin's proposals for large increases in state sales taxes had run into opposition from the Democratic majority in the Senate, as well as from many Republicans in both chambers. In 1991, the situation changed in three important ways. First, Martin was proposing a far smaller tax hike. Second, his budget office pegged the difference between projected revenues and anticipated spending in 1991–92 at $1 billion—a fiscal gap far larger than in past years. Finally, the Mavretic coalition was no longer in charge in the House. Ideologically, Speaker Dan Blue and his top lieutenants were for the most part to the left of previous Democratic leaders and committee chairs. They were more willing to consider tax increases in general and less willing to rely solely on higher sales taxes, which they saw as regressive. In general, Senate Democrats were more concerned than their House counterparts about the consequences of raising personal taxes or corporate income taxes on business recruitment, entrepreneurship, and investment. As for the Republicans, few expressed enthusiasm for Martin's local-option sales tax. But they welcomed the governor's clear declaration about going any farther. "I was most excited about his firm resolve that he would actively oppose any other tax increase," said Rhyne.

The governor confirmed that position a week after his State of the State address, when the NCAE and the SEANC called for higher pay raises. "I think it would be very difficult to justify an even bigger tax increase than what I've proposed on people who are out of work, or have a member of their family unemployed, in order to provide bigger pay increases to our folks who do have a job," Martin explained.

The gulf between the two parties proved wide. Gardner worked with Rhyne, Senate minority leader Bob Shaw, and joint caucus leader Art Pope to develop an alternative budget with no state or local tax increases at all. Its $300 million in additional budget savings relied on further cuts in school administration and construction, lower contributions to health and pension plans, higher tuition increases, and the idea of converting part of the BEP into block grants, thus giving local districts less money in exchange for greater flexibility in spending it. Meanwhile, the NCAE and other groups allied with legislative

Democrats castigated Martin for proposing only $143 million in new spending. They argued for far larger tax increases to fund as much as $848 million in new spending on the BEP, school construction, and major pay raises for teachers and state employees.

In early March, the Economic Future Study Commission released its report listing several policy options for lawmakers to consider. Some of them—such as reforming the budget process, phasing out principal and teacher tenure, and preferring across-the-board tax cuts to targeted tax incentives for business—pleased Martin and the Republicans. Other options—such as expanding the sales-tax base to include services and giving localities more taxing authority—drew plaudits from Democrats and liberal groups.

When appropriations committees began work on their own budget plans, they pledged to cut at least $400 million from the continuation budget for 1991–92 before resorting to state tax hikes. Legislative leaders also signaled that the governor's proposed swap of a local-option sales tax for lost tax reimbursements would go nowhere. The war of words between the two sides escalated when Democrats criticized Martin for hiring former state GOP chairman Frank Rouse for a vacant post at the Department of Transportation. Martin responded defiantly. "Neither you nor your editors nor legislators who are sniveling about all this are going to tell me who's going to be hired," the governor told reporters at one of his regular Thursday press conferences.

The budget talks continued throughout March and April. Martin, Gardner, and Republican legislators insisted that a large tax increase would hurt North Carolina's economy and suggested that cabinet secretaries—including Estell Lee, who replaced Jim Broyhill at the Department of Economic and Community Development—be given more "management flexibility" to save money. "Budget crises like we have right now come and go," Gardner said. "We will get out of this. We will get out of it probably in the next year. Taxes are forever." Democrats said the General Assembly was the proper place to identify specific cuts, and that preserving state programs was worth the extra taxes. Speaking to a skeptical audience at a luncheon hosted by the John Locke Foundation in Raleigh, Speaker Dan Blue defended the legislature's "conservative fiscal approach" of combining tax hikes with spending restraint. "We couldn't balance the budget with cuts alone—the hole was too deep," he said.

Indeed, the fiscal situation took another turn for the worse in May, as new projections indicated the state would receive $729 million less revenue

MARTIN CONDUCTS AN APRIL 25, 1991 PERFORMANCE OF THE CHARLOTTE
SYMPHONY AT QUEENS COLLEGE (NOW UNIVERSITY). MARTIN FAMILY PHOTO

than forecast through the end of the 1990–91 fiscal year. State budget analysts
concluded that the 1989 Tax Fairness Act, a bipartisan bill intended to be
revenue-neutral, had inadvertently cut income taxes by as much as $300 mil-
lion. Once again, the administration was forced to delay tax-refund checks, to
tap reserves, and to move a state pay date into the 1991–92 fiscal year, for which
the gap between expected revenue and requested spending was now $1.2 billion
(or $2 billion in 2015 currency). Martin responded by calling for hundreds of
millions in additional cuts—endorsing several of the recommendations Gardner and legislative Republicans had previously made—but Democrats had already shifted their focus to taxes. Some House members pushed a plan to raise
marginal taxes rates to as high as 9 percent for personal income and 8 percent
for corporations. Senators preferred to raise state sales and excise taxes or even
institute a state lottery.

As the two sides tried to reconcile their revenue packages, Martin, Rhyne,
and other Republicans opened the door a crack by offering to consider whatever the Democrats came up with on taxes, in return for enactment of the
Goldston-Pope cap on spending growth and passage of a gubernatorial veto

referendum, which had once again passed the Senate but stalled in the House. But if Democrats refused to budge, they said, cooperation would be impossible. "They have the authority to adopt a budget on their own," the governor said of the Democrats. "They've got all the marbles. They've got all the footballs. They've got all the baseball bats. They've got all the other metaphors that you want to use. They've got the cows, and the chickens, and the turkeys."

After weeks of negotiations, the House and Senate struck a deal on July 9. It contained $638 million in tax increases in 1991–92 and $739 million when fully implemented in 1992–93. The package pushed the sales-tax rate up a penny to six cents, raised the top personal income rate to 7.75 percent from 7 percent, did the same thing for the corporate rate (while adding a temporary surcharge), and levied $25 million more in excise taxes. The budget included expansion funds for both the BEP and Senate Bill 2, but much more for the latter. Overall, authorized operating spending actually went up by 1 percent, or roughly $100 million, in the first year of the biennium, but that was far less than the average increase of nearly 9 percent a year the operating budget had experienced over the previous decade. With capital spending included, the total General Fund budget was now scheduled to decline by 3.1 percent in fiscal year 1991–92 and then to rise 4.4 percent in 1992–93. One of the few consolations for fiscal conservatives was the adoption of a formulaic rainy-day reserve fund, as Goldston and Pope had proposed. As for non-budget issues, Martin made little headway. The veto amendment failed again in the House, as did an amendment on judicial selection. Republicans from western districts helped kill Martin's proposed Mountain Area Planning System. On the other hand, the General Assembly agreed to create a new 13-member authority to propel and govern the proposed air-cargo and manufacturing complex.

As the 1991 session came to a close, the governor was feisty—and more clearly aligned with the politicians and activists of his own party than he had been since 1989. Instead of accepting more sweeping proposals for budget savings from his administration and other Republicans, Martin said, the Democratic legislature had opted for large tax hikes on households and businesses, a move that threatened to hamper the state's recovery from the recession. "Those of us who are on the conservative side have a political obligation . . . to point out the flaws in what the General Assembly has done," he told reporters after the passage of the budget and tax hikes. "We will do that. It's a gold mine for Republican candidates in 1992."

CHAPTER TWELVE

HOME, SCIENCE, AND SENIOR STATESMAN

On February 18, 1991, Senator Phil Gramm of Texas visited Raleigh. A free-market economist who had served with Jim Martin in the House, Gramm was now chairman of the Republican Senatorial Campaign Committee. He came to North Carolina to sound out potential candidates to run against Terry Sanford in 1992. And like many Republicans inside and outside the state, Gramm had not yet given up the dream of Martin's returning to Washington in triumph as the junior senator from North Carolina.

Sanford was clearly vulnerable. An RSCC poll showed that only 26 percent of the state's voters were committed to reelecting him. Gramm told Martin the North Carolina race was the most promising among five Southern contests Republicans would target for the 1992 cycle. Although he knew Martin had said repeatedly he would not run, Gramm told the governor that if he had "a St. Paul–type experience on the road to Damascus," Republicans would "be happy about that religious experience." It was a clever way of pitching the devout son of a Presbyterian minister. But it didn't work. Instead, the two men discussed other potential candidates and how Martin could help unify the GOP around the primary victor. Gramm then talked with Lieutenant Governor Jim Gardner, who hadn't yet committed to running for governor. Gramm had already met in Charlotte with the city's two-term mayor, Sue Myrick, and in Greensboro with another former congressional colleague, Gene Johnston.

Gardner opted for the gubernatorial race. Myrick and Johnston did, in the end, run for Senate. They lost the nomination to Lauch Faircloth—like Gramm a Democrat turned Republican—who went on to defeat Sanford in the 1992 general election with the help of both the Congressional Club and the political organization run by Brad Hays. The governor's party-building work and personal assistance to Faircloth helped propel him to victory. Indeed, Martin's first conversation with Faircloth about the Senate race was on February 19, 1991, the day after the governor's meeting with Gramm.

Martin was glad to help his beloved Republican Party succeed. But his own days on the ballot were over.

BACK TO THE FUTURE

It was a relief. The governor's second term had been far more tumultuous and stressful than the first. His offer of a grand bargain on taxes, spending, and education reform was rebuffed by Democratic leaders and many members of his own party. He was burned in effigy and ridiculed in song. A relatively minor probe of the activities of his research office produced the major embarrassment of his "cough syrup" press conference. The onset of recession in 1990 brought rising unemployment, broadening deficits, and falling approval ratings.

On the other hand, the second term had also brought policy successes for Martin and his administration: the Highway Trust Fund bill, significant appropriations and bond issues to combat prison overcrowding, the creation of the Department of Environment, Health, and Natural Resources, and the displacement of top-down education reforms like the Basic Education Program with the local flexibility and accountability measures contained in Senate Bill 2.

Moreover, while the stressful demands of the second term had kept him busy, Martin still made time for family, golfing and sailing trips, and the ceremonial duties of the job, from which both he and Dottie often drew immense pleasure. The Executive Mansion in Raleigh continued to attract a wide variety of events and visitors. For example, conservative columnist and *National Review* editor William F. Buckley, who had interviewed Martin on his PBS program, *Firing Line*, came to town to play harpsichord with the North Carolina Symphony at a fundraiser to endow the "Governor and Mrs. James G. Martin Principal

FORMER BRITISH PRIME MINISTER MARGARET THATCHER VISITS WITH UNITED STATES SENATOR JESSE HELMS AND JIM AND DOTTIE MARTIN. COTSWOLD PHOTOGRAPHERS INC. PHOTO USED BY PERMISSION

Tuba Chair." Jim and Dottie weren't intent on leaving Raleigh because they disliked it. They simply wanted to go home to Lake Norman and a rhythm of life less interrupted by meetings, speeches, and incessant campaigning.

As early as the fall of 1991, Martin was thinking about the next step. At 56, he had accomplished a great deal but still had plenty of time and energy to devote to new pursuits. While returning to campus to teach was not a practical option, a college presidency would certainly have made sense. His friend Lamar Alexander had become president of the University of Tennessee after leaving his governorship in 1986. Terry Sanford had spent 16 years as president of Duke University between his tenures as governor and senator. Ultimately, however, Martin decided to apply his academic and administrative talents in a different setting: a medical research laboratory.

After leaving the post of budget director in late 1990, former First Union chairman Cliff Cameron had become chairman of the research development board overseeing the James G. Cannon Research Center in Charlotte. It was located at Carolinas Medical Center, which had recently become a full-fledged teaching hospital and changed its name from Charlotte Memorial Hospital. Members of the teaching faculty, physicians, and medical residents used the Cannon Center's facilities to conduct laboratory experiments in basic science and to explore potential clinical treatments. Cameron had always planned only a temporary role there. From the start, he urged hospital executives and board members to recruit Jim Martin to replace him. They didn't take much convincing. The chairman of the Charlotte-Mecklenburg Hospital Authority was Martin's longtime friend and supporter Stuart Dickson, chairman of the company that owned the Harris Teeter supermarket chain. Another influential board member of the hospital authority was Rusty Goode. Even without these connections, the prospect of a former governor and congressman returning to Charlotte to oversee the research center would have been too attractive to pass up.

Following extensive discussions in late 1991 and early 1992 with Carolinas Medical Center president Harry Nurkin, Martin agreed to fill the position when his term of office concluded. The Charlotte-Mecklenburg Hospital Authority announced the decision on March 23, 1992. "We're very fortunate to know what the future holds so that we will not be distracted from the job at hand," Martin said, which was to "devote full attention to my top priorities" during "this ultimate year of my administration."

ONE MORE DEBATE
ON EDUCATION REFORM

What were those priorities? Martin put education reform and fiscal restraint at the top of his list. By March 1992, the fiscal effects of the recession had begun to ease. State revenues were running slightly ahead of forecasts. By May, the state budget office was projecting a modest surplus of $150 million. In his budget revision for the 1992–93 fiscal year, Martin proposed $38 million more for the performance-pay provisions of Senate Bill 2, as well as 2 percent increases in base pay for teachers and state employees and money to hire additional workplace inspectors at the Department of Labor—a response to a September 3, 1991, fire at a chicken plant in the Richmond County town of Hamlet that took the lives of 25 workers who couldn't exit the building because the fire doors were locked. To offset the fiscal impact of these expansion items, the governor relied on $29 million previously earmarked for BEP expansion, another round of tuition increases, and reducing the number of, and pay for, vacant positions across state government. In addition to his operating-budget changes, Martin recommended that the legislature approve a $300 million bond referendum for capital improvements at University of North Carolina campuses.

Although the North Carolina Association of Educators and the State Employees Association of North Carolina protested the 2 percent pay raises as far too low, the General Assembly didn't attempt to outbid Martin on the issue. But legislative leaders flatly rejected his transfer of education-expansion dollars. "We're not going to cut the BEP funding," said Martin Nesbitt, cochairman of the House Appropriations Committee. "That is a high-priority item with us."

The House and Senate finalized the budget on July 8, 1992. General Fund operating spending rose 7 percent for the 1992–93 fiscal year, to $7.9 billion. Republicans criticized the plan for adding hundreds of new positions, arguing that it illustrated why the 1991 tax hikes had been excessive and economically damaging. "Those of us who vote against it," House minority leader Johnathan Rhyne said, "believe it takes the state in the wrong direction." While the Democratic legislature didn't enact Martin's proposed transfer of education funds, it did take steps to strengthen Senate Bill 2 by giving individual schools the authority to develop improvement plans, rather than vesting the power in school districts, as the original legislation had done. Martin welcomed the move. Lawmakers followed his lead on another issue, too, albeit with a lag time. They denied his request to put a $300 million bond for UNC system capital needs on the November 1992 ballot. A year later, however, they authorized and voters approved $310 million in bonds for UNC, along with $250 million for community colleges, $145 million for water and sewer projects, and $35 million for parks.

Meanwhile, events outside North Carolina suddenly removed two of the most difficult items on Martin's to-do list.

On June 10, 1991, the United States Supreme Court refused to reverse a lower-court ruling that blocked states from closing their borders to the shipment of hazardous wastes. Under the Constitution, the appeals court had ruled, only Congress had the authority to regulate interstate commerce. South Carolina and Alabama could no longer enforce their ban of hazardous waste from North Carolina. The pressure to locate an incinerator in the state dissipated. It was never built. As for low-level radioactive waste, fiscal and legal developments suddenly broke in North Carolina's favor as well. In May 1992, the South Carolina legislature and Governor Carroll Campbell decided not to close the Barnwell disposal site as scheduled at the end of the year. Instead, they extended its life for at least three more years, citing the fact that North Carolina's facility had been delayed. (It didn't hurt that South Carolina's state and local governments, just as cash-strapped as those in other states, would receive nearly $90 million a year from disposal fees.)

Then, on June 19, 1992, the Supreme Court announced its decision in *New York v. United States*, a case involving a proposed nuclear-waste facility in that state. It found that Congress had overstepped its bounds in 1985 by compelling states without disposal sites to take ownership and legal liability for radioactive waste produced within their borders. Although the justices ruled that Washington could offer financial incentives for building disposal facilities, the liability rule was the primary motivation for North Carolina and most other states to take action. When the rule disappeared, so did efforts to locate other disposal sites. North Carolina and South Carolina continued their legal wrangling after Martin left office, but no new regional-compact site for low-level radioactive waste was ever constructed.

Another major capital project on the governor's to-do list did advance during his "ultimate year": the proposed air-cargo complex eventually known as the Global TransPark. The General Assembly had created a new authority during the 1991 session to oversee the project. Martin appointed Rusty Goode president of the authority, which spent late 1991 and early 1992 surveying potential sites. Public officials and civic leaders in Charlotte and the Piedmont Triad made the case for their respective international airports, each of which already had active air-cargo operations and developable land. Given that the complex was an inherently risky venture, they argued that putting it in a major metropolitan area would make it more likely to attract the necessary industrial tenants—and make it easier to repurpose the new landing strip and land parcels if tenants never arrived. On the other hand, some state leaders feared that trying to put a massive new air-cargo complex in a heavily populated area might lead to the kind of vocal opposition and interminable delays that had plagued the hazardous and low-level radioactive waste projects. They looked favorably on proposals from rural counties in eastern North Carolina to convert small municipal airports or military installations such as Goldsboro's Seymour Johnson Air Force Base. In those areas, local residents would be less likely to oppose as a nuisance a project that backers promised would bring tens of thousands of jobs and put hundreds of millions of dollars' worth of developed property onto the tax rolls.

Authority members weighed the pros and cons of the various locations. "If we had one perfect site that could meet all those requirements, it would be an easy choice," Martin said at an April 1992 meeting of the authority in Chapel Hill. With influential legislators heavily favoring a rural site in the east—where, they argued, the need for economic development was greatest— the authority announced its decision in May: the project would be developed at the little-used Kinston Jetport. A large swath of eastern counties would be included in a Global TransPark Development Zone, where automobile owners would pay extra registration fees to help fund the project's development and business-recruitment costs.

The announcement of the Kinston site did nothing to silence the project's critics, who included some legislators, as well as fiscal conservatives outside government. Armed with an armful of maps and charts, the governor told a John Locke Foundation audience in Raleigh on July 24 that the project was reasonable and affordable. "We will not delude ourselves into investing more than is justifiable in this concept," Martin said in response to a critical article the foundation had distributed a few weeks earlier, "but neither will we be so foolish as to squander a brilliant idea and let some other state harvest what we have sown."

As the General Assembly convened for the last session of Martin's tenure, his administration experienced a final changing of the guard. The initial change, the most consequential, had actually started a few months earlier with the February resignation of Secretary of Corrections Aaron Johnson and several other top officials of the department after a state probe into purchasing irregularities. Although Johnson was not personally involved, the events had occurred under his watch, and he felt compelled to resign. His replacement was Lee Bounds, a retired criminal-justice professor who had served in the same post under two previous Democratic governors. Then, in May, shortly before the start of the legislative session, Alan Pugh became secretary at Crime Control and Public Safety after Joe Dean resigned to pursue his campaign for attorney general as the Republican nominee against the Democratic candidate, former district attorney Mike Easley. Similarly, in late August, Secretary of Revenue Betsy Justus resigned to campaign for the office of state treasurer as the Republican nominee against incumbent Democrat Harlan Boyles. Martin asked former legislative lobbyist Ward Purrington to head the department for the final four months.

ONE MORE ELECTION CYCLE AS GOVERNOR

Talk of the possibility that Jim Hunt might return to the Executive Mansion had started right after Martin's reelection in 1988. Hunt administration veterans spent much of 1989 and 1990 urging him to declare early. In response, Hunt offered public words of praise for other potential Democratic candidates such as Attorney General Lacy Thornburg. But he refused to rule out a run if they failed to catch fire. "I'm obviously very concerned that the Democrats be successful in 1992," he told the *N&O* in early 1990. "That is all I intend to say right now." By March 1991, however, Hunt was less circumspect. That's when, with his permission, friends sent out letters soliciting the opinions of past Hunt campaign donors about a gubernatorial run—and asking for money. By June, the former governor was ready to announce. Thornburg responded caustically. He described Hunt as damaged goods after the 1984 Senate campaign and suggested he couldn't win.

Throughout all this, everyone assumed that the Republican nominee to replace Martin would be Jim Gardner—and everyone was right. At the 1991 state GOP convention, held in early June in Wilmington, Jack Hawke was reelected for another two-year term as party chairman, again with broad support among all Republican factions. A highlight of the event was a banquet honoring Martin and featuring a video tribute entitled "Thanks for the Memories." But the focus was as much on the future as on the past. The governor did his part to set the stage for a Gardner-Hunt matchup in 1992. Criticizing the former governor's record on education and other issues, Martin suggested during his remarks to the convention that, in contrast to the Three Musketeers' motto, "All for one and one for all," Hunt's motto should be, "All for one and that's all."

Throughout 1991 and into the spring of 1992, Thornburg tried his best to make it a real Democratic race. The voters didn't cooperate. When primary day arrived on May 5, 1992, Hunt won 65 percent of the vote. Gardner won 82 percent in the GOP gubernatorial primary. The nomination battle for the United States Senate was much closer, Lauch Faircloth getting 48 percent to Sue Myrick's 30 percent and Gene Johnston's 17. In addition to Joe Dean getting the GOP nod for attorney general and Betsy Justus for state treasurer, two other Martin administration alumni won Council of State primaries that day. One was Nelson Dollar, who became the Republican nominee for commissioner of labor, to face Democrat Harry Payne, who'd been part of the Mavretic coalition in the House. The other was Art Pope, who'd worked on the Martin campaign in 1984 and in the governor's office in 1985. Now a state representative and joint caucus leader, Pope clinched the Republican nomination for lieutenant governor in a competitive race against two House colleagues, Representative Doris Huffman and former representative Trip Sizemore. In the fall, Pope would face another House colleague, Dennis Wicker, himself the winner of a highly contested Democratic primary that included Representative Jim Crawford and state auditor Ed Renfrow.

Martin returned to the campaign trail in the fall of 1992 with vigor, hoping to boost Republican prospects in North Carolina even as the three-way presidential race among George H. W. Bush, Bill Clinton, and Ross Perot made a decisive turn in Clinton's favor after the Democratic convention in mid-July. "If you want to keep moving forward, elect Jim Gardner," Martin told campaign audiences. The lieutenant governor in turn promised to build on the governor's legacy. "Jim Martin has done incredible things in eight years," Gardner said. As for Hunt, his 1992 campaign mixed the promise of new reforms, particularly on education, with reassurances about fiscal discipline. He clearly recognized that during his years out of office—and particularly during the turbulent debates in Washington and Raleigh about tax hikes—the issue had grown in importance to voters. "There are limits to what government can do," Hunt said during the 1992 race, pledging to attract business and volunteer support to any new initiatives. It proved difficult for Gardner to score points against Hunt on the issue. The only major tax increase during the Democrat's first eight years as governor had been a 1981 hike in the gas tax to fund highway construction. The Gardner campaign attacked it in an ad but couldn't find traction. After all, the legislature had done the same thing in 1989 at Martin's behest and with Gardner's backing.

Hunt was careful never to offer a clear defense or endorsement of the massive General Fund tax-hike package of 1991. That package would cause North Carolina Democrats a great deal of grief—but not Hunt, and not in 1992. Despite his loss to Jesse Helms in 1984, Hunt had proven to be a political force of nature. Thanks to his natural gifts as well as excellent strategic advice and staff execution, Hunt had held his party's traditional constituencies together throughout the turbulent 1970s and early 1980s. In 1992, he brought them back together into another winning coalition—one that included moderates and business leaders who had supported Martin but weren't as comfortable with Gardner. Hunt's campaign was also better funded and better timed.

Although a strong top-of-the-ticket showing had given state Republicans a significant boost in the previous three presidential cycles, Bush managed only 43.4 percent in North Carolina on Election Day, November 3—enough to edge Clinton (42.7 percent) for the state's electoral votes but not nearly enough to help GOP candidates down the ballot. Hunt won 53 percent of the vote for governor, with Gardner getting 43 percent and Libertarian candidate Scott McLaughlin claiming the rest. All the Republican candidates for Council of State fell short as well, as did Bev Lake's second attempt to win election to the North Carolina Supreme Court, although Bob Orr did win reelection to the court of appeals. In congressional and legislative races—the first after the adoption of controversial redistricting plans—the big news of 1992 was the lack of news. From the 12th District race, Democrats gained a seat in the United States House delegation, but it was a newly created one. The four Republican incumbents were reelected. In the General Assembly, Democrats gained three seats in the Senate while losing three in the House.

Considering Faircloth's defeat of Democratic icon Terry Sanford in the Senate race and the weak performance of the GOP's national ticket in North Carolina, the results weren't devastating to state Republicans. But for Martin, they weren't exactly a warm send-off either. He had helped build a party capable of competing with the Democrats in state and local races. The 1992 outcomes didn't fulfill the promise of all that work. Even as he met with Hunt to plan another transition—this one in the opposite direction—Martin was determined to do his part, as a candidate recruiter and "coach," to bring the North Carolina Republican Party farther along. He didn't know how long it would take.

He couldn't have imagined the first big success would come only two years later.

As in late 1984, the transition talks between the Martin and Hunt camps were professional and largely noncontroversial. It would be going too far to call them cordial, however. During the campaign, Hunt had questioned Martin's effectiveness in recruiting business and his record on education and crime. But the public statements of the Democratic governor-elect weren't the main problem. During the last several months of the gubernatorial race, Gardner campaign staffers and Martin administration officials had experienced numerous incidents—phone calls, letters, questions from reporters, and gossip at business events and dinner parties—that led them to believe the Hunt campaign was getting inside information. Republicans remembered the discovery of the phone tap at the Executive Mansion in late 1984 and wondered if something similar might be afoot.

On October 22, 1992, Martin and Jim Trotter held a meeting at the mansion with representatives of the Gardner campaign to inform them of credible evidence that two of Hunt's former law partners in Rocky Mount, Charles Lane and former North Carolina Supreme Court justice Phil Carlton, had been receiving intelligence on the Gardner campaign from a Hunt supporter, Beverly Smith, who was using a scanner to eavesdrop on phone calls made by Gardner's son Chris. Even though Martin had the mansion and administrative offices repeatedly swept for bugs, he decided to hold his briefing for the Gardner aides on the porch outside the mansion. "Maybe it was just prudence," he explained. Lane and Carlton later admitted their involvement in what the media termed "Scannergate." In reality, the Hunt campaign got far more useful intelligence about Gardner and the Republicans from leaks, rather than from eavesdropping. Still, it happened. And it strained relations between the two sides, although it never got personal between the two governors. "I respected him," Hunt later said of Martin. "He had done some really good things."

For the last event the Martins hosted at the Executive Mansion, they planned a secret twist that even Dottie's assistant, Sarah Lofton, didn't know about ahead of time. With many of the governor's top aides, campaign supporters, and friends dressed to the nines, the staff served an initial course on fine china and beautiful crystal. Then the servers returned—their formal wear exchanged for red shirts, kerchiefs, and straw hats—and to the guests' great surprise began removing the plates, silver, and table decorations. Out came red-and-white tablecloths and buckets of fried chicken. "The theme was, 'We started out great, but now it's time to go,' " Dottie explained.

On January 9, 1993, Jim Martin attended his last function as governor of North Carolina: Hunt's inauguration. "Dottie and I want you to know how grateful we are to the people of North Carolina for what has been our tremendous experience here, with the challenge, the thrill, and the satisfaction of these last eight years," Martin said in his farewell address. He listed the policy accomplishments of which he was most proud: making education funding the state's top budget priority, initiating the new intrastate program of four-lane highways, promoting economic development, and reorganizing state government. He also urged Hunt to keep pursuing the gubernatorial veto and to continue the initiatives Martin had begun near the end of his term, including the Global TransPark and developmental preschool for at-risk four-year-olds. "Just as you so kindly expressed confidence in the future eight years ago as you left this office to my care," he told Hunt, "in that same spirit I express to you the same confidence today as you return to the responsibilities of this office and we depart. May the grace of God and the strength of the people be with you."

And with that, Martin departed his office and Raleigh—but not community service or public life.

NEW JOB, FAMILIAR ROLES

Jim and Dottie were delighted to return to their Lake Norman home for good. He was also relieved to be out of the political spotlight for the first time since 1966. That didn't mean Martin would be slowing down, however. He threw himself wholeheartedly into his new job at the Cannon Research Center. Although the role was originally described as chairman of an oversight board, Martin actually became Carolinas Medical Center's vice president for research, a job he held from 1993 to 2000. One irony about the position was that the research center's laboratories made extensive use of animals including sheep, goats, chickens, pigs—and rats. When it opened its doors in 1992, it endured an initial wave of criticism from groups such as People for the Ethical Treatment of Animals. But these were not experiments to test cosmetics or invent new foods. The center's researchers sought to cure diseases and develop medical therapies. The general public largely shrugged off the criticism. As for Martin, the man who once had warned against banning consumer products "at the drop of a rat" was entirely comfortable with the idea of promoting human health through rigorous, replicable experiments. Laboratory animals were useful surrogates for testing new medications and procedures before assessing their advantages in human clinical trials. As he followed the studies done at the center and asked researchers questions about their discoveries, he was always looking for innovations that could be patented and marketed. Several were during his tenure.

The potential value of such medical research became much more personal to Martin in 1994, the year after he came to the Cannon Research Center, when his beloved brother Joe was diagnosed with ALS. "He didn't want it to be presented as a fatal diagnosis," Martin later told the UNC Center for Public Television, "but as something you could continue to live with and to be a part of the family." Watching Joe's brave struggle with the disease for 12 years, until his death in 2006, inspired Jim, other family members, and many in the Charlotte community. They founded the Joe Martin ALS Foundation and helped launch the Carolina ALS Center at Carolinas Medical Center.

As the year 2000 approached, Martin thought about retiring. He'd be turning 65, after all. But then Harry Nurkin and the Carolinas Medical Center board approached him with another job offer: vice president for government relations. He'd no longer be required to shoulder administrative duties. Instead, Martin would help manage relations with state and federal policymakers—a critical task, given that Medicare, Medicaid, and other government health plans accounted for a substantial share of annual revenues. He would also be called upon to represent CMC at meetings and in policy debates on such subjects as state regulation and medical-malpractice reform. Martin said yes to the idea. He stayed at CMC for another eight years, retiring in 2008.

Even then, he wasn't done working. He agreed to become a senior advisor to the McGuireWoods consulting firm in Charlotte and continued to serve on corporate and nonprofit boards for organizations ranging from Duke Energy, Family Dollar Stores, and the North Carolina Biotechnology Center to the Charlotte Symphony, the Charlotte Area Science Network, the North Carolina Research Campus in Kannapolis, the North Carolina Masonic Trust Board of Trustees in Greensboro, and the Pope Center for Higher Education Policy in Raleigh.

After changing roles at the hospital in 2000, and particularly after his "retirement" in 2008, Martin found more time to devote to his grandchildren and to personal interests such as sailing, golfing, and writing. In 2011, he began working on a book about two of his favorite subjects: science and religion. Growing up in a Presbyterian minister's home, studying and teaching chemistry, and debating both scientific and moral issues over the course of 26 years in public office had given Martin a great deal to think about, and had served as excellent preparation for organizing and communicating those thoughts. "Science is a modern and valid means of Revelation of God's great power," he argued. "Science observes and explains the nature of God's work in His universe and in us." In the book, Martin wasn't afraid to challenge liberals and conservatives, Democrats and Republicans, believers and unbelievers. The Bible is "not a scientific textbook," he stated, but neither was there "an irreconcilable conflict between science and religion, as they are revealed from the same God." Borrowing a turn of phrase from an English rabbi, Martin observed that "science takes things apart to see how they work," while "religion puts things together to see what they mean." From evolution and climate change to abortion, vaccination, and other issues of life and death, Martin insisted that people trust the evidence of their senses and study the accumulated knowledge of thousands of years of scientific discovery—including discoveries such as the Big Bang, DNA, and the physical fine-tuning of the universe, whose first causes have continued to be not only unexplained but unexplainable by the scientific method. "Science can reveal evidence for belief, pointing us to God," he concluded in the book, slated to be published in late 2015. "Thank God for Science."

Throughout his years with CMC and McGuireWoods, Martin remained active as a civic leader. The former governor was often asked to lend his name to political causes, such as the bipartisan opposition to a state-run lottery, and to help resolve political disputes. For example, Mecklenburg County voters in 2005 said no to a $427 million bond issue for school construction. In response, local officials asked Martin to chair a School Building Solutions Committee to develop an alternative. It comprised 35 members appointed by county commissioners, school-board members, and mayors representing a variety of parties and viewpoints. Martin said right off the bat that for the committee's work to be valuable, its goal should be a plan endorsed by a "substantial supermajority" of the members. Over the next several months, he sought to produce precisely that result—and succeeded, as 32 of the 35 members signed on (some Republicans added their names in response to personal attacks on Martin by a Democrat on the school board). After some to-and-fro with the county commission and the school board, the committee's efforts produced a capital program that included debt financing, pay-as-you-go, and various cost-saving recommendations.

AN ATHLETIC SCANDAL—AND MORE

The debate about school construction in Mecklenburg County was a local matter. Some years later, Martin was drawn into a different dispute—one that would play out on the national stage.

While chairing the board of another organization, the Institute for Defense & Business in Chapel Hill, he had gotten to know Holden Thorp, a fellow chemist who became chancellor of UNC–Chapel Hill in 2008. Two years after Thorp took the job, allegations of improper gifts to UNC football players by sports agents led to embarrassing revelations, staff resignations, NCAA fines, and criminal charges. It soon came to light that the improprieties extended beyond financial gifts. Football players were getting impermissible help with their college studies as well. One player seeking to have his eligibility reinstated, Michael McAdoo, inadvertently exposed that he had plagiarized a paper for his Swahili class. That in turn led to the disclosure of other plagiarized or ghost-written papers, "independent study" courses within the Department of African and Afro-American Studies (AFAM) for which students got passing or even high grades for doing no real work, and traditional lecture-style courses for which the lectures never actually occurred. The department's chairman, Julius Nyang'oro, admitted to creating the fake classes and other frauds, later attempting to justify them as heroic efforts to help disadvantaged and minority students.

At first, UNC officials tried to contain the damage by commissioning an internal review. A May 2012 report listed improprieties of one kind or another with more than 50 AFAM courses and identified a department administrator, Deborah Crowder, as playing a key role. But as the *News & Observer*, in particular, kept producing new revelations, it became apparent to university leaders that their internal review was insufficient. In August 2012, Thorp asked Martin to work with the consulting firm Baker Tilly on an external review. They were asked to determine when the plagiarism and no-show classes began in the department Nyang'oro chaired and whether or not something similar occurred with other faculty members and departments. Martin agreed to serve as a volunteer on a project that would last two months. It actually took four—and proved to be far from the last word.

Given what they understood to be a time constraint, Martin and the consultants did not attempt to read all the tens of thousands of email records or answer all questions surrounding the scandal. Another major constraint was that the two main actors in the tragedy/farce, Julius Nyang'oro and Deborah Crowder, refused to participate, on the advice of their attorneys. Still, using 84 interviews with university personnel and a large trove of academic records analyzed by a computer algorithm, the Martin–Baker Tilly probe discovered that the fake classes and other academic fraud had started much earlier and involved many more students than originally thought. Its December 2012 report identified more than 200 lecture-style classes that were confirmed as, or suspected of, having never met, dozens of independent studies with no real work required, and hundreds of suspicious grade changes dating as far back as 1994. The report also concluded that Crowder had likely graded some of the papers herself, despite being an administrator, and that no other department had operated like AFAM, although several offered relatively easy classes disproportionately populated by athletes.

The Martin–Baker Tilly report was a substantial addition to the public record and advanced the UNC story in many ways. Yet it proved controversial. To understand why requires a trip back in time. During the first year of Martin's second term as governor, in 1989, an NCAA investigation of the basketball program at North Carolina State University had found that some players had sold shoes and game tickets for cash. Other violations involving recruitment and academic rules were also alleged but not confirmed, although a subsequent commission found that head coach Jim Valvano—also the university's athletic director—and his staff should have watched their players' academic performance more closely. At first, the UNC system forced Valvano to resign as athletic director but let him remain head coach. As governor, Martin had no authority over these decisions. But he spoke out publicly on the issue. While questioning whether or not Valvano's holding both jobs had anything to do with it, Martin said that "if it makes everybody feel better to hire a different person as athletic director, that's OK with me." His main point was that "academic standards must not be compromised" to serve the goals of athletic departments.

Even as a Davidson professor back in the 1960s, Martin had been critical of colleagues who gave out easy grades. It "devalued the currency" of university scholarship, he argued. But he didn't see athletics per se as the problem. In early 1990, it came out that several of Valvano's players had engaged in a point-shaving scheme. Amid rising calls for Valvano's firing, Martin on March 3, 1990, attended what proved to be the coach's last game, and made a point of publicly shaking Valvano's hand as the home crowd cheered. "I told him I was his friend," Martin explained, "and I'm all for him." The governor also felt a certain kinship with the coach, as both were being excoriated by the *N&O*. While concerned about systemic problems within college athletics, Martin didn't believe Valvano was personally responsible for misbehavior by his players or the effects of competitive sports on academic standards as a whole.

When he agreed to Holden Thorp's request to conduct the review in 2012, then, Martin had no reason or intention to whitewash academic problems on the Chapel Hill campus. (Wolfpack fans alleging otherwise were likely unaware of Martin's prior friendship with Valvano, who passed away from cancer in 1993.) Indeed, in the years since the 1989–90 controversy at North Carolina State, Martin had become even more concerned about rampant grade inflation and other evidence of egregious declines in academic standards across American higher education, only some of which involved athletes. He saw the disclosures at UNC–Chapel Hill as another example of this pervasive problem—and his review as an excellent opportunity to call public attention to it.

But Martin's report to the Board of Trustees on December 20, 2012, did not generate the press coverage and public reaction he expected or intended. His choice of words proved critical. "This was not an athletic scandal," he told the trustees. "It was an academic scandal, which is worse." While Martin said that academic advisors in the Athletic Department knew that "something fishy" was going on in the AFAM courses—and that a couple had even tried to defend the plagiarized term papers to Martin as appropriate, given the disadvantaged backgrounds of the students involved—he found no evidence that the scheme had been initiated by those advisors or anyone on the coaching staff. He also cited the presence of non-athletes in the classes as evidence that they weren't simply set up to aid the sports program. A major cause of the scandal, Martin explained, was that UNC–Chapel Hill leaders did not subject AFAM to the same scrutiny they applied to other campus departments because of the "hot political conception" of the department and a desire not to be accused of racism. Not only was there no external supervision, but the department lacked basic internal structure such as regular faculty committees and meetings.

Furthermore, Martin had learned about a claim made in the original UNC internal review: that officials from the Athletic Department had come to the university's Faculty Athletic Committee to express concern that their students were being enrolled in so many independent-study courses at AFAM. "They claimed they were told not to worry about it, that it was up to each instructor to determine how a course will be presented," Martin said later. After interviewing athletic officials and the two professors present, Martin concluded that a conversation had occurred. Based on the recollection of just one of the professors, however, Martin further concluded that the athletic officials had in fact been told not to worry about the independent-study courses. "That's where we made a mistake," Martin admitted. The other professor didn't remember it that way, and the Athletic Department's claim became hotly contested. Martin decided to include it in his report. In retrospect, he said he should have avoided drawing any conclusions absent further corroboration. Also, within minutes of making his verbal presentation to the trustees, Martin realized he had mischaracterized the claim by stating that the Athletic Department had expressed concern to the faculty committee about lecture courses not actually meeting. During the question-and-answer session after his presentation, Martin informed the board he'd made an error—the Athletic Department's stated concern was about independent studies, not fake lecture courses. He later corrected the report text.

The uproar following the release of the Martin–Baker Tilly report guaranteed that much more would come. In February 2013, Holden Thorp announced plans to leave Chapel Hill to become provost at Washington University in St. Louis. A year later, his replacement, Carol Folt, and other university officials launched another outside review of the scandal. It was headed by

Kenneth Wainstein, a former Department of Justice official. In the meantime, Nyang'oro had been indicted for fraud. The district attorney agreed to drop the charge if Nyang'oro spoke truthfully to Wainstein. Crowder was also given immunity from prosecution in exchange for her cooperation. The Wainstein investigation was given a large budget, a long time frame, and a wide purview. And his team went through all the email records Martin and Baker Tilly had not. Not surprisingly, then, the subsequent Wainstein report released on October 22, 2014, answered many questions Martin's report did not and could not. It turned out that the fraudulent classes had begun about a year earlier than indicated by the Baker Tilly analysis. Wainstein also discovered via recovered emails that while Nyang'oro and Crowder were indeed the central actors in the drama, other professors and staff members (including academic advisors in the Athletic Department and former head football coaches John Bunting and Butch Davis) were aware of all or part of the academic fraud at AFAM and either encouraged it or chose not to rock the boat by reporting it.

Confronted with the additional information Wainstein and his team had found, Martin was generous in his praise. "It was a very thorough study," Martin said. "You have to be impressed with the detail that they were able to bring out that wasn't previously available." But he insisted that, given the constraints of time, budget, and noncooperation imposed on his earlier review, he remained proud of his role in probing the affair. Wainstein, for his part, expressed his respect for Martin's prior work, noting that without the interviews with Nyang'oro and Crowder, he couldn't have gotten "the answers we needed" about the extent of the scandal and the participation of academic counselors. "Am I infallible? No, of course not," Martin later reflected. He shouldn't have included the Athletic Department's claim as a fact in his report, and should have expressed himself more clearly when characterizing the scandal. It was a "fair criticism," he also admitted, to argue that he shouldn't have said, "This was not an athletic scandal."

But again, Martin's purpose was not to exonerate UNC or excuse the disproportion in plagiarized papers and fake classes by athletes. To observe that the scandal extended beyond athletes into an entire academic department—thanks to the malign neglect of university officials fearful of discussing politically tinged issues such as affirmative action and AFAM—was not, in Martin's mind, to downplay its significance. On the contrary, he saw it as a tremendous blow to UNC–Chapel Hill's reputation and a manifestation of the woes plaguing higher education as a whole. "There was something here far worse than just athletes taking advantage of easy courses," he said. The fact that the vast majority of athletes in the insubstantial AFAM classes were black illustrated the nature of the problem—and the great disservice the practice did to athletes and non-athletes alike. "I could have said, 'Not only is it an extraordinary athletic scandal, but it is also an incredibly damaging academic scandal,'" Martin said ruefully. That would have communicated what he meant more effectively. The academic scandal was "worse than any athletic scandal before or since."

HOWEVER SLOWLY, THE REPUBLICANS ASCEND

In yet another role, Republican senior statesman, Martin was to experience both the thrills of victory and the agonies of defeat.

Beginning with the 1994 cycle, he frequently helped party leaders recruit candidates for federal, state, and local offices and then gave them pointers on how best to hire staff, craft messages, and handle themselves on the campaign trail. He and the other former Republican governor, Jim Holshouser, were routinely asked to serve on steering committees or advisory panels for gubernatorial and Senate candidates. They sat in on meetings and conference calls, read polls, and offered advice.

In many cases, the candidates or political consultants involved had once worked on Martin's campaigns or in his administration. During the 1990s and the following decade, an increasing number of these Republican campaigns were successful. It was particularly gratifying to help Bob Orr, Bev Lake, and other friends (including Mark Martin and Barbara Jackson, both of whom had served Governor Martin as legal counsel) win election to the North Carolina Supreme Court, producing and maintaining a Republican majority. He was also delighted to see many Martin administration alums win election to the General Assembly and local offices. In the first midterms after Martin left office, the 1994 cycle, Republicans won a majority in the House for the first time since Reconstruction and nearly won a majority in the Senate as well. Although part of a national Republican wave, the North Carolina GOP's legislative gains were among the largest in the nation. Its candidates ran vigorously against the Democrats' 1991 tax increases. They pointed out that, even as the national economy recovered and the state treasury filled up with new revenue in 1993 and 1994, the General Assembly had refused to roll back the tax hikes. The Republicans' new House majority lasted until 1998—a bad national cycle for the GOP—after which control of the state legislature eluded Republicans for another decade. However, this was at least in part an artifact of gerrymandering. In the 2000, 2002, and 2004 election cycles, GOP candidates actually polled more votes than Democrats for one or both chambers, yet ended up with a minority of the seats.

The bigger disappointments lay with losses that couldn't be chalked up to adverse political cartography: races for governor. Jim Hunt easily won reelection in 1996 over state representative (and future congressman) Robin Hayes. In 2000, Attorney General Mike Easley won a competitive race against former Charlotte mayor Richard Vinroot, an ally and friend of Martin's, then won reelection easily in 2004 against former Senate minority leader Patrick Ballantine, despite a strong showing on the North Carolina ballot by other Republican candidates such as President George W. Bush and victorious United States Senate candidate Richard Burr.

In 2008, another Republican with strong ties to Martin, longtime Charlotte mayor Pat McCrory, fell short in his gubernatorial run against Lieutenant Governor Beverly Perdue. It was a bad year for GOP candidates nationwide, thanks to the onset of the Great Recession and the historic candidacy of Barack Obama, yet Perdue's margin of victory was only 3 points. Nevertheless, the race capped a frustrating 20-year stretch for Martin and other Republicans forced to watch a succession of Democrats hold the state's top elective office.

Hayes and Ballantine may have been doomed from the get-go because of national trends, fundraising disadvantages, and the inherent difficulty of defeating incumbents. But in the open-seat races of 2000 and 2008, Vinroot and McCrory had raised significant sums and worked hard to emulate Martin's "constructive conservatism" model from 1984 and 1988. While criticizing Democratic tax increases and espousing fiscal restraint, they had also promoted significant new initiatives for education reform and transportation improvement. In both cases, however, their Democratic opponents successfully muddied the waters on fiscal policy by pointing to Charlotte's relatively high tax burdens and spending levels as evidence that the city's mayors might not be trustworthy stewards of the state treasury. In the 2000 race, the Easley campaign even ran ads and sent mailers suggesting it was Vinroot, not Easley, who'd be more likely to raise state taxes if a budget gap developed. To some extent, Martin himself had contributed to the GOP's messaging problem by proposing sales-tax hikes in an attempt to strike grand bargains with the legislature. On state spending, the Democratic campaigns in 2000 and 2008 used the same line of attack: that the Republican candidates' support for structural reforms in education—performance pay, decentralization, and parental choice—meant they could not be trusted to fund public schools adequately.

Just two years after McCrory fell agonizingly short in his bid to recapture the Executive Mansion for the state GOP, however, Republicans achieved historic victories in the 2010 midterms by taking control of both chambers of the General Assembly for the first time in more than a century and achieving a 50–50 split in the control of county governments across the state. Richard Burr, who in 2004 had recovered the United States Senate seat Lauch Faircloth lost to John Edwards in 1998, won reelection in 2010, while Renee Ellmers defeated incumbent Bob Etheridge in the Second District, giving Republicans six of the state's 13 House members. The 2010 cycle featured a national wave for the GOP—a reaction against the passage of the Affordable Care Act and other unpopular policies associated with President Obama. But as in 1994, Republicans in North Carolina outperformed their counterparts in most other states by recruiting stronger candidates, running better campaigns, and developing a message that combined fiscal conservatism with reform proposals on education and infrastructure.

Facing a new and energetic Republican legislature intent on rolling back tax increases and other policies enacted during her first two years in office, North Carolina governor Beverly Perdue struggled to regain her footing. The state's languid recovery from the Great Recession had already pulled her approval ratings into the danger zone. The ensuing battles with the General Assembly did little to improve them. In late 2011, facing a likely rematch with Pat McCrory, Perdue declined to run for reelection. Democrats turned to Lieutenant Governor Walter Dalton as their standard-bearer. An effective legislator and capable politician, Dalton proved inadequate to a daunting task. On Election Day, November 6, 2012, McCrory was elected governor with 54.6 percent of the vote—a showing that fell between the 54.3 percent Jim Martin had won in 1984 and the 55.1 percent he got in 1988. Sue Myrick's son Dan

Forest was elected the first Republican lieutenant governor in 20 years as well. Thanks to favorable district maps and superior candidate recruitment, fundraising, and messaging, Republicans won nine of the 13 races for the United States House, upped their legislative margins to 77–43 in the North Carolina House and 33–17 in the state Senate, and became the majority party in county governments by winning 53 commissions, as well as numerous elections for sheriff, clerk of court, and other offices.

Republicans had never been so strong in North Carolina. In the eyes of Pat McCrory and many other party leaders—including the newly elected governor's political consultant, Jack Hawke, who tragically passed away soon afterward from cancer—they had finally fulfilled the vision Jim Martin and an earlier generation of party leaders and activists had worked so hard to bring to fruition.

Martin was among the cochairs of McCrory's transition team in late 2012, counseling him on the importance of assembling a good staff and the need to let the General Assembly take the initiative on some issues. After McCrory's first year on the job, Martin praised him as an energetic governor who "thrives on the excitement of debate and getting things done." McCrory, in turn, frequently lavished praise on the last Republican to serve as governor before him. "He's been my mentor," McCrory said in late 2014 at an event commemorating a new collection of Martin artifacts at the North Carolina Museum of History. "I constantly seek his advice. He's a true role model of a public servant."

EPILOGUE

A CATALYST FOR CHANGE

The word *catalyst* has two standard definitions. *The Oxford English Dictionary* describes the first one, the literal one, like this: a catalyst is "a substance that increases the rate of a chemical reaction without itself undergoing any permanent chemical change." The second definition, the figurative one, describes a catalyst as "a person or thing that precipitates an event."

While catalysts abound in nature, the term itself is of relatively recent vintage. It was coined in 1835 by Swedish chemist Jöns Jacob Berzelius, who helped lay the foundations of modern chemistry. For example, he devised the familiar notation system for molecules (e.g., H_2O). Berzelius also encouraged collaboration and innovative thinking by running a laboratory, leading the Royal Swedish Academy of Sciences, and engaging in extensive correspondence with other scientists across Europe. Berzelius, in other words, served as a catalyst in the development of modern science.

His fellow chemist James G. Martin did the same in his chosen fields of academia and politics more than a century later. As a young Davidson College professor, Martin proved a natural leader and helped propel reforms of the college's curriculum. As a candidate and county-commission chairman during the 1960s and early 1970s, Martin played an important role in precipitating the rise of Republicans as an electoral force and governing party in Mecklenburg County during tumultuous times. Through the creation of the state's first regional council of governments and his service as the first Republican president of the state's association of county commissioners, he soon extended his influence beyond his home county. After his election to the United States House of

Representatives in 1972, the young congressman survived his party's Watergate debacle to make his mark as an advocate of applying sound science to public policy, as an opponent of federal overregulation and encroachment on local and private prerogatives, and as one of the architects of the supply-side tax reforms of the late 1970s and early 1980s.

In 1984, Martin overcame a 37-point deficit to Rufus Edmisten after the May primary to win a convincing 54 percent of the vote for the office of governor of North Carolina. Following many battles with the Democratic legislature, an impressive 1988 reelection victory over Bob Jordan, and spirited efforts to help GOP candidates in the challenging midterms of 1986 and 1990, Martin left the North Carolina Republican Party stronger by virtually every measure than when he entered the Executive Mansion. After the elections of 1992, the GOP had both United States Senate seats, four of the state's 11 congressional seats, 53 seats in the 170-member General Assembly, and its first toehold in elected judicial posts. Republicans would build on this impressive base just two years later, in 1994, by winning control of the North Carolina House, almost capturing the North Carolina Senate, taking their first majority of the state's congressional delegation, winning their first elections for the North Carolina Supreme Court (Bev Lake and Bob Orr), winning two elections for the court of appeals (Mark Martin and Ralph Walker), and achieving majorities on 42 of the state's 100 county commissions.

CONTRASTING HELMS, HUNT, AND MARTIN

But focusing on electoral outcomes misses the real import of Jim Martin's career in public life. For one thing, the rise of the North Carolina Republican Party after Martin's tenure as governor did not follow a straight, upward line. Democrats controlled the Executive Mansion for the next 20 years, until Pat McCrory's victory in 2012. Republicans suffered the same losing streak in elections for lieutenant governor until Dan Forest's win in 2012 and scored only limited victories in other Council of State offices. At the legislative level, the Republican breakout of the mid-1990s wasn't sustained. Although control of the General Assembly remained highly contested from the 1998 midterms to the 2008 cycle, Democrats came out on top every time, thanks to a variety of factors (including gerrymandering and even a bribe paid to a Republican legislator to change parties after the 2002 election). Republicans managed only to hold steady in county elections during the same period, although they did make impressive gains in municipal politics and reached a majority on the North Carolina Supreme Court in 1998 (which they've held ever since).

It wasn't until the 2010 cycle, then, that the state GOP had its next big surge—and not until 2012 that it achieved simultaneous power in all three branches of state government, as well as most North Carolina counties. Obviously, Jim Martin's gubernatorial career from 1984 to 1992 couldn't have been the immediate cause of Republican triumphs in 2010 and 2012. The relationships among these events are more complicated than that, and more interesting. Describing them requires that one distinguish between Republican competitiveness in federal elections—for the United States Senate and House and the state's electoral votes for president—and Republican competitiveness in state and local elections. There are, naturally, common denominators. Successful candidates for any office must raise sufficient funds. They must avoid fatal gaffes. They must get out the vote of their electoral base while swaying undecided voters with effective messages conveyed through advertising, direct appeals, media coverage, and peer-to-peer campaigning (which has enjoyed a resurgence, thanks to social media and technology platforms that support cost-effective canvassing).

But the content of those messages isn't the same. Candidates seeking to serve in Washington focus on a different set of issues—and describe them in a different way—than candidates for state or local offices do. In the North Carolina context, journalists and political analysts often point to the pivotal 1984 Senate race between Jesse Helms and Jim Hunt to illustrate the dichotomy. While Hunt initially emphasized his work as governor on matters such as education and economic development, the Helms campaign set the agenda early with attack ads on such emotional issues as school prayer, forced busing, and the federal holiday for Martin Luther King. The strategy was intended to define Hunt ideologically as left-of-center while also exploiting differences between his words and deeds to question his candor. "Where do you stand, Jim?" was the big question of the campaign. Hunt responded with attack ads of his own, including a series of spots linking Helms to anticommunist death squads in El Salvador. That Helms ultimately won the 1984 contest is typically explained either by arguing that Hunt decided too late and too reluctantly to "stoop" to the senator's level, or by observing that Ronald Reagan's strong showing in North Carolina—he won 62 percent of the state's presidential vote in 1984—pushed Helms over the finish line.

The purpose here is not to recapitulate the wide-ranging debate about the 1984 Senate race. Rather, the point is that while Jesse Helms spent many years perfecting the craft of running federal campaigns in North Carolina, Jim Hunt spent many years perfecting the craft of running state campaigns. The latter tried to make the jump to federal office. He lost. If Helms had ever wearied of Washington politics and tried to return home to run for governor, his fate might well have been similar to Hunt's. How would his signature campaign issues and tactics have matched up with those of an experienced state politician promising to reform public education, improve the state's infrastructure, or restructure the state's prison system? Probably not very well.

It was Jim Martin, not Helms or Hunt, who was able to make the transition successfully. "I think all of his collective experiences helped him see things from a telescopic range," said his former communications director, Karen Rotterman. That range allowed him to connect the conservative rhetoric North Carolinians expected from Republican candidates with the practical solutions they wanted from governors. After Martin, some Republicans followed his lead as they ran for state or local offices. Many succeeded. Others tried to run Helms-style campaigns for such offices. Many lost.

This is not a commentary on the relative merits of the two GOP leaders or a brief for moderation. Left-leaning analysts like to distinguish Martin from Helms by calling the former "moderate" and the latter "conservative." But the distinction isn't accurate. By any reasonable standard, Jim Martin was a conservative congressman. During his 12 years in Washington, he averaged an American Conservative Union rating of 87 percent. Using a methodology based on bill sponsorship—more revealing, in a sense, because many bills never make it to floor votes—the transparency website *GovTrack.us* rated Martin as significantly more conservative not just than the average congressman during his tenure but than the average Republican member. It was no accident that Martin joined Newt Gingrich as one of the original members of the Conservative Opportunity Society.

As he turned his attention to running for and then serving as governor, Martin retained his general philosophy of fiscal conservatism and his Reagan-era interest in reforming the tax code to promote economic growth and opportunity.

But he also devoted himself to the effective provision of services such as public safety, education, and infrastructure. Voting against increased federal action on these fronts as a congressman was not to suggest they were unimportant. To Martin, and to most modern conservatives, they are proper and important areas for state and local action—areas where private providers should be employed whenever practical, certainly, but where public agencies are often used to deliver services directly at the lowest possible cost commensurate with a high level of performance.

THE FRUITS OF CONSTRUCTIVE CONSERVATISM

As a Republican governor in what had been a strongly Democratic state, Martin enjoyed remarkable success in translating his policy agenda into law. Some of the victories came during his eight years in office. Although the corporate income-tax rate was higher when he left than when he arrived (over his strong objections), business inventories and some intangible assets were removed from the local tax base. The payroll tax was also lower. His vision of education reform based on budget flexibility, local control, and high standards became the bipartisan consensus in Raleigh by his second term, replacing the previous emphasis on school inputs and statewide standardization found in the Basic Education Program. Martin explained the change in thinking this way: "Our educational system itself, not the availability of resources, was the real problem." During his tenure, North Carolina expanded its prison system and the use of alternative sentences, reorganized state government, and launched a massive expansion of the state road network with the Highway Trust Fund, which Martin described as his "single biggest achievement." The legislature opened more of its deliberations to public scrutiny, adopted a true rainy-day reserve, and curtailed pork-barrel spending. Fewer state employees were hired according to their political affiliations and pressured to make political contributions to keep their jobs.

Longtime North Carolinians generally remember the Martin era as one of progress and success for their state—and for good reason. From 1985, the year of his inauguration, to 1993, the year his last budget was implemented and he departed, North Carolina's economic performance was impressive in both absolute and relative terms. In personal income adjusted for inflation and population, for example, North Carolina experienced an 18 percent gain from 1985 to 1993, compared to a national average of 10 percent and a regional average of 14 percent. This annual rate of increase was the largest under any North Carolina gubernatorial administration since the 1960s (as well as under the subsequent Hunt, Easley, and Perdue administrations) and exceeded the national and regional averages by the largest spread in state history.

It would be erroneous to attribute such trends entirely to the actions of Martin and his Republican administration, or even to state government as a whole. National, international, and private-sector trends explain much of the variation in a state's economic growth over time. Moreover, to the extent that state policy influences economic performance, some of the effects take many years or even decades to materialize. Nevertheless, Martin's policies and economic-development work clearly played an important role in North Carolina's impressive performance during these years. And more importantly from a political standpoint, North Carolinians came to associate good economic times with the governor then in charge in Raleigh.

Martin's influence on public policy extended far beyond the end of his term. In many cases, while he may not have scored a legislative victory on a particular issue during his governorship, he successfully framed it for future action. During the 1990s, bipartisan majorities in the General Assembly phased out the state sales tax on food and the rest of the intangibles tax, ended the state's abortion fund, enacted the gubernatorial veto, and expanded parental choice in public education through the creation of charter schools. On performance pay for teachers, this period saw some progress with the implementation of school-wide teacher bonuses for schools performing at or above expectations under the new ABCs of Public Education system (which was based on the structure of Senate Bill 2), although concerted action on the Career Ladder and performance pay for individual teachers had to wait until the McCrory administration in 2013.

That Governor Martin won so many of the policy debates he engaged in is directly related, then, to his importance as a builder of the North Carolina Republican Party. His blending of pro-growth tax policies with a coherent strategy for improving core public services—an approach Martin called "constructive conservatism"—served to give an entire generation of Republicans the tools they needed not only to win elections for local and state offices but also to govern effectively. "Because he was a successful governor, the Republican Party benefited from that," Jim Hunt later reflected. "The image he gave the GOP was good."

Martin's achievements weren't sufficient by themselves to put the Republicans in power in state government. Indeed, for a time, other factors conspired to block the party's continued rise. Perhaps the most important one was Hunt's own skillful tack to the center during his third term. Shortly after the GOP legislative gains of 1994, he proposed an income-tax cut larger than the one Republicans had campaigned on, as well as another cut in the state payroll tax. (In fact, the three largest tax cuts in North Carolina history were enacted under Martin in 1985, Hunt in 1995, and McCrory in 2013.) Still, as Republicans applied and refined Martin's constructive-conservative approach in their local and state campaigns, they gained ground. Once they gained it, following his example helped them keep it.

"A BRIDGE TO FULL POLITICAL CITIZENSHIP"

This is not a criticism of other North Carolina Republicans. It is an observation, and hardly a unique one. One veteran Congressional Club activist observed that while the careers of Jesse Helms and Jim Martin were both significant factors in the rise of the North Carolina Republican Party, their roles were distinct. They played on the same team, in other words, but in different positions. Due in part to circumstances but also to personal strengths and temperaments, Helms primarily played defense. He specialized in exposing bad actors and stopping bad ideas. On the other hand, Martin more often looked for opportunities to play offense. Indeed, one of the reasons he decided to run for governor was that he saw more such opportunities in Raleigh than in the nation's capital.

"It's not that one was bad and the other was good," the Congressional Club activist said of the contrasting approaches of Helms and Martin. Instead, they were complementary. State Republicans needed a political talent such as Helms to help detach North Carolina voters from their longstanding allegiance to the Democratic Party. But his Senate campaigns on national and international issues "didn't build the infrastructure of the party" for success in down-ballot races, the activist said. That was Martin's contribution. He was "a bridge from the minority mentality to full political citizenship as a Republican in North Carolina."

So far, this discussion has focused on the definition of a catalyst as someone who precipitates an event. But the literal definition, from chemistry, is that a catalyst increases the rate of a reaction without undergoing any permanent change of its own. To suggest that Jim Martin never changed throughout his life would be an absurd overstatement. When considering Martin's political career as a whole, however, the continuities are striking. For example, his role in brokering the Democratic-Republican coalition in the North Carolina House after the 1988 elections was a familiar one. He'd helped assemble bipartisan coalitions to enact the Reagan tax cuts in the early 1980s and to stop the saccharin ban in the late 1970s. He'd even hammered out his own bipartisan coalition on the county commission in 1969, despite being in the minority. Gifted with a remarkable intellect and a facility for communicating complex ideas with catchphrases and examples, Martin often used public forums as a tactic for building consensus, starting with his first term as a Mecklenburg commissioner and including his leadership of a school-construction task force in the same community four decades later. Whether in local, state, or federal office, he advocated a consistent set of policies: balanced budgets, savings reserves, pro-growth tax policies, local control, and applying sound science to energy and environmental issues. Even the low points of Martin's political career exhibited continuity. When he let accusations of personal impropriety provoke him to anger, his resulting public comments didn't always serve him well. And when he tried to work out thorny problems or design "grand bargains" by himself, rather than consulting a wider network of people before staking his position, he tended to experience legislative setbacks.

From the vantage point of 2015—nearly half a century after Jim Martin made his first run for partisan office in 1966—the GOP appears to have the upper hand in North Carolina politics. It's an outcome most Republicans in the 1960s would have seen as improbable. Yet it happened. As Martin and his peers looked at the state GOP victories of 2012 and 2014 with elation and pride, however, other North Carolinians felt as Martin once had as a young man: on the outside looking in. Aggrieved but determined Democrats across the state were in 2015 doing precisely what Martin and his allies had done a half-century earlier. They were recruiting new candidates, creating new organizations, planning new campaigns.

Their task was not as daunting as Martin's. North Carolina Republicans weren't nearly as firmly entrenched in 2015 as North Carolina Democrats had been in 1966. Martin helped overturn a near-monopoly on political power by one party. To the extent he and other Republicans were successful, what came next wasn't another monopoly on power by their own party, but rather true partisan competition. Of course, even close contests must have victors. North Carolina Republicans won most of the elections from 2010 to 2014. But the upcoming games promised to be highly competitive.

As a party trailblazer and coach, Martin hoped the GOP winning streak would continue. But as another example of the consistency that marked his time in public life, he viewed the North Carolina Democrats' efforts to compete in 2016 and beyond in philosophical terms. "According to my original philosophy, that's healthy," he said, because political cultures ought to be "fluid" rather than static, with "two parties vying with one another, bringing out their best candidates, sometimes missing that responsibility and having to pay for it."

Throughout his political career, Jim Martin both fostered and thrived in such a culture. In the process, he set an example for North Carolinians of all persuasions to study, admire, and emulate.

ACKNOWLEDGMENTS

One of the earliest biographers of political figures—or of anyone, for that matter—was the Greek historian Plutarch, who lived from the years 46 to 127. His works chronicled the lives of emperors, generals, and elected leaders of Greece and Rome. Like most authors, Plutarch was a voracious reader. "Books delight to the very marrow of one's bones," he wrote. "They speak to us, consult with us, and join with us in a living and intense intimacy."

I've always felt this way. My parents say that around the age of three, I could frequently be found squatting on the floor with a volume of the *World Book* encyclopedia spread open. I couldn't read all the words, but I could look at the pictures and scrutinize the maps. Although the Internet has placed more words, pictures, and maps at our fingertips than ever before, I find that it hasn't replaced the sublime tactile experience of sitting down with a cherished old book or thumbing through an unfamiliar one. If you've read this book on a screen, I offer my thanks. I hope you found its stories fascinating and thought provoking. But if you're holding a hard copy of *Catalyst* in your hands, *salute*! You and I have something in common.

As I researched the life and times of former North Carolina governor James G. Martin, I spent a lot of time in front of screens. I scanned online databases and archives. I read newspapers and other records on microfilm. I used search engines to explore connections among key individuals and events. I could not have completed the book without these tools. But I also spent many hours with paper copies of source materials—books, monographs, transcripts, photographs, correspondence files, and notebooks produced by Martin or staff members of his administration—in my hands or laid out on tables. In addition,

I watched many hours' worth of videotapes of Martin's televised speeches, debates, and campaign ads. Most of these materials were provided to me by the subject himself or by his wonderful wife, Dottie. I'd also like to thank the archivists of the James G. Martin Papers of the Southern Historical Collection at the University of North Carolina at Chapel Hill's Wilson Library, as well as the kind and helpful librarians who assisted me at the State Library of North Carolina in Raleigh, the microfilm collection at UNC–Chapel Hill's Davis Library, and the Robinson-Spangler Carolina Room at the main branch of the Charlotte-Mecklenburg Library.

Much of this book, however, was based not on materials written or recorded by someone else but instead on interviews I conducted over the course of three years with several dozen individuals. They included Jim and Dottie Martin, Jim Hunt, former attorney general and secretary of state Rufus Edmisten (as it happens, a distant cousin of mine), veterans of Martin's congressional office and gubernatorial administration, political professionals who worked both for and against him, reporters who covered him in Washington and Raleigh, and many, many others. I'm greatly indebted to them.

Naturally, while I appreciate the assistance of all the persons I interviewed or whose writings I used, only I am responsible for the conclusions I drew from the information they provided—and for any mistakes made in transcription or description.

This is not a commissioned biography. That is, while Jim Martin gave generously of his time, personal records, and ideas, he did not hire or arrange for me to write this book. Nor did he ask for or receive editorial control over the finished product. At my request, he did read a draft of each chapter. There can be no more authoritative source for facts about his life, of course, so I wanted to make sure I neither misstated information I included nor omitted information I should have included. Being a former college professor, Martin also couldn't help correcting the many errors of spelling and grammar he discovered, for which I was grateful and embarrassed in roughly equal measure. But he made recommendations, not commands. And he fully understood and accepted my desire to provide alternative points of view about his decisions, positions, campaigns, and achievements. Having read this book, you know a great deal about Jim Martin's beliefs and motivations. You know what his political rivals and critics thought and said about him, too. During 26 years in public life as a county commissioner, congressman, and governor, Martin had many impressive accomplishments. He also experienced setbacks. "To make no mistakes is not in the power of man," Plutarch observed, "but from their errors and mistakes the wise and good learn wisdom for the future."

In addition to those who assisted this project by providing records, sitting down for interviews, or pointing me in the right direction, thanks are also due my former colleagues and fellow board members at the John Locke Foundation, where I worked when I began researching the book, as well as my new colleagues at the John William Pope Foundation, where I started a new job as president at the beginning of 2015 after 25 years at JLF. They offered suggestions, technical assistance, or encouragement as I sought to complete the book while shouldering my other professional responsibilities. My heartfelt appreciation also goes to my friend John Thomas and the organization he leads, the E. A. Morris Charitable Foundation, which helped support my research for the book. I can't offer sufficient praise to the folks at John F. Blair, Publisher, in Winston-Salem for believing in this project and bringing it to market with such professionalism, elegance, and care. They include company president Carolyn Sakowski, editor in chief Steve Kirk, designer Debra Long Hampton, and publicist Sally Johnson. I'm immensely grateful to my brother David Hood and my good friends Mark Dearmon, Art Pope, Lindsay Hollandsworth, and Neal Rhoades for reading the finished product cover to cover and providing invaluable help in improving the narrative, boiling away the extraneous material, and strengthening my argument. (And make no mistake, there is an argument here. If you'll pardon another observation from Plutarch: "The mind is not a vessel to be filled, but a fire to be kindled." Whether you agree or disagree with my thesis, I very much hope you find your fire kindled by it.)

Most of all, I offer thanks to my family: to Alex and Andrew, for putting up with Saturdays and Sundays without someone to chauffer them around or to pummel in games of chance or skill; to Jerri, for having to rehearse her various performances (both balletic and comedic) without me along for musical accompaniment or moral support; and to the wonderful woman who became my bride shortly after I began this project, Traci Hood. She was another of my manuscript readers and editors, a task for which the former high-school English teacher was eminently qualified.

SOURCES AND METHODS

All of the direct quotes in this book came from recorded and transcribed personal interviews, previously published books or transcripts, or articles published by the *Washington Post*, the *Charlotte Observer*, the *Charlotte News*, the Raleigh *News & Observer*, the Greensboro *News & Record*, the *Winston-Salem Journal*, the *Fayetteville Observer*, the *Wilmington Star-News*, the *Hendersonville Times-News*, the *Lexington Dispatch*, the Lumberton *Robesonian*, the *Statesville Record & Landmark*, and other newspapers.

Space considerations precluded the inclusion of endnotes. However, I have attributions for every direct quote, available upon request by contacting me at JohnMcDonaldHood@gmail.com. In addition, here is a chapter-by-chapter description of major sources and methods.

PROLOGUE:
A SECOND SOUTHERN STRATEGY

I obtained accounts of the Blackberry Farm meeting not only from Jim Martin but also from published accounts in the *Washington Post* and elsewhere, as well as a transcript of the March 25, 1987, edition of William F. Buckley's *Firing Line*. Insights about modern Southern politics came from Merle and Earl Black's *The Rise of Southern Republicans* (Cambridge, MA: Harvard University Press, 2002) and David Woodard's *The New Southern Politics* (Boulder, CO: Lynne Rienner Publishers, 2006).

CHAPTER 1: STRONG BONDS
AT THE START

Jim and Dottie Martin were the primary sources for the details of their early lives, supplemented by articles from *The Davidsonian*, other newspaper accounts, and the recollections of former Martin students such as John Napier, who later served with Martin in Congress.

CHAPTER 2: A PROFESSOR TURNED POLITICIAN

A doctoral dissertation by Elaine Allen Lechtreck, "Southern White Ministers and the Civil Rights Movement" (Union Institute & University, Cincinnati, OH, 2007), provided critical background on Arthur Martin's role in the racial politics of South Carolina. Details of Jim Martin's campaigns for, and service on, the Mecklenburg County Commission came primarily from county records of budgets and referendum results, contemporaneous coverage in the *Charlotte Observer* and the *Charlotte News*, and Martin's recollections.

CHAPTER 3: THE REPUBLICAN BREAKTHROUGH

Campaign coverage in the *Observer* and the *News* proved essential here, as did recollections about the late Brad Hays from Paul Shumaker, Alan Pugh, and other former colleagues and allies. I checked county records to confirm Mecklenburg budget figures.

CHAPTER 4: "AT THE DROP OF A RAT"

In addition to the Charlotte-area media, the *Statesville Record & Landmark* was an important source for reconstructing the major events and controversies occurring during Martin's early years in Congress. Background and details about the battle over the Food and Drug Administration's regulation of artificial sweeteners came from rules and reports published by the FDA, articles published by *Chemical Heritage* magazine and the American Council on Science and Health, and a transcript of the April 21, 1977, event at the American Enterprise Institute.

CHAPTER 5: THE REAGAN CHAIN REACTION

For the history of the supply-side movement and the Kemp-Roth tax cuts that became central to the Reagan economic plan, I relied on Brian Domitrovic's *Econoclasts: The Rebels Who Sparked the Supply-Side Revolution and Restored American Prosperity* (Wilmington DE: ISI Books, 2009) and my friend Marty Anderson's inside account of the birth of Reaganomics, entitled *Revolution* (New York: Harcourt, 1988). Details about Martin's role in the Conservative Opportunity Society came from Mel Steely's *The Gentleman from Georgia: The Biography of Newt Gingrich* (Macon, GA: Mercer University Press, 2000). A blow-by-blow account of the nuclear-freeze debate came from contemporaneous news accounts and Douglas Waller's *Congress and the Nuclear Freeze: An Inside Look at the Politics of a Mass Movement* (Amherst, MA: University of Massachusetts Press, 1987).

CHAPTER 6: THE OTHER CAROLINA RACE OF 1984

Extensive interviews with Martin, Rufus Edmisten, Jim Hunt, Bill Cobey, and other participants in the 1984 campaigns formed the core of this chapter, along with contemporaneous news accounts. I also had a lengthy phone conversation with Jack Hawke and a brief conversation with former governor Jim Holshouser about these events. Sadly, both passed away before we could schedule sit-down interviews. Accounts of the various 1984 campaigns by Rob Christensen in *The Paradox of Tar Heel Politics* (Chapel Hill, NC: University of North Carolina Press, 2008) and Tom Eamon in *The Making of a Southern Democracy* (Chapel Hill, NC: University of North Carolina Press, 2014) also came in handy.

CHAPTER 7: DIVISION LEADS TO ADDITION

Interviews with Karen Hayes Rotterman, Arlene Pulley, Tim Pittman, Art Pope, and other Martin campaign staff provided critical details about the general election. Coverage by the Associated Press, the Raleigh *News & Observer*, the *Wilmington Morning Star*, and the *Fayetteville Observer* supplied most of the direct quotes of Martin and Edmisten on the campaign trail.

CHAPTER 8: GOVERNING BY TWISTS AND TURNS

The first volume of Governor Martin's collected speeches and papers, edited by Jan-Michael Poff and published in 1992 by the North Carolina Division of Archives and History, was an invaluable tool in reconstructing the major events and controversies of his first gubernatorial term, as were documents at the State Library of North Carolina and the James G. Martin Papers (#4392) at UNC–Chapel Hill's Southern Historical Collection. Interviews with cabinet secretaries and staff members were helpful in describing the gubernatorial transition and the first legislative session.

CHAPTER 9: FINDING A FORMULA FOR SUCCESS

Interviews with Phil Kirk, Paul Shumaker, Jim Trotter, Tom Ellis, Terrence Boyle, and Art Pope were particularly important here, in addition to Governor Martin's recollections and the aforementioned archives. I also made extensive use of budget documents from the governor's office and the Fiscal Research Division of the North Carolina General Assembly. Details about the early organization of the Bob Jordan campaign came in part from Ned Cline's *The Man from Mount Gilead: Bob Jordan Helped Give Public Service a Good Name* (Mount Gilead, NC: privately printed, 2011).

CHAPTER 10: "BETTER SCHOOLS, BETTER ROADS, BETTER JOBS"

In addition to Cline's biography and other sources already mentioned, campaign coverage by the *News & Observer*'s Steve Riley and Rob Christensen, the *Wilmington Morning Star*'s John Wood, and the AP's John Flescher provided many of the quotes from Martin and Jordan on the campaign trail. Dawn Lowder, Tim Pittman, Jim Trotter, and other staffers provided useful insights on the interaction between the campaign and the administration.

CHAPTER 11: A NEW COMBINATION OF ELEMENTS

Joe Mavretic provided indispensable background on the events leading to the overthrow of House speaker Liston Ramsey and the subsequent coalition in the North Carolina House. Firsthand accounts of the "cough medicine" press conference from the governor, the first lady, Tim Pittman, Nancy Temple, Chris Fitzsimon, and Rob Christensen supplemented my own recollections of the event and its aftermath. The second volume of Martin's speeches and papers (edited by Jan-Michael Poff and published by the Division of Archives and History in 1996) supplied many of the governor's quotes for this chapter. Aaron Johnson's autobiography, *Man from Macedonia* (Bloomington, IN: WestBow Press, 2010), supplied background on his tenure as secretary of corrections.

CHAPTER 12: HOME, SCIENCE, AND SENIOR STATESMAN

Martin and Hunt were generous in their recollections of the 1992–93 transition—and in praise of each other's professionalism during the process. I included quotes from Martin's forthcoming book on science and religion with his permission.

INDEX

Abbott, Anthony "Tony," 19, 21, 29-30
Abbott, Susan, 21
ABCs of Public Education, 312
Administrative Procedures Act, 171, 172, 178
AFAM, 298, 300, 302, 303
Agnew, Spiro, 70
Agresta, Phil, 42, 44
Aiken, SC, 60
Alexander, Hugh Quincy, 27
Alexander, Kelly, 41, 42
Alexander, Lamar, 2, 5, 6, 186, 202, 223
Alexandria, VA, 74
All the King's Men, 148
Allen, Arch, 207, 208
ALS, 296
American Chemical Society, 113
American Conservative Union, 92, 310
American Council on Science & Health, 92
American Enterprise Institute, 82, 90
American Legislative Exchange Council, 174-75
American Tobacco Company, 228
Anderson, Gene, 180
Anderson, John, 101
Anderson, Martin, 97, 98
Andrews, Ike, 64
Archer, Bill, 94
Atkinson, Sam, 30, 33, 34, 35-36, 42, 49, 51-52

Bahakel, Cy, 58
Bailey, Allen, 55
Bailey, Doug, 2, 3
Bailey, Jack, 208
Baker Tilly consulting firm, 299-303
Baker, Gene, 161
Ballantine, Patrick, 304
Ballenger, Cass, 119, 122, 149
Baltimore, MD, 41
Bank of America, 12
Barker, Peggy, 74
Barnes, Henson, 247, 255, 258, 263
Barnwell, SC, 190, 252, 289
Bartlett, Bruce, 95
Bartley, Robert, 95
Barwick, P.C., 205
Basic Education Program. *See* BEP
Bayh, Evan, 219
Beason, Don, 263, 265

Beatty, Jim, 58-59, 61, 63, 65, 66, 67, 69, 70, 71, 72
Belk, John, 58, 119
Belk, William Henry, 17
Bellmon, Henry, 6
Bennett, Bert, 132, 165
Bennett, John, 165
Benton Convention Center, 240
Bentsen, Lloyd, 95
BEP, 168-69, 177, 179, 186, 187, 198, 210, 229, 249, 252, 277-78, 281, 283, 285, 311
Berzelius, Jöns Jacob, 307
Beta Club, 14
Beta Theta Pi, 16
"Better schools, better roads, & better jobs," 224
Biden, Joe, 165
Billings, Rhoda, 191-92, 197, 201
Bingham, Laura, 203
Black, Earl, 4-5
Black, Merle, 4-5
Blackberry Farm summit, 1-4, 201
Blackburn, James, 124
Blue Sky Curriculum, 21
Blue, Dan, 167, 174, 231, 232, 238, 276, 280, 281
Blythe, Frank, 30, 34
Board of Governors, 219
"Boll weevil" Democrats, 103
Bounds, Lee, 291
Bowen, William, 19
Bowles, Erskine, 223
Bowles, Hargrove "Skipper," 64-65, 70, 71, 72, 131, 223
Bowles, Lawrence, 74
Boyd, Bill, 222
Boyles, Harlan, 164, 291
Bradshaw, Bob, 53, 55, 59, 65, 70, 120, 121, 130, 156, 162, 193, 194, 199-200, 205, 220, 221, 272
Branch, Joseph, 196, 197
Broder, David, 5, 6
Brookshire, Stan, 39, 41, 56
Brown, Kevin, 220, 247, 260
Browning, Robert, 197
Broyhill, Jim, 27, 64, 74, 80-81, 103, 121, 122, 192, 196, 197, 201, 203, 247
Broyhill-Funderburk primary, 275
Brubaker, Harold, 121
Bryant, Donald, 65
Bryant, Linda, 250
Buchanan, Monroe, 246
Buckley, William F., 6, 25, 285

Bunting, John, 302
Burgener, Clair, 107, 109
Burr, Richard, 121, 304, 305
Bush, Barbara, 210
Bush, George H. W., 194, 218, 221, 236, 269, 292, 293
Bush, George W., 304
Butterfield, G. K., 129

Calhoun, Pat, 65
Cameron, C. C. "Cliff," 55, 56, 158, 174, 175, 176, 182, 267, 276, 277, 287
Camp Miniwanca, 19
Campbell, Carroll, 2, 6, 201, 223, 239, 289
Campbell, John A. "Gus," 30, 34, 36, 38, 42, 49, 52, 54, 55, 57, 58-59
Candidate, The, 73
Cannon Research Center, 287, 295, 296
Cannon, Charles "Charlie," 22, 29
Canton, NC, 226
Career Ladder, 145, 169, 186, 187, 210, 211, 213, 249, 250, 252, 253, 257, 258, 268, 312
Carl, William, 222
Carlton, Phil, 294
Carolina ALS Center, 296
Carolina Inn, 225
Carolinas Medical Center, 33, 57, 287, 295, 297
Carter, Jimmy, 86, 91, 92, 95, 97, 98, 101, 114, 179, 237
Carville, James, 237
Catholic Mercy Hospital, 57
Cats, 246
Center for Rural Economic Development, 199
Central Board of Scientific Risk Assessment Act, 113
Central Piedmont Community College, 48
Central Piedmont Regional Council of Governments, 40-41, 44, 47, 48, 51
Chambers, Julius, 49-50
Champion International Paper Company, 226-27
Charles Lathrop Parsons Award, 113
Charlotte Area Fund, 38-39, 42, 43, 44
Charlotte Junior Women's Club, 69
Charlotte Memorial Hospital. See Carolinas Medical Center
Charlotte News, 34, 44, 52, 57, 69, 70, 71, 83, 92, 93, 100, 137
Charlotte Observer, 22, 38, 44, 47, 52, 70, 100, 102, 103, 126, 139, 149, 179-80, 200, 233, 240 241

Charlotte Symphony, 16, 21, 163
Charlotte-Mecklenburg Charter Commission, 40
Charlotte-Mecklenburg Hospital Authority, 287
Charlotte-Mecklenburg Schools, 32
Cheney, Dick, 107, 109
Chicago, IL, 41
Christensen, Rob, 200, 209, 266-67
Christian Endeavor Society, 12
Clarkton Tobacco Festival, 136
Clayton, Ivie, 173
Clements, Bill, 6, 201
Cline, Ned, 218
Clinton, Bill, 292
Coats, Dan, 107
Cobb, Larry, 55, 256, 269
Cobey, Bill, 119, 120, 122, 153, 201, 203, 247, 259
Coble, Howard, 153
Cochrane, Betsy, 173, 244, 272
Col-Cor, 124
Coleman, Noble, 39
Columbus Corruption. See Col-Cor
Committee on Constitutional Integrity, 172
Committee on Interior & Insular Affairs, 75
Committee on Science & Astronautics, 75
Committee to Ensure Good Government, 55
Comprehensive Environmental Response, Compensation, & Liability Act, 100
Conder, Richard, 258
Congressional Club, 27, 84, 85, 119, 120, 184, 192, 196-97, 204, 205, 206, 207, 221, 222, 313
Conservative Club, 27
Conservative Opportunity Society, 2, 107, 310
Consolidated University of North Carolina, 219
"Construction Work in Progress," 144
"Constructive conservatism," 26, 312-13
Cooley, Harold, 28, 36
Cooper, Roy, 246
Cornelius, Preston, 108-9
Cost-Benefit Analysis, 113
Council of Economic Advisors, 95
Cox, Edward, 70
Crane, Phil, 94, 107
Crawford, Jim, 292
Crews, Charlene, 120, 160

Cromer, Charles, 244
Cross, Mike, 163
Crowder, Deborah, 299, 302
Crumpler, John, 223
Cullen, Robert, 115
Cunningham, John Rood, 20
Currin, Sam, 208, 274

Dalpiaz, J.A., 205
Dalton, Walter, 140, 305
Danforth Foundation, 18
Davidson College, 3, 10, 11-12, 14, 17, 19, 20, 21-22, 78
Davidson Elementary School, 50
Davidson, Chalmers, 21
Davidsonian, 22
Davis, Butch, 302
Davis, Laura, 223
Davis, Lawrence, 259, 263, 264, 265
Dawkins, Donald, 243
Dean, Joe, 157, 172, 291
Delaney Clause, 89, 90, 113
Democratic Leadership Council, 165
"Democrats Forward" task force, 165
Dent, Harry, 70
Denton, Donald, 41
Department of African & Afro-American Studies. *See* AFAM
DeVane, Dan, 243, 244
Diamont, David, 243
Dickson, Stuart, 287
Diels-Alder reaction, 19
"Displaced Pastors," 25
Dole, Bob, 113, 218
Dole, Elizabeth, 186
Dollar, Nelson, 121, 292
Dorman, Marvin, 158, 183, 277
Dorsey, Patric, 156, 170
Dorton Arena, 222
Doster, Joe, 34
Downs, Glen, 208
Drexel Heritage Furniture Company, 156-57
Drury, Elizabeth, 159
Dryden, John, 267
Du Pont, Pete, 5, 218
Dukakis, Michael, 219, 227, 236
Duke Power, 129, 140, 141
Duke University, 12
Duncan, Allyson, 274
Dunn, Winfield, 2

Earnhardt, Dale, 273
Easley, Mike, 219, 274, 291, 304, 305

East, John, 28-29, 36, 85, 102, 119, 184, 192, 196
East, Priscilla, 196-97
Eastminster Presbyterian Church, 17
Ebenezer Associate Reformed Presbyterian Church, 9
Economic Future Study Commission, 272, 277, 281
Economic Recovery Tax Act, 104, 105, 108
Edmisten, David, 144
Edmisten, Jane, 125
Edmisten, Linda, 148
Edmisten, Rufus, 131-51, 181, 123, 124, 125, 126, 127, 128, 129, 130, 230, 267, 308
Education for All Handicapped Children Act, 87, 88
Edwards, John, 305
Eisenhower, Dwight, 4
Ellis, Tom, 85, 119, 120, 192, 204, 205, 206, 207, 208, 222, 256
Ellmers, Renee, 305
Emerging Issues Forum, 227
Emory University, 4, 12
Environmental Protection Agency, 102, 103
Equal Rights Amendment, 143
Ervin, Sam, 34, 77, 79, 125, 129, 143, 172
Esso Research and Engineering Company, 17
Etheridge, Bob, 201, 249, 305
Etheridge, Larry, 165, 256
Eudy, Ken, 203, 215, 223, 229

Eure, Thad, 151, 156
"Evil empire," 113
Executive Mansion, 164
Exum, Jim, 196, 197, 198, 274, 275

Faculty Athletic Committee, 301
Faircloth, Lauch, 118, 132, 135, 123, 124, 125, 126, 127, 129, 223, 284-85, 292, 293, 305
Fannin, Paul, 95, 97
Fayetteville Observer, 161
FDA, 89, 91, 102
Federal Food, Drug, & Cosmetic Act, 90
Feldstein, Martin, 95
Fetzer, Tom, 256
Firing Line, 6, 285
First Presbyterian Church (Raleigh), 164
Fiscal Integrity Act, 83

Fitzsimon, Chris, 232, 265
Flaherty, David, 86-87, 162, 204, 270
Flescher, John, 224
Fletcher School of Diplomacy, 3
Folt, Carol, 301
Food & Drug Administration. *See* FDA
Food Quality Protection Act, 113
Ford Foundation, 38
Ford, Gerald, 74-75, 84-85, 95, 119
Forest, Dan, 305-6, 308
Forrest Gump, 9
Fourth Circuit Court of Appeals, 50
Franklin, Bill, 159
Fredericksen, James, 20
Freemasons, 38
Frenzel, Bill, 94
Friday, Bill, 133, 274
Fuller, Dottie, 74, 160
Funderburk, David, 192, 196

Galifianakis, Nick, 64, 71
Gallent, John, 19
Gamble, John, 48
"Gang of Eight," 201, 214
Gantt, Harvey, 25, 128, 224, 274, 276
Gardner, Chris, 294
Gardner, Jim, 28, 36, 44, 45, 63, 64, 116,
    121, 184, 208, 222, 234, 241, 242, 243, 245,
    247, 256, 260, 277, 280, 284, 291, 292,
    293
Gardner, Sherwin, 90
Garner, NC, 235
Gas tax, 255
General Fund tax relief, 176
Georgius, John, 213
Gephardt, Richard "Dick," 165, 219
Gill, Jim, 31
Gilmore, Tom, 118, 123, 126, 127, 128, 132
Gingrich, Newt, 2, 3, 5, 107, 310
Global TransPark, 277, 289-90
Golden Corral restaurants, 222
Goldsboro, NC, 41
Goldston, Bill, 234, 255, 279, 283
Goldston-Pope spending cap, 282
Goode, Seddon "Rusty," 162, 192, 221,
    249, 287, 289
Goodman, Arthur Jr., 87, 88
Goodykoontz, Bill, 22
GOPAC, 5-6
Gore, Al, 113, 219, 274
Gorsuch, Anne, 103
Governor's Efficiency Study Commis-
    sion, 167, 189, 196

GovTrack.us, 310
Grady, Robert, 256
Graham, Jim, 138, 222
Gramm, Phil, 284
Gramm-Rudman-Hollings Balanced
    Budget Act, 110
Granville County, 272, 273
Green, Jimmy, 118, 123, 124-25, 126, 127,
    128, 134, 135, 136, 159, 230, 239, 240, 267
Greensboro, NC, 41
Greenville, NC, 217
Greenwood, SC, 17
Gregg, Judd, 107, 113
Gregory, Charlie, 114
Greider, William, 111
Grimsley, Joe, 129
Groveton High School, 74
Grubbs, James Elbert, 12

H.R. 3456, 104
Hair, Liz, 87, 92
Hall, Billy Ray, 178, 214
Hamlet chicken plant fire, 288
Hamlet, NC, 288
Hanning, Howard Jr., 274
Hardison, Harold, 201
Harrell, Bernie, 161
Harrelson, Tommy, 203, 260
Harrington, Jim, 156, 185, 186, 249, 255,
    260
Harris, Ken, 29, 30, 103
Harris, Ollie, 276
Harris, W.T. "Bill," 49, 51-52
Hart, Gary, 219
Hasty, Pete, 243
Hatcher, Eddie, 233
Hawke, Jack, 64, 72, 120, 121, 138, 146, 149,
    160, 161, 164-65, 182, 183, 184, 206, 207,
    208, 212, 220, 221, 257, 274, 291, 306
Haworth, Howard, 156-57, 190, 198, 199,
    201, 249
Hayes, Karen. *See* Rotterman, Karen
    Hayes
Hayes, Robin, 304
Hays, Brad, 4, 59-60, 63, 65, 66, 70, 74,
    93, 115, 116, 119, 120, 122, 128, 130, 131,
    145, 148, 162, 184, 192, 193, 197, 200,
    206, 220, 225, 232, 237, 238, 257, 262,
    263, 264, 285,
Hazardous Waste Treatment Commis-
    sion, 190
Hazardous-waste disposal, 251-52, 261,
    272, 289

Helms, Jesse, 7, 64, 71, 72, 76, 84, 95, 97, 117, 118, 119, 120, 131, 135, 142, 143, 151, 153, 184, 208, 221, 245, 262, 274, 275, 276, 293, 309, 310, 313
Hendon, Bill, 102, 109, 153, 201
Hennigan, Daniel, 49, 52
Hickman, Harrison, 146, 223, 236
Hickman, Marcus, 29, 30, 65, 72
Hickory, NC, 253
Higgins, John, 161
Highway Patrol, 256
Highway Study Commission, 249
Highway Trust Fund, 7-8, 156, 175, 176, 186, 248, 255-56, 257, 260, 285, 311
Hill, Richard, 19
Hinnant, Darrell, 272, 273
Hodges, Luther Jr., 51, 65, 66
Hodges, Luther Sr., 217
Holding, Lewis "Snow," 182
Holshouser, Jim, 63, 64, 70, 71, 72, 115, 117, 118, 119, 131, 146, 256, 303
Hood, W. A. "Lex," 30, 34
Hooper, Ruby, 128
Hoover, Daniel "Dan," 116, 149, 151
Hope, Bob, 210
Hope, Dolores, 210
Horton, Hamilton, 205
Hotline, The, 3
Huffman, Doris, 292
Hughes, Charles "Charlie," 120, 160, 161, 248, 261-62, 263, 265
Humphrey, Hubert, 44, 45
Hunt, Guy, 6, 201, 261
Hunt, Howard, 77
Hunt, Jack, 246
Hunt, Jim, 72, 86-87, 102, 114, 117-19, 123-25, 128, 132, 134, 138, 151, 153, 154, 164, 170, 217, 223, 227, 229, 243, 244, 245, 274, 291, 293-95, 304, 309, 310, 313
Hunt, Sam, 217, 243, 255, 262
Hunter, Clyde, 31
Hurricane Hugo, 260-61

Independent Presbyterian Church (Savannah), 9, 10, 12
Individual Savings & Investment Act, 105
Ingram, Alan, 42
Ingram, John, 118, 123, 124, 126, 127, 128
Institute for Defense & Business, 298
Iran-Contra affair, 218
Ives, Wesley, 135

Jackson, Barbara, 303
Jacobs, Timothy, 233

James G. Cannon Research Center. *See* Cannon Research Center
"Jim Martin Listens" tour, 138
Jobs Creation Act, 82-83, 97
Joe Martin ALS Foundation, 296
John Locke Foundation, 281, 290
Johns Hopkins University, 88
Johnson, Aaron, 157-58, 187-88, 250-51, 290-91
Johnston, Frontis, 19, 29, 30
Johnston, Gene, 102, 109, 247, 284, 292
Johnston, Randy, 223
Jonas, Charles Raper Jr., 58, 68
Jonas, Charles Raper Sr., 27, 28, 53, 58, 74, 81
Jones, Charles Andrew, 27
Jones, Paul, 74, 161
Jones, Walter Jr., 28, 36, 243, 244
Jordan Lumber & Supply, 217
Jordan, Bob, 140, 153, 154, 158, 162, 165, 166, 170, 172, 174, 175, 178, 189, 192-93, 195, 198, 201, 203, 210, 211, 216-19, 222-23, 225-26, 227-29, 231-36, 239, 240-42, 245, 246, 247, 262, 308
Jordan, Everett, 28, 65
Judicial Standards Commission, 252
Junior League of Raleigh, 163
Justus, Betsy, 210, 272, 291, 292

Kaplan, Harry, 165
Kasarda, Jack, 272, 277
Keith, Lisa, 162
Kelly, David, 42, 44
Kemp, Jack, 3, 76, 82-83, 94, 97, 107, 109, 110, 218, 221
Kemp-Roth bill, 97, 98, 99, 100, 104
Kennedy Covington law firm, 29
Kennedy, John, 95
Kennedy, Teddy, 91, 92
"Kennel Club," 246
Kentucky Derby, 229
Keynesianism, 95-96, 100
Kilgo, John, 70
Kimbrough, John T., 23
Kincaid, Don, 269
Kincaid, Randy, 99-102, 108
King, Coretta Scott, 232
King, Margaret, 81, 93, 108, 146, 156, 220
King, Martin Luther Jr., 41, 231
Kinston Jetport, 290
Kirk, Phil, 156, 190, 203-4, 209, 213, 247, 260, 263, 269, 272
Kissinger, Henry, 3
Knott, J. T., 166

Knox, Charles, 132, 159, 230
Knox, Eddie, 55, 118, 123, 124, 125-26, 127, 128, 129, 130, 131-33, 135, 139, 140, 151, 166, 193
Knox, Frances, 132
Kuralt, Wallace, 39

Laffer, Arthur, 95
LaGuardia Airport, 83-84
Lake Norman, 16-17, 20, 73, 116, 145, 262, 286, 295
Lake, I. Beverly Jr., 102, 119, 161, 175, 183, 193, 274, 276, 293, 303, 308
Lake, I. Beverly Sr., 35, 126
Lane, Charles, 294
Laughery, Jack, 215
Laurinburg, NC, 243
Lawing, Craig, 134
Lawrence, Melinda, 230
League of Conservation Voters, 141
Leake, George, 41, 42
Lechtreck, Elaine, 25
Lead Teacher, 258
Lee, Estell, 281
Lexington Dispatch, 70, 142
Liddy, G. Gordon, 77
Lofton, Jim, 65, 74, 160, 161, 182, 183-84, 204
Lofton, Sarah, 161, 294
Long, Huey, 148
Lott, Trent, 3, 76, 81-82, 83, 107, 109, 110
Louisburg, NC, 221-22
Louisville Presbyterian Theological Seminary, 10
Love Canal, 100
Lowder, Dawn, 221, 248
Lowe, Charles M., 42, 43, 44, 45, 46, 48, 49, 51-52
Lyons, Schley, 69-70

Mack Truck, 228
Mack, Connie, 2
Manning, Howard E. "Howdy" Jr., 242
Markey, Ed, 110-12
Martin Machine, The, 66
Martin, Adele, 11
Martin, Arthur Benson, 54
Martin, Arthur Morrison Jr. "Bubba," 12, 13, 15
Martin, Arthur Morrison Sr., 10-12, 13, 17, 25, 115, 163
Martin, Ben, 21, 164, 210, 214, 222
Martin, D.G., 153

Martin, David Grier "Grier," 20, 22, 29, 30, 40, 65
Martin, Dorothy Ann McAulay "Dottie," 17-19, 30, 53, 54, 66, 72-74, 103, 116, 137, 151, 161, 164, 174, 209, 246, 262, 265, 285-86, 295
Martin, Emily Wood, 21, 74, 214
Martin, James Grubbs Jr. "Jimmy," 19, 50, 66, 74, 161
Martin, James Grubbs Sr.: abortion funding, 177, 213, 259, 312; Blackberry Farm summit, 2-4; campaign ads, 238; campaign style, 136-37, 200; chemistry, 14-15; completion of I-40, 133, 143-45, 185, 241; childhood, 9-15; Davidson town council, 23-24; debates, 143-44, 225, 240; EPA appointment, 102-3; Delaney Clause, 89-90; dissident Democrats, 243-44; drug policy, 67; education, 168-70, 277-78, 311; Equal Rights Amendment, 143; first inauguration, 162-63; football, 13-15; forced busing, 67; Charlotte-Mecklenburg government consolidation, 56-57; Highway Trust Fund, 248, 311; infant mortality, 279; judicial appointments, 252; management approach, 182; Mecklenburg County commission, 29-38, 46-47; M. L. King holiday, 142, 231-32, 238; M. L. King memorial service, 41-42; music, 13, 20; nickname, 11; phone tap, 155; prison issues, 187, 213, 250, 253, 270; Republican Research Committee, 110, 111; research-office controversy, 275; run for Congress, 53-55; sailing, 209, 214-17, 229, 238; school desegregation, 49-50; science, 75-76; taxes, 82-83, 154, 166-68, 173, 174, 177, 188, 198, 212, 213, 251, 254, 259, 280, 312; term limits, 171; throat infection, 264-66; UNC scandal, 298-303; veto power, 171-72, 177-78, 179, 252, 271-72; Vietnam policy, 66-67; vs. Preston Cornelius, 108-9; vs. Randy Kincaid, 99-102; waste disposal, 155, 189-91, 214, 251, 259; Watergate, 79-80; whistle-stop tour, 146-47
Martin, Joseph B. III "Joe," 12, 21, 53, 116, 148, 153, 156, 162, 182, 192, 220, 296
Martin, Joseph B. Jr., 10-11
Martin, Mark, 303, 308
Martin, Mary Grubbs, 12, 13
Martin, Neal A., 12, 21

Martin, Patricia Higgins, 161
Martin-Baker Tilly probe, 299-303
Martinez, Bill, 6
Martinez, Bob, 201
Mary Reynolds Babcock Foundation, 38
Massachusetts Institute of Technology, 3
Maulden, Julia, 37
Maupin, Tony, 207
Mavretic, Joe, 167, 244, 246, 247, 253, 255, 268, 269, 276, 280
Maxwell, Charles, 92-93, 98
McAdoo, Michael, 298
McAulay, Ben, 17
McCarty, Barry, 205, 206, 207, 208
McClister, Michael, 223, 236-37
McColl, Hugh, 12, 162
McCoy, Henry, 159
McCrory, Pat, 7, 121, 140, 304-6, 312, 313
McGovern, George, 64, 67, 69, 76, 117
McGuire Nuclear Station, 68
McGuireWoods consulting firm, 296, 297
McKay, Bill, 73
McLaughlin, Scott, 293
McMillan, Alex, 103, 153
McMillan, James B., 50, 55
McNamara, Rae, 170
McWhorter, Ned, 226-27
Mecklenburg County Commission, 2
"Mental Contests," 14
Meredith College, 224
Michel, Bob, 109
Miller, George, 174
Miller, Glenn, 118
Mills, Wilbur, 95
Milwaukee Sentinel, 112
Miner, Bob, 17-18
Mitchell, Burley, 271
Mizell, Wilmer "Vinegar Ben," 45, 64, 78, 80
MLK holiday commission, 232
Mondale, Walter, 1, 138, 139, 219
Monroe, Lee, 161, 249
Montreat, NC, 17
Moore, Dan K., 35, 126, 128
Moore, Herman, 55
Moore, Jeanelle, 164
Morgan, Robert, 79, 102, 179
Mount Gilead Town Council, 219
Mount Gilead, NC, 217
Mountain Area Planning System, 279, 283

Moynihan, Daniel Patrick, 113
Mt. Zion Institute, 13, 15
Muchmore, Lynn, 183
Mundell, Robert, 95, 96
Myers, Charles, 42, 44, 45, 46, 47, 49, 51-52
Myers, Lew, 159
Myrick, Sue, 224, 274, 284, 292, 305
Myrtle Beach, SC, 235

Nader, Ralph, 88, 90, 101
Napier, John, 21
National Academy of Sciences, 113
National Association of Evangelicals, 112
National Conference of Catholic Bishops, 111
National Education Association, 111
National Governors Association, 199, 265
National Review, 6, 25, 26, 82, 95, 285
National Rifle Association, 127
National Toxicology Program, 92
NCAE, 169, 249, 250, 253, 253, 258, 259, 280, 288
NCCBI, 172-73, 257, 260, 269
Neely, Chuck, 207, 208
"Neighbors Program," 81, 93, 146
Nesbitt, Martin, 201, 258, 288
New York v. United States, 289
News & Observer (Raleigh, NC), 116, 131, 146, 149, 188, 196, 200, 209, 233, 261, 266, 267, 299
News & Record (Greensboro, NC), 161, 188, 202
Nixon, Richard, 44-45, 51, 69, 70, 76-78, 118
North Carolina Association of Broadcasters, 144
North Carolina Association of County Commissioners, 48
North Carolina Association of Educators. See NCAE
North Carolina Citizens for Business & Industry. See NCCBI
North Carolina Commission on Jobs & Economic Growth, 178, 198
North Carolina Highway Users Conference, 143
North Carolina Justice Center, 230
North Carolina Low-Level Radioactive Waste Management Authority, 273
North Carolina Museum of Art, 189, 277
North Carolina People, 133

North Carolina School Boards Association, 169
North Carolina School of the Arts Jazz Ensemble, 163
North Carolina Symphony, 189, 285
North Carolina's Blueprint for Economic Development, 198
North Wilkesboro, NC, 224
Nunn, Sam, 165
Nurkin, Harry, 287, 296
Nyang'oro, Julius, 298, 299, 302

O'Herron, Ed, 65
O'Neil, Tip, 133-34, 179
Obama, Barack, 105, 304
Office of Citizen Affairs, 230
Office of Risk Assessment, 113
Old Brick Church, 9
Olson, David, 200
Omicron Delta Kappa, 16
Operation Switch, 193
Orr, Robert "Bob," 121, 186, 242, 293, 303, 308
Osborne, Wallace, 42, 44, 45, 46, 48, 49, 51-52
Ovens Auditorium, 41
Oxford, NC, 228

Parent to Parent program, 210
Parker, Francis, 191, 197
Parrigin, Lyman, 17
Patterson, Ernest, 22
Patterson, Jane, 132, 155
Payne, Harry, 203, 246, 292
Peace College, 224
Pearce, Gary, 225
Pearson, Ernie, 148
Pekarek, Nancy, 248
Perdue, Beverly, 304, 305
Perot, Ross, 292
Perpetual Elections Amendment, 193
Peterson, M. W. "Pete," 30, 34, 36, 37-38, 42, 45, 48, 49, 52, 54, 55, 58, 59
Petty, Richard, 146
Phi Mu Alpha Sinfonia, 16
Phillips, Craig, 37, 161, 164, 169
Pigeon River, 226
Pine Needles Lodge & Golf Club, 181, 260
Pinehurst, NC, 227
Pittman, Tim, 161, 220, 224-25, 247, 264-65
Plyler, Aaron, 201, 195

Poe, William, 55, 58, 61
Poole, Greg, 167
Pope, Art, 121, 161, 256, 272, 279, 280, 283, 292
Pope, Claude, 203, 247
Potter, Robert, 30, 34, 36, 42, 55
Poucher, Cherie, 207-8
Powers, Helen, 157
Prather, David, 247-48
Presbyterian Hospital, 57
Preyer, Richardson, 126
Price, David, 142
Price, W. R. "Monk," 14
Princeton University, 3
Princeton, NJ, 18
Pritchard, George, 27
Prochnaw, Fritz, 144
Public Citizen Health Research Group, 90
Public School Forum of North Carolina, 249
Pugh, Alan, 122, 159, 184, 291
Pugh, Richard, 122, 159
Pulley, Arlene, 136, 159, 230, 248
Purcell, Bill, 25
Pure Food & Drug Act of 1906, 88
Purloined letter, 147-49
Purrington, Ward, 183, 204, 244, 291

Raleigh Hilton Inn, 150, 151
Raleigh Inn, 150
Ramsey, Liston, 142, 154, 158, 166, 167, 170, 173, 179, 195, 201, 214, 222-23, 243, 244, 246
Rand, Tony, 195, 201, 234, 235, 242
Rauch, Marshall, 134, 251, 257, 276
Rauscher, Frank, 90
Ray, James Earl, 41
Reagan Revolution State 2, 4
Reagan, Ronald, 1, 84, 94, 98, 101, 103, 112, 114, 117, 119, 131, 137, 138-39, 151 179, 201, 218, 241
Reason, 95
Redford, Robert, 73
Redman, William, 173
Renfrow, Ed, 222, 263, 264, 265, 292
Republican Governors Association, 3, 6, 201
Republican National Convention (Kansas City), 85
Republican Research Committee, 110, 111
Republican Senatorial Campaign Committee, 284

Republication National Committee, 4
Research Triangle Park, 173
Reynolds, Alan, 95
Rhodes, Thomas, 157, 247
Rhyne, Johnathan, 244, 256, 269, 277, 280, 282, 288
Rice University, 4
Richardson, Jim, 129
Ringe, Don, 121, 200, 220, 239, 264
Rise of Southern Republicans, The, 5
Ritchie, Michael, 73
RJR Nabisco, 228, 235
"Roads to the Future" plan, 195
Robb, Chuck, 165
Roberson, William, 132
Roberts, Karen, 74
Roberts, Paul Craig, 95
Robertson, Pat, 218, 221, 222
Robesonian (Lumberton), 233
Robinson, Bill, 42
Robinson, Bradshaw & Hinshaw, 53
Robinson, George, 203
Rohrer, Grace, 156, 204
Rolling Stone, 112
Roosevelt, Teddy, 89
Rose, Charlie, 203
Rostenkowski, Dan, 104
Roth, William "Bill," 95, 97
Rotterman, Karen Hayes, 120, 121, 137, 160, 161, 247
Rotterman, Marc, 121, 247
Rouse, Frank, 48-49, 156, 200, 281
Rousselot, John, 94
Royall, Ken, 166-67, 173-74, 201, 268
Royster, Vermont, 184
Rubik's Cube, 152
Rural Economic Development Center, 214
Ruth, Earl, 45, 64, 80

Saccharin Study, Labeling & Advertising Act, 91
Sanford, Terry, 38, 63, 117, 125, 128, 134, 197, 201, 217, 223, 246, 262, 265, 284, 286, 293
Santo, Ron, 91
Sara Lee, 228
Savannah, GA, 9
Savings & Investment Act. *See* Jobs Creation Act
Sawyer, Wendell, 171
"Scannergate," 294
School Building Solutions Committee, 297-98

School Improvement & Accountability Act. *See* Senate Bill 2
Schwarzenegger, Arnold, 210
Scott, Bob, 44, 45, 64, 92
Scott, Kerr, 125
SEANC, 280
Second Southern Strategy, 1-8
Senate Bill 2, 179, 258, 260, 278, 283, 285, 288, 312
Senate Subcommittee on Health & Scientific Research, 91
Seymour Johnson Air Force Base, 290
Shallcross, John, 28
Shaw, Bob, 120, 280
Shelton, Charlie, 221
Sherrill, Wilma, 161
Short, Milton, 58, 79-80, 88
Shumaker, Paul, 60, 121, 140, 193, 220-21, 224, 225, 263
Simmons, Cynthia, 223
Simon, William 95
Sion Presbyterian Church, 10, 12
Sitton, Claude, 266
"Six-year itch," 165-66, 194, 201
Sizemore, Trip, 256, 269, 292
Smith, Beverly, 294
Smith, Charlie, 127, 128
Smith, Donald, 191
Smith, Jay, 120
Smith, Meredith, 260
Smith, Wade, 165
Smith, Zachary, 65
Smoky Mountain British Brass Band, 163
Snider, Reitzel, 31, 71-72
Southern Governors' Association, 193, 199, 260
Southern Pines, NC, 181, 224, 260
Southern Republican Exchange, 5-6, 201, 224, 248
Southland Ramblers, 273
Speight, Marvin, 132, 135-36
Spending Limitation Act, 99
St. Paul's Baptist Church, 42
Stahl, Donald, 30, 31
Stallings, Livingstone, 48
Stam, Skip, 255
Stamey, Peggy, 170
State Employees Association of North Carolina, 243, 288
State of the State address, 167-68, 216, 248, 250, 252, 279
Steiger, Bill, 94, 98, 99
Stein, Herbert, 95, 96

Steward, Carl, 124
Stith, Thomas, 122, 161
Storrs, Tom, 167
Stott v. Martin, 231
Stott, Bobby, 230
Stuart, John, 208
Sughrue, Jim, 220
Summers, Brenda, 203, 228
Sununu, John, 2, 3, 6
Superconducting Super Collider, 228
"Superfund," 100, 252, 261
"Supersub," 201
Supply-side economics, 96
Sutton, Charlie, 74
Swann v. Charlotte-Mecklenburg Board of Education, 50, 52, 54-55
Swann, James, 50

Talton, John, 223
Tarrance, Lance, 120, 220
Tax Equity & Fiscal Responsibility Act, 106
Tax Fairness Act, 258, 282
Tax Fairness Study Committee, 251
Taylor, Betty Sue, 120
Taylor, Charles, 276
Taylor, Pat, 64-65, 131
Teeter, Bob, 2, 3
Temple, Nancy, 247, 260, 263, 264
Thornburg, Lacy, 138, 172, 178, 230-31, 263, 264, 265, 266, 291, 292
Thornburgh, Dick, 2, 3, 6, 194
Thorp, Holden, 298, 299, 300, 301
Thrower, Henry, 30
Tillis, Thom, 121
Trotter, Jim, 122, 161, 179, 182, 184, 204, 294
Tufts University, 3
Ture, Norman, 95, 104, 106
Turlington, Ed, 165, 200, 203
Turner, Frank, 274

UNC Center for Public Television, 232, 296
Union of Concerned Scientists, 111
United States Chamber of Commerce, 82
United States Supreme Court, 50, 289
University of Edinburgh, 10
University of Minnesota, 12
University of North Carolina at Charlotte, 37
University of Paris, 10
Uplift Day Care, 278

Valvano, Jim, 299-300
Van Every, Philip, 55, 61-63
Van Hecke, James, 223, 229, 245
Vander Jagt, Guy, 94, 107
Vaughn, Earl, 191
Veale, Max, 120, 137, 148-49
Verna, Peter, 66
Vinroot, Richard, 121, 304, 305
Voting Rights Act, 142

Wainstein, Kenneth, 302
Walker, Bob, 107
Walker, Johnny, 72
Walker, Ralph, 308
Wall Street Journal, 82, 95, 184, 210
Wallace, George, 45, 63
Wallace, Mason, 30, 32, 34
Wanniski, Jude, 95
Warren, Jim, 48
Warren, Ray, 171, 194, 231
Warren, Robert Penn, 148
Washington Post, 5, 112
Washington, DC, 41
Watergate, 76-78
Waters, Monroe, 135, 159
Watkins, Billy, 167, 171, 172, 173, 176, 201, 212, 214, 222, 223, 243, 244, 246
Ways & Means Committee, 81, 82, 84, 88, 94, 104
WBTV, 68, 74
Weatherly, Harry, 34, 36, 37
Webb, John, 197
Weber, Vin, 107
WECT-TV, 223
Weldon, NC, 41
Wells, Phil, 223
Wertz, James, 43
West Georgia College, 3
West Potomac High School, 74
Wheeler, Larry, 170
Whelan, Elizabeth, 92
Whichard, Willis, 197-98
White House Inn, 72
White Memorial Presbyterian Church, 155
Whitfield, Paul, 42, 49
Wicker, Dennis, 171, 292
Wide World of Sports, 58
Wildflower program, 210
Williams, Harry, 148
Willoughby, Colon, 264, 265
Wilmer, Henry, 55, 57, 59
Wilmington Morning Star, 150

Wilmington, NC, 41
Wilson, J. G. Jr., 170-71
Winnsboro, SC, 9, 12
Winston-Salem, NC, 41
Witherspoon, E. E., 70
Wolfe, Sidney, 90, 91, 101
Wolfe, Tom, 184
Wooglin, 78
WRAL-TV, 265
Wrenn, Carter, 119, 192, 204, 205, 206, 207, 208
Wrightsville Beach, NC, 239

Yates, Graem, 61, 63
"Year of the Family," 194
YMCA, 111

Z. Smith Reynolds Foundation, 38
Zablocki Resolution, 111, 112
Zablocki, Clement, 111, 112